Mary L Cort

Siam

The Heart of India

Mary L Cort

Siam
The Heart of India

ISBN/EAN: 9783742886590

Manufactured in Europe, USA, Canada, Australia, Japa

Cover: Foto ©Andreas Hilbeck / pixelio.de

Manufactured and distributed by brebook publishing software (www.brebook.com)

Mary L Cort

Siam

THE HEART OF FARTHER INDIA.

BY

MARY LOVINA CORT,
A Resident of Siam.

NEW YORK:
ANSON D. F. RANDOLPH & COMPANY,
38 WEST TWENTY-THIRD STREET.

COPYRIGHT, 1886, BY
ANSON D. F. RANDOLPH & COMPANY.

EDWARD O. JENKINS' SONS,
Printers and Stereotypers,
20 North William St., New York.

TO

CHULALANGKORN,
Supreme King of Siam,
THE WISEST AND BEST RULER THIS KINGDOM HAS EVER KNOWN;

THE DEAD MISSIONARIES,
WHO OPENED THE DOORS OF THIS LAND TO THE WORLD;

THE LIVING MISSIONARIES,
WHO TOIL IN THE PATIENCE OF HOPE;

THE MILLIONS OF SIAM,
WAITING TO BE UPLIFTED;

HER LITTLE DARK-EYED CHILDREN,
AMONG WHOM I SPECIALLY LOVE TO LABOR;

THIS SKETCH

OF THEIR BEAUTIFUL LAND, IS,
FROM THE HEART OF FARTHER INDIA,

Dedicated
BY THEIR FRIEND
THE AUTHOR.

PREFACE.

Having lived since 1874 in Siam, the writer has thought that a new volume on this interesting land might not be unwelcome to the intelligent reader.

Events must first occur before they can be chronicled. History is composed of the accumulations of the past, and no matter at what date we appear on the scene there is much of interest that we can only know through the written records or verbal reports of our predecessors.

To these two sources I am indebted for much that will appear on the following pages. I therefore acknowledge with gratitude my obligations to all who have consciously or unconsciously contributed of their thoughts or words to enrich my book.

In the field of literature every new book must make its own way. It cannot go in the beaten paths of others. New hands will handle it, and new eyes and hearts will scan its pages and take in its contents. I hope, therefore, along with what I have written myself, to carry a few old truths and incidents to many fresh readers.

All I ask for my book is that it be read, while I trust that through its perusal this hitherto almost unknown land may become more familiar to the busy, wide-awake world of to-day. M. L. C.

Petchaburee, Siam.

Since writing the above I have come home to America on a brief visit, and before my book goes to press I wish to add that the last chapter, New Siam, has been finished since my return and I refer the reader to it for the very latest and best information.

During a late visit to Washington, I called upon the President. In the course of our conversation he remarked: "America should be on the most friendly terms with Siam. When you see the king again, please extend to him my most cordial greetings."

It is indeed true that Americans have ever received from the present sovereign, and his illustrious father also, the most kindly treatment, and it is in consideration of this, and because of my boundless hope for the future of both king and kingdom, that I have ventured to dedicate this volume to His Majesty Chulalangkorn.

M. L. C.

DENVER, COL., 1886.

CONTENTS.

CHAPTER I.
The Start, ... 1

CHAPTER II.
On to Siam, ... 5

CHAPTER III.
The King's Realm, ... 14

CHAPTER IV.
Products, ... 22

CHAPTER V.
Bangkok, ... 29

CHAPTER VI.
Peeps into Palaces, ... 42

CHAPTER VII.
Some Kingly Customs, ... 54

CHAPTER VIII.
Disposition of the Dead, ... 64

CHAPTER IX.
A Royal Cremation, ... 72

CHAPTER X.
The Supreme King of Siam, . . . 88

CONTENTS.

CHAPTER XI.
SIAMESE LANGUAGE AND LITERATURE, . . . 98

CHAPTER XII.
THE KING'S BIRTHDAY, ... 108

CHAPTER XIII.
SIAM'S RELIGION, ... 114

CHAPTER XIV.
IDOLS, ... 131

CHAPTER XV.
MONASTERIES OR WATS, ... 138

CHAPTER XVI.
MORE ABOUT WATS, ... 148

CHAPTER XVII.
BUDDHIST SHRINES, ... 153

CHAPTER XVIII.
THE BUDDHA FOOTPRINT, ... 162

CHAPTER XIX.
THE PEOPLE AND THEIR HOUSES, . . . 166

CHAPTER XX.
HOLIDAYS IN SIAM, ... 178

CHAPTER XXI.
SIAMESE TIMES, SEASONS, AND CUSTOMS, . . 193

CHAPTER XXII.
ELEPHANTS, ... 201

CHAPTER XXIII.
THE YOUNG AND OLD FOLKS OF SIAM, . . . 212

CHAPTER XXIV.
CURIOUS THINGS, ... 223

CONTENTS.

CHAPTER XXV.
SIAM'S CENTENNIAL EXPOSITION, ... 228

CHAPTER XXVI.
PETCHABUREE, ... 233

CHAPTER XXVII.
WALKS ABOUT PETCHABUREE, ... 243

CHAPTER XXVIII.
THE ROYAL CAVE, PETCHABUREE, ... 255

CHAPTER XXIX.
DRINKING THE WATER OF ALLEGIANCE, . . 260

CHAPTER XXX.
THE TEMPLE OF THE SLEEPING IDOL, . . . 265

CHAPTER XXXI.
LOTUS-LILIES, ... 269

CHAPTER XXXII.
CHRISTIAN MISSIONS IN SIAM, ... 280

CHAPTER XXXIII.
THE CHURCH IN SIAM, ... 294

CHAPTER XXXIV.
OUR SCHOOLS IN SIAM, ... 301

CHAPTER XXXV.
MEDICAL MISSIONS, ... 314

CHAPTER XXXVI.
LIFE ON THE COMPOUND, ... 323

CHAPTER XXXVII.
THE PRESS, ... 332

CHAPTER XXXVIII.

Laos, the North-Land, ... 337

CHAPTER XXXIX.

The Captive Laos in Siam, ... 355

CHAPTER XL.

Seetone and his Angel-Bride, Monora—A Laos Legend, ... 370

CHAPTER XLI.

Buddha's Crystal Tooth, ... 373

CHAPTER XLII.

New Siam, ... 378

Appendix, ... 385

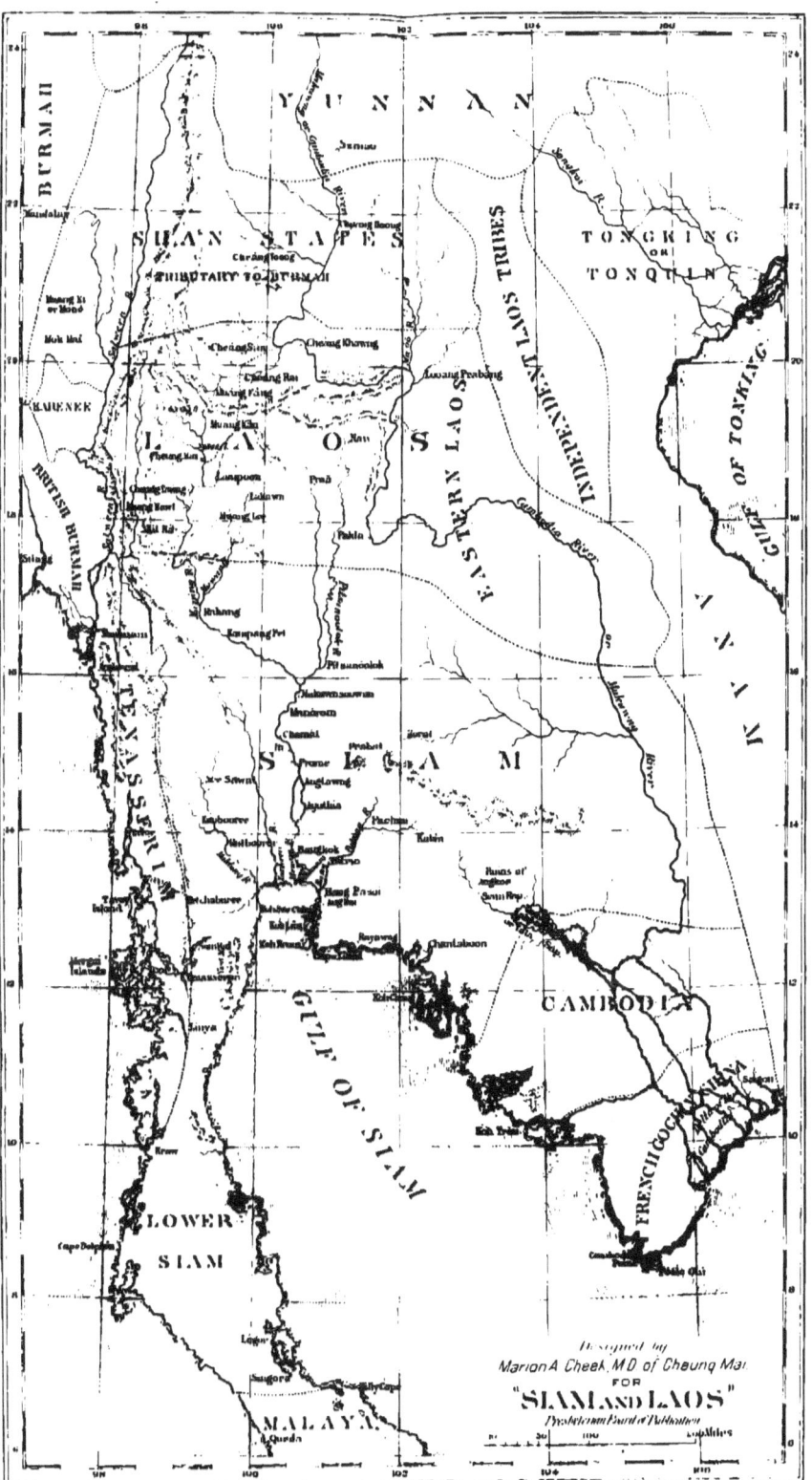

SIAM.

CHAPTER I.

THE START.

SIAM is not an old land, renowned in song and story. Indeed it is so new, has so lately come within the ken of western nations, that very few books in European languages have been written about it. Perhaps, all told, they would not number a score.

The native records are so legendary, so full of palpable falsehoods, that even the grains of truth, mixed with stones and sand, and which have been washed down the stream of time from the past, must be sifted and rubbed and polished before the pure gold of their worth appears.

I shall not, therefore, attempt a history of this tropical land that smiles in the sunshine of a perpetual summer, nor shall I carry you back into the dim past and try to trace for you the succession of kings who have lived and reigned and died in the centuries that are gone forever.

No, I have no time for that; neither would you have leisure to read so much at the threshold while I am beckoning you to follow through the open door into the Siam of to-day.

There were many dear friends who bade me a tearful farewell when I left my home in Colorado that pleasant evening in July of 1874, and started on my long journey to Asia. But there were few to bid me " God-speed," because they thought I ought to stay at home and labor among the "heathen at the door." I think some one is tempted to say this to nearly every man or woman who sails on a mission to a distant shore. I told them they might all be home missionaries, but that I was willing to go and labor among the foreign heathen to whom they would not be sent.

I have found nothing but God's disappointments in all my Siam experiences, and they are always better than our fears, and in the end prove to be full of blessing. God has always taken care of me and given me ever so many things to be glad for, and He helps me to open my eyes and heart to see and take them in.

I started from home alone. Just beyond Cheyenne I overtook Dr. Cheek and Miss Grimstead, and they accompanied me to the end of my journey.

At San Francisco we met Dr. and Mrs. Ellinwood, and we had the pleasure of their company to Yokohama. They were going round the world to visit mission stations, and carry tidings home to the churches. We have always been sorry they did not come to Siam, but thankful that we met them by the way, and at this late date acknowledge a debt of gratitude for their words of cheer and encouragement.

On our ship was a large astronomical party going to the East to observe the transit of Venus. The steamer *Alaska* was a pleasant home for us all.

We had a very fair voyage, just twenty-five days from shore to shore, and yet I think I will never forget how glad we were to see the green hills of Japan rising from the sea; we had sighted Fuji Yama, that landmark in the "Sunrise Kingdom" long ere the shore line was visible.

We tarried in Yokohama a day or two, and were welcomed as kindly by the missionaries as though we had been old friends. We went to ride in *ginrikishas* through Curio Street, saw all manner of rare and wonderful things; visited a tea house where the workmen were preparing green tea on great copper plates; laughed to see the comical little children playing in the streets, with their odd, old-fashioned clothes, and wide, wide sleeves, and babies big and little strapped to their backs.

Then we went through the beautiful inland sea, down to Canton, where we spent six weeks waiting for a steamer to Siam.

How we enjoyed our visit in that miserable old Chinese city! There we met many of "God's folks" who still labor for the heathen, and the better we knew them, the more we loved them; we would like to have pitched our tent in the Celestial Empire, and gone forth with the reapers to bind the sheaves in that wide harvest field; but, among the last messages sent to us from New York ere we started, were the words "Go forward," and how dared we halt, or even dream of standing still when we had not yet reached the end of our journey?

I was betrayed into writing, however, in one of my letters from Canton, that had I come with no definite point in view, I am sure I should have chosen this as my home, for there is great need of more workers, and this is such a pleasant place in which to be, and there can be no boundary to your work except the utmost limit of your strength. The mission circle is large and happy, and their homes good and comfortable.

But over against these pleasant blessings of God's provision and tender care, we must not forget that these heathen cities are horrible in comparison to the very filthiest portions of the foreign quarters in America. The streets are narrow and full of bad odors; the native houses small, gloomy, and damp; the people wretched, ignorant, and sinful. Their idol worship is before you continually, for altars and shrines are built at nearly every doorway, and their temples tower like palaces above the miserable huts in all parts of the city. Some of the most gorgeous temples are black with the smoke of incense that is kept constantly burning upon their many altars, and they are so thronged with worshippers that you can scarcely pass through them.

In Canton, with its streets and water-ways constantly

swarming, the fact is driven home to your soul that if one city can hold so many human beings, the heathen world must indeed have millions, and *millions*, and MILLIONS.

We are always saying good-bye to somebody, and so the day came when we must leave Canton. We had a pleasant trip of a few hours down the Pearl River, past the Chinese cemeteries with their countless graves, built like immense horseshoes; past the rice fields, the pagodas, the forts, on, on to Hong-Kong, that English city on a Chinese island. Here we saw the unlading of a ship by coolies. Everything was borne off either in their hands, or on their backs and shoulders. Men are too plenty to admit of hand-cars, trucks, or drays.

The city of Hong-Kong is built on a hillside, and from our ships as we lay at anchor in the roadstead, looked quite beautiful, especially at night, with the gaslights flashing up and down the streets. I am sorry now, that although I was at Hong-Kong twice, I never set foot on shore. It is like a bit of Europe waiting at a doorway of the Celestial Empire, and people of the "Middle Kingdom" can there catch glimpses of what life may be on the other side of the world.

CHAPTER II.

ON TO SIAM.

We left Hong-Kong on the 14th of October, about four in the afternoon, and at five passed the *Alaska* lying high and dry near the Aberdeen docks, where she had been tossed on shore in the late typhoon. We felt sorry for the poor old ship, but thanked God for the quiet passage and happy time we had had on board.

We were safe in Canton during the terrible typhoon of 1874, that almost destroyed Macoa, strewed the shores of China with wrecks, and filled the harbor at Hong-Kong with sunken ships. News went home that the *Alaska* was wrecked, and the passengers lost. Until letters reached home from China my friends all supposed me dead.

The following midnight we saw the lights off Cape St. James. Soon we had the pilot aboard and were steaming up the river to Saigon. The daylight disclosed green banks on either side, and little brown monkeys peering at us from the branches of the trees. Palm-trees clustered on the plain, and we saw the little mat huts where the Anamites dwell.

We found Saigon quite a modern-looking place, with its fine two-storied brick houses, its wide streets, its horses and carriages. There are trees along the streets, and lamp-posts at every corner marked in French, "*Rue*" so and so. This is a French port, and the religion is Roman Catholic, of course. I saw one of the little stone chapels with its cross almost as soon as I arrived. There are many priests here and a large convent. All the natives who join the Catholics wear a peculiar black dress, so they are known wherever met. We remained here nearly two days. The captain secured a two-horse carriage from a friend, and with a coachman and footman of some unknown nationality we all went out for a drive. We visited the Botanical Gardens, which are quite beautiful, but not very well kept. Although the city covers a great deal of ground it is not closely built, and the whole place had the appearance of being overgrown with weeds and verdure. There were some beautiful places, especially that of the Governor. We passed the barracks and saw the soldiers drilling on the parade-ground. Poor fellows, far, far from home, they have a hard, rough life of it, with none to help them to be good.

When praying for missionaries in foreign lands do not forget the other strangers sojourning here. There are hundreds, yes thousands of Europeans in these Eastern countries. The temptations that surround them are fearful, and often overwhelming; and the seamen, they too should have a warm place in the hearts of God's people.

Shortly after leaving Saigon we entered the Gulf of Siam, and found the smoothest, brightest sea we ever saw. Scarcely a ripple broke the surface of the water, and the very air was still and slumbrous as though sleeping under the southern sky. We passed Pulo Obi early in the morning, and during the day saw several beautiful rocky islands: one called White Rock, against which the sea waves dash angrily when beaten by storms, but they do not wash away the beautiful green moss that covers their tops.

Yesterday we sailed S. E., to-day we go N. W., and the sun sets on the other side of the ship. As I watched the light die out and the twilight deepen, I thought of my old home far, far beyond the sunsetting.

One day a little boat was seen bobbing up and down on the waves. They signalled to the ship, and she hove to, and when the sorry craft came alongside, the poor passengers begged to be taken on board. They proved to be three Chinamen who had drifted out to sea, and had been tossing about for seventeen days. Their small native boat, such as we commonly see in rivers and canals, perhaps not more than fifteen feet long, was half full of water, and they had nothing to bail it out with but a cocoanut-shell. They were nearly famished; they had only seven sweet potatoes and about a pint of drinking water left. They had eaten nothing for nearly two days. They said they were saving the potatoes for fear they would starve! After putting their cargo, several old bags and a box, on board, they climbed on to our ship, and then set their old crazy tub afloat, and the sailors amused themselves shooting at it till it could no longer be seen.

On the morning of the fourteenth day after leaving Hong-Kong we found ourselves outside the bar at the mouth of the ma-nam Chow Payah, waiting for the tide to rise so we could cross over and steam to Bangkok. It is a mistake that travellers must here take little boats and be rowed up the river. It may have been so in the olden time. Indeed I have heard that the Siamese were afraid to have "fire-ships," as they call them, come to Bangkok, and to prevent it they had great chains stretched from shore to shore, and three Chinese junks laden with stones were sunk across the mouth of the river, and are to this day a source of danger and annoyance. But now, large steamers at high tide cross the bar and sail on and on through a wide, deep, open river and cast anchor in the very heart of the Siamese capital.

We were four and a half hours going up to Bangkok, but it would take me a long time to tell all the strange things we saw, and the thoughts that filled the mind and heart. I have no journal of that time, and my first impressions of this wonderful land to which God had led my willing feet, were all sent home in letters, and I cannot rewrite them now. But let me quote a page or two from Bayard Taylor's "Siam." The author visited Siam in 1857 in one of the vessels of the United States East Indian Squadron, and was present at the exchange of ratification of the treaty made in the previous year. He enjoyed advantages such as I have never had of seeing the royal life in the capital, and of visiting places of interest, sacred and historic. He seems to have ascended the river in the old-fashioned way—a row-boat, but here is his own story:

"There is enough to be seen in Siam if only it could be described. But nothing is harder than to convey in words the indescribable charm of tropical life and scenery; and it was in this, in great measure, that the enjoyment of my month in Bangkok consisted. Always behind the events which occupied us day by day, and behind the men and things with which we had to do, was the pervading charm of tropical nature, of soft warm sky, with floating fleecy clouds, and infinite depths of blue beyond them, of golden sunlight flooding everything by day, and when the day dies, its sudden death, of mellow moonlight as if from a perennial harvest moon; and of stars that do not glitter with a hard-pointed radiance, but melt through the mild air with glory in which there is never any thought of twinkling. Always there was the teeming life of land and sea, of jungle and river; and the varying influence of fruitful nature, captivating every sense with sweet allurements.

"It was drawing toward the middle of a splendid night in May when I found myself among the palms and temples of this singular city. It had been a tiresome journey from the mouth of the river, rowing more than a score of miles against the rapid current; and if there could be monotony in the wonderful variety and richness of tropical nature, it might have been a monotonous journey. But the wealth of foliage, rising sometimes in the feathery plumes of the tall ereca-palm—of all palms the stateliest—or drooping sometimes in heavier and larger masses, crowding to the water's edge in dense impenetrable jungle; or checked here and there by the toil of cultivation; or cleared for dwellings—was a constant wonder and delight. Now and then we passed a bamboo house, raised high on poles above the ground, and looking like some monstrous bird's-nest in the trees, but they were featherless bipeds who peered out from the branches at the passing boats; and not bird's notes, but children's voices that clamored in wonder, or were silenced in awe at the white-faced strangers. Sometimes the shining roofs and white walls of temples gleamed through the verdure, suggesting the magnificence and beauty which the statelier temples of the city would exhibit. Bald-headed priests, in yellow robes, came out to watch us.

"Superb white pelicans stood pensive by the river side, or snatched at fish, or sailed on sunny wings with quiet majesty across the stream. Or, may be, some inquiring monkey, grey-whiskered, leading two or three of tenderer years, stops to look at us with peculiar curiosity, as at some singular and unexpected specimen, but stands ready to dodge behind the roots of mangrove trees in case of danger. It will be fortunate for the traveller, if, while he is rowing up the river, night shall overtake him; for besides the splendor of the stars above him, there will be rival splendors all about him. The night came down on me with startling suddenness—for there is no twilight within the courts of the sun, just as I was waiting at the mouth of a cross-cut canal, by which, when the tide should rise a little, I might avoid a long bend in the river. By the time the tide had risen, the night had fallen thick and dark, and the dense shade of the jungle made it yet thicker and more dark.

"Great fern-leaves grew on either side of the canal and almost met over our heads. Above them towered the forest trees. Among them rose the noise of creatures countless and various. But the jungle, with its darkness and dim, had such a beauty as I have never seen equalled, when its myriad fire-flies sparkled thick on every side. I had seen fire-flies before and had heard of them, but I had never seen nor heard of anything like these. The peculiarity of them was that they clustered, as by one concerted plan, on certain kinds of trees, avoiding carefully all other kinds, and then, as if by signal, they all sent forth their light at once, at simultaneous and exact intervals, so that the whole tree seemed to flash and palpitate with living light. Imagine it! At one instant was blackness of darkness, and the croaking jungle. Then suddenly on every side flashed out these fiery trees, the form of each, from topmost twig to utmost bough, set thick with flaming jewels.

1*

"This peculiarity of Siamese fire-flies was noticed long ago by old Kämpfer, who speaks concerning them as follows: 'The glow-worms settle in some trees like a fiery cloud, with this surprising circumstance, that a whole swarm having taken possession of a single tree, and spread themselves over its branches, sometimes hide their light all at once, and a moment after make it appear again, with the utmost regularity and exactness.'

"The lapse of centuries has wrought no change in the rhythmic regularity of this surpassing exhibition. Out in the river once again, the houses on shore began to be more numerous, and presently they crowded together in continuous succession; and from some of them the sound of merry laughter and of pleasant music issuing, proved that not all of the citizens of Bangkok were asleep.

"The soft light of the cocoanut-oil lamps supplied the place of the fire-flies. Boats large and small were passing swiftly up and down the stream; now and then the tall masts of some merchant ships loomed through the darkness. I could dimly see high towers of temples, and broad roofs of palaces, and I stepped on shore with a half-bewildered feeling that I was passing through some pleasant dream of the 'Arabian Nights,' from which I should presently awake.

"Even when the flooding sunlight of the tropical morning poured in through my windows, it was hard to realize that I was not in some unreal land. There was a sweet, low sound of music filling the air, with its clear, liquid tones. And joining with the music was the pleasant ringing of a multitude of little bells, ringing I knew not where. It seemed as if the air was full of them. Close by was the palace of a prince, and somewhere in his house, or in his court-yard, there were people playing upon instruments of music made of bamboo. But no human hands were busy with the bells. Within a stone's throw of my window rose the shining tower of the most splendid temple in Bangkok. From its broad octagonal base to the tip of its splendid spire, it must measure, I should think, a good deal more than two hundred feet, and every foot of its irregular surface glitters with ornament. Curiously wrought into it are forms of men and birds, and grotesque beasts, that seem with their outstretched hands or claws, to hold it up. Two-thirds of the way from the base, stand four white elephants, wrought in shining porcelain, facing one each way toward four points of the compass. From the rounded summit rises like a needle, a sharp spire. This was the temple tower, and all over the magnificent pile, from the tip of the highest needle to the base, from every prominent angle and projection, there were hanging sweet-toned bells, with little gilded fans attached to their tongues; so swinging that they were vocal in the slightest breeze. Here was where the music came from. Even as I stood and looked I caught the breeze at it. Coming from the unseen distance, rippling the smooth surface of the swift river, where busy oars and carved or gilded prows of many boats were flashing in the sun, sweeping with pleasant whispers through the varied richness of the tropical foliage, stealing the perfume of its blossoms and odor of its fruits, they caught the shining bells of this great tower, and tossed the music out of them. Something like this Æolian tower there must be in the adjacent kingdom of Burmah, where the graceful pen of 'Fannie Forrester,' Mrs. Judson, has put the scene in verse:

> "'On the pagoda spire
> The bells are swinging,
> Their little golden circlets in a flutter
> With tales the wooing winds have dared to utter,
> Till all are ringing
> As if a choir
> Of golden-nested birds in heaven were singing;
> And with a lulling sound
> The music floats around
> And drops like balm into the drowsy ear.'"

This description of the temple bells of Bangkok belongs to the great pagoda at *Wat Chang*. It is the most imposing in the city, and is the one usually found in illustrated books and articles on Siam. The great pagoda, or *prachadee*, as the natives call them, seems to be of no use. It is simply to look at, and in this the old saying holds true, "that distance lends enchantment," for a nearer view dispels the illusion of granite, and of pure white marble; and even of porcelain elephants and gold and silver bells.

I do not think there is any entrance to the interior except just under the dome-shaped summit, where there is a cruciform room, through the openings of which at each of the four arms, the "porcelain" elephants protrude their huge trunks into the upper air. Beneath this it is a solid pile of brick and mortar, and the elaborate ornamentation of the outside is principally plaster, cunningly applied by the deft hands of Chinese workmen. There are flowers formed of bits of china and shells, and there are rows of whole plates and saucers, disposed around the pagoda, or sticking in the plaster up and down the shining pillars. They are the ancient suggestion, perhaps, of the modern plaques which now adorn the inside walls of the most elegant houses at home.

You can ascend to quite a height on the outside by climbing the steep narrow steps connecting the balustered galleries which completely surround the prachadee. When I was there I climbed till I was tired, and yet far above me were the elephants, and I could hear the tinkle of the bells, which are hung so high up that the trouble of getting them would be more to the thief than they are worth, for they are neither gold nor silver, but a sort of bell metal which no doubt holds the precious metals in very small percentage. I was so fortunate as to find one of the "little golden fans" that had dropped from its delicate fastening, and was surprised to find it larger than my hand, and heart-shaped like the leaf of their sacred *poh* tree, both the tree and foliage of which are similar to the cotton-wood with which we are so familiar in western America.

I have now been safely anchored in my mission station since the 20th of November, and you may be surprised to hear that I came "every step" of the way from San Francisco to the boat landing of my new home at Petchaburee by water. I consider myself quite a sailor after traversing nearly nine thousand miles of ocean and sea, river and canal. It required just forty-two days of water travel for my trip. Although I left Denver the 19th of July, I did not reach Petchaburee till the 20th of November, because I tarried by the way. My stay was very pleasant both in Japan and China, and the two days I spent in Saigon, Cochin China, I will never forget. That French port is more like a civilized city than any other I have seen on this side of the sea. These Eastern lands are more beautiful than I ever dreamed of, and Siam is not a whit behind any of the others. I was enchanted with it the very first evening, when, through the moonlight, we sailed up the river to Bangkok. The pure white gleam of the temples and pagodas, the cool shadows of their sacred trees, the silvery ripple of the river water, and the constant flash and sound of the fireworks put off in honor of the king, with now and then a strain of native music, were sights and sounds so novel to me, that thoughts and memories of all the Eastern romances I had ever read filled my mind; and my heart wondered at the seemingly strange Providence that had brought me into their very midst.

CHAPTER III.

THE KING'S REALM.

SIAM is a small kingdom in the North Torrid Zone, lying wholly within the tropics. Its entire area is but 190,000 square miles, not twice that of the Centennial State of Colorado, and is bounded on the north and west by the Laos provinces, Burmah and the Bay of Bengal; on the east by Anam and Cambodia, and on the south by the Gulf of Siam and the Malayan States.

It is the very heart of Farther India, but it does not seem to furnish the life-blood, the strength and vitality of that spur of the world jutting into equatorial seas, for foreign blood from western nations is beating at the extremities, as witness Singapore and Saigon, and we hope that soon the rising tide will overflow the heart and stir its sluggish streams to new and purer life.

The kingdom stretches from about the 4th to the 20th or 22d degree of north latitude, through a length of some 1,300 miles; its greatest breadth is about 450 miles, while at the Isthmus of Kraw it is not more than 50 miles. It is across this narrow neck that the French are trying to gain permission to cut a canal, a measure which the rest of the world should highly commend. But the project is opposed by all the English advisers at the Siamese court. They know too well the fate of Singapore should the carrying trade between China and the rest of the world flow across the Gulf of Siam direct to the Indian Ocean. They know, too, that Saigon and Hue may both become points of great commercial interest, and the French have the advantage on that coast. It is already three decades since this canal was first spoken of, and it may be years before it becomes an accomplished fact.

French agents have been at Bangkok, and the king graciously assisted them to survey the proposed route, sending the party down the coast in royal steamers, and in other ways showing his usual amiability.

Siam has six principal rivers, the Bangpakong, Chow Payah, Tacheen, Ma Klong, Petchaburee, and Chantaboon, besides many smaller streams, and almost innumerable canals, forming extensive water-ways, which are the chief thoroughfares throughout the kingdom. The bulk of all travel is performed by boat, as well as the transportation of goods or produce from one province to another. There are no railways and no established stage-coaches from one city to another. Within the last year or two hacks have been running in the capital, over the new roads which are being constantly extended and improved under the present energetic young ruler. It was during his royal father's reign in 1864, that the first road, worthy the name, was opened for travel in Bangkok.

As one leaves the capital, the roads become mere elephant trails, or bridle and foot-paths through the jungle. Around provincial towns, of course, there are a few roadways worn into ruts and gullies by the two-wheeled rice-carts which bear the harvests from the fields to the granaries. But for long, pleasant roads, stretching for miles and miles over hill and dale, the traveller sighs in vain.

The natural scenery of Siam is rather tame. Around Bangkok a dead level of rice-fields and fruit gardens, along the southern seacoast it is a little more rugged, while off to the north, near Laos, it is diversified by river and lake, hill and mountain. The latter are misty, sleepy-looking elevations, which would not be worthy of the name except that they are so far from the high and lofty Himalayas as to stand without a rival. None of them are high enough ever to be covered with snow. Indeed, I think the verdure creeps to the very summits. There are many volcanic islands along the gulf coast, mostly covered with thick jungle and inhabited by wild beasts. Fishermen sometimes venture into their quiet coves, but one might explore many a one without finding a single human habitation. Some of these islands are singularly beautiful, rising like mountains of verdure from the deep blue sea. As you approach them you can see the lovely sea-shells, and living corals, deep, deep beneath the waves, and the brightly-colored fishes sporting in the clear waters.

Siam has a few good harbors, and the gulf is seldom visited by those terrible typhoons which strew the China seas with almost yearly wrecks. Her larger rivers are navigable for some miles from their mouths. But where they empty into the sea there is usually a bar, which must be crossed at high tide by all large vessels.

All Siam's rivers flow through valley basins, or rather low-lying plains, and overflow their banks in the rainy season. The most rain falls in September, and during the next two months there is scarcely a path or street in Bangkok that is not overflowed at high tide with water nearly knee-deep. The whole country near the coast presents the appearance of a lake, with trees, houses, and temples peeping out of the water. Boats go everywhere. People lie in their houses and fish, and a traveller arriving in September or October, might ask, "Where is the *Land* of the white elephant?" All he can see is Siam in solution. Thousands of square miles are watered and enriched by these annual floods, and made so fertile as to rival the most productive regions of the earth.

All tropical fruits, plants, and cereals grow here in the richest profusion. Food is so cheap and abundant that no one need starve to death in Siam.

"A more healthy city than Bangkok cannot be found in all the tropics."

"The climate of Siam is genial and healthy."

"From November to February the weather is delightful, and the thermometer is seldom below 64° Fahrenheit. March and April are the hottest months, but the thermometer does not rise as high as might be expected in this latitude. I have never seen it over 98°."

The above quotations are taken from good authorities, and I will add one more to let the misinformed world see what old residents, of twenty and forty years' sojourn, think of Siam's delectable climate:

"Do not represent the climate of Siam as insalubrious. People die here, so they do everywhere else, except in heaven. Here people sometimes die of fever, of dysentery, of cholera, and sometimes men dig their own graves by the brandy bottle, cut their throats with the broken glass, and then stumble into it. The report that Siam is unhealthy is a libel on the climate."

This last is from Rev. Dr. Dean, who came to the East half a century ago, and is still living, a hale old man of nearly eighty, in Bangkok.

The seasons are two, the hot and cool, or wet and dry. The northeast monsoon blows from November to May, when the wind changes, and the southwest monsoon blows until the next November. The northeast monsoon greatly modifies the heat of March and April, and makes the Siamese mid-summer months endurable. The nights in Siam are almost always cool and comfortable.

I do not hesitate to say, after a happy, healthful residence of ten years in Siam, that foreigners, with care and temperate habits, can live here to a good old age, and keep as well as in any other land. But if they are too lazy, or keep too busy to take proper exercise, are intemperate in eating and drinking, spend their nights in dissipation and sin, and their days in needless exposure to the sun, they can lie down in their graves under the palm-trees before they are forty years old; yea, even before they are thirty, as many a Bangkok grave will testify.

The climate is just as healthy as that of Missouri, Illinois, or Kansas, and, with the exception of a few months each year, as pleasant as that of Colorado. Indeed, I never spent more delightful days under the shadow of the Rocky Mountains than I have seen here under the shadow, I might almost say, of the equator!

There are eight old people, Americans, in Bangkok to-day, who have spent from twenty to forty years here already, and one of them has never been out of Siam since she arrived, nearly thirty-five years ago, and all these are just as hale and hearty, and as strong, as old folks of their age in their native land.

Dr. Ernest A. Sturge, our resident physician, says he thinks there are as many fatal diseases in the United States as here, perhaps more; neither small-pox nor measles are usually fatal, while there are diseases which are never found here—diphtheria, and pneumonia, and yellow and scarlet fever, for instance.

Siam is capable of supporting a much larger population. No regular census has ever been taken, and we have never heard her people numbered higher than ten millions, and sober, matter-of-fact minds are apt to say six or eight millions. There are vast tracts of unwatered plain, and dense, uncut jungle, all of which might be reclaimed and cultivated by industry and perseverance; but thus far there has been no necessity for this, and these broad lands lie wild.

But the Chinese are immigrating in large numbers; twenty thousand of them are said to come here every year, and the majority remain. Other nationalities are flowing in across the borders, and through all the open ports, and are working changes, the end of which we do not yet see. All these people are attracted to Siam by her fertile soil, her fruitful gardens, her forests of teak and other useful and precious woods; her mountains strewn with jewels; her mines of gold and tin, lead and coal; her almost inexhaustible fisheries; her mild government, and the free, untrammeled life they are permitted to lead; while it is a notable fact that all foreigners fare better than the native population. Their privileges are greater, and their taxes less oppressive. They are not drafted into the army, and are not subject to the beck and call of every officer and nobleman in the unlimited ranks above them, for the real native Siamese are branded like beasts with the mark of their masters. Although they call their land "*Muang Thai*," the "Kingdom of the Free," all are slaves; all have masters; from the highest to the lowest, except the king upon his throne.

Notwithstanding the wonderful proclamation of freedom, of which one writer has given such glowing and heart-thrilling accounts, the Siamese are a nation of slaves to-day. How could such a proclamation, if it was ever uttered, be anything but a dead letter to a people who do not wish to be free, and who, if forbidden to sell themselves, their wives, and children, would consider it a great oppression?

Besides native slaves, there are, according to one authority, one million two hundred thousand prisoners of war, and their descendants, held in hopeless captivity, and made to serve three months out of every year. No effort is made by their respective countries for their redemption. They settle down in the land of their captivity, and, in time, learn its manners and customs, language and religion; and, intermarrying with the poorest classes, gradually lose their nationality, and become a part of Siam's heterogeneous people. Pure, *bona fide* Siamese are very rare.

The most important river in the kingdom is the one at Bangkok, called by the natives the Chow Payah, but known to the world as the Ma-nam. The latter is a common Siamese name for all rivers. "*Ma*" means mother, and "*nam*" waters, and thus the Chow Payah is, like other rivers, a "*ma-nam*." The Chow Payah rises among the mountains of Yunan, and flows south for eight hundred miles, and empties into the Gulf of Siam. It waters a wide, fertile valley, and along its banks are clustered most of the population of the kingdom. Its commerce and wealth, royal power and glory, culminate in Bangkok, the capital city.

As we trace back the annals of Siam, we must steadily ascend the ma-nam Chow Payah, and approach nearer and nearer those northern lands and races from which the indolent and unambitious Siamese descended. On its banks are ruins of former capitals, and, as each in its turn was abandoned, the newer cities crept closer and closer to the sea, and, in the same proportion, they came nearer to the rest of mankind. They seemed to be escaping the exclusiveness of the Celestial Empire, and reaching out hands for help and sympathy to the waiting world.

But, as is usual with newly-opening countries, it was not the best exponents of the outside world who first found their way to these shores; and it is a sad fact that many Europeans who came hither did not bring a blessing with them, but a curse, and were a disgrace to their native lands.

The Portuguese, with their love of adventure and dominion, were the pioneer visitors to Siam. They came in the beginning of the sixteenth century, and, being kindly received by the king, they settled in considerable numbers in Ayuthia, which was then the royal city, and in other provinces, and, for nearly one hundred years, enjoyed unmolested the advantages of commerce and diplomacy accorded them by the sovereign.

Then followed the Dutch, and afterward the French, who, in the time of Louis XIV., endeavored to seduce both the king and his people into an alliance with France and

Roman Catholicism. But a singularly honest Jesuit priest, less wily or ambitious than most of his order, had already taught that "the king's heart is in the hand of the Lord, as the rivers of water; He turneth it whithersoever He will." And so that old heathen king, nearly two hundred years ago, was able to withstand the flatteries of the French monarch, and to reprove Louis XIV. for meddling "in an affair which seems to belong to God," even the conversion of a soul.

In 1854, Sir John Bowring negotiated a treaty between Siam and Great Britain, and very soon after the United States of America secured a treaty through her ambassador, the Hon. Townsend Harris. And now this kingdom is in treaty relations with nearly all the civilized countries in the world, and their resident ministers and consuls occupy posts of honor and influence at the capital.

The coming of American missionaries to Siam long before—bringing with them Western civilization, good morals, and the pure and holy Word of God—prepared the way for the formation of these treaties, and made the work of the ambassadors a comparatively easy task. There was no need of gun-boats, of powder and shell. It was "peace and goodwill" that won the hearts and confidence of these Orientals. And if Commodore Perry, off the shores of Japan, on board his ship of war, sang,

"Praise God, from whom all blessings flow,"

much more should Sir John Bowring and Mr. Harris have sung the same glorious Doxology when, not only Siam's ports, but all her inland cities and towns, were thrown open with a welcome to the foreigner.

CHAPTER IV.

PRODUCTS.

"ITHAMAR," Land of Palm, might well be applied to Siam, for everywhere you look will be seen their graceful plumes, swaying in the tropic air. "Palms in cluster" dot the wide, fertile plains of all Southern Siam, and far to the north they are found, and in Laos the cocoanut palms are very large and productive. On the Maklong River there is a place called the "City of Twenty Thousand Palms." They fringe the rivers and canals through all the water-ways of the entire kingdom, and under the trees are seen the sugar camps, where the sweet sap is converted into that delicate luxury. The Palmyra, betel, cocoanut, and attap palms are the common varieties.

The betel furnishes the nut which these Orientals eat with lime, cera leaf, and tobacco. The yield in Siam is immense, and great cargoes are shipped to India and China, where the same disgusting habit prevails.

The Siamese cocoanuts are large and meaty, and great quantities of them are marketed even in Europe and America.

The "palm wine," of which you may have dreamed as something cool and delicious, is a very insipid, sweetish sap, and what we get here is flavored with the smoked bamboo joints in which it is gathered. When fresh, it is simple and harmless, but if allowed to ferment it soon becomes an intoxicating liquor. It is procured by squeezing and tapping the long spathe, or spike, containing the embryo blossoms and fruit, which are "full of sap," and are found near the top of the palm-tree, just under its crown of leaves. It is very dangerous work to climb up twice each day—to bring down the full vessels in the morning, and place the empty ones there in the evening—for the flow of sap is most copious during the cool, dewy night. When tapped they can be kept flowing for several months, by occasionally cutting a little bit from the wound, thus opening it afresh. Every part of the palm-tree is useful, and it is considered one of the greatest blessings God has given to mankind, and hence, no wonder an old Eastern legend says: "As the palm branches rustle in the night-wind, they murmur the sweet words, 'Jesus, Jesus.'"

Our gardens are full of tropical trees and flowers—the bamboo, the tamarind, the pomegranate, the banana, and the cactus. The air is sweet with the fragrance of tuberoses and shrubs, and the cypress swings its scarlet bells by the smooth, white walks, while the oleanders are crowned with great clusters of pink and white blooms. They grow without care, just as they do in Palestine. I love to think that the oleanders blossomed and brightened all along the shores of Galilee, where the Saviour loved to walk in the long-ago days of His sojourn upon earth. Perhaps He gathered them in His hands sometimes, or maybe the little children brought them to Him when He laid His hands on their heads, and blessed them.

I have some fragrant white flowers on my table that were gathered on the mountain at sunset. They have a luscious odor, like ripe peaches, and are very beautiful, with their white and pink veined leaves and golden heart. But I always feel sorry when I see them, for I know that in all the heathen temples these flowers, that Christ made, are placed as offerings in the open hand of Buddha.

One day a boy appeared at the school-room window, and handed me a cluster of blossoms from a century plant (aloe). It has been standing in our mission compound for years.

We noticed, several months ago, signs of flowering. It threw up a slender spike, five inches round at the base, and gradually lessening to the height of over twenty feet. About four feet from the top it began to branch, and now presents the appearance of a beautiful flower-tree on the top of a long pole. The flowers are small and delicate, and hang pendant from the branches like little bells. They measure about one inch across, and are composed of six petals, six stamens, and a three-lobed, fleshy pistil. The prevailing color is pea-green, verging to creamy white at the edge of the petals. The stamens are covered with golden pollen on little caps of brown velvet. They have a delicate odor, reminding one of the flavor of a delicious apple, and perhaps this, with its spiny leaves, induced the Siamese to call the plant "foreign pineapple."

We have flowers of almost every name and hue, beautiful in color and rich in fragrance. Orange blossoms and magnolias, camellias, crepe myrtle, Honolulu creeper, passion flower, lotus and other water-lilies, foliage plants, and vines and flowering trees of almost infinite variety; and generations of ferns, orchids, and parasites. Besides all the tropical flowers, many of whose names and forms I never knew before coming to Siam, there are many of the dear home favorites, that have been introduced by foreigners, such as roses, geraniums, dahlias, verbenas, pinks, morning-glories, and honeysuckle. The Siamese idea of beauty is a paved yard, or a ground plot in which not a spear of grass is allowed to grow. They are very fond of flowers, but they plant them in pots, or have a few blossoming trees.

The fruits embrace all the rich and luscious varieties usually found in the tropics. Some of them we must learn to like, and it takes as long, almost, as to learn the language; but when you once like them, oh, how you do like them! Pineapples, oranges, custard-apples, pomegranates, limes, plums, guavas, some fifty varieties of bananas and pumpelows, a large species of orange (*citrus decumana*), one of my favorites, and nowhere better than in Siam. In the Southern United States it is called the shaddock. We have also "The mangosteen, most delicate and most rare of them all. It grows only in Siam, and the lands adjacent to the Straits of Sunda and Malacca. The mangosteen is Siam's peculiar glory. Beautiful to sight, smell, and taste, it hangs among its glossy leaves the prince of fruits. Cut through the shaded brown and purple of the rind, and lift the upper half as if it were the cover of a dish, and the pulp of half-transparent, creamy whiteness stands in segments, like an orange, but rimmed with darkest crimson where the rind was cut. It looks too beautiful to eat, but how the rarest, sweetest essence of the tropics seems to dwell in it as it melts to your delighted taste!" And then, richest of all, is the durier, a large fruit with a thick, prickly rind. If the mangosteen is prince of fruits, this is surely king. Inside it is divided into distinct lobes, each containing several large seeds surrounded by pulp. The odor of the fruit is terrific, reminding one of onions and elderly eggs. But the flavor! Richest cream, and walnuts, and other indescribable essences, produce the matchless durier!

Siam is rich in other products—spicy peppers, cloves, nutmeg and mace, cardamums; cotton, sugar, medicines, dyestuffs, gamboge, stielac, pitch, rice, beeswax, ivory, fish, bird's-nest, gutta-percha, tiger skins and bones, buffalo horns, tumeric, teak lumber, eagle-rose, and sapan woods.

Among her vegetables we find corn, peas, radishes, lettuce, cabbage, celery, onions, garlic, squash, melons, citron, cucumbers, egg-plant, okra, beans, tomatoes, turnips, sweet potatoes, and yams. There are no carrots, beets, parsnips, nor cauliflower. But there are many native vegetables, new to us, that we learn to eat and relish, too. There are no grapes or berries, and only two kinds of nuts, cocoa and peanuts, but both of these are very plentiful. Tea grows wild; but I do not think it is ever cultivated, as it can be bought already prepared from China so cheaply. A great deal of tobacco is raised.

The forests and jungles abound in wild beasts. There we find the elephant, tiger, bear, wildcat, monkey, porcupine, deer, buffalo, wild boar, gazelle, squirrels, chipmunks, and even wild horses. Of birds there are many, and with brilliant plumage, and some of them are sweet singers; larks, swallows, doves, pigeons, parrots, mocking-birds, cat-birds, peacocks, crows, Java sparrows, jays, woodpeckers, kingfishers, hawks, snipe, plover, owls, heron, quails, buzzards, bats, and wild ducks, chickens, and geese. This land, like all tropical countries, is infested with snakes, lizards, and creeping things. They are not more dangerous than those of America, and I have never heard of a foreigner coming to his death on their account; neither have the crocodiles swallowed any of our company since the earliest years of missionary effort, and I do not think they ever will in the future. I have been stung more than once by a scorpion, and the pain is no worse, and the wound heals as quickly as the sting of a wasp. Flies, which were the delight of the brightest summers at home, are seldom seen in Siam, but we have a goodly number of mosquitoes, and ants are found everywhere, but they are splendid little scavengers, and so are the crows, vultures, and lizards; and the latter are more afraid of us than we need be of them. Of domestic animals there are dogs, cats, horses, goats, donkeys, cattle, and buffalo. The cows are not milked, as the Siamese have no use for milk, and the buffalo are trained to work in the fields like oxen. The cats are very queer; some of them have blue eyes, and little knots of tails, or no tails at all. There are also chickens, ducks, geese, and turkeys. In the market we can buy pork, beef, mutton, venison, buffalo meat, fowls, and fish of almost endless variety, fresh, salted, and dried, besides prawns, shrimps, lobsters, crabs, oysters, turtles, frogs, eels, and devil-fish. The natives think the latter is quite a delicacy. They also eat white ants, turtle and crocodile eggs, mushrooms and snails, and silk-worms. They are, moreover, so advanced in civilization that, like the French, they eat horseflesh when they can get it.

The mineral products are gold and silver, lead, iron, tin, copper, and antimony. The country is also rich in coal and petroleum. And there are quarries of white marble, and other useful stones, jewel mines and mountains, and buried treasures, hidden under the ruins of many an old temple or Buddhist pagoda.

There is a great deal of gold in Siam, but whether it has all been dug from her own mines, or imported, I cannot say. But we do see golden buttons, ear-rings, girdles, chains, armlets and anklets, beads, crowns, and betel trays, boxes, bottles, tea-pots, cups, goblets, plates, vases, pots, candlesticks, spittoons and cigar-cases, all pure beaten gold. There are golden hair-pins, and fans inlaid with gold and set with gems, garments of cloth-of-gold with jewelled buttons, saddles, bridles, and all sorts of both horse and elephant trappings, ornamented with that most precious metal. There are golden umbrellas, and a golden chair and sceptre for the king, golden idols, and pagodas overlaid with gold; paper with gold-foil pictures; and I once saw a love-letter, in which the first sentence was written in letters of gold. Gold-leaf is put up in the temple doors as offerings to the gods, and pasted on coffins as signs of love for the dead. Gold mining at Kabir, and other places, is carried on in the crudest manner possible. There are a few silver mines, but the Government is forced to buy Mexican dollars to make their coin at the Royal mint.

The people often dig up treasure that has been hidden by former generations, perhaps by misers or priests, or people who fled at the approach of the invading armies, and never returned for their own. Silver basins, knives and swords, and scissors with brass or silver handles, and old, old coins and ornaments, are thus discovered. It is quite common to bury money at the present day, for robbers are very bold, and there are no banks or safe deposits in Siam where the poor can hide their store. After a fire, the people often return to the ruined site, and dig up their pots of coin.

CHAPTER V.

BANGKOK.

BANGKOK is the Royal City, the capital and metropolis of this kingdom. There the old barbarous splendor of the realm culminated, and there the new life sprang up that is beginning to throb to the utmost bound of the sleepy old kingdom.

Bangkok is built for about six miles on both sides of the noble river, Chow Payah, and is thirty miles from the mouth, but in reality not more than half that distance from the sea. The downward current of the river is very strong, but the rising tides force the water back into the creeks and canals that intersect each other all over this semi-aquatic city, which, like the "Queen of the Adriatic," depends more on her water-ways for travel and transportation than on streets of solid ground. Ships of the heaviest tonnage anchor on either side of her wide river, and there are steamers, gun-boats, yachts, tugs, and innumerable smaller craft, of every variety.

One unique feature of this curious city, as of several others in Siam, is her floating houses. They are built of light wood, and thatched with the leaves of the attap palm (*Cocos Nipa*). They are buoyed up by bamboo rafts, and moored to the bank, or to posts driven into the mud. They are nearly all occupied as shops or stores, and here you can purchase your supplies with very little trouble, by stopping your boat and pointing out what you want in the wide open room before you, or having the goods handed in to your own boat for inspection.

You could spend days, yea, weeks, in sight-seeing in and around Bangkok, and yet go everywhere in your own boat.

There are some grand old temples, moss-grown and covered with mold, hidden among the sacred groves and lotus ponds, and others newly built, or repaired, shining in all the glory of gilt, fresh plaster, and Chinese paint. But whether old or new, haunted by pariah dogs, and bald-headed Buddhist priests, both alike, in great measure, the meanest of their kind, for every man who is too lazy to work enters the priesthood, where he is always sure of a living, and carries in his heart an expectation of a good place in the next world, which, I fear, is not so sure as his daily rice.

It is said that there are ten thousand of these drones in Bangkok alone, and one can easily believe it, for you meet them everywhere, and there are hundreds of temples and monasteries to shelter and support them.

Of the city's half million people, perhaps nearly one-half are Chinese, Hindoos, Malays, and other foreigners, of whom less than three hundred are Europeans.

When Bangkok was founded in 1782, the king's palaces and all the principal buildings were erected on the left bank of the river, but now the royal palaces of both the first and second kings are on the other side, also the famous temple of the Emerald idol, and Wat Poh, with the royal mint, the museum, the forts, arsenals, the post and telegraph offices, the best streets, drives, markets, and stores.

Merchants like best to have a river front for their houses, but all cannot secure this, and of late years the king has allowed many to establish themselves within the walls of the city.

The walls are fifteen feet high and twelve broad, and surrounding the city proper extend some four and a half miles. This wall is pierced by sixteen large gates and forty-seven smaller ones, and defended by sixteen octagonal forts, two stories high, and having two and three tiers of portholes. Within the city walls are palace walls, thick and high, with double doors and frowning forts, and in this most carefully guarded enclosure are the grand royal palaces of the king and queen, and scores of other palaces for the royal harem, that "City of Women," of which we have so often heard. The armory and the royal mint are both within the palace walls. It is estimated that the city walls enclose one hundred thousand souls; this leaves four or five hundred thousand outside, and if the city were attacked or besieged, it would be impossible for such a multitude ever to find shelter behind the gates.

Bangkok is situated upon a plain which is almost a dead level; there are no hills or mountains to relieve the eye in any direction. This plain is covered with rice fields, vegetable gardens, fruit and spice orchards, and gardens of betel, cocoanut, banana, and other tropical trees; orange, mango, coffee, and nutmeg. The soil is alluvial, and very rich and fertile, and the annual inundations prevent it from becoming worn out and unproductive; nevertheless, especially in the betel gardens, the natives often use rotten fish as a fertilizer, which produces anything but "spicy breezes," as the evening air drifts through the quiet groves of palm. But if you are so fortunate as to be gliding through moonlit canals in other parts of the city, where the flower-gardens and orange-trees are blooming in beauty and fragrance, every sense is filled with delight, and one could almost wish they might drift through such enchanting ways forever.

Like all Oriental cities, Bangkok has few sanitary laws, and such as have been enacted are seldom strictly enforced; yet it is acknowledged to be one of the healthiest cities in the East, and the cause is mainly due to the ebb and flow of the tide in the ma-nam Chow Payah, which cleanses the water-ways and carries the refuse seaward.

The streets are nearly all very narrow and crooked, and

only adapted to the Siamese, who until lately never pretended to use carriages, and always walked single file. They are also very uneven, with here and there great holes, crossed by rough stepping-stones, and during the highest tides are overflowed with water, sometimes knee-deep, for several hours each day. But the people go barefoot, and can pull up the waist-cloth to the desired height, and so never dream of improvement.

There are, however, a few wide, pleasant streets that deserve the name, and on the king's side of the city they are long enough to furnish six or seven miles of good driving. They are kept in tolerable repair, and in the dry season sprinkled through the heart of the city to lay the dust, and at night lighted by lamps and patrolled by watchmen and police.

The Chinese are very clannish, and settling together have given to some portions of the city quite a "Celestial" appearance. Their streets are close and dark, some of them covered overhead, and filled with real Chinese odors, principally onions, *samshoo*,* and opium.

But the people are industrious and enterprising, and do most of the work and control much of the wealth of Bangkok, outside of what is in the hands of the kings and nobles. Some of them have acquired titles and live in palaces, and own steamships and mills. They have their temples and joss-houses, their religious fêtes, processions, and festivals. Their holidays are recognized by the Government, and are granted the same privileges enjoyed by the Siamese national days. Their secret societies are many and formidable, one especially, called the *Ang Yee*, which sometimes threatens the peace of the kingdom and often disturbs that of the city. Its members seem banded together for mutual protection *in wrong-doing*.

---

* Chinese liquor.

I consider the Chinese the privileged class in Siam; they fare better in every respect than the ordinary natives; for this reason we find many of the latter cultivating queues and trying to pass as Chinamen. There is also a Mussulman's Square in Bangkok, where the Mohammedan Hindoos live and die. Their houses are built of brick, and the little stalls of shops are filled with many curious and useful things. All are merchants or peddlers. They have mosques and retain their old religion and old home habits as much as possible. They keep the long, long fasts, and go on pilgrimages to Mecca.

Bangkok is quite cosmopolitan, and her motto seems to be, "Live and let live." She is growing to be more and more European, with her Lord Mayor, her marshals, constables, courts, and judges; her military guard inside the city walls, and her land and water police; her hacks and 'busses, her regular steamer to Ayuthia, and another down the coast to Anghin, Bangplasoi, Patriew, and Chantaboon. There is a custom-house and officers, lighthouse, cable, telegraphs and telephones, gas and electric lights, and a system of signals by which news and calls for help can be readily transmitted. There are charts of the great river, maps of the city, and lately a Siamese General Directory has been completed.

The king's army and navy have their headquarters in Bangkok, and consist of the royal bodyguard, one squadron of cavalry, two battalions of infantry, and one company of artificers and sappers, three field officers, five aides-de-camp, eight in the regimental staff, eight lieutenants, nine sub-lieutenants, and thirteen cadets. In connection with the Royal Guards is a surveying department, composed of three foreigners and two native assistants. Then there are the artillery, elephant troops, and marine corps, with twelve gun-boats carrying thirty-nine guns. The Siam *Supporter*, of eight hundred and twenty tons, is the largest, and carries ten guns. There is a fort at Paknam intended to guard the approach to the city. In times of peace it may do pretty well as a health resort for soldiers, but in case of war it would never prove a Gibraltar.

The city is of considerable commercial importance. During the reign of Pranang Klow, which extended from 1824 to 1851, the king and his chief ministers of state had control of the commerce of the country, and entirely monopolized the trade between Siam and the outside world. They owned and loaded Chinese junks which made annual trips between Siam and China. But finding these awkward vessels too unwieldy, they essayed to build better ones of their own. In 1835 the late ex-regent, then an energetic young noble, had built and presented to the king the first square-rigged vessel ever made and owned in Siam. Others were built in rapid succession, and both European and American vessels purchased, which served as models for the native workmen. But it was not until 1855 that the first steamer was built here.

The aim of the Government was to keep the dreaded and hated Europeans out of their capital, but they were compelled to employ them to command their vessels, as the Siamese are very poor and ignorant sailors. These vessels soon unfurled the Siamese flag in Singapore, the Netherlands, East India Islands, and the ports of China. But that old selfish policy, so detrimental to the true interests and prosperity of the kingdom, has long since been abandoned, and commerce has been relieved of many of its former restrictions; still it is not as free and encouraging as the present day demands.

There are now five steamers making regular trips to Singapore and back, and seven that cruise between here and Hong-Kong. There are forty-four Siamese merchant vessels flying the Siamese flag, but commanded by German or Danish captains; with other occasional steamers.

In the olden time, say fifteen or twenty years ago, there were a few American ships in port, but now their appearance is so very rare that they are made the topic of a special newspaper article. Last year we saw the following:

"It appears that Siam, which has little trade with Europe, has still less with the United States. The records of the consulate state that there has been but one direct shipment from Siam to the United States the past four years. Some few American commodities, such as kerosene, oil, flour, canned goods, light vehicles, pumps, weighing scales, firearms, and sewing-machines, find their way thither in foreign bottoms through other markets."

English and German ships do most of the carrying trade to and from foreign lands. In 1882 the imports amounted to $7,104,361. Of course opium and liquor head the list, the first amounting to $481,862, and the second, $302,020. Kerosene oil comes next with $39,443. There were nearly $25,000 worth of silk Chinese trousers, and over $37,000 worth of umbrellas. But this last item is not to be wondered at when we remember that the sun is likely to shine every day in the year (as it did actually in 1883) in Siam, and the rain to fall six months out of the twelve.

Some one has said that kerosene oil is the most effective civilizer that was ever introduced into Japan, because it lightened the darkness of millions, adding to their hours of peaceful labors, and thus increasing their wealth and happiness. I am not prepared to say quite as much for its power in Siam, but it is wonderful to all how the oil-lamps have taken the place of the smoky, fitful torch, even in the huts of the poorest. As none but the best oil is ever shipped, we never hear of an explosion.

The steamships with cargoes "entered" at the Siamese Custom-house in 1882 were 238, of 135,920 registered tonnage; sailing vessels with cargoes, 103; Chinese junks, 151; steamers entered in ballast, 10; sailing vessels in ballast, 57. Total number entered, 559; value of cargoes as already stated, $7,104,361. In 1881 there were 585 vessels with cargoes worth $6,279,484.

The exports amount to a little more, averaging a little over two-thirds of a million per month. The greatest value, I noticed, was for July, 1883, when the report was $1,120,539. The principal articles are rice, sugar, pepper, and peas; rose, ebony, teak, sepan, and agilla woods; salt and dried fish; mussels and shrimps; hemp; ox and buffalo hides, horns, bones, and hoofs; elephant and rhinoceros hides and bones; tiger and other skins; cardamums, cotton, gamboge, sticlac, indigo, gumbenjamin, lotus and other seeds; tobacco, tamarinds, betel-nuts, cocoa and ground-nuts; turtle shells, raw silk, fish maws, sharks, armadillo and snake skins, birds'-nests, ponies, and cattle.

The street scenes are often very comical. The houses in the markets are so made that the front can all be taken down in the daytime, and the whole inner room and its contents exposed to view. If they have counters, they fill nearly the whole room, which is often not more than ten by eight feet, and upon it the merchant sits in the midst of his goods. The whole family, which usually lives in or back of the store, comes and goes at its own sweet will; and often the baby's hammock is swung from the ceiling, and the little one is cared for while customers are waited on. All sorts of trades are carried on in sight of every passer-by. You stop at a restaurant or bakery, and you see the inmates prepare the food or cake before your very eyes. The blacksmiths and tinners are hammering for dear life; and the tailors cutting and sewing, but always on the alert to sell a needle or a half dozen buttons.

In the barber-shops you can see the luckless Chinaman squirming and making faces while he sits on a high stool with neither back nor foot board, and has his ears picked, his head and eyebrows shaved, and his eyelashes and beard pulled out. The gamblers squat in fascinated groups, too intent on their game to look up or care who sees them at the nefarious business. The liquor-jars, too, are out in the street, and the people stop and drink with as much indifference as if it was water from a public fountain. Pigs, dogs, cats, and children throng these thoroughfares; there is no danger from horses or carriages, the streets are far too narrow to admit them, and all are willing to turn out of the way for the children.

It is not necessary to go to the Fiji Islands to see babies dressed in scarlet pocket-handkerchiefs, for that is a favorite costume in Siam; and although I have never seen one in an old umbrella-cover or a flour-sack, *a la* Panama, nor young men like the Japs, with stove-pipe hats or ladies' bonnets, yet there are other combination suits just as ludicrous, viz.: bracelets, anklets, and a woolen hood; a birthday suit and a warm, comfortable cigar; a waist-cloth and a lace sofa-tidy for a scarf; and there goes a pretty nobleman who failed to finish his toilet before he left the house, for he is followed by a train of servants carrying his hat, shoes, and umbrella, and others bearing his betel-box, his cigars, teapot and cup.

We meet Chinese, Siamese, Laos, Cambodians, and Karens, and now and then a disdainful Hindoo, who, no matter what caste he belongs to himself, seems to feel quite sure every one else he meets is a "pariah."

We sometimes hear shrill, falsetto voices above the din of the multitude, and passing on to where the crowd is so dense you can hardly force your way through, you will see a stage thrown across the street, and a band of Chinese eunuchs, dressed as men and women; mandarins and slaves performing some wonderful tragedy, with both action and voice raised to the highest pitch. Jugglers also come into the street, treading fire, and climbing knife-ladders in their bare feet, and piercing their cheeks with daggers. Here wander the sick and the lame, the leprous and crazy, and the blind, dumb beggars; for Buddhism, that is too gentle and benevolent to kill a dog or let a sick cat starve, but will nourish them in its temple grounds, has never taught its adherents to build homes and hospitals for poor, distressed human beings, but leaves them to die in the streets.

Often we see an idol-procession: a great gilded Buddha seated cross-legged on a litter, and carried, with shouts and beating of drums and gongs, to see how hot the sun is, and how much rain is needed. Again you will see him enthroned in the roadways, and an altar before him loaded with gifts, and burning incense-sticks, while Siamese theatricals are being performed for his entertainment. All such plays and performances are free. Some nobleman or rich person hires the troupe, and then thinks he makes merit by letting others see the performance for nothing. All that is necessary is the stage and an awning. There is no curtain even, and the actors array themselves in public. One would almost think it was counted in as a part of the play.

But it is out upon the river that every phase of city life displays itself. It is the splendid highway of commerce, of trade, of fashion, and of journeys. The palaces and temples have their gates upon the river. Out upon the river come the kings in their great dragon boats, that look like centipedal monsters with uplifted heads. As these strange craft make swiftly toward one, and the sharp, startling cry of the dusky and almost naked oarsman, breaks upon the ear, no second exhortation is required to clear the way for royalty. Out upon the river come the kings for coronation or for burial. Out upon the river come the priests to visit or to beg or to perform their priestly functions at some distant shrine or temple. Out upon the river come the peddlers with their merchandise, and the hucksters with their various supplies. Out upon the river for a visit or a purchase or an airing all must go who live in

Bangkok, as you would go out upon Broadway or upon the avenue, if you are living in New York. Until lately the river frontage of palaces was nothing but a group of scraggy boat-houses and servants' quarters; but now better ideas prevail, and good landings and graceful salas or porches, with here and there a dooryard, may be seen.

There are some beautiful private gardens in Bangkok, adorned with fountains and statuary, fish-ponds, lotus-lily lakes, and cages for birds and animals. They are pleasant parks in the midst of heathenism, and foreigners are allowed to visit them frequently. The Minister of Foreign Affairs gives delightful garden parties, and invites all the missionaries and other foreigners. There are arbors covered with flowering vines, furnished with seats for the weary. There are tables and garden chairs of iron, painted some pretty color. They also furnish music and refreshments, the latter prepared at a European bakery, and including many of the good things of the home-land, even ice-cream and cake.

The Royal Museum is open every Saturday from twelve M. to half-past four P.M., and so is the king's garden at the Saraurom Palace, except when the Buddhist sacred day falls on Saturday. Bands of music are in attendance, and it is a favorite resort. Occasionally the king gives a garden party there to distinguished guests. When the Duke of Mecklenburg was in Bangkok he was entertained and saw the white elephants there in their royal trappings of scarlet and gold. Several alligators are kept in a pond near one of the gateways. A new building for rare plants has been erected; and just lately the guests of a brilliant garden party dined there, surrounded by twenty-six varieties of orchids all in bloom, while two royal bands discoursed pleasant music. The croquet and tennis lawns are carefully preserved. Princes and nobles often give birthday parties, and also invite foreign guests at the opening of new palaces, or when their children have their topknots shaved off.

There is very little foreign society in Bangkok, and what there is, seldom meets except at church or on some public occasion, for it is a city of magnificent distances, especially if the tide happens to be against you both going and returning.

There is an English chapel where the missionaries hold regular services on the Lord's day. The Ladies' Library is kept in this chapel, and is opened once a week for the exchange of books. It contains thousands of volumes in English, French, and German. Near by is the foreign cemetery. The plot of ground was given by the late king in 1853, and already there are quite a number of graves. Many of them are filled by dear little children who were called away before they knew the sin and sorrow of the wicked land in which they were born; others are graves over which parents might weep forever, of wild, wicked sons, who ruined soul and body with the vices and indulgences of this idolatrous and voluptuous city, and who, with natural force abated, and eyes bleared and dim, died before their heads were gray; sailors, too, who expired in this strange land, far from home and friends, some on shipboard, and others whose bodies were recovered from the water.

There, too, are many "asleep in Jesus"; those old saints, Drs. Jones and Bradley, with their wives, who, one might almost say, were "the beginning of the Gospel" in Siam, and grouped about them are others who finished their course and were translated. Caswell, French, and Chilcott; Mary Campbell, whose bright young life, like that of Mr. Benham, was quenched in the deep waters of the Chow Payah; and David MacLaren, who last year was called to wear the victor's crown, when he had but just buckled on the armor, and as a Christian soldier was preparing to storm Satan's citadel. All are sleeping side by side, waiting for the resurrection, while the palm-trees, like stately sentinels, guard the spot, and the sunshine and the rain, the rush and the whirl of the heathen capital are alike unheeded.

Besides the legations in England and America, the king has an Envoy Extraordinary and Minister Plenipotentiary at the courts of Continental Europe; Consuls-General in London, Paris, New York, and Hamburg—all foreigners; also consulates in Calcutta, Hong-Kong, Macao, Lisbon, Mauritius, Penang, Rangoon, Saigon, Singapore, Batavia, Bordeaux, Marseilles, and Vienna, and the different powers in treaty relations with Siam also have their representatives, legations, consulates, and agencies in the royal city of Chulalangkorn.

Bangkok is no longer the sleepy old city of fifty years ago, when the events of greatest interest were the capture of a white elephant, the consecration of an idol, the burning of an old king or the enthronement of a new. It has been awakened by the call of the Western world, and will never again sink into the former lethargy.

CHAPTER VI.

PEEPS INTO PALACES.

The king and his royal family do not live in that utter seclusion and privacy which characterize the imperial household of his celestial neighbor, the Emperor of China. Although the doors are not thrown wide open to all who would come and go, yet it is always possible to gain an audience with the king; and even the queen is not invisible, though dwelling in her private palace within the triple-walled "City of Women." And whoever meets their majesties are sure of a gracious reception.

In the fall of 1882, the United States Minister, Mr. Halderman, secured a private audience for the old and new missionaries. Quite a reinforcement had reached us; some for Siam proper, and others who had Cheung Mai as their objective point.

At the appointed hour we left our boats at the Noblemen's landing, and were escorted by officers through the great gates of the city wall into the palace enclosure, to the new and beautiful "Maha Prasaht Chuck Ree," "the Three-towered Palace." It is a magnificent building lately completed and occupied by the king. It took five days to consecrate it with holy water and the merit-making offerings of incense, blessings, and benedictions. These Buddhist ceremonies were performed in the various throne-halls and in the royal sleeping apartments. Some Buddha relics were enshrined in an idol, and they bore aloft in grand procession the royal white umbrella. The king enjoyed the orthodox number of baths in showers of consecrated water, and the putting off and on of royal attire; and after sitting on the eight designated points of the compass, finally ascended the gorgeous throne, and received anew the congratulations of his people. There was a distribution of new decorations to princes and nobles; there were feasting and music and mirth, and the usual Siamese theatricals for the entertainment of the thronging multitude.

The new palace is a combination of European and Siamese architecture, and the roof is singularly beautiful, with its glazed tiling and highly ornamental pagoda towers. On the front wall is a large medallion portrait of the king, and bronze elephants guard the royal entrance. Going up the broad stairway, past fluted pillars, statuary, flower-stands, and the gaily dressed Laos pages, we entered the waiting-room. The floor was of black and white marble, the furniture covered with maroon leather and stamped with the royal seal. A crystal chandelier depended from the centre of the frescoed ceiling. Gas-burners were all about the walls, and lighted up their tinted surface, and flashed back from the polished arms and armor hanging there. As we tarried, some young princes entertained us, and tea was served from silver trays in cups of delicate china, gold-rimmed and marked with the king's monogram. When ushered into the royal presence we were introduced by Minister Halderman, and the king shook hands with each one. Then our minister made a short address, during which he said, "These are representative Americans, and at home we have fifty millions more! They were good citizens there, and I assure you they will be true and loyal to your Majesty's government here." The king requested Mrs. Dr. Bradley, who sat on his left hand, the place of honor in Siam, to tell us that " he was glad to see us, and to welcome so large a company to his kingdom, for Americans aided in the prosperity and advancement of his realm. And although he did not hold to our religion, yet he welcomed us as teachers of that which is wise and good." Dr. McGilvary took occasion to thank him for his interest in the Christians at Cheung Mai, and his proclamation of religious liberty to the Laos. His Majesty replied that "he wished to maintain the principles of his father, and to uphold his royal policy." Mrs. Dr. Bradley then spoke of Miss Campbell, the young missionary to the Laos, who was drowned; and that now four other ladies were on their way to the north to take up the work, and then added, "I believe Siam will become a Christian nation, and when that glad day comes I will be ready to go home." "I fear," said the king, "that will not be for a long while yet." She continued: "We desire the king and his people to be very happy. Rulers and their subjects in Christian lands are much happier because of Christianity." The king laughingly rejoined, "I think that the Czar of Russia is not so happy as the King of Siam."

The hall in which the audience was given is large and beautifully decorated. A sort of family gallery appeared on the walls in the portraits of the king and queen and notables of former reigns. Here and there were bronze and marble statues, flower-stands, and lamps. The furniture was upholstered in pink silk brocade, which contrasted finely with the gleaming marble tables.

Before leaving the palace, we were requested by one of the princes to write our names in the king's autograph album under date of our birthdays. Taking leave of royalty, we were escorted through the dusk of evening to our boats and carriages by the royal guardsmen, bearing lighted tapers.

Now we will take a long look backward, more than half a century, and see what an old French bishop writing in 1829 has to say:

"The palace consists of many buildings surrounded by a triple wall. The care of the outside gates is confided to men. The inner gates are guarded by Amazons. These women are not reckoned among the wives of the king, but receive pay and rations like soldiers. In the third enclosure is a remarkable garden, and containing in miniature a representation of the world as they imagine it to be—woods, mountains, cultivated fields; a sea with islands, vessels of war and merchantmen of every nation; a city, a village, a bazar, a market held by the ladies of the palace, a fortress with cannon, religious temples, manikins representing all the different nations of the earth in their costumes; all quadrupeds and birds, and all the rare trees and plants they can produce. They call it the 'Garden of Delights,' or 'Terrestrial Paradise!' It is on the model of that at Peking.

"As there are persons enclosed here who have never seen the world, and who never will see it, they have thus an imperfect notion of what it contains. It is illuminated at night by lamps. The ladies of the harem retire to the garden and amuse themselves there, if they please, till morning."

I will also let you read some letters from my friends, and through them catch glimpses of what you may never behold with your natural eyes:

"It was on one of Siam's hottest afternoons that we made our toilets with unusual care, and set out to pay our respects to Her Majesty Somdet Pranang Klow, Queen Sawang Wattana ('Radiant Light'). As we came into the palace grounds the glare from the white glittering walls was blinding, and the hot sanded walk almost burnt through our shoes. So we quickened our steps, and passing around the front of his majesty's new palace, soon came to the heavy gate that is the entrance to the little city of three thousand women, the harem of the King of Siam.

"A number of soldiers on the outside, and a number of women on the inside of this gate keep guard, and see to it that no one enters without a royal permit. As our escort was in the habit of going daily at this hour to give lessons in English to the queen and her sister, the guard evidently concluded that she had permission to take the present visitors with her; so we spoke pleasantly to the different persons who sat or stood about, and, unchallenged, passed into a walled city within a walled city.

"The impression at first was far from pleasant as we passed along the narrow paved streets, where scarcely a shrub, or even a green blade of grass is to be seen; and between the high doorless and windowless walls, which are the ends and not the fronts of the houses. The dwellings seemed to be in pairs, with the fronts facing each other, and a gateway leading into a little narrow alley, which is common to both houses.

"This little city is not without its tradespeople, its markets and shops. Apparently everything that native women need to buy can be found spread out on the pavement for sale. In one place we noticed panungs,* scarfs, kerchiefs, and various kinds of native and foreign cloth; in another there were baskets of fruit and vegetables, betelnut and cinleaf and tobacco, and further on baskets of fish and buckets of rice.

"On our way we went down one street and up another; turned a corner here and crossed a street there, till at last we came to a kind of open court-yard, and to the steps of a handsome building, which looked quite different from those we had passed, because it has cheerful windows and hospitable-looking steps leading up to the wide-open doors. The court-yard is covered with grass, and flower-pots are on the steps and in the windows. Numbers of women were sitting on the broad stairway and around the doors; they did not rise as we came near, but simply gave themselves a little shuffle, as if they meant to make room for us to thread our way through among them.

"The first room at the head of the steps is her majesty's private chapel, and was all arranged for services. We did not enter, because the yellow priests in their yellow robes were already there, seated, tailor-fashion, on beautiful divans covered with yellow silk.

"We stood waiting for a moment, when a messenger came with an invitation from the queen to go up to her own drawing-room. We gladly turned and followed the messenger through a wide hall to the back of the building, and then up a flight of narrow winding stairs, and, strange to say, here, on the stairs, and in that awkward place, we met the queen and her sister as

---

* Siamese waist-cloths.

they were on their way down to '*fung tate*'—listen to the Buddhist service. Then and there we were introduced to two apparently very unassuming young ladies; neither of them looked to be more than sixteen years of age, but in reality the queen is twenty and her sister eighteen. In person they are of delicate frame, and under the medium height for Siamese women. They are quite graceful and good-looking, and so much alike that although I have seen them several times since, I am never sure that I know one from the other.

"The royal ladies politely excused themselves and passed down to the chapel, and we were taken up to a very pretty, cheerful drawing-room. Everything was handsome and in good taste, rather than costly and splendid. The beautiful carpet, chairs, sofas, and tables, were all of foreign make, and so were the mirrors, pictures, and other ornaments. Heavy satin curtains were looped up at the sides of a doorway into another room, and through that half-curtained way we caught but a glimpse of her majesty's bed-chamber, with its lovely lace-curtained bed, and furniture to match that in the drawing-room. There was only one thing that was truly Oriental, and that was the deportment of her majesty's maids of honor. Of course, they are of the highest rank in the kingdom; the youngest sister of the late king was one of eight or ten who were passing in and out, and seemed to be the special favorite. Some of them remained in the room all the time we were there, and some came up with the queen from the preaching. But no matter whether the queen was in the room or not, these maids of honor dropped to their knees the moment they came to the door, and walked around that way as long as they remained in her majesty's apartments. Although this custom has long since been abolished in the king's presence, as the ladies of the royal household are more conservative, it is still kept up in the women's apartments.

"The religious services lasted perhaps an hour, and then the queen came up, followed by a number of young princesses. She came into the room very quietly, and took a chair on the opposite side of the table from where we sat, and at once entered into conversation in an easy, social way. I noticed that when the court ladies who had been to '*fung tate*' came in, the others greeted them with a quiet, '*Bang songe boon hi*' ('Give us a share of your merit').

"The heir-apparent, who is perhaps three or four years old,

was soon brought in in the arms of his nurse, and, of course, he was then the object of attraction. He came and sat on my knee, but as his only dress was what nature gave him, with the addition of a few gold ornaments, I held him rather awkwardly, and soon gave him back to his nurse.

"As the queen was supposed to be now ready and waiting for her lesson, we took our departure, and as gracefully as possible bowed ourselves backward out of her presence.

"We left the palace feeling that we had enjoyed a pleasant interview with a very agreeable but by no means a powerful personage.

"On another occasion we called at one of the ordinary houses of this little city. We turned from a narrow street into a gateway, and found ourselves in a narrower alley, not particularly clean and tidy, with the front door of one house on our right, and that of another on our left. We could but wonder if such near neighbors are always good friends! On going up the narrow little steps and entering, we were met by a number of women and girls all busy decking themselves out in an unseemly mixture of native and foreign finery. It was a gala day with them, one of the rare occasions when they were allowed to see the king and the other inhabitants of his palace. The only room that we saw was small and dark, and just then was in a state of extreme confusion; betel trays, spittoons, open trunks, and all manner of clothing were jumbled together over the floor. The women and girls were talking in a very loud tone, and evidently too much excited to entertain foreign visitors; so in a short time we bade them good-bye, and turned our steps homeward once more through the narrow streets."

The king has several palaces situated in different parts of his realm. An old one at Petchaburee, a newer one at Ratburee, and one not yet completed at Bang Pa In, an island in the Chow Payah, north of Bangkok. It was during a pleasure trip to this island that the late queen was accidentally drowned. In a letter dated, "en route for Cheung Mai, December 20, 1882," there is this notice of the new palace:

"Last Friday we passed one of the king's summer resorts, where he is having a palace built. The man who is superintending the work showed us through a part of the house. It is a beautiful structure, and looks as if it might be the summer residence of some American millionaire. It is built of teakwood, and the outside painted in brown and white bars. Some very pretty landscapes in water-colors, and some oil paintings adorn the walls. Two of the rooms are separated by lace and brocatel curtains, and at one end is a large bay-window. The chairs are cushioned and covered with old gold and blue brocaded satin, and there are several handsome French mirrors. The women's apartments are in the rear of the king's palace, also a plain white marble monument erected in honor of the late queen. The grounds are enclosed by a neat fence and laid out in flower-beds."

Near this palace is a new Buddhist temple built in modern style and seated with pews, perhaps the first Buddhist temple ever furnished with such accommodations for worshippers. Turning to an old letter, I read:

"In the evening we went to the temple, a handsome building, just like a Catholic church, without the cross or the belfry. There were stained glass windows and a foreign bell, rung by a rope from below. We were told that we could not be admitted until the priest who kept the keys would return to open the temple for service at nine o'clock at night. We therefore returned to our boat and waited. Soon the sweet tones of the bell rang out over the water. We did not wait for the second bell, not caring to attend service at that hour, but went up at once, and found the temple lighted with lamps. There were fifteen chandeliers with sixty-eight lamps, but only a few were lighted. An image of Buddha was placed where the pulpit would be in a Christian church, and several small images were in niches along the walls at each side. On the left is the king's seat, and on the right one for the priest, who reads the Pali services. The floor is laid with black and white marble. All was kept very neat and clean.

"The priests invited me to play the organ, and finding it had a crank I accepted; and the melody of a lively German march echoed from the roof. I noticed that most of the tunes it played were waltzes and polkas."

There are no "zenanas," strictly speaking, in Siam, and even the ladies in the royal harems are often allowed to go outside the walls and witness state ceremonies. Of course, they occupy retired positions—often behind curtains or screens—and are not allowed to mingle with other spectators. But they are there, and with ears and eyes take in a great deal to carry back to their quiet, monotonous life in the palace, and to think and chat about till the next fête day. They have very little to occupy their time; no sewing to do; no studying of fashion plates, or deciding which "love of a bonnet" to buy. The Siamese costume has been essentially the same for centuries, in palace and in hut, with only a difference in the number of cloths possessed, and the cost and texture of the material; and one garment often suffices for the royal ladies of the harem even as it did for revellers in France in the olden time.

In such undress assemblages, with sometimes the slight addition of a silken scarf, do the ladies of the royal harem often meet. But of late years changes are busy even there, and I have heard whispers of foreign costumes which the ladies have "tried on," again and again, to the infinite amusement of all beholders. The day is coming when they will not only order them from England and France, but wear them afterward; and even learn to appear in public, that is, outside the walls of their own private palaces, dressed in more modern garments. A few of them wear lovely dressing sacques, ruffled and embroidered, and silk and satin jackets edged with costly lace, and fastened with gold buttons and jewelled brooches. They are not so loaded down with gold chains and rings as they used to be, but what they do wear is more costly and of delicate workmanship. Many Siamese women are jewellers, and make exquisite articles of pure, beaten gold, but their setting of jewels is still quite rude.

Hindoo and other peddlers often find admittance, and

tempt the ladies to do a great deal of shopping in their own apartments. Some learn to embroider, and do fancy-work. They make wax and paper flowers for crematories and temple decorations, and the loveliest chandeliers, lambrequins, table-covers, and even curtains of lace-work of natural flowers threaded and netted in beautiful patterns. When one remembers that their festivals often last for days and weeks, we can see that the frequent renewal of such fragile ornaments must consume a great deal of time. Some, indeed, are not above preparing fancy confections, and sending their slaves out to sell them. Others read novels, poetry, and plays, and spend countless hours in gambling. Sometimes there is a flirtation with some gay and reckless prince or noble outside. But if discovered the penalties are very severe. I have heard of both parties being put to death. The latest instance of flirting resulted in the disgrace of both; the flogging of the young nobleman, and banishment from the capital; while the lady who dared be faithless to her faithless king, was condemned to wear chains and cut grass for the royal elephants all the rest of her life.

After the king's visit to Petchaburee in 1876, we were on the mountain one evening, and were admitted to the empty palace. We were interested in seeing the little pens set apart for the king's wives. They were side by side, and made of teak boards. They were no larger than the state-room of a steamer, and had but one little door, and this opened into the large room in which they were set, like so many little boxes on the floor, for the board walls of these stalls did not reach half-way to the ceiling. Is it not dreadful to think that women, our sisters, are thus crowded together like stalled cattle, and kept for the sinful pleasure of one man!

A dear little pupil in one of our schools was telling me of her older sister, who was presented to the king when she was fourteen, and has been in the palace ever since. She has an annual gift from the royal treasury of some sixty dollars, and a slight monthly allowance besides. Her father sends her rice, and she has some of her other food from the royal kitchen. It is not true that these women each have separate palaces. They huddle together, sometimes five or six in one house, with their relatives and servants. Those of higher rank may live more retired, and they also receive more from the royal treasury. But many of them are rich in their own right, and do not depend upon the king for support; and, indeed, they are not responsible for their presence in the king's household, having had nothing to do with it, except, perhaps, to consent, with a child's foolish heart, to the flatteries and representations of their designing relatives, who in Siam, as in some other lands, are always anxious to get their daughters "married off," not particularly caring what they get them married into. So we must pity more than we blame these poor, blind, helpless women for living as we find them.

They are called "Forbidden Women," because they are not allowed to go outside the gates without permission from the king himself, and this privilege costs a good sum, for they are in the habit of "tipping" all who attend them, and these are Amazons, guards, servants, and old women, who go and return with the royal lady, or "Nang Harm." I know of one who went to visit her dying father and it cost her nearly fifty dollars, more than half her yearly allowance. Their mothers and younger sisters may dwell with them in the palace, and their own children, though they be sons, until they are four or five years old, and then they are sent outside to the care of relatives or royal nurses.

Every year new maidens are admitted to the privileged circle, and those who are growing old, slipping up toward twenty-five or thirty, or have no children, are invited to take the first step downward and become attendants and waiting-maids of younger and brighter girls. Thus at an age when a true and earnest-hearted woman of the West has but reached her full, ripe womanhood, her sisters of the East are cast off as old and childless, and are become as "a woman forsaken and grieved in spirit, and a wife of youth that wast refused." And, saddest of all, they know nothing, these poor palace women, of their "Redeemer, the Holy One of Israel; the God of the whole earth," whose kindnesses are everlasting, and whose love and mercy are unbounded.

Oh, the cruelty, the bitterness, the irony of such transfers; 'tis only because these poor creatures know of no other life that they submit to it with a sort of dumb patience.

Almost my last work before leaving Siam, was the preparation of a book entitled "Stories of Jesus." It was published in Bangkok, and bound up with illustrations sent from London. Through General Halderman, our United States Minister to the Court of Siam, I presented twenty copies handsomely bound to the queen, and received from the king himself, a letter of acknowledgment and thanks for the gift. Let us hope that these "Stories of Jesus" may enter into the hearts of the inmates of the king's palaces, and thus proclaim the Gospel to those who are hidden away from our personal influence, and help brighten the lives of some poor souls groping in the darkness and gloom of a Buddhist harem. It is a significant fact, in this connection, that Buddhism offers no salvation for woman. The best it can do for her is to hold out the false hope that in some of her future transmigrations, she may be born a *man!*

CHAPTER VII.

SOME KINGLY CUSTOMS.

It is a great deal of trouble to be a king, and no doubt those who wear the crown and bear the royal sceptre, often long for the quiet and liberty of the less regally favored ones of their realm.

Just think, for instance, of having one's head shaved in the presence of thousands, and having to undergo various baths and changes of apparel before the very eyes of assembled rank and nobility. But such custom has decreed to be the fate of all Siamese monarchs, and the rule for past centuries has been almost as inflexible as the laws of the Medes and Persians.

The removal of the topknot from the head of a young Siamese prince marks the boundary between childhood and manhood, and is accompanied by imposing ceremonies which last for days and cost immense sums of money. They affect even the most remote provinces, for the governors are expected to grace the fête with their presence, and also bring gifts according to their rank for the young prince.

Gaudy processions are one of the chief features of almost every public Siamese ceremony, and when the present king, Chulalangkorn, whose name, by the way, means "Regal Topknot" or "Royal Hairpin," or something of that kind, was deprived of his forelock, the procession was unusually long and magnificent.

The customary mount representing Meru, which is supposed to uphold the heavenly worlds, was constructed in the palace gardens. It was formed into grottos and caves, and ornamented with shrubs and flowering plants. On the summit was a graceful pavilion, draped with costly curtains and glittering with gilt and tinsel; at its foot were artificial animals, among which the white elephant and the sacred white ox were conspicuous.

On the appointed day the prince, richly attired and loaded down with the weight of golden chains and shackles on hands and feet, was borne in state, seated in a gilt and jewelled sedan-chair, between a body-guard of richly-dressed noblemen. Before him in the hands of their bearers sparkled and flashed the gold umbrellas and fans, and some stately Brahmins marched carrying golden vases filled with parched rice, which they strewed to right and left in token of plenty. Following them were Amazons from the "City of Women," and twelve maidens in cloth-of-gold; surrounding three lovely girls, two of whom bore branches of gold and silver covered with bright leaves and flowers, and the other a superb peacock's tail brilliant with its argus eyes and ever-changing colors. Two young noblemen carried golden lotus-shaped vases, in which nestled fabulous birds, whose song is said to entrance even beasts of prey. They were followed by troops of boys, their shoulders fairly covered with gold collars and necklaces, and others dressed as Chinese, Malays, Hindoos, and English; the king's Japanese body-guard, some infantry and pioneers.

All along the outside of the line marched thousands of men representing Buddhist angels to guard the procession in its march through the imaginary forest to the sacred mountain. They were frightful-looking angels with their black faces, hands, and feet, protruding from their conical caps and queer gauze robes. This was but a part of the *cortège*. Behind the prince's golden throne were young girls bearing his betel-box, spittoon, fans, and swords, and others carrying the many golden vessels indicative of his high and royal rank. Then there were troops of children in fanciful costumes; maids of honor; and ladies of the harem crowned with gold, and neck, hands, and arms sparkling with jewels of great worth and beauty. On and onward reached the pageant, gradually decreasing in rank till naught was left but bands of women representing different nationalities, or real captives from all tributary provinces, including the Karens and Laos, and slaves of the prince.

At the foot of the mountain there was a comic play representing an encounter between the kings and chiefs who desired to witness the august ceremony, and some hideous monsters riding on eagles. The king himself and several of the principal ministers of state took part in this drama. When the inquisitive chiefs and rajahs were disposed of, the king received the prince, and setting him in the place of honor, the people offered homage. Then royal ladies conducted him down the marble steps to a golden basin where two maidens bathed his feet in pure water.

He next proceeded to the Maha Prasaht, where are deposited the bone relics of his royal ancestors. In an inner chamber of the temple he was seated on a costly carpet before an altar, upon which incense tapers slowly burned, filling the space with their smoke and dull, heavy fragrance. In his hands were placed some Buddhist texts inscribed on a palm-leaf, and a ball of unspun thread which was made to encircle the sacred hill, the temple, and the head of the prince himself; from thence nine strands extended to the altar and into the hands of the attending priests.

It was not, however, till the morning of the third day, that the tuft of hair was severed from the brown pate. This was done in the early morning amid the clang of trumpets and blowing of conch-shells; after which he was clad in white and bathed in a fountain whose streams ran through those sacred beasts at the foot of the mountain.

He was again arrayed in white silken robes and led by ladies of rank to the pavilion on the summit, where the king waited to bestow his royal blessing. With one hand raised to heaven and the other on the bowed head of his son, he solemnly uttered words in Pali, which may be translated thus:

"Thou who art come out of the pure waters, be thy offences washed away! Be thou relieved from other births! Bear thou in thy bosom the brightness of that light which shall lead thee, even as it led the sublime Buddha, to Nippon, at once and forever!"

Feasting occupied the rest of the morning. About noon the prince took his place between two standards bearing a sort of five-storied tray, upon each of which was arranged cooked rice, cakes, fruits, and scented flour. A new procession was formed which marched round and round the prince and the standards nine times. Seven golden candlesticks with lighted candles were passed from one princely hand to another as they joined in this mystic circling, and as oft as they came in front of the enthroned prince they waved their lights before him.

A Brahmin priest then gave the royal lad a spoonful of rice sprinkled with cocoanut milk, and then, anointing his right foot with oil and flour, exhorted him to be brave and manly, and conduct himself well in the battle of life.

This ended the ceremony, and while receiving the congratulations of relatives and friends, they poured at his feet richest treasures of gold and silver coin. These lavish gifts might almost aggregate the entire expenditure. And thus, by a cunningly devised network of giving and receiving, and mutual merit-making, the whole kingdom is entangled in the meshes of Buddhism and self-deception.

A few years later when this same royal lad was duly chosen to succeed his father, he with the Grand Council of the kingdom, invited foreign ladies and gentlemen to witness all the ceremonies of the coronation which had, till then, been accounted too sacred for any to behold save a select company of princes, princesses, and lords of the land. The coronation took place November 11, 1868, as the Brahmin astrologers had decreed that was the most propitious time.

"It was nearly 8 A.M. when the foreign guests were allowed to pass into a small triangular court, facing one of the doors of the inner audience hall. In front of this door was an elevated platform richly gilded, and upon it there was placed a very large golden basin; within the basin was a golden three-legged stool. Extending over the platform was a beautiful canopy, and above the canopy towered the nine-storied umbrella, tapering in the form of a pagoda. In the centre of the canopy was a vessel of consecrated water, said to have been prayed over nine times, and poured through nine different circular vessels. This water is collected from the chief rivers of Siam, at a point above tidal influences, and is constantly kept in reservoirs near the temples in the capital. In the vessel was a tube or syphon, representing the pericarp of the lotus lily after the petals have fallen off. At a flourish of crooked trumpets, the king-elect descended from the steps of the hall, arrayed in a simple waist-cloth of white muslin, with a scarf of the same material thrown over his shoulders, and took his seat upon the tripod in the golden basin. A Brahmin priest approached him and offered some water in a golden lotus-shaped cup, into which he dipped his hand and rubbed it over his head. At this signal the sacred waters from above the canopy descended in a shower-bath upon his person, representing the Buddhist angels raining blessings upon His Majesty. A Buddhist priest then poured a goblet of water over the king. Then came Brahmin priests who did the same. Next came the chief princes, uncles of the king; next two aged princesses, his aunts. The vessels used by these royal personages were beautiful conch-shells, rimmed with gold. Then came the nobles in graded rank, each with a vessel of different material: gold, silver, china, and earthenware. Then, last of all, the prime minister with a vessel of iron. This finished the royal bath, and the young king descended from the stool in a shivering state, and was divested of his wet cloths, and arrayed in regal robes embroidered with gold and studded with diamonds. In the south end of the coronation hall was an octagonal throne, whose sides corresponded to the eight points of the compass. He first seated himself on the north side, passing round toward the east. In front of each side of the throne was crouched a Buddhist and a Brahmin priest, who presented him with a bowl of water, of which he drank, and anointed his face. At each side thy pronounced a blessing, to which he responded with a prayer."

The *English Governess*[*] secured a translation of this part of the service from the royal father of the king, as it had also been a part of his own coronation.

Priest.—"Be thou learned in the laws of nature and of the universe."
King.—"Inspire me, O Thou who wert a law unto Thyself."
P.—"Be thou endowed with all wisdom and all acts of industry."
K.—"Inspire me with all knowledge, O Thou the enlightened."
P.—"Let mercy and truth be thy right and left arms of life."
K.—"Inspire me, O Thou who hast proved all truth and mercy."
P.—"Let the sun, moon, and stars bless thee."
K.—"All praise to Thee, through whom all forms are conquered."
P.—"Let the earth, air, and water bless thee."
K.—"Through the merit of Thee, O Thou conqueror of death."

He was then conducted to the north end of the hall, and was seated upon another throne more gorgeous and beautiful, and then the insignia of royalty were presented to him by his uncle, Prince *Chowfa Maha Mala*.

First came the sword, then the sceptre, then two massive gold chains which he suspended around his shoulders. Then came the heavy gold crown, sparkling with jewels, which the king placed on his own head, and then at that instant he was proclaimed Supreme Sovereign of Siam!

---

[*] Mrs. Leonowens.

Then came the gold slippers, the fan, the umbrella, and two large rings set with diamonds, which he placed on his forefingers. Then the different Siamese weapons of war were presented, which he simply received and handed back to the waiting courtiers. The Brahmins delivered a short address, to which he briefly responded.

When the gifts were distributed by the new king, the foreigners were allowed to walk up to the throne one by one, and receive from His Majesty's own hand the gold and silver flowers which he was pleased to give them. But the king's court, and all the high princes and nobles, were prostrate before him, and obliged to scramble for the royal presents thrown among them broadcast by the king. The coronation ceremonies of the second king of Siam are similar to those of the first, except that the Supreme Ruler places the crown upon the head of his second. Shortly after the coronation a new king always makes a tour of the city walls. He is borne outside on a kind of litter, seated on a golden throne, covered with a glittering canopy. He is arrayed in all the regal robes, and moves along with great pomp and splendor, and in passing throws gold and silver coins among his thronging subjects. They behold his face, they see his glory, and they bow down and worship him.

An old tradition says that when a new second king is chosen he leaves the mansion which he has occupied to take possession of the palace of his predecessor. But on going to the city he finds the gate shut, and is obliged to ungird his sword and scale the wall before he and his *cortège* can enter.

The following is a Siamese schoolboy's description of a royal ceremony:

"There is a curious ceremony which the Siamese call '*krachat.*'* When the King of Siam wishes to perform this

---

* A kind of basket.

he commands the princes of the royal family to make the large baskets for him, and they must buy useful things to furnish them and make them more beautiful; for example, rice, dried fish, peppers, onions, garlic, sugar, cakes, sweetmeats, and robes for the priests. When they have prepared the baskets, they carry them to the place which the officer has built, and set them up in a long row. The places which they build are covered with red and white cloth for awnings, to protect them from the sunshine and the rain. When all are finished the king goes to see them, and signs the names of the princes who are the owners of the large baskets, and then appoints a day to let all the people come and look at them in the royal palace. The king invites many priests, also, who are in high rank to the palace, for he wishes to listen to the preaching for seven days. When the priests have finished their preaching, the king gives the presents to them. In all these baskets are some very curious things to look at. One was made in the shape of a cart, with two buffaloes, which were covered with tobacco instead of hair, to draw it, and the eyes of the buffaloes were made of brass dippers that were painted black and white. The owner had put many useful things in the cart. Also, there was the figure of a man that was covered with dried peppers, and wore spectacles on his nose, sitting in front of the cart. Another was a tree basket that had many useful things hanging along its branches, such as lamps, augers, saws, knives, handkerchiefs, cigars, and matches. One or two contained automatic dolls running round and round, in and out of the small doors in the baskets; and some other baskets had dolls that were covered with many pennies like the savages, and large birds that had silver and copper coins instead of feathers, and many more curious things that I cannot now remember. At night the owners lighted a fire round the baskets, and two of them had electric lamps that made a good illumination till early in the morning. Then they extinguished them all. But near the end of the week the king invited thirty-two priests to come and cast lots for the baskets, and then he distributed them according as the priests drew lots. When the king had finished there was a great ceremony on the seventh day."

These Krachat festivities are of annual occurrence. Last year the royal demonstrations were of a peculiarly interesting nature, and were connected with ancestral worship. They were in honor of the king's great paternal grandfather, who reigned in peace and prosperity over this kingdom precisely the number of years, months, and days that the illustrious grandson, the present sovereign, had then reigned. Thirty large baskets containing thank-offerings for discourses delivered, were prepared. They were cylindrical in shape, over eight feet in diameter and more than sixteen feet long.

The ceremonies in honor of the royal ancestry of the present dynasty began August 15, 1883. On the eve of this great day, fifty-eight priests performed Buddhist services and chants in the throne hall. The following morning they returned and breakfasted at the palace, and on that day five hundred priests took part in the ceremonies for the benefit of the departed grandfather. The same afternoon there were joyous demonstrations in honor of the present reign in the throne hall, Chakree Maha Prasaht. Here thirty-one priests chanted the praises of Buddha, and the next morning they were feasted at the palace. The following afternoon burning tapers were passed round in connection with the ceremonies of anointing the white umbrella suspended above the royal throne. Thirty Buddhist sermons were read in the next three days, ten each day; and each of the readers received one of the large baskets with their costly contents. The Minister of Foreign Affairs sent an invitation to the Diplomatic and Consular Corps to attend the public audience at which the princes and officials in full uniform would present their congratulations to the king as on his birthday. On that occasion General Halderman, the dean of the Diplomatic and Consular Corps, presented the following address:

"YOUR MAJESTY:

"The Diplomatic and Consular Corps whose organ I am, have especial pleasure in tendering to Your Majesty on this 'red-letter day' of Siam's history, their warmest congratulations, associated with their best wishes for Your Majesty's continued health, happiness, and prosperity."

'At noon and six P.M. of that day, salutes were fired in honor of the coincidence.

The Krachat festival is usually held in the seventh Siamese month, and the people observe it in a much more simple way than obtains within the palace walls. It is but another of their numerous ways of making merit. Formerly the poor scrambled for the food and clothing, but now they scramble for tickets and take whatever they call for. Sometimes persons will throw themselves away by putting their name on a ticket and becoming the slave of the fortunate grabber. But instead of serving they redeem themselves, and the price, be it great or small, is placed in the hand of their quondam master, and I have also heard that if a slave has merit enough to thus secure the name of their master, their own liberty is granted and their debts forgiven.

When persons of the highest rank are ill, the king visits them, and sends the royal physicians to care for the patient. If death ensue, the king goes immediately and helps to bathe the body and prepare it for the urn in which it rests in state until the cremation, when His Majesty graces the occasion with his presence and ignites the funeral pyre. When the king dies all his subjects must shave their heads and put on white in token of mourning.

CHAPTER VIII.

DISPOSITION OF THE DEAD.

Siam is one of the few lands where the dead are cremated or burned. There are many strange and curious customs connected with the rite and the general disposition of the dead. Those who die a natural death may be cremated without having been buried; but cholera victims, suicides, those who die by accident, and mothers who perish in child-bed must all be buried first; while those who are executed are neither buried nor burned, but are thrown to the dogs and the vultures. They are considered as having lost all merit, and even their nearest relatives will not own the corpse.

Little children are often buried and forgotten—that is, the grave is lost—for they never have headstones or monuments. Sometimes the bodies of children are thrown into the river or sea, especially still-born infants, as a punishment for having caused their mothers so much trouble and anguish for nothing. The little body is put in a rice-pot, and a plantain leaf tied over the mouth, and then set afloat. Such a craft went by one day. The body inside had swollen and forced its head up through the plantain leaf. The little face looked too pitiful as it went bobbing up and down on the waves, hurrying on to the sea.

The Siamese coffin is an oblong box, the same width from end to end, and as much as two feet deep. The bottom is made of slats, and there is usually no lid. It is papered inside and out, or covered with white cloth and gilt trimmings. When it is finished a lighted wax taper is fastened at each of the four corners, and the workmen ask,

"Whose coffin is this?" It is supposed to respond, "I belong to the body of the dead." Three nicks are cut in the edge of the box as a proof of ownership, and then it is taken to the home of the dead. Sometimes the tapers are not lighted at all, and again they are put out almost immediately, and reserved for future use. All sorts of deceptions are practiced at a funeral, and every device adopted to save expense, notwithstanding the appearance of lavish expenditure for the dead.

At times the interment is a mere pretence. The grave is dug and all is made ready as for a real funeral. The body is bathed, the feet and hands bound together, and a cord fastened round the waist. These three cords are "to bind the ghost so it cannot return and trouble any one." Money is put in the mouth to be used on the journey to the next world, and rice, salt, and betel are placed in the coffin, which is lowered into the grave and allowed to remain "as long as it takes to cook rice," then it is hoisted out and burned. They believe it takes the soul seven days to reach heaven, so prayers and services are kept up, hoping thereby to help it on the way. I heard a Christian native pray for an old woman who had been dead several days, and she seemed very much surprised when I spoke to her about it, and told her that prayers only availed for the living. It is very hard for them to rid themselves of all the old ideas and superstitions.

The burning-places are supposed to have spirit masters called "Yi Talee" and "Ta Kala"—"Grandmother and Grandfather Cocoanut-shell"—and the old custom was to toss thirty-three "beahs" or little cowry-shells on the ground as the price of it. Now that shells are no longer used as money, they toss a small copper coin worth half a cent. Before the burning the body is carried to an open porch, called a *sala*, in the temple grounds, and the people gather about it. Buddhist priests are hired to recite the good deeds of the dead, to chant and mourn. White cloths are folded and laid upon the chest of the corpse, which it is supposed to give to the priests. They go up one by one, and each helps himself to a cloth until all are gone. The chief mourner, or master of ceremonies, also distributes plates, cups, and other articles as he sees fit. The body is then taken to the pyre, and carried three times round the wood to confuse the ghost that it may not return the way it went. The body is often placed face downward to prevent the escape of the spirit. The corpse is bathed by the relatives and friends by pouring cold water over it, and it is then sprinkled with an odorous yellow powder called "cummin." This bathing and powdering are never omitted, even though it is nothing but a few old bones they intend to reduce to ashes. A green cocoanut is opened, and the milk poured over the remains. The friends send up trays of betel and tobacco all prepared for chewing; these are emptied into the coffin. The fire is lighted, and is a signal for the friends to come forward with torches, tapers, incense-sticks, and fire-crackers; and so amidst confusion, smoke, and flame the body is consumed. The clothes of the deceased are often burned, too, but sometimes they are tossed back and forth three times through the flames without letting them fall to the ground, to purify them, so that they may be worn by those who remain. Many bodies are just laid on the wood and burned without a coffin, the vultures and crows circling overhead, watching and waiting for a morsel; they often get it, too, for some, before they die, bequeath their flesh to the vultures and dogs as a last act of merit, and it is cut and torn from the bones in the presence of many witnesses.

Those who should be the mourners seldom shed a tear, or manifest the least sorrow. I have seen them go about among the crowd, with their shaved pates and white garments, laughing and smoking, drinking tea, or chewing betel, and telling of other cremations that were more or less "sanook" (enjoyable) than the present. Within three days after the cremation the bones are gathered up, and placed in an urn, or tied in a rag to be kept as sacred relics, and to make merit over, just as Roman Catholics keep the relics and bones of their supposed saints, and teach the credulous to believe they are sacred.

What I have described are the ordinary cremations. Of course the princes and nobles have more imposing ceremonies, and spend thousands of dollars where the poor spend tens. They have theatrical performances, puppet shows, and fireworks for days and weeks in succession. Sometimes the body is prayed over and worshipped for months, as in the case of the late queen and her child. They lay in state almost a year, while the *Pramane* was erected for the cremation; and the preparations on a royal scale completed. I will reserve for another chapter an account of the royal cremation I witnessed in Bangkok in 1881. But I will here insert a page or two from one of my old journals written in 1875:

I have been out through the hot August sun to witness my first cremation service. It was held in a grove near a heathen temple, and was horrible enough. The body was that of an old woman about ninety-six years of age, and had been kept four days without ice or any preservative. A funeral pyre was built of bamboo poles, and ornamented with carved work made of the pith and soft layers of the plantain, and with pieces of cloth. It was built with square corners, and was two stories high, the upper story being covered with earth to prevent its taking fire. Upon this was piled about half a cord of close-fibered solid wood, that burns well, emitting great heat.

The people were scattered about in groups, sitting on the grass, and under bamboo sheds. There were many yellow-robed priests sitting cross-legged, and almost as impassive as images of Buddha, on a raised platform in a *sala* or open porch. The people were busy laughing and talking and chewing betel, or smoking little cigarettes and drinking tea. After a great deal of whispering and looking at us, they brought us a tray filled with little cups of tea. This we had to drink for politeness' sake, though we took it with but little relish. The general appearance of things reminded one of an American camp-meeting, but we saw no Christian ministers, and there were no hymns nor prayers. The religious services were all over before we arrived.

The body was placed in a rude box face downward, and was resting under a canopy far from us on the other side of the grounds. No one approached it except the Buddhist priests, who marched by single file and gazed upon it "that they might have an opportunity to think on death." Fires were burning here and there, at which the joss-sticks and torches were to be lighted. Meantime they furnished "lights" for numberless cigarettes.

The only sign of mourning was the newly shaven heads of the relatives. They did not even wear the white waist-cloth which has been the national badge of mourning for past centuries. Presently the native players struck up their heathenish music, and four men who wanted to make merit by the act, came bearing the body. The box was quite deep. It had no cover, and the bottom was made with open slats to admit the flames. It was suspended by loops at the corners from two bamboo poles which rested on the naked shoulders of the men. They marched slowly three times round the pyre and then mounted it with their burden, nearly upsetting the whole affair by their awkwardness, while some boys with an eye to economy were tearing the white cloth from the sides of the pyre. The body was placed upon the wood, a cocoanut was opened and the milk dashed upon the head of the corpse, and then the nut was divided and thrown away that no one else might use it. Trays of betel and tobacco were thrown on the body, and pieces of wood, joss-sticks, and incense, while whole bunches of fire-crackers were tied to the corners of the light railing which surrounded the enclosure, and set to popping. The custom, I have heard, is for the nearest relative, or chief mourner, to apply the first torch, but here all seemed to go pell-mell with their fire-brands, as though anxious to have the old lady burned as quickly as possible. I only saw two that shed any tears, and they were granddaughters of the deceased. The wood burned rapidly, and soon the whole pile was enveloped in flames and smoke. There were two men who watched the fire, and dashed water upon the coffin to preserve it as long as possible. In a very short time they began to punch the body with a long bamboo pole to see if it was burned. It was an awful sight, but we thought we might never see another burning, and yet we wanted to know just how the natives did these things. The fire roared and the flames leaped higher and higher. With shuddering we thought also of the poor widows of India, thousands of whom have mounted burning funeral pyres, and perished with the body of their husband, rather than endure the living death, with its agony and wretchedness, which always fell to the lot of the widowed in that dark and wicked land.

As we still gazed the box burst open, and part of it fell off. Through the flames and smoke appeared the white skull and cheek-bones and the deep black sockets where the eyes had been. They held themselves aloft as if the head had been thrown back and the neck twisted. That gaunt figure of Death peering at us from the midst of the fire we could endure no longer, especially as the man with his pole pushed it over again among the burning wood. We turned away in utter disgust, feeling sure we desired no such cremation services for any of our dear friends. Meanwhile the vultures gathered on the adjoining trees or circled about in the sky overhead. As we walked home I could not but think of the quiet, peaceful graves in America covered with grass and flowers, in comparison with the little jar of charred bones they will scrape from the ashes, or the little bundle of them they will tie in a rag and hang up in the pagoda or temple. These bones will be brought out occasionally for merit-making. They will be sprinkled with holy water and prayed over by the hired priests, while the relatives who have gathered to pay their respects to the remains, will give their attention to the performers in the *lacon* or theatre, who are always hired to be present.

Cremation is forbidden by royal mandate during the prevalence of cholera. In 1881-2, when it raged so fearfully in Bangkok, very many of the bodies were not even buried or coffined, but were hurried away to Wat Sah Kâte, "that garbage field of Buddhism," and piled up within a walled enclosure, resembling the Parsee towers of silence on Malabar Hill, Bombay, strewn with quick-lime, and left to decompose. Others were rudely boxed and piled in open *salas*. They were numbered, and the owner's name registered, that when the plague was over the remains might be claimed and burned.

And—oh, horrors!—they tell that in the former reign portions of many of the bodies of cholera victims were put down in salt pickle, and sold through the outside provinces as food. Those who purchased supposed it was beef or buffalo meat. When the horrid traffic was exposed the king had the offenders beheaded, thus showing that he was just so much better than cannibal kings who take part in such ghastly feasts. This is the only kind of cannibalism that is ever practiced by the Siamese, except that a few of the most ignorant and superstitious men eat the roasted liver of such dead bodies as they believe have been bewitched, that they themselves may be forever proof against witchery.

The Siamese believe that to neglect the cremation is to doom the dead to everlasting servitude, and cut them off from all possibility of further transmigrations of the soul. They believe in a monster—a sort of god of the nether world—having a human body and a dog's head, and he has to sit with his feet in the fire. The souls of those poor mortals whose bodies have not been cremated, after death, are his servants, and must carry water over a long bridge in wicker baskets to pour on his feet to keep them from being consumed. As soon as the body, or bones even, are burned, the soul is freed from its bondage to him. They say there are times when he has very few attendants left, and then he sends out his army for new recruits. The army attacks the people as an epidemic, usually cholera, and they die by thousands. The relatives who are left are afraid to burn the bodies for fear they themselves will then be called upon to carry water for the monster. They think he knows all their names and places of abode. If a poor wretch recovers from cholera, they say the soldiers, by mistake, caught the wrong person.

They know of no real way of escape, but this is what they try. The fearful ones agree to be his relatives. They get red and yellow strings from the priests, and bind them on neck and wrist and ankle for signs that they belong to the demon's family, and should not therefore be made his slaves. Then, too, they take sticks and strings and make a little cart, with clay oxen to draw it, and a clay figure for each member of the family. These they put in the cart, with gifts and offerings of tobacco, betel, fruits, and flowers; then, taking all away out in the rice-fields, they send it to the demon, figuratively, with some sort of a ceremony. But in reality it is left in the fields. The birds or mice eat the fruit, the flowers wither, the little images are beaten with the rain, or crumble "dust to dust," while the sticks and strings remain longest as witnesses of their ignorance and folly.

Oh, how many refuges of lies man has tried to make for himself since he turned his heart from the living and true God! The natives think we are very cruel to bury our dead friends, and then leave them in the grave forever. Cremation, to us so horrible, is to them the last service of love they can render the departed, and it frees the soul from the thraldom of the body, and opens before it a glorious future of possible births in brighter and better worlds.

If we knew all their superstitions, their doubts and fears, we could pity them more, and would not be so quick to censure them for not believing all we tell them. It is hard to throw away all that you have heard and believed in your past life, and trust implicitly in the new things that are told you by strangers.

CHAPTER IX.

A ROYAL CREMATION.

In contrast to the scenes described in a former chapter, read this account of the cremation of Her late Majesty the Queen of Siam, and of Her late Celestial Highness the Infant Princess Chowfah Kanabhorn. It occurred in 1881, and is the last burning I have witnessed.

The proposed visit of the King of Siam to the United States of America will be remembered by many, and also how suddenly that visit was postponed. A great sorrow fell upon him in the accidental death by drowning of his queen and infant daughter in the river Chow Payah in May, 1880. There was mourning in the palace and sympathy throughout the kingdom. The royal remains were kept till March of the following year, when they were disposed of by grand cremation ceremonies, which were more elaborate and expensive than any ever before known in Siam, costing, it is said, a half million dollars or more.

The main features of these cremations in high life are essentially the same from generation to generation, because everything is ordered to be done "according to the ancient royal custom." The remains were embalmed and placed in a sitting posture in urns prepared expressly for the purpose—the inner one of copper, the outer of gold, each having openings through which the air could circulate and liquids escape. In time bodies thus exposed become perfectly dry. The liquids are caught in large brass basins and carried off in procession from time to time, and burned with incense and fragrant woods. The ashes are then rolled into balls, and borne with great ceremony to the river bank before a certain temple, and then thrown into the water. These urns were then placed upon a platform amid the blowing of trumpets and conch-shells, and other heathenish rites. Around them were arranged all the rich and costly jewels, vessels of gold and silver, and other precious things, insignia of royalty, which had belonged to the dead during life. Through all the months they sat in state in their golden urns upon the platform the funeral dirge was performed before them morning, noon, and night of every day, and wailing women appointed from the palace came in quartettes four times each day and night to weep and mourn, to sing the funeral hymns and chant the excellencies of the deceased. Relays of Buddhist priests preached every day, and chanted through the night in their sacred Pali language.

Meantime the whole kingdom was astir with preparations for the grand burning, and even the foreign merchants sent orders to Europe, China, and America for thousands of dollars worth of goods to be used as presents, or to be sold to the thronging multitudes. The king's messengers were dispatched to all the provinces, and to the tributary states, making known his wants. The people acknowledge his right to everything he desires, and so hastened to supply his needs, that they might not incur his royal displeasure, and also to manifest their respect and fealty to their sovereign.

Long weary months were consumed in gathering materials and erecting the temporary buildings considered necessary. But when all was complete the effect was dazzlingly beautiful, especially that of the great central building called the *Pramane*. It was cross-shaped and finished " after the similitude of a palace," with wings and pagoda spires and beautiful roofs all covered with gilt paper, and ornaments that sparkled and flashed like gems in the tropical sun.

Here is a more minute description, partly gathered from the local press:

The Pramane buildings are located between the first and second kings' palaces, and are bounded by wide, pleasant streets. On one side are twelve large and twelve small towers, from which are displayed fireworks every night. There are posts connected with wires, and when the king appears at his pavilion, men holding in their hands a bunch of peacocks' feathers, perform the perilous task of walking these wires. All successful performers are rewarded by the king. Here, too, are long bamboo sheds where tea, water, and other refreshments are furnished to the natives free. And on another street halls are provided where princes, nobles, and foreigners are all entertained at the royal expense. Tables are set, and regular warm meals served with soups, fish, meats, vegetables, and all the delicacies of the season, including fruit, cake, ice-cream, lemonade, and even wines and liquors for those who indulge in such hurtful drinks.

Beyond these halls and nearer the centre of the grounds is an elegant pavilion covered with crimson cloth, gilt-edged, the curtains of which are looped gracefully to the many pillars. The king comes here every afternoon and meets his assembled courtiers, and the foreign representatives, and with them witnesses the various sports designed for entertainment, such as men walking on wire cords, the fencers and boxers, and contests with different kinds of weapons; the Chinese, Siamese, Peguan, and other plays that are being enacted. While here gold and silver coins, presents of ornaments and lottery tickets are scattered among the crowds, who scramble with great zest, each one anxious to get the most. The king personally makes presents of choice and costly articles to those in his immediate presence. The ceremonies lasted eleven days, and the value of gifts to spectators and contestants, repeated day by day, is no trifling sum.

The enclosure is surrounded by a high bamboo wall, having wide gateways at the east and west. On each side of the gates are five seven-storied umbrellas; two of them are golden, two silver, and one crimson. From gate to gate there is one continuous roof, forming a long open hall all round the inside. The wall on the inner side of this long hall is painted with scenes from the great Indian work which has been translated into Siamose and is known as the Ramakien. Rows of lamp-posts also extend from gate to gate.

The enclosed area is covered with a thick mat of bamboo slats to prevent the possibility of a muddy surface should heavy showers of rain fall during the ceremonial days. From the gates to the central building, the bamboo slats are covered with a softer mat of rattan, making a pleasant path for the bare feet of the thousands who crowd the place. The walk is also protected by an awning.

The ascent to the four wings of the central building is by sixteen steps. These steps are matted, and on either end of each step stands a pot filled with beautiful shrubs or flowers. The landing of the second story runs all round the Pramane, and is bordered with lamps and flower-pots. The ceilings of these halls are beautifully decorated, and from them are suspended three lines of five chandeliers each, and between them pendant flower ornaments, looking so fresh and beautiful that the beholder would hardly dream they were artificial.

The central spot formed by the convergence of the four halls has an imposing grand-stand or altar. On this are placed the gold and silver idols, images of Buddha, and heirlooms of the deceased, and relics of their ancestors. The altar is surrounded by a rail, with lamps and candle-stands, and is decorated with pairs of gold five-storied umbrellas. On the very top are two apparently golden stands, upon which will be enthroned the royal remains intended for cremation. Over them hang seven-storied white umbrellas, called Sawatrechat. These can only hang over images of the Buddha or royal personages. The ceiling above the altar is bright red, highly adorned with golden ornaments. It serves to bring out the chandeliers, the white silk umbrellas, and the lovely flowers with wonderful effect. This central space may at any time be closed from public gaze by drawing the rich curtains of cloth-of-gold, that are now looped in graceful folds so as to expose the costly treasures on the altar.

The walls of the building are covered with pretty paper, also the great pillars which support the roofs; those beautiful roofs rising tier on tier, and crowning every sacred and royal building in Siam. We noticed many beautifully worked mottoes in scroll wood frames. They were embroidered with black silk floss on white satin, and placed on exhibition by Lady Payah Bashakarawongse. Some of them are very good, as witness the following: "Three things to admire—intellectual power, dignity, cheerfulness. Three things to be prepared for—change, decay, death. Three things to hate—cruelty, ignorance, ingratitude." The floor of the Pramane is covered with Brussels carpet of the richest, brightest colors.

In one of the king's apartments, roofed with red, are three altars. The middle one is to receive the bone relics of the former kings of Siam. Over it is suspended a gorgeous white silk umbrella, studded with jewels; on the side-altar relics of eminent persons, not royal, but related, will be placed; and on the other a prominent priest will sit, and go through certain formal rehearsals of Buddhist precepts. Under this same roof are rooms specially designed for the king, and grandly decorated and furnished. Many beautiful and costly paintings adorn the walls, and brackets holding stuffed birds, and plants, and golden figures representing scenes from the Ramakien. The sofas and chairs are covered with rich damask, and the floor with velvet carpet. Marble stands and quaintly carved tables abound. The doorways and openings are all draped with black curtains, bordered with white. One door opens into a hall, filled with rich and costly presents, which the king himself will bestow; another doorway gives access to a sleeping-chamber, with its regal adornments and all the conveniences for rest and slumber. From these apartments of the king there is entrance to another complete set for the queen, and furnished in the same royal manner. The couches, bed, tables, and mirrors are beautiful indeed. All the halls and apartments are lighted with many windows, on the leaves of which are painted imaginary beings. Hanging from the upper sill of each window is a basket of beautiful artificial flowers.

In the basement or ground floor of the grand Pramane building are many rooms, and at each corner is a hall in which are artificial mountains and streams, and pots of flowers trailing their graceful vines and clusters of bloom over the wall. Mirrors are so arranged as to reflect and multiply every object, and at night the whole is illuminated with gas. One room represents a shop where Siamese theatrical masks are made, and has lifelike figures of the workmen and proprietor. At another place may be seen a Chinese mason, and his coolie handing him mortar in a little basket. Then an earthenware manufactory, where are tiles, bricks, and pots in all stages of formation, and completed articles exposed for sale. Carpenters, gilders, smiths, weavers, tailors, and workmen of nearly every trade may be seen. Some of the figures are very striking and natural, and display a good degree of artistic ability.

When all these arrangements were completed, the remains of the late queen and princess were borne in catafalque and procession, with great pomp and ceremony, from their temporary resting-place in the palace to the Pramane, where they were placed upon the funeral pyre. It would be impossible to estimate the number present at this imposing Buddhist pageant. All who could be spared from their homes in a city of more than five hundred thousand inhabitants, and multitudes from all parts of the kingdom who were in the city to honor the highly esteemed queen, were out. This is the only statement that can give an approximate conception of the vast numbers who crowded all the streets of the city converging to the palace during this (Sabbath) day and night, the most important time of all the ceremonies. The attendance of foreigners was general, except the American missionaries and the Roman Catholic priests.

All the Europeans who held official positions as representatives of their respective home lands, endeavored to display to the utmost their rank in the burdensome uniforms under which they groaned. The heat was intense, and the dust barely endurable. At 10 A.M. companies of soldiers dressed in blue, carrying their arms with fixed bayonets, advanced; these were followed by lines of lictors, on each side of the street, holding bundles of rattans. They were dressed in blue, with white hats and blue bands. Next came companies of spearmen, holding their weapons under their arms, the sheathed spear pointing to the ground behind them, the swordsmen with their weapons in the scabbards. These were dressed in white coats and hats, and had a band of black crape on the right arm.

His Majesty the king now appeared, attired in mourning, seated in the royal sedan; he held his black hat in his hand, and passed with uncovered head in recognition of the respect shown him by the standing group of foreign gentlemen and ladies, who bowed as he came in sight. The king's children, an interesting and pretty group, were borne in a gilt palankeen by twelve men, immediately behind their royal father. These were followed by a regiment of soldiers in red jackets, marching with fixed bayonets.

After the king had passed, preparations were made to clear the streets for the real procession, the great object of attraction for the day. We noticed here acts that merit no other name than brutal cruelty. It was manifest that all the temporary buildings lining each side of the street were appropriated for particular parties. The public of all nationalities were invited to attend and honor the occasion, but were cautioned not to interrupt or in any way impede the procession. Such a general invitation attracted immense crowds, and, as far as could be observed, they meant to be obedient to the directions given, and the street was left free for the procession. But, after the king had passed, on the opposite side of the street were assembled scores of people who pressed upon each other to look at the foreigners, and to get a good sight of what was yet to come. Some rude native officials, with rattans, went to this crowd and began to strike at the inoffensive people, and some well-dressed native women joined in the merciless cruelty of beating them from their elevated position with slats of bamboo. It created a shudder, and called forth cries of "Shame! shame!" from the kinder-hearted foreign spectators. It would have been much more reasonable if those who seemed to be possessed of some authority had indicated a less conspicuous, but equally suitable, place of observation for these innocent, but well-intentioned onlookers.

Soon the sound of slow and plaintive music was heard; the band came in sight, preceded by an ensign-bearer. He was supported on either side by tassel-bearers. All were dressed in deep mourning, even the drum was draped in black. This band was followed by three companies of soldiers. The officers had broad bands of black crape on the sleeve. The soldiers wore black coats and white trousers. All were barefoot, and stepped slowly and solemnly. These were followed by many companies in black suits, with red trimmings, white hats, and light-colored leather pouches. The royal body-guard formed a hollow square about the royal pavilion, and protected all avenues of access to the king. A second band approached, dressed in black, with yellow lacings and tufts in their hats. They were followed by companies in black, with red trimmings and white hats, all bearing their arms reversed. These armed companies were forty minutes in passing, and represented the military.

His Royal Highness Somdet Chowfah Bhanurangsi Swang Wongse now made his appearance, and took his place with his foreign guests. He was clad entirely in black. A band, dressed in white, now led the naval force of the kingdom, which consisted of many companies of sailors, all in white, except their black badges. These were followed by civilians, Siamese ministers, and other high state officials, in white coats, with gold sashes and a crape badge. Their breasts were adorned with resplendent orders, foreign and Siamese. This part of the pageant was fifteen minutes in passing.

An artificial rhinoceros and lines of men, representing celestial beings, known as *Tawadahs* or Buddhist angels, with conical white hats, having one horn like the unicorn, now filled the streets. Both beast and angels were carrying small gilt houses, filled with presents for the priests. There were native soldiers in the style of old Siam, holding flags and streamers of all shapes and colors; others wearing coats of grotesque designs, and bearing poles, to which were attached long white and yellow cloths, also for the priests. Others wore red caps and jackets, and were drawing carts, on which were placed pretty little gilded houses, full of presents.

Minute guns were now being fired, indicating that the urned remains of the queen and her daughter, a princess of the highest possible grade, were being removed from their temporary resting-place at Wat Poh, to be conveyed to the gorgeous cremation building. They were preceded by piles upon piles of priests' robes, borne upon men's shoulders, four men to each gilt palankeen. On each side of the street were all sorts of imaginary beasts, partly human, and bearing the same burdens of merit-making gifts for Buddhist priests. Some of these creatures were horrible, and had faces of many colors. After these imps came another band of Buddhist angels (Tawadahs), with their white horned caps, each one holding a trident, the tips of whose prongs were all crowned with white lotus lilies. Next a band of drummers, dressed in red, and each one striking his drum with a mournful cadence as he marched. They were followed by more Tawadahs in white; then came bands of instrumental music, and bearers of the sacred five and seven storied umbrellas, called *chats*, signs of approaching royalty.

The head-priest's elaborately gilt and spired car, drawn by men and horses, approached, surrounded by gold umbrellas. Its windows and door were hung with golden curtains. The chief-priest, the king's uncle, sat in state, with open palm-leaf book before him, but passed by in silence, followed by a train of Siamese mourners in white, and with closely-shaven heads. The second car was drawn by six horses and forty men. The standard and umbrella bearers were dressed in green. A very near relative of the queen was in this car. The third car contained the youngest brother of the dead queen. These cars were very much alike in general appearance and accompaniments. Number four was the car of cars, and the greatest object of attraction. Its style and costliness transcended all the others. It was overlaid with pure gold, and set with jewels. It contained the gold urn, sparkling with gems, which held the body of Her late Celestial Highness the Infant Princess Chowfah Kanabhorn. The car was six-storied, and gold umbrellas were placed round it, tier after tier. The fifth car was also six-storied, costly and beautiful, of the same material as the preceding one, and held the urned remains of Her late Majesty the queen. The car of the princess passed before that of the queen, as the child ranked higher than the mother who bore her, because her father was king and her mother queen of Siam, while the queen, although she had a kingly father and husband, was not the daughter of a queen, but of a lady of high rank in her father's harem. It was some time after her brother had taken her to wife before she was herself elevated to the royal throne.

A strip of silver cloth, about six inches wide, extended from the high-priest, through the cars of the living to those of the dead, where it was placed in contact with the urns. This forms, they think, the mystical union between the sacred Pali books, the living and the dead.

These cars were followed by the surviving brothers and sisters and servants of the deceased queen. All were dressed in white, and had their heads shorn. There were several other cars in the procession, two of them holding what seemed to be empty urns, designed, doubtless, for use when the cremation takes place. In another was the fragrant sandal-wood for burning the corpses. The wood was cut in short lengths, and the ends gilded. These cars were followed by bearers of umbrellas of all colors—green, yellow, white, red, and blue—and more and more gifts for

4*

priests, all of them merit-making offerings, supposed to benefit the dead. Among the gifts were numerous boats on carts drawn by men, and figures of lions, tigers, elephants, and fabulous creatures never seen alive on earth, in air, or water; and every beast bore its offering of yellow robes for the priests of the Buddha. The procession now stopped, but the street up and down as far as the eye could reach was filled with the wonderful pageant.

The consuls of the treaty powers and the other foreign residents present witnessed all that was transpiring, and had in view the Pramane buildings, the king's pavilion, the soldiers, the plays, and other imposing scenes that were being enacted. The various theatrical troupes were in full play; the favorite parts were taken from the Ramakien, an Indian mythological romance, to which I have already referred. After this all were refreshed with lunch at the prince's tables.

At half-past two the consuls and their suites and other foreign visitors were allowed to enter the Pramane, and see the placing of the gold urns on their golden altars. The piece of narrow silver cloth already mentioned, was attached to the urns, and extended to the floor on either side, and then out the east and west wings of the building to the steps, where the ends rested on piles of sacred books. These visitors were afterward conducted to the west hall of the grand Pramane, and had an audience with the king, who gracefully thanked them for their attendance, and the honor they had conferred in assisting him in these last sad tokens of respect to his loved and departed ones.

Buddhist priests were everywhere more numerous than the army, counting all the soldiers, both military and naval forces. They had swarmed from all parts of the kingdom to chant prayers and recite moral lessons, to see the wonderful royal cremation, but principally to have a share in the spoils.

It used to be the custom for all Siamese mourners to dress in white and shave the head, but at this time, in imitation of Western ways, the king and princes and many others wore black and did not shave. Others shaved and wore white, but added a band of black to the sleeve.

In the evening, near sundown, the second king came with his courtiers to the first king's pavilion, where they held a private audience or exchange of greetings. In a few moments the latter appeared before the assembled multitudes and received their salutations. His arrival was the signal for activity; the wire walkers, the jugglers, the theatre actors all resumed their parts with spirit. In front of the king was a lion dance and tiger antics, represented by a Hindoo's contest with a tiger, which attacked him while drawing water at a well. Soon two horsemen appeared and engaged in a game of tilting. Meanwhile, presents were being distributed in all directions. As night came on the king ignited a quick fuse, which placed the grounds in a blaze of light, and a large variety of interesting fireworks passed off in succession. A company of men danced with lotus-flower lanterns in each hand, and others, representing a huge serpent, performed before the king. This latter is truly a barbaric invention. A jointed framework is made in the form of a huge serpent, some twenty or thirty feet long, covered with paper, and painted in colors to look like the spots and scales of a snake. The mouth is set wide open, and painted red, to appear as frightful as possible. Lighted lanterns are hung inside, and the whole is animated by men, who bear it about, following as nearly as possible the natural movements of a serpent. Globe lanterns, like balls of fire, roll about the ground, and the hideous monster makes vain attempts to swallow them.

A group of the royal children accompany the king on all these grand occasions, and receive much paternal attention, but their mothers must all remain in the background. The very queen who has been advanced to the place of the dead woman does not appear in public as such while she lives. It is only her dead body and her bones that are thus honored, and paraded through the streets and water-ways of the royal capital.

The ex-regent, and ministers of state, and leading officials are all very gracious in their recognition of and attentions to foreigners, and they treat the ladies and gentlemen with equal politeness. It is not to be wondered at that the common people envy the foreigners who receive so much respect and consideration while they are seemingly neglected, yea more, oppressed, sorely so, by those of the nobility who are unscrupulous and overbearing.

The many repeating arms of modern invention may be seen in position to enforce good behavior, and make it to the interest of the people to be law-abiding, peaceful, and honest amid the many temptations which the lavish display of gold and silver and jewels presents. The bristling Gatling gun, capable of clearing extensive ranges, is a wonderful and logical pacificator.

The king and his court did not retire, nor the immense crowd disperse till a very late hour. And quiet did not settle upon the scene at all, for hundreds of watchmen, officers, and servants were left on guard. Gamblers were still intent on their games, and singing and laughter could be heard through the night, mingled with the chanting of the Buddhist priests in different parts of the Pramane.

I was present the next day and saw them lower the grand altar, and remove from it all costly and precious things. The outer golden urns were taken away, and the copper ones covered by others made of carved sandal-wood, very delicate and beautiful, and festooned with garlands of fresh flowers. Natural flowers, white and fragrant, were substituted for the artificial ones in the dome above the altar, and this was surmounted by a crown resplendent with gems.

Spices and fragrant powders were strewn about and incense-sticks placed among the sandal-wood under the urns. A fuse was laid from the altar to where the king sat in state, and when the time had come for "offering up the sacred flame," he ignited the fuse with holy fire from the palace. Soon all that was left of the dead queen and her child was enveloped in the devouring element. The princes and nobles were standing near with lighted wax-candles, fragrant tapers, and flowers of sandal-wood in their hands. Each stepped up and threw their offering upon the pyre. There was a flourish of trumpets, the band struck up a funeral dirge, and the wailing women commenced their awful, mournful lamentations, but their cries were soon hushed. Men stood by watching the fire and dashing water upon it, to prevent the flames from rising too high and destroying the Pramane. The building is never burned. They are careful that nothing is consumed but the wood and the remains.

The cremation began a little after six P.M. In the evening, after the foreigners and other guests had dined at the prince's table, the king again made his appearance and the usual presents and sports were dispensed.

It is the custom to throw limes and hollow nuts, with silver coins and lottery tickets inside, among the crowd, and let the people scramble for them; but the foreigners were waited upon by the king's brother, Chowfah Noi, who kindly placed the limes and nuts in our hands. To the foreign officials, and to those whom he delighted to honor, the king gave with his own hand many beautiful and costly articles. Some friends of mine thus received three sets of mythological figures in gold, a gold vase and a gold bird, an elegant gold locket with the Siamese word for "cremation" engraved on the outside, a silver tray, and a black bag with forty nuts in it, each containing a silver coin, while their children drew a set of gold buttons, a pretty smoking-cap, and other articles of beauty and worth. The gifts drawn were almost infinite in their variety and style, and most of them costly. I saw jewelled rings and pins, gold and silver boxes and bottles, vases, trays, cups, teapots, goblets, all of silver and gold. I received a gold ear and tooth pick, encased like a pencil, and a handsome little castor, besides several silver coins. Then there were rooms filled with gifts for the priests, bottles, lamps, clocks, tables, chairs, Japanese and Chinese writing-desks and cabinets, lacquered and inlaid with pearls; tea sets, trays, boxes, priestly robes and fans, umbrellas, shoes, mats, teapots, lanterns, and bags and iron bowls for holding the rice and fruit given them every morning. We could not help laughing, as we noticed among their merit-making gifts, patent oil stoves from America. The manufacturers little dreamed they would ever be used in Siamese monasteries to make tea for Buddhist priests.

The ceremonies lasted over a week, and there were rope-dancing, jugglery, pantomime plays, side-shows, theatres, feasting, preaching, praying, chanting, gambling, and tilting, all going on at the same time in the most disgusting jumble. The bodies were burned the eighth day. The charred bones were collected and put in small golden urns, to be kept by the royal family. It is said the present king has the bones of his ancestors, for several generations back, preserved in this way; and one day of the ceremonies these old bones were marched out in procession; also a reputed tooth of Buddha. If all the Buddha's reputed teeth are genuine, he must have had several sets, with double rows above and below. And just here I may remark that the king's foreign physician says there are enough of Buddha's bones in Bangkok alone to make two skeletons!

The next morning the urned bone relics were placed on state palankeens, and were conveyed through the west gate, in procession, to the royal barges at the priests' landing. The ashes were also gathered up after the burning, and I saw the procession of forty-seven gaily-decked boats which accompanied the royal barges as they bore them down the river to the temple of Wat Yanawarahm, where the ashes were strewn upon the water.

The five-storied altar was re-erected in the Pramane, and the bone relics were placed upon it in a golden Busabok. Some precious relics of Buddha, a tooth perhaps, and bone relics of His late Majesty the King Pra-Chaum Klow, and Her late Majesty the Queen Somdet Pra-Tape Surindramat, and of the Celestial Princess Chandra Monton, and the statue of the Celestial Prince Isiriya Longkorn, were brought in state from the grand palace and placed in the king's pavilion. Afterward the bone relics of Prince Unukarn and Pra Ong Nopahug were brought there also.

The ceremonies, plays, distribution of gifts, preaching, chanting, and fireworks continued for three more days and nights. The principal performances in the Pramane were recitations by the priests of portions of the Buddhist work know as the Apbhidharma.

On the morning of March 20th all the relics were removed, also the precious things, and conveyed thence into the palace. In time the Pramane building was taken down, never to be used again. And thus ended the royal cremation of 1881. It was truly a gorgeous affair. The king outdid himself in lavish display and distribution of costly gifts. I do not think Bangkok ever witnessed such extravagance before, and we hope she never will again. The kingdom cannot afford such expensive cremations.

CHAPTER X.

THE SUPREME KING OF SIAM.

PRABAT SOMDET PRA PARAMEND MAHA CHULALANGKORN KATE KLOW CHOW-YU-HUA is the high and honorable title of His Majesty the First King of Siam, ruling in this good year of our Lord, 1884. He was the ninth child of his royal father, was born under the sacred white umbrella, and first saw the light within the palace walls, September 21, 1853. His father, the late King Maha Mongkut, had a very large harem, and among the women who composed it were thirty-five royal mothers, who bore him eighty-four children, thirty-five sons and forty-nine daughters.

Of all the young princes, Chulalangkorn had the highest rank, and the very night of his father's death he was chosen by the *Sanabodee*, the highest nobles of the realm, to succeed his royal sire. Maha Mongkut died October 1, 1868. His body was embalmed, and he sat in state till March, 1870, when his remains were cremated according to all the Buddhist rites and ceremonies.

The young king was first crowned and ascended the throne November 11, 1868. Five years later, after having spent some twenty-one days in the Buddhist priesthood, he was again crowned November 16, 1873. This was necessary to comply with the customs of the country. The king, as well as every officer in the Government, must at some time in their lives have been a priest; and when a man enters the priesthood his former life, with all its social honors and position, must be renounced, even to a throne, a crown, and sceptre, if he have them. Therefore, after the king's stay in the monastery, it was necessary that he be recrowned, and again invested with all the appointments of royalty. This was a unique experience, as few kings are ever twice crowned sovereign over the same people.

It was during the ceremonies of his second coronation that he issued the manly proclamation, abolishing the abject prostration of all persons in the royal presence. When the gorgeous curtains of cloth-of-gold were slowly parted, the king was seen seated on the throne, dressed in royal robes, and the glittering crown upon his head. The princes and nobles crouched before him on all-fours, bowed their heads to the ground, and lifted their clasped hands in adoration for the last time, for after reading the decree against that most debasing custom they rose *en masse*, and stood before their sovereign like men. At that time, also, the Chula Chaum Klow Order was established, and all who have been decorated with this Order are to assemble annually in the royal palace, and do homage to the statues of the four dead sovereigns of the present dynasty.

The present king is the fifth of the dynasty, and the fortieth in succession since 1350, when Ayuthia, the former capital, was built. Bangkok, the present capital, was chosen in 1782, and in 1882 the king celebrated the centennial with great pomp and ceremony. It was one of the grandest events in Siamese history, and reflects unusual credit upon the young king and his nobles, from the very fact that they were willing to break through old-established customs, and attempt and carry through so successfully a nineteenth-century celebration.

In March, 1872, the king visited Singapore and Batavia, and in December of the same year he sailed for Calcutta. These glimpses of the outside world gave him wider views of mankind, and better ideas than he could ever have entertained shut within the boundaries of his own small realm. In 1880 he intended to visit Europe and the United States of America, but the drowning of the queen and consequent sorrow and confusion in the kingdom detained him here.

When the sad news of President Garfield's death reached Bangkok the flags of the different foreign consulates were placed at half-mast, and up and down the river, on the king's yacht *Vesatri*, and the Siamese and foreign shipping, similar evidences of impromptu mourning were visible. By the king's command, three of the royal princes waited upon the American Consul-General, and expressed to him His Majesty's great regret at the death of the President, and his warm sympathy for Mrs. Garfield and family, as well as for the American nation. He has recently shown the same courteous respect and sympathy for Queen Victoria in her sorrow for the death of her youngest son, the late Duke of Albany.

In his early boyhood the King of Siam was instructed in English by Mrs. Leonowens, the governess at his father's court. After the removal of his topknot he was made a "nane," or novitiate, at the Buddhist temple for a season. Afterward he was transferred to a separate palace of his own. Here, among other tutors, we find that good old man, Mr. Chandler, who, we have no doubt, tried to impress the heart and mind of his princely pupil with the highest and noblest truths.

The government of the land is such that it behooves the princes and noblemen to secure as close relations as possible with the king. They, therefore, present their young daughters to him by scores. If pleasing to the king, they are taken for wives; if otherwise, they remain in the women's department. It is through these channels that the strange "City of Women," of which we hear so much, is supplied with inhabitants. Thus, nearly all the men of high rank are fathers-in-law to the king. It is said that no native woman in all the realm is forbidden to the king except his mother. The queens are always his own sisters.

The King of Siam must be ranked among the most humane and liberal of heathen monarchs, and his government is of the mildest form. His father proclaimed religious liberty throughout Siam, and the king himself is the only one in Siam to-day bound to be a Buddhist, for at his coronation he vowed to uphold and support that religion. After the cruel death of the Laos martyrs, the present king granted the same precious boon of religious liberty enjoyed in Siam, to all his northern tributary provinces. He has ever proved himself a kind friend to the missionaries, and manifests his good-will and respect for them in numberless ways. He welcomes them to his kingdom, and encourages them in their work. In a private audience granted to a large company of American missionaries in the fall of 1882, at the new palace, I heard him praise them for their good works in Siam. Elsewhere I have spoken of his generous gift to the Girls' School Building in Petchaburee. Since then he has called Dr. S. G. McFarland, one of the oldest missionaries, to take charge of a royal school at the capital. During the cholera in 1881, he had dispensaries opened all over Bangkok, and free medicines were distributed to the poor, distressed populace. After the terrible earthquake in Java and among the islands south of Singapore, the king contributed one hundred catties of silver (over $4,000) to the relief of the homeless sufferers, and his queen gave fifty catties more. Again and again has he helped to send home the wives and children of Englishmen in his employ, and no sooner had the son of Mrs. Leonowens returned to Siam than the king gave him Government employment.

In 1862 his royal father established a mint, and flat silver coins were issued, bearing the elephant on one side and the royal umbrellas on the other; but since Chulalangkorn's accession to the throne a new die has been cast, and the coinage now bears on one side a fine profile portrait of the king. The postage stamps bear the same regal face. Copper coins are also made at the mint, which take the place of shells and bits of lead of Old Siam.

July, 1883, was made memorable in the history of Siam by the opening of telegraphic communication with the rest of the world via Saigon. As far back as 1866 the British entered into an agreement to connect Bangkok with the world via Singapore, but that line is not yet complete. The French, however, have secured that boon to Siam through their energy and perseverance. In that same year a local post was established in the capital. . The king has since extended it to all important points, and Siam is now entitled to, and holds a place in, the great Postal Union.

We hear that the bottom of the letter-boxes are made of sandal-wood, to impart fragrance to the missives, and thereby cultivate a taste for letters. When letter-writing becomes common, a great revolution will have been effected among the people. At first the postal privileges of Bangkok were very much abused by evil-minded persons sending anonymous letters in which they even cursed princes and nobles in whose presence they would not have dared to utter a word. Heavy packages of trash were also sent, and the charges collected on delivery.

The houses in the principal cities, and along the larger rivers, canals, and roadways have all been numbered, to facilitate the delivery of letters, and the people must also assume distinctive names and titles. Now there is no difference between the names of men or women, married or single, and it is almost as hard to find the owner of a letter addressed to "Dang" as one sent to "John" in New York would be. Very neat postal-cards, with the king's seal, are also used in Bangkok, or "Krung Tape" as the natives call their royal city.

The king has an army and a navy, both very small, of course, and representing but little fighting force; yet more than she needs, for Siam is an independent kingdom, in treaty relations with most of the great powers; and has strength enough to keep her tributary states in subjection and power to hold her own, unless France or England conclude to take her under their protection, and in such an event all her male population could not resist their power, because they are without discipline or patriotism.

The king has sent an embassy to England and Europe, and quite a number of Siamese boys are being educated abroad. He has a sort of parliament, called the "Sanabodee," composed of the highest princes and nobles, who meet in night sessions and attend to affairs of state. The country is divided into fifty-eight provinces, the governors of which are appointed by the king without regard to hereditary descent. They are usually chosen from among men in and about the capital to whom the king wishes to show some special favor. The golden vessels—cups, goblets, tea-pot, spittoon, etc.—of which the former governor was so proud, revert at his death to the king, and are bestowed upon the new ruler as insignia of his office.

These fifty-eight provinces are portioned out to three principal ministers of state. The Kalahome, or Prime Minister, has the west and southwest provinces, and charge of the army and navy. Puterapie, or Minister of the North, because his provinces lie there, has charge of the habitations and dwellings of the people. The Praklang, or Lord of the Treasury, has a certain control of the exchequer, and of all foreign interests and trading vessels; also of the provinces of the southeast. The Laos states to the north and the Malay states in the south, which are tributary to the king, are governed by their own princes, whose titles are confirmed by the king, and they seem to be under his direct care.

The king's power is almost absolute. He makes laws and establishes customs, which his ministers sanction, and his people abide by and suffer. He seems to think that the land and its inhabitants are for him and him alone, and his merit is so great that he deserves their service, their property, and their lives. Therefore, as his subjects say, he "eats the kingdom." Taxes are very heavy and oppressive, and often to get money to pay them the people sell themselves, their wives or children, into perpetual slavery.

The crown is not hereditary in a European sense, nor is a queen ever allowed to reign. In 1829 and 1830 a queen mother acted as regent, until she with her paramour conspired against the young king, her son, and put him to death. She placed her lover upon the throne. He only reigned five months, and was assassinated, and she herself cast out. The Sanabodee, or Royal Councillors, always select the successor to the throne. He must be a prince of the realm, but not necessarily a son of the dead ruler. Sometimes the second king is elevated to the rank of supreme king. Siam, Cambodia, and Laos all have first and second kings, and there are records of third kings in several of the past reigns. It is not at all strange that in families of from fifty to eighty sons there should be several aspirants to the throne, each claiming an equal right to the sceptre. We suppose they have to note the day, and the hour even, when the sons are born to determine which are the elder. The priests, who are very good at making up stories, claim that the "Siamese sovereigns are lineal descendants of Buddha, and that the people themselves have sprung from his earlier disciples. Thus ruler and people are alike interested in the support of a religious system which is identified with their own origin." One of the king's titles is the "Lord Buddha."

From all that can be learned the second king is a very expensive honorary adjunct of Siamese royalty. He has no responsibility in the Government, and no special power except among his own personal adherents. He has a court and harem and all the pomp of royalty, one-third of the revenues (?), and receives almost equal honor with the first king. He is a sort of shadow, and yet he is not always a true reflection of the mind and purpose of his sovereign. One can but regret that the present second king, a man of varied knowledge and rare ability, should by his very exaltation be lifted above all power to help and benefit his countrymen. He is forty-five years old, while the first king is but thirty. He is the prince, George Washington, so often mentioned in connection with his talented father, the late second king of the former reign, who was also a full brother of Maha Mongkut.

The King of Siam is not so secluded as most Oriental monarchs, and yet he cannot go and come at his own sweet will like other men. He is dependent on his princes and nobles for nearly all the information he receives, and of course it is colored more or less by the medium through which it passes. There are no independent vernacular newspapers published by natives, and the only one in the kingdom is edited by a foreigner, who is careful to praise and flatter more than he condemns. Besides, he cannot know what is passing among the natives as a Siamese could.

The king has a royal printing-press and a court journal, but we hear of no literary efforts such as distinguished his father. He has made a few translations, among others the "Arabian Nights," which his subjects read and many of them believe. His speeches read very well, and it is significant that he always closes them with these words, "May that Power which is Supreme in the universe keep and guard all of you and grant you all prosperity and bliss." He has several beautiful palaces and a royal steam yacht. He has several lordly white elephants, with gorgeous trappings, and many ordinary elephants; Australian horses, with saddles and bridles of the finest workmanship, mounted with gold and silver, and some of them set with jewels. "The saddle for the king on state occasions is made of the finest white doeskin, the royal arms of Siam being worked on the sides and seat in heavy gold bullion. The gold mountings, the white leather, and the rich scarlet cloth and trimmings have a chaste, yet magnificently rich appearance. The state harness is beautifully mounted with silver, with the royal crest, and surmounted with small figures of elephants in gold. A set for the Queen of Siam, and similar ones for the young princes, are of quieter, but none the less admirable, designs." He has also some beautiful carriages and splendid boats. When the king, in his royal barge, dressed in his glittering robes of state, with the jewelled crown upon his head, and followed by thousands in boats hardly less beautiful, goes out upon the river to make his annual temple visitations, it is one of the most gorgeous and imposing scenes to be witnessed in Siam. The choicest things from foreign lands have been brought to furnish his palaces—beautiful pictures, vases, statues, chandeliers, carpets, and furniture. His gold and silver plate and some of his jewels are magnificent, and he is constantly adding to their store.

There is no national debt, and the royal vaults hold uncounted treasure. "The Siamese are at peace with all the world. Their great occupation is the cultivation of their land; their great hope its development. From the king down they entertain admiration and friendship for the United States. His Majesty has ordered a huge block of native marble to be cut and sent to Washington for the National Monument. He has also placed his brother, Prince Devawongse, in charge of the preparation of a series of articles and illustrations of Siamese life and people, which he intends to present to the United States Government, to be placed in the National Museum." He also sent some rare and costly things to our Centennial Exhibition.

Chulalangkorn is small and slightly built, with a pleasant face and graceful manner. He is well formed, and always appears dressed in excellent taste. The new costume is semi-European, for although he has adopted shoes and stockings, hat, coat, and underwear, he still retains the native "*panoong*," or waist-cloth, which, I must own, is, when neatly draped, much more graceful and comfortable, too, than the pantaloons of Christendom. The present dynasty is more progressive than any previous one, and the now reigning king is far in advance of his predecessors, and indeed of all his regal neighbors, except the Mikado of Japan; and the nation is slowly, but surely, swinging into the light of civilization, knowledge, and true religion. God bless the King of Siam, and may his sons outshine even their royal father.

5

CHAPTER XI.

SIAMESE LANGUAGE AND LITERATURE.

The Siamese language is neither full nor expressive. It is a tonal language, and for that reason harder to acquire than one whose words must simply be remembered in order to be used. It is monosyllabic to a great extent, and has five tones, some say seven. By the aid of these five tones nearly every word that is a single syllable can become five distinct words, each capable of a primitive, derivative, and figurative meaning. In this respect the language has a striking resemblance to the Chinese. Siamese is a jargon made up from the languages of the neighboring races. Chinese, Cambodian, Laos, and Malay have each contributed largely. Many words from the Pali and Sanscrit have been introduced through the Buddhist religion, and it is constantly being enriched by the adoption of very many words from the European and other learned languages capable of expressing truths in all departments of science.

The teachings of Christian missionaries are giving new meanings to old words, in order to make plain the divine truths and doctrines of God's Holy Word, and they are sometimes even compelled to invent or compound words to express thoughts which have hitherto had no place in the pagan mind and heart. It seems almost impossible to apply any of the known rules of grammar to this language. As a rule, it has no terminations to indicate case, tense, and mood, number, or person. All these things are to be learned from the context, tone, or gesture.

In Siamese, as in all languages, there is a chaste and

refined use of words that ought to be employed by all persons in all places, without reference to the accidental position of the parties speaking. There is here, however, in Siam, a humiliation which the brutally arrogant demand of those whom they require should honor them, and which only the helpless and oppressed must necessarily yield: as degrading prostrations, and the use of words, epithets, and phrases that exalt the tyrant and degrade the speaker. There is one expression which I specially abhor. It is, "*Pome krap tow*," or "*Pome krap fa prabaht.*" It denotes the most abject humility, and signifies that the person speaking abases himself so as to place the hair of his head, the most sacred possession of his body, under the very soles of the feet of the person spoken to.

In the presence of royalty, princes, and great nobles, the commoner is expected to use such expressions as belong to what is called the court language. Then there are so-called holy nouns and pronouns used only with reference to the king and the Buddha, and we, perforce, must use them when we speak of God and Christ, else the Creator is degraded below the level of the creature. Sometimes, even after one has the holy nouns and pronouns all right, you may inadvertently use a pronoun in reference to yourself which so exalts you that the rest of your speech appears as burlesque.

The Siamese abounds in metaphors and similitudes, and native writers and speakers seem to pride themselves on the volubility of their repetitions, and the multiplication of similes, and as they have neither a Webster nor a Worcester as a standard, each one spells to please himself. Two or three years of honest, conscientious study will furnish the student with enough knowledge of Siamese for all ordinary purposes. Some of our missionaries have been able to preach the first year, but of course the first efforts are not supposed to have edified the hearers very much.

There is a laughable story of one who was preaching to a great crowd in one of the market-places of Bangkok. He imagined he was making a deep impression and so increased in earnestness and rapidity of utterance. The natives listened, as they always will, believing there is merit in the mere fact of letting the sound fall upon the ear. Presently he heard a man on the edge of the crowd say: "He is a great talker, truly, but I can't make out what language he uses!" And with this flattering (?) remark he turned and left. The disconcerted speaker soon closed his remarks and departed likewise.

We have a comical old teacher of Siamese at Petchaburee, who is trying to learn English. The following is a list of words which he gives with their meanings, all in English: "*Wig:* hypocrite hair. *Flattery:* a good kind of curse-word. *Whiskey:* sin-water. *Gold:* a very good thing. *Blew:* a wind-verb. *Kick:* a foot-verb. *Bow:* a salute-verb. *Howl:* a dog-verb. *Kiss:* a salute-verb. *Preach:* a missionary-verb. *Murmur:* an old-man-verb. *Fickle:* a boy-verb. *Hop:* a frog-verb. *Liar:* a bad adjective of boy. *Modesty:* a good adjective of girl. *Vine:* a string-tree. *Cunning:* a good word of philosophy-man. *Spider:* master of the web. *Daughter:* a girl-son. *Bullet:* son of a gun. *Sponge:* water foam. *Angel:* God's boy. *Large:* an adjective of preacher. *Thin:* a bad adjective of body. *Adulterate:* a bad adjective of lying man. *Admonition:* word of Bible. *Comfort:* word of mother to crying child."

When foreigners came to Siam they found that the language had for centuries been reduced to writing. The spoken and the written language are alike, and the written and the printed characters are the same. The written language in Cambodian characters is composed of forty-four alphabetic symbols, or consonant letters, with seventeen vowel-points above and below the line, after the model of, the ancient Hebrew. The characters are written like English from left to right, and if on ruled paper always below the line. The words are run together, unbroken by spaces, points, or capitals. The pages are numbered, and there are marks to denote the beginning and end of the paragraphs. It is easy to learn to read so that the reader can understand, but to make it intelligible to others is quite another matter, especially if the hearers are natives.

There are various kinds of books. The most elegant are said to be written, or rather engraved, on tablets of ivory, but I have never seen any of those. Some are made of long strips of coarse paper, either white or black, and folded together something like a fan. These are written with gamboge or soap-stone pencil, which can be erased, or with the ordinary lead-pencil and ink. Others, mostly sacred books, are written with a brass or iron style, on carefully prepared palm-leaves, and rubbed with ink and oil to bring out the characters. Sometimes the letters are gilt, and the edges of the leaves are also gilt, or colored with vermilion. They are placed in order on strings, and when read are usually laid upon a table or cushion, to preserve them, it is presumed, from the injurious moisture of the warm hand, or, more likely still, the reader is too superstitious or indolent to hold them. The preparation and copying of these sacred palm-leaf books is considered a work of great merit. Some perform the work themselves, others hire it done, but all derive merit from the gracious work. We have little idea of the labor and "passionate patience" required for work of this kind. We, with our steam-presses that multiply copies with the rapidity of thought, smile with grim pity at the small accomplishments of years of careful labor. What are called the "weak hands of delicate women" have wielded, and are wielding, a mighty power with no greater weapon than the stylus or pen. They work like coral builders in the deep, their lives soon over, and accomplishing they know not what, while round about them beat forever the mighty waves of God's infinite purposes, and with them, and by them, yea, even in spite of them, His grand schemes are rounded and complete. It is enough! We might never have been, and yet God has made us immortal in the midst of His glorious unfoldings.

"In Japan there is a sect of Buddhists whose priests wear the ordinary dress and marry. Many of them are thus allied to the nobility, and even to the royal family, and the great mass of people in Japan belong to this sect; but the fashionable religion of the chiefs is still the system of Sin Lo, the latest development of which has been preserved in a work by a learned Japanese woman of the twelfth century." There are old books of poems, written ages ago by Buddhist nuns, which are still preserved and venerated among the scriptures of the worshippers of the Buddha.

The noble ladies of Siam to-day spend much of their time in writing, or copying rather, the sacred books for the Buddhist temples and monasteries. But few of them know what they are writing, or understand a single word traced by their style. They are blind devotees, toiling in the dark. Their work does not enlighten their hearts nor open their eyes to see the glorious things of God, nor do their pages prophesy aught of the future blessedness of those whose sins have been washed away in the blood of Christ.

Besides these written books there are now a great many printed ones. Some have been done by Siamese and others by foreigners. There has been a Government press for a great many years, and from it used to issue some very strange articles. But the first Government document ever printed in Siam was April 27, 1839. His Majesty Somdet Pra Nang Klow, who was then reigning king, had published at the mission press and put in circulation nine thousand copies of a proclamation against the importation of opium. Thus, an old heathen king, nearly half a century ago, tried to protect his subjects from the direful effects of that trade which England still upholds. The first Siamese calendar appeared in 1842; two years before, the first steamer anchored in the Gulf; and the first newspaper was started in 1844, not by Siamese, however, but by the American missionaries, and the first number was dated "July 4th." At present (1885) there are only four papers in the kingdom—the *Daily Advertiser*, begun in 1868; the *Siam Weekly Advertiser*, which came out a year later; and the "*Sayahm Samai*," a vernacular paper, scarcely three years old. All three are printed by S. J. Smith, of Bangkok. The royal printing-office publishes a Siamese newspaper once a week. The price is $6.60 per year. It is a very small sheet, and contains little besides court news. Besides these the past has seen almanacs, calendars, newspapers, and one or two magazines, all short-lived, for lack of encouragement and financial support. In 1874 one of the princes began a Siamese paper, called the "*Darunawaht*." It proposed to furnish both home and foreign news, and to be interested in the arts and sciences. But the paper was too spicy and wide-awake for Old Siam, and it died at the end of its first year. The kingdom has not advanced far enough yet for a free press. But, with the telegraph and post-office in successful operation, there must needs be some more direct means of communication with the people, and the newspaper is sure to come into favor and exert its mighty influence here as in all enlightened lands.

The late king, Maha Mongkut, while still a priest in the temple, had a small press, and printed Buddhist books, quite a number of which have been translated into Siamese. "It was 330 years after the Buddha's death when the

Three Pitakas * were for the first time reduced to writing. Before that they were handed down from generation to generation by word of mouth. It is very doubtful whether at the time Guatama lived the art of writing was known in the southern valley of the Ganges; but the Buddhists believe that he composed works which his immediate disciples learned by heart in his lifetime, and thus handed down."

Siam is supposed to have been converted to Buddhism by monks from Ceylon in 638 A.D. The present Siamese know nothing of any former religion which may have obtained among them, and all are now absorbed in the various sects of the Buddhist Church. It is curious to note just here that although Siam owes her religion to Ceylon, centuries after its introduction a king of that island sent to Siam for teachers to impart a better knowledge of Buddhism to his own degenerate subjects. At least so says old Siamese history. Whether the story has any foundation in fact, or is only told to show the superior merit of the Siamese Buddhists, I cannot tell.

Pra Chow Song Tam, a priest-king, and the founder of the second dynasty, who reigned from 1603 to 1628, versified the history of the Buddha before his deification, and later, during the reign of the illustrious *Pra Narai*, we read of an ambassador who was sent from Siam with a royal letter to the court of France.

There is a well-written Siamese History extending from A.D. 1351, almost to the present. It begins with an absurd story and tells of a wonderful drum, which almost equalled "Alladin's lamp," and throughout there are many signs and wonders recorded with the utmost faith, because they are believed in by this superstitious people; yet aside from

---

* The Three Pitakas, or Collections, are of the canonical books of the Southern Buddhists.

all this, the greater part of the history may be accepted as reliable.

There is a court historian who chronicles passing events. They are not made public, however, but are laid away in the royal archives. We cannot tell when, if ever, the history of the late reign will be published, but we know that already the name of Maha Mongkut has passed into history, and all future readers on Siam will know more or less of his erratic character. He was quite a literary celebrity himself, and his fame has spread throughout the kingdom. He seemed anxious to prove himself pre-eminently a man of letters. He wrote a great deal, both in Siamese and indifferent English, and we often see quotations "from the pen of Maha Mongkut." He was very arbitrary and would have liked to have had the world of letters bow to his diction and orthography. He claimed to be an authority in Sanscrit, and perhaps did know more of that language than any Siamese now living. He was a great admirer of Martin Luther. He set himself up also as a reformer of the Buddhist religion, and revised many of their sacred books to make them accord more with scientific facts. It is remarkable that all false religions may be improved, and made better than their originals, while the more Christianity reverts to the original, the purer and holier we find it.

Almost every *wat*, or Buddhist monastery, has a library building, and it is usually well stored with books on religion and medicine. The Buddhist scriptures are considered by some to be very voluminous indeed, but good authority* says that by actual counting of words

—"the Buddhist scriptures, including all the repetitions, and all those books which consist of extracts from the others, contain rather less than twice as many words as are found in our Bible; and a translation of them into English would be about four

---

* T. W. Rhys Davids.

times as long. The repetitions, however, are so numerous, that without them the Buddhist Bible is probably even shorter than ours."

It is a mistake to consider all books in Buddhism scripture, as much so as it would be to call all Christian literature Bible. Many of the sacred books of the Southern Buddhists have been translated into Siamese. Others are the Pali or Sanscrit text in Siamese characters, which the priests in the temples learn to read by rote. Indeed, some can repeat chapters and whole books, without knowing the meaning of one-quarter of the words. And these "vain repetitions of the heathen" are the "much speaking" so highly censured in our Bible. One has to live for a time among Oriental heathens to properly understand that grandest of books. The ignorance of the priests was not unknown to Maha Mongkut, a priest-king, who spent no less than a quarter of a century of his eventful life in a monastery. He once called the Siamese priests "ignorant and blind leaders and dunces."

His Highness Mour Rochodey went with an embassy to France and England, and wrote an account of the voyage and their reception at the foreign courts, which has been read with pleasure by thousands since. He died in 1867. There are also histories of Cambodia, Pegu, and Burmah, and a very fabulous one of China, which they read and reread. There are books of etiquette, and maxims, proverbs, and medicine. They have also translations from old Indian and Hindoo romances, and there are scores of the vilest and most immoral plays, which they read with avidity, and never tire of seeing performed in the native theatres. Of poetry in its highest and noblest sense they know nothing, but they have volumes of rhymes which they read, as indeed they do all their books, aloud, and in a sing-song tone, more for the sake of the jingle than for any meaning they may contain.

The former Foreign Minister and the late ex-Regent were rival translators, each one trying to do more than the other, and through this emulation they have furnished the people with quite a number of books, not specially useful, however, nor likely to lift them above the ordinary low level where they found them.

To the Christian missionaries, earnest-hearted and persevering, the foreigner owes nearly all his thanks for books which will in any way help him in the acquirement of the language. Among these Bishop Pallegoix's Dictionary stands first. It gives the Siamese words and their meanings in French, Latin, and English. It was printed in Paris in 1854, and nothing better has since appeared. The MS. for another Siamese Dictionary has lately been sent to Europe. The American missionaries have prepared ordinary school-books. Some of them are printed with maps and illustrations. There is a physiology and United States history not yet published. Of their religious books I shall speak in my chapter on the missions.

CHAPTER XII.

THE KING'S BIRTHDAY.

The present King of Siam was born in Bangkok, September 21, 1853. I happened to be in the capital in 1880, and there witnessed the festivities and illuminations in honor of his natal day. As he is a royal personage, they were kept up for three days and nights. Oriental kings are privileged to add three years to their ages, because old age is held peculiarly honorable in all these lands. Whether the King of Siam avails himself of this right or not I do not know.

The illuminations were beautiful all through the palace grounds and up and down the river. There were such mottoes as "God save the King," "God bless the King," and "Long live the King." There was a lighthouse traced against the sky in brilliant jets of flame, Siamese seal, gates ajar, pagodas, crowns, and letters. The shipping was specially brilliant, the hulks outlined with lamps, and the rigging ablaze with golden light from the deck to the masthead. There was music, also, and fireworks.

The last night there was a party at the "Sumran Roone Palace," "The Happy Shelter," where General and Mrs. Grant were entertained during their visit to Siam. The missionaries were all invited. There were only about twenty foreign ladies present, but a great many foreign gentlemen, and there were crowds of Siamese princes and nobles, dressed in their elegant court clothes, made of silk and velvet and cloth-of-gold, set with jewels. But not one Siamese woman appeared. We looked over the magnificent rooms, the beautiful palace walls, the rich furniture, the marble floors, all standing out in the brilliant glare of the new electric lights, which blazed like suns from the lofty ceiling, and we thought of the gross darkness which still enveloped the people, and especially the women, and we questioned, "What good is in all this show?" The nation can never "arise and shine" while the mothers, wives, and sisters are trodden under foot.

I cannot fully describe the grandeur of the palace, the music, the lights; the flowers, ferns, and lilies, arranged over ice in crystal boxes; the sparkling fountains, which threw their bright spray over artificial grottos and fairy bowers; the rich and costly furniture, the lovely adornments, paintings, and statues; the sumptuous table, glittering with gold and silver plate, china, and glassware. The viands, too, were many and delicious, having been prepared under European supervision. This is the first party at the palace that I have attended, although invited nearly every year. And yet I have part of the promise, "Thou shalt stand before kings for My Name's sake." People of the Western world cannot appreciate the honor of being able to "stand before kings," instead of lying prostrate before them, as was so lately the custom here in Siam.

During the birthday celebration we went one day to the Royal Museum, which had been newly opened to the public. The display of curiosities was good. There are many stuffed animals and birds from other lands, and cases of costly gold and silver ornaments set with gems; Chinese bowls and dishes of many curious and beautiful shapes and colors; some geological specimens, and rude, uncut gems from native mines; elephant-tusks and trappings, some captured battle-flags and armor on the wall, old-style saddles and bridles, swords, spears, bows and arrows. We noticed toys and dolls, images and idols, and a full-length portrait of the king, and near by a marble bust of the same. There is also a nucleus of a fine English library. The king came to the museum, and was greeted by all the people. He passed from room to room, followed by his courtiers and four of his little children—nice little ones, bright-looking, and smiling pleasantly.

The following extracts from the letter of a friend who attended the birthday party the previous year, are worthy a place on my pages in this connection:

"This season is a gala time for the entire nation, and is annually celebrated with great splendor and show. For several days preceding the festivities the rain fell almost unceasingly, the heaviness of the showers seeming to indicate the closing up of the six months' rainy season; but the evening of the 20th which ushered in the all-important day, the rain ceased so suddenly, and so obligingly refrained from falling to any amount during the entire time of the celebration, that the superstitious natives ascribed it to the great 'merit' His Majesty had made—probably by gifts to the priesthood or visits to the heathen 'wats'—and that the favoring of the weather-god boded for the future happiness of the king, and the continued prosperity of his kingdom. It will be difficult for me to give you even the faintest idea of these strange, brilliant Oriental scenes, which almost beggar description, for if the Siamese can be said to excel in any one thing, in their present degraded condition as a nation and people, it is in their display of fireworks.

"On the evenings of which I write the Royal Palace was brilliant with multitudinous flashing lights, trimmings of greens and flowers, and waving flags. On the masts of the steamers lying near the palace, from point to point, in and out, around the hull, were brilliant lights, making the steamers resemble things of life as they lay on the water. Conspicuous for its beauty was the pleasure steam-yacht of His Majesty.

"The different boat-landings vied with each other in their illuminations; many of the designs were particularly noticeable. The skeleton of a building thrown up and literally covered with small lights, resembled a house about to be consumed. At another place, amid the scarlet of waving flags and surrounding lights, flashed out 'God save the King,' written in English; 'Vive le Roi' glittered from the front walls of the French consulate. At one point I noticed the figure of a Buddha, so perfectly represented by the lights that the features were distinguishable. Far off in the distance one could tell the position of 'wats' or temples by the spires, tipped with blazing balls of light. Above all from behind the clouds peeped the moon, with veiled face, as if she feared to compete with such brilliant, though transient earthly glory.

"Amid the firing of cannon from the palace forts, which took place at intervals throughout the morning of the real birthday, the king received the congratulations of the various consular representatives, and of others who desired to pay him that respect.

"The evening of the 22d the festivities terminated in a reception, which is annually given to the foreign community by the Minister of Foreign Affairs, a Siamese nobleman of great wealth, and bearing the title of *Kromatah*. Nine oclock P.M. found us in our floating carriage, among a crowd of other boats, in front of the magnificent palace of the Kromatah, which was ablaze with light. Matting, covered with a strip of Brussels carpet, ran even to the water's edge. Up this I was conducted by the usher, through the halls, saloons, and windings, till I stood at the door of the dressing-room, where a Siamese waiting-woman received me. Ah, the chasm between the hovel and the palace! I could almost imagine myself in fairyland for the time. Handsome mirrors reflected my form on every side; a blue and white carpet covered the floor; soft divans, on which one could dream hours away, were scattered here and there; a bed, hung with blue tapestry, attracted admiration; while in a still smaller room could be found every *et cetera* that the most fashionable belle would demand in making her toilet. Was I in heathendom?

"The palace is built somewhat after the European style, with many quaint designs of architecture. The saloon in which the guests were gathered was paved with mottled marble, and throughout the rooms were scattered articles, curious, rare, and costly. I saw, too, portraits of Queen Victoria, Napoleon Bonaparte, the late Pope, William of Germany, Bismarck, and other celebrities; specimens of Siamese and Chinese workmanship were conspicuous. Upon one of the centre-tables in the large saloon were displayed in all their wonderful beauty and fragrance two of the *Victoria Regina* lilies, which, though not indigenous to this soil, are cultivated in the private garden of our host, the Kromatah. Bubbling fountains, swinging punkahs (a sort of large fan suspended from the ceiling), pleasant conversation with people of different nationalities, made the hours fly rapidly, and soon the bursting of sky-rockets and the strains of the national anthem announced the arrival of the king. Ere we were aware the graceful form of His Majesty, dressed in the most unostentatious manner, followed by his courtiers, stood in the midst of the guests, who with one accord rose to meet him. In a dignified manner he passed around the group, shaking hands and speaking a word or two to those in the inner circle. Passing through the rooms, he soon returned to the saloon, where Dr. William Dean, in the name of the company gathered to do honor to His Majesty, offered him their hearty congratulations and best wishes. The king, in a cordial manner, replied in his native language, and soon after bowed a final adieu to all. His eldest and favorite child, the Princess Civili, about twelve years of age, accompanied her royal papa."

Here is a copy of the paper presented to the King of Siam on his recent birthday, signed by the American citizens of Bangkok:

"We, the undersigned citizens of the United States residing in Siam, beg leave to present to His Majesty, the King of Siam, our congratulations on this, the anniversary of His Majesty's birthday, and to offer our best wishes for his continued health and happiness and the prosperity of his kingdom. We congratulate Your Majesty on the friendship and good-will of all other nations for the kingdom of Siam, and for the progress of civilization in this kingdom. Boats and bridges have been built to facilitate travel, ships and steamboats have been constructed for navigating the various surrounding waters, canals have been dug for bringing timber from the forests and opening new regions of the country for cultivation, elegant palaces have been erected for His Majesty and the nobility, improved buildings have been made for the market-places and the dwellings of the people, and a general air of progress is apparent to recent visitors to Siam, and especially to older residents of the country.

"With respectful deference, we beg to suggest to Your Majesty that a still higher improvement, and a pledge of still greater prosperity to Siam, might be secured by abolishing the gambling-stalls, the spirit-shops, and the sale of opium. These are the prolific sources of poverty, theft, and disloyalty.

"We renew our congratulations for His Majesty's good health, wise government, and prosperous reign, and pledge our prayers for his continued happiness and growing kingdom."

CHAPTER XIII.

SIAM'S RELIGION.

Buddhism is said to exist in greater purity in Siam than in any other land at the present day. If this be true, then here we may look for its best and noblest fruits. But what we see is selfishness, indifference, indolence, and vice. Buddhism is a heartless religion, and has no soul. It acknowledges no God and no Creator, and its founder taught that each one must work out his own salvation by the performance of good deeds, and acts of self-denial, whereby all desire and all ambition is crushed and the man reaches *Nipon*, exemption from transmigrations, the attainment of never being born again, and therefore exemption from a succession of deaths. They will not let us call it annihilation, for they insist that the existence still continues, but in an unconscious, indifferent state. What a cheerless, hopeless future! And when it is remembered that the attainment of even this, is only for those who perfectly follow the teachings, and walk in the "Paths," we do not wonder that even the best and most austere of Siamese Buddhists when questioned as to their hopes for the future, reply, "It is all dark."

As they know not the real God, and will not love and serve Him, they have exalted Buddha far beyond his deserts, and attribute to him many superhuman qualities. Guatama, or *Somana Kadom*, as the Siamese call the last Buddha, was the son of an Indian prince, and is reputed to have been born in Northern India, in the province of Oudh, within one hundred miles of the city of Benares, in the fifth century before Christ. He left the palace and gave up all its royal pleasures for a life of meditation and poverty. He claimed to have attained Buddhahood and then began to teach the way to others. There is no doubt that he taught many pure and beautiful truths, but as his teachings were not reduced to writing for several centuries after his death, many things may be ascribed to him which he never uttered.

"He recognized no caste as did the Brahmins, and he taught the old Indian and Egyptian doctrine of the transmigration of souls. His doctrines created quite a revolution in India, a land accursed by caste and licentiousness, but they were eagerly accepted by many earnest souls. His missionaries went forth preaching the doctrines, but the further they went the more they were corrupted. Dissensions arose among his disciples and the order was divided into two streams, northern and southern. The first flowed through Thibet, China, Corea, and Japan. The southern stream overran Ceylon, Burmah, Siam, Cochin-China, and parts of the Malay Archipelago. Like a river that flows through many soils, dissolving them all, and corrupting its own waters, so is Buddhism. It is thick and turbid with the superstitions of every land it has entered. The Christian missionary meets to-day not the original purity of life, but the vilest of sin and the grossest of lives in men who profess what Buddha himself would never recognize. Buddha's faith, and the Buddhism of to-day, are two different things." *

What is here said of Buddhism in Japan, I can also say of it in Siam. Here, it is modified by the beliefs of all the commingling nations. It is very tolerant and will adopt and teach anything to please the people to whom the lazy priests look for their support. The masses in Siam are ignorant of most of the tenets and doctrines of the very religion in which they profess to believe. They live in constant fear of all kinds of invisible spirits, ghouls, satyrs, fairies, and water-sprites. Lying is always permissible, and

---

* Rev. W. E. Griffis.

at times highly recommended. The Siamese are polygamists. They cast off their old wives and marry new ones "with none to molest or make them afraid," and so it often happens that a man cannot remember the names of all his wives or children, nor tell who are dead and who are living.

The missionaries can tell these people much they have never heard about their Buddha. Their sacred writings are sealed up in a foreign language, and even if translated thousands could not read them. It is a mistake to suppose that all the Siamese know how to read. There is no missionary spirit among the priests of to-day. They do not go from house to house teaching for the sake of instructing the people and making them better, as history says Buddha and his early disciples did. They do no voluntary work. They must be hired and paid well, besides being feasted before every service. They do not take up a collection, as we understand that term, yet by sticking coins into a wax candle, offerings are made which ultimately fall to the priests. They are forbidden to touch money, but they spread a fold of their sacred robe over their hand, and the money is laid on the cloth, or one of the temple boys who are their constant followers is appointed to receive it.

The Buddhist religious services are usually conducted in open porches on the temple grounds and are accompanied by bands of music, native theatres, and often gambling. They freely acknowledge that it is a sin to have these things mixed up with religious rites, but say the people will not come without them. The natives—dressed in their best, and well supplied with betel, which they chew incessantly and give and take with the utmost politeness—sit on the edges of the porch or on the ground, in the shade or sunshine just as it happens, and laugh and talk and gossip while the priests on the platform are preaching away in their loudest tones and most exalted style. "Pi fung tate"—

go to hear preaching—does not mean to a Siamese that he is to listen at all, but simply that the sound of the words may fall upon his ear. Why should they listen—the words are in an unknown tongue, the sacred Pali, and as they say, "Mi cow chi"—it does not enter the heart.

It is very easy for the admirers of the "sublime teachings of Buddha," who sit in the light and glory of Christian England and America, to imagine their benign influence upon the millions of the East, where they have been repeated through the centuries. But we who are nearer, enshrouded by its gloom, in the very midst of the darkness, see and know how vain are these repetitions, and how impossible that they should affect the lives of those who hear but the sound of words they cannot understand. The very priests who speak them have learned them by rote, and might not be able to translate a dozen sentences. Occasionally the sermon is in Siamese, but they choose priests who are good talkers and can tell stories to make the audience laugh, and the sober parts of the discourse are exhortations to the impossible observance of rites and ceremonies in order to make merit. Every act of a Buddhist's life is a selfish one, and is believed in some unknown way to augment his merit. I even knew of a woman who was robbed, comforting herself by saying, "Never mind, in my heart I will devote the stolen money to Buddha, and make merit by it."

When we say that all Siamese are Buddhists, it is "necessary to decide not only what is Buddhism, but also whether a firm belief in one religion should or should not be nullified by an equally firm belief in another. Almost every Chinaman would probably profess himself a believer in the philosophy of Confucius, while he would also worship in both Buddhist and Tao temples." In Siam they are equally inconsistent. This religion claims more followers than any other in the world, but perhaps "not one of the five hundred millions, who offer flowers now and then on Buddhist shrines, who are more or less moulded by Buddhist teaching, is only or altogether a Buddhist." There are many sects, and they do not worship nor believe alike. Monks and nuns dwell in the monasteries. The monks are called "Pra," and the nuns "Ma Chee." Like all man-made religions Buddhism was at first opposed to the admission of nuns, considering women too inferior to enter the pale of the sacred order. But as the Buddha's wife, Yasodhara, was one of the first nuns, it may be that she used her womanly arguments to effect her purpose, as did Mrs. Mahomet, years after, when her husband was formulating another religion which was for the sole benefit of men. Not that Mahomet's wife became a nun, but she had some teachings in the Koran arranged more to her taste. Bergh's "Society for the Prevention of Cruelty to Animals" is often laughed at as a modern upstart, while the humane are advised to look at Buddhism as the perfection of that theory. Let us look at it for a moment and what shall we see? Animals that have been wounded, or hurt in any way, left to suffer and starve to death; cattle goaded until the blood runs down their sides; dogs scalded and beaten and cut; bull-fights, cock-fights, fish-fights, and the wounded and vanquished cursed and often turned adrift. Many Buddhists will not take life, it is true, but they torment and wound to within an inch of it, and then laugh at the sufferings of the poor creature, or watch it unmoved, from day to day, as it lingers on.

Just when this religion was introduced into Siam we cannot tell—some say A.D. 638, and that it was brought by missionaries from Ceylon. The Siamese themselves acknowledge their debt to Ceylon, or Koh Lanka, as they call that island; and I have elsewhere recorded the legend that Ceylon was formed by a clod of earth that dropped from Lord Buddha's heel as he stepped over the Bay of

Bengal from India to Siam. No wonder Buddhism made such strides in the early centuries, if its founder could thus travel with more than the speed of the wonderful "seven-league boots." It is hard to tell how they reconcile this apparent contradiction. If, as the legend says, Buddha came to Siam, he would teach the religion himself, and the island of Ceylon was not in existence till after his transit. It seems to be on the strength of this legend that they claim one of his sacred footsteps on Mount Prabaht. But, as a writer on Buddhism has naively remarked, "It is true that those early writers were not capable of making due distinction between that which they thought ought to have happened and that which actually occurred; it is true, even, that what they thought highly edifying is often miraculous and not seldom absurd and childish." It is said that at the age of seven Buddha could take an elephant by the tail and throw it a long distance; he could rise at will and sit cross-legged in mid-air; he could divide his body into innumerable portions, and from each would flash light. He destroyed a dragon by burning odors before it. He shot with a bow that 1,000 men could not bend, and the twang of whose string was heard 7,000 miles. But that he ever performed a miracle for the benefit or good of any one except himself is not recorded. And although he has been dead for centuries, and is now deified, no one pretends that he ever could, would, or should help his worshippers.

Guatama was only one of a succession of Buddhas. In their sacred books there is a list of twenty-four who preceded him. In the Pali and Sanscrit the word Buddha is always used as a title, not as a name. After the death of each Buddha his religion flourishes for a time, and then decays, till it is at last completely forgotten, and wickedness and violence rule over the earth; the world then gradually improves until a new Buddha appears, who again preaches the lost truth. After 5,000 years shall have elapsed since his rediscovery of the truth under the Po tree, a new Buddha will again open the door of Nirvana to men, his name being Maitreya, the Buddha of kindness, or the Unconquerable One. As the present century falls near the middle of that cycle of 5,000 years, it may be that Buddhism is at its very worst, and that is why its glorious teachings, so full of light and beauty, are so at variance with the abominable lives and the darkness and superstition of its votaries.

For twelve centuries the "Light of Asia" has been shining on this favored kingdom, and yet the further we penetrate in our search for good fruits, for justice, mercy, and love, for purity of heart and life, the more are we convinced of the utter rottenness and deadness of the whole system. It reminds me of the corpse of a dead king enthroned in the Pramane, surrounded by all the insignia of royalty, guarded by the new sovereign, and worshipped by the priests and people, but waiting for the fire, when the golden casket will be removed, and the putrid mass they proudly called their king will be reduced to a handful of ashes. The corpse of Buddhism is also waiting in state for the sacred fire to ignite its funeral pyre—the fire from heaven—and it will surely come. It is kindled already. The Unconquerable One has invaded the realm, and many hearts are owning him Lord!

To Buddha, it is said, the trees rendered homage at his death, letting fall upon him fragrant flowers out of season, and bending lovingly over him with their sheltering branches; and who can wonder that the story adds that the angels in the sky dropped heavenly flowers and sang heavenly songs to strengthen him. After his death at the age of eighty, the miracles and exaggerations increase, and the former especially are evidently influenced by the desire to make the Buddha's funeral rites as splendid as those of a Chakrawarti king. The body refuses to be moved until the gods indicate the direction in which it is to be carried; it refuses to burn till the venerable Kasyapa, the old and faithful head of the Order of Mendicants, arrives. Three times, with his monks, he paces reverently round the pile on which the body of his dead master lies, and stands with bent head opposite the feet. Then the pile takes fire of itself; and, when everything except the bones have been consumed, showers from heaven extinguish it.

The later accounts relate that, as Kasyapa stood by the feet of the revered teacher, he fell into the mystic trance of Dhyana; and when he recovered from the trance, prayed to see once more the sacred feet on which the thirty-two signs of a Chakrawarti were visible. He had scarcely uttered his prayer when the coverings unrolled themselves, the coffin opened, and the feet came out like the full moon emerging from the bosom of a dark cloud. The whole assembly burst into loud applause on seeing this matchless prodigy. Kasyapa and his monks reverently placed the sacred feet upon their heads, after which the feet withdrew, the coverings replaced themselves, and the coffin and the pile resumed their natural appearance.

Once, while sailing above Petchaburee, we stopped at a rest-house on the river bank. The posts and ceiling were nicely painted, and here I saw this pictured legend in all the glory of red and yellow Chinese paint. There were the funeral pyre and the coffin, the protruding feet, and old Kasyapa and his monks, with bare head and feet and yellow robes. As I had not yet read the legend, I could not understand the picture. I asked the natives, who crowded round to see us, what it meant. But their knowledge of the past and their ideas of Buddhism are very vague and imperfect, and they could not throw much light on the story. They only knew that it was one of Buddha's miracles. If we but knew their beliefs and legends, the strange and grotesque pictures all over the temple walls, and traced on salas, halls, and porches, would have a new and peculiar interest to us. There are pictures and images of Buddha everywhere. Once only have I seen an image of any other god, and that was the three-faced god Brahm, in a hall near the Buddhist temple in the lotus gardens of Bangkok. I have heard of one in this province, a stone image of Brahm, which, it is said, fell from heaven, and is now lying neglected in an old deserted temple ground, but I have never seen it.

The Siamese are gross idolaters, worshipping these images and bowing before them with clasped hands and faces to the earth in the most abject manner. Daily offerings are placed before them, and flowers laid in the ever open palm of the Buddha. They are enthroned at all the royal ceremonies, and when the oath of allegiance is taken, the priests present hold in their hands a sacred cord which connects them with the image. They are carried in processions, and preside at fêtes and feasts; they are taken to the fields to see the parched earth when the land suffers from drought. When Petchaburee was burned, and the governor's treasures carried out into his garden, he set an idol there to guard them. Once each year they are bathed and sprinkled with perfume, and many of them presented with new scarfs and coverings. The natives write letters to dead friends, and lay them across the shoulder of the image, believing it will safely carry the message to the departed. An oath or a vow taken before an idol is considered irrevocable.

That the very highest and most intelligent look through the image to Buddha as the real object of worship, may perhaps be true. But they are such a small number, that the Siamese Buddhists, as a nation, must be classed among veritable pagans.

In the old history of Siam there is a story of a gold image of Buddha that was cast in 1380, and which weighed

141,000 pounds, and this, if of pure gold, would be worth the incredible sum of $30,000,000. They also tell of another image fifty cubits high, made of gold and silver and copper. But of course we receive these stories doubtfully, because there are no traces of these images to-day, nor after-stories of their destruction, and the largest and grandest idols now are only brick and mortar, thinly, very thinly, overlaid with gold-leaf, and set with jewels of questionable value. The famous Emerald Idol at Bangkok, brought from Laos and said to have fallen from heaven, with a diamond in its forehead and diamond eyes, is so far up beyond the sight of vulgar eyes, that, like the really beautiful statue of the Goddess of Liberty on our national capitol, you have to believe in it because people say it is there, and you see a dim outline in the height above you. Then, too, it is so dark in the temple that I have never been able to distinguish if the image is green or black. It is held very sacred by modern Siamese, and is kept in the royal temple where the princes and nobles of the realm gather twice each year to drink the water of allegiance and swear fidelity before their king.

One may gain a pretty fair idea of their belief from the following translation of the Siamese Oath of Allegiance:

"We, the slaves of the Lord Buddh, beg to offer to His Majesty, Prabaht Somdetch Pra Chula Chaum Klow, the King, this our personal oath, pledging our loyalty, in the immediate presence of the god Buddh, the sacred teachings and the sacred priests.

"We entreat the deity which protects the sectioned white Umbrella (the insignia of royalty), and the guardian deities of all other places throughout the kingdom, to observe with their godlike eyes, and hear with their godlike ears, the pledges we make to Prabaht Somdetch Pra Chula Chaum Klow, the King, who has been crowned and placed upon the throne, and who, observing the ancient royal usages, treats graciously the priests, the ministers, and royal descendants, the official servants of His

Majesty, military and civil, within and without, the provincial governors and their subalterns, the rulers of territories, states, and the entire population living within His Majesty's dominions. Hence it is proper that we gratefully perform our official duties, under His Majesty's feet faithfully, free from rebellious acts, physical, verbal, mental.

"If we, the slaves of our Lord Buddh, are not firmly fixed in true natural gratitude, or if we meditate to His Majesty, Prabaht Somdetch Pra Chula Chaum Klow, the King, with body, words, or in disposition, or if we disclose our minds to the people or rulers of other regions that are hostile, and plot that others do evil to Prabaht Somdetch Pra Chula Chaum Klow, the King. If we see with our eyes, hear with our ears, or know that others are about to do evil to His Majesty, and do not bring forward the subject for investigation, so that it may be specially brought to the knowledge of His Majesty, but delay with evil intent, with ingratitude, and lack of honesty, and with evil purposes toward Prabaht Somdetch Pra Chula Chaum Klow, the King, who is so full of great mercy and incomparable graciousness:

"We pray the deities of lands and forests; the guardian deities; the atmospheric deities; the goddesses who care for the earth, especially the powerful deities who are located where is the great white Umbrella, emblem of royalty, may plague us with evils, destroy our lives, effect our destruction and death by breakage, by severance; cause our death by lightning and thunderbolts, by royal weapons, the powerful royal sword, by poison, and the power of land and water animals; let there be some opportunity for the destruction of the perfidious ones; let swift destruction come; let us not escape all great disasters, and consequences of all localities, which those who have the power can inflict for all offences. We beseech the power of the deities to plague with poisonous boils, rapidly fatal, and all manner of diseases, the dishonorable, perverse, and treacherous, plague with untimely, wretched, and appalling deaths, manifest to the eyes of the world; when we shall have departed this life from earth, cause us to be sent and all to be born in the great hell, where we shall burn with quenchless fire for tens and hundreds of thousands of ages and limitless transmigrations; and when we have expiated our penalty there, and are again born in any world, we pray we may fail to find the least happiness in worlds of pleasurable enjoyments; let us not meet the god Buddh, the sacred teachings, the sacred priests, who come to be gracious to animals, helping them escape misery, reach heaven and attain a cessation of births and deaths; should we meet them, let them grant us no gracious assistance.

"If we remain firmly established in gratitude and honesty, and do not meditate the rebellion and evil that has been rehearsed, we beg the land, the forest, and the atmospheric deities, and the four great guardians of the world, whose power extends to all the worlds of the gods, to the sacred foundations, forces and rulers of powerful nations, and the deities stationed in the great white Parasols of royalty, and the guardian deities that protect His Majesty by night and by day, and the deities that protect the palace, and the deities stationed to protect the twelve royal treasuries, and all the deities, the armories, and ministers, and great royal property; we entreat you all to assist, and protect us who perform all official duties faithfully; grant us prosperity and happiness in this and in other worlds; cause us to escape all the diseases and calamities that have been enumerated.

"We have received from His Majesty this water, pledging ourselves, therefore cause us to possess clear, unalloyed happiness, and to escape from all diseases and maladies; and grant us eminent prosperity, and brilliant, happy, fruitful lives, prolonged into very great age; then let us die in happiness resembling sleep, with an awakening in the abode of the gods, in the enjoyment of godlike possessions in heaven, for hundreds of thousands of ages and limitless species of beings.

"When we die and depart from the heavenly and god-worlds to be born again in human worlds, let us abound with goods, glorious and limitless possessions, and distinguished attendants in accord with our desires.

"We entreat the Lord Buddh, the sacred teachings, and the sacred priests, to grant the fulfillment of our desires in the way of heaven, and escape from the successions of life and death, and their attendant miseries, together with our fidelity and gratitude."

Buddhism is undoubtedly the best of all heathen religions, and in many, very many things,—especially its rites and ceremonies; its priests and monks and nuns; its monasteries and gorgeous temples; its robes and vestments; its feasts and fasts and processions; its idols, altars, candles, incense, holy-water, and bells; its purgatory; its works of merit and almsgiving and penances; its sworn poverty, but marvellous wealth; its self-denial and mortification of the flesh; its adoration of relics, shrines, and angels; its prayers for the dead and canonization of old saints; its literal buying of salvation,—it so closely resembles the Roman Catholic Church that it is no matter of surprise that she has admitted Buddha to her calendar, and ordered him to be worshipped as a saint on every 27th of November, under the title of St. Josophat.* But to have been made a Catholic saint is not the only curious fate which has befallen the great teacher. He takes his place also in a quaintly illustrated old book, called "Dictionnarie Infernel," as the man in the moon, or rather the "hare in the moon." The origin of this legend, which is very old, appears traceable to one of the Jataka stories, in which the future Buddha is a holy hare who keeps the Sabbath and exhorts his fellow hares to charity and piety. One Sabbath, after exhorting them to give a part of their food to the hungry, and then recollecting that men cannot eat grass, he resolves, if necessary, to give away his own body. The god Sakra, aware of this high resolve, comes in the form of a Brahmin and begs; but when the hare really offers himself and jumps into the fire, the fire does not burn him. Then Sakra, saying, "O wise hare, let your virtue be known to the end of the world!" splits open a mountain and taking the sap draws a picture of the hare on the disk of the moon. The Japanese always see a *hare* in the moon. This story is given both in Pali and Sanscrit, and, perhaps modified, in

* For authority on this and other statements and legends concerning Buddha, see "Buddhism," by T. W. Rhys Davids.

Edwin Arnold's sacrifice of Buddha to feed the hungry tigress and her whelps.

There are many legends especially dear to Siamese Buddhists. First among them is that concerning Buddha's birth, which says that "after seven days of fasting and seclusion the pure and holy Maya dreams that she is carried by archangels to heaven, and that there the future Buddha enters her right side in the form of a superb white elephant." It was predicted that "the child will be a son, who will be a Chakrawarti, a universal monarch; or, if he becomes a recluse, will be a Buddha, who will remove the veils of ignorance and sin from the world; one who will make all worlds glad by the sweet taste of the ambrosia of Nirvana." It is easy to see, therefore, why Siam has the burly form of the white elephant on her flags, her coins, her medals, and her temples, and why the living animal is held in such sacred honor. Edwin Arnold, in his "Light of Asia," pandering to the poetic tastes of his English readers, makes the incarnation transpire through the descent of a star which enters Maya's side and becomes the "Enlightener of the World."

I saw a picture of Buddha in one of the halls on Palace Mountain, at Petchaburee, in which flames of fire are bursting from the top of his head, flames which cast a red and lurid glare over the canvas at least, if not through the kingdom of Siam.

To show how old some of their customs are, here is the story of the ploughing festival, found in both the Nepalese and Ceylonese accounts. The great king Suddhodana goes out to celebrate the opening of the season, and the prince, Buddha, is taken with him. In the rejoicings the baby is neglected. It then seats itself cross-legged on the couch, and falls into a mystic trance. Though the shadows of all other trees had turned, the tree under which it sat still shaded the child. From this old myth the Siamese declare that to this day the Po tree never casts a shadow. They keep up the ploughing festival, too. When God sends the rain and the earth is made soft with showers, the king, who is the acknowledged civil head of the church, sends a Government officer to each province. The priests go out with him to some of the royal rice-fields, and there eat their morning meal. After this they bless the fields, and the officer ploughs a furrow or two, and then any farmer can begin his spring work. When we remember that history places Guatama's birth five hundred years before Christ, we see how time-honored is this custom of the ploughing festival!

It is frequently stated that Buddhism is supported in Siam at an annual cost of $25,000,000. With a population of 10,000,000, this would only be $2.50 *per capita*. One could easily imagine their religion cost them more than that. We seldom go out but we meet persons on their way to or from the temples, and they never go empty-handed. The most fragrant flowers; the largest, ripest, and most luscious fruits; the whitest rice; the most savory curry and daintiest sweetmeats; the richest and best of all food and drink, are daily offered. Scores of people, who may never have a coat or jacket for their own bodies, will yet buy yards and yards of white cloth, and give it for funeral and other ceremonies, or dye it yellow for the priests. It is estimated that at least ten thousand priests are supported in Bangkok, and I heard a gentleman say a few days ago that in a fishing village near here, numbering some six hundred inhabitants, they support no less than forty priests in their temple. This would be equal to every fifteen Americans supporting a minister, but with this marked difference in the two countries, that the priest has better food and clothing than any of his parishioners.

Besides all that is given at the temples, they feed hungry dogs and cats and beggars, and their spirit-offerings are found daily by the wayside, hanging to the branches of the trees, or set in little idol-houses in the midst of their gardens. Then they set up banners, pennons, and spirit flags. During the dreadful cholera of 1881 and 1882 these flags were to be seen at almost every house, signifying that the inmates were in league with and willing to worship the evil spirits, and should on that account not be stricken with death by the spirits' terrible cholera. Also for miles through the city streets little lanterns were strung up to tall bamboo poles, and there they twinkled and shone all night long to guide the spirits through the air, so they need not descend into the streets below to trouble or molest the people. They also believe in charms, shells, and bones. Almost every imaginable event in life, and their very plays and pastimes, call for some religious observance, and they usually demand more or less outlay. Our hearts are filled with pity for them, bound hand and foot in superstition and sin, and religious ceremonies which neither break the one nor take away the other.

Buddhism has no Saviour, no Helper, no one to hear prayer. Some of our latest converts, when asked why they came to us, said: "We are sinners, and we hear that your God helps." Another said once: "I have studied many religions, and I have found no god that loves as your God loves." Ah! that is it; and just here we see the mighty power of Christianity.

Buddha had a long and active ministry of forty-five years, and died honored and revered at fourscore among his disciples. Christ, after a short ministry of three and a half years, was cut off, ignominiously crucified, despised and rejected of men. But by the divine power of His Godhead He came off more than conqueror; and by His glorious resurrection He abolished death and brought life and immortality to light, and by the boundless power of His almighty love He subdues His bitterest enemies, and makes them His loyal, faithful subjects, ready even to die for the honor of His matchless name!

They say that Buddha attained Nirvana, but not one cry of suffering humanity ever disturbs his repose, or turns his heart with quick throbs of love and pity, or stretches forth his hand to save. But Christ ever liveth to make intercession for us, and while we are yet speaking He hears, and before we call our requests are granted. What is Nirvana compared to that heaven where Christ dwells—in whose presence there is fulness of joy, and at whose right hand there are pleasures forevermore! Since Christ is true, and His the only way to escape from death and reach that "glad city of peace" which all souls long for, let us do with our might for these poor Siamese Buddhists, and help sound the glad tidings through all the kingdom.

CHAPTER XIV.

IDOLS.

ALTHOUGH one of the common maxims of the priests of Siam is, "Make no idols of any kind," yet the land is full of images. We see them everywhere, the almost universal type—motionless, senseless, inane Buddhas. But it is a mistake to suppose they are all images of Guatama. The Siamese, like most worshippers of the Buddhas, believe in past, present, and future gods; and while Guatama is the latest incarnation, and his images are more numerous than any others, still we often see images of past Buddhas, as "*Mok-a-lah*" and "*Salee-boot*," on either side of Guatama's idol, and the image of "*Maitre*," also called "*See-ahn*" by the Siamese; the future Buddha of kindness and mercy, who is supposed to be living a happy life in heaven now, but who will ultimately attain Buddhahood and reach the matchless state of Nirvana. His image is usually distinguished from others by having a five or seven storied umbrella over it. The worship of all these images is "utterly contrary to the original teaching of Guatama, which knew nothing of God, taught that *Arahats*, holy men, were better than gods, and acknowledged no form of prayer."

Among the famous idols of Siam the image at Wat Pra Kêan, at Bangkok, perhaps stands at the head. Then there are the gigantic sleeping idols, one at Wat Po one hundred and fifty feet long and forty feet high, entirely overlaid with plate gold; and its companion in Petchaburee, of equal bulk, which I have described at length in another place. I have also heard of a monstrous image above Ayuthia, the old capital, said to be two hundred feet high. But I think this must include the pedestal and mount upon which it rests. It sits in the usual listless tailor-fashion, with its broad, flat-bottomed feet folded in the lap. It is the largest idol in Siam, but it is abandoned by its former worshippers, and the walls of the old temple which once enclosed it have crumbled into decay. It is called a "*Pra-Pa-le-li*" because it is to perpetuate the legend of Guatama's hermit life, when he was still a *Prasudong* in the forest, where the elephant and the monkey ministered to him. Images of these two devout animals were originally crouched at its base, as you can still see them in attendance on a similar Pra-Paleli in the Royal Cave at Petchaburee. In its lonely desertion it reminds one of poor old Dia Butze, the colossal bronze Buddha of Japan, which has borne the storms of six centuries, and been worshipped by millions of benighted souls.

In the old Siamese history we read that there was a famine in 805 (A.D. 1444), and rice sold for $1.50 a bucket—about four times the usual price; and the reigning king, to please the gods and avert another famine, instead of helping the poor and needy subjects of his realm, "cast five hundred and fifty images of Buddha, representing him in so many previous states of being, before he became divine." About forty years later, in the reign of *Rama Tibawdee II.*, a large standing idol was cast. It was fifty-two feet high. The face was six and a half feet long, and about five feet wide. It was nearly eighteen feet across the breast. The metal of which it was made—a composition of gold, silver, iron, brass, and lead—weighed fifty-three thousand catties. The gold with which it was covered alone was two hundred and sixty-eight catties, equal to $219,600! The gold over the front lacked but one-sixteenth of being absolutely pure. When finished it was consecrated and given the name of "*Pra Seesunpet*"—the

"All-knowing One." But in this year of our Lord 1884 all that remains of the "All-knowing One," and the temple and grounds devoted to his use and service, is the old site covered with ruins, about which clings but the memory of a name—"Wat-Praseesanpetdaram."

The twentieth king in the first dynasty "made three golden idols and two silver ones. When finished he had a grand festival, with boat-races and idol-processions for seven days." From those olden times down to the present all the kings of Siam have made idols and worshipped them, and while I write to-day, no doubt many new ones are in process of formation.

Embedded in some of these images, especially those made of brick and mortar, they have pretended bone-relics of the Buddha, and just this morning my Siamese teacher was telling me that at the end of this dispensation the widely scattered relics of Guatama will assemble in one place, "bone to his bone" (as Ezekiel saw in the valley of vision), and forming a perfect human frame, will become a component part of the new incarnate Buddha-Maitre, who will then appear to bless the world!

During a late visit to Bangkok I secured the following essay, written by one of the students[*] in the King's School, on "Idols and Idol-makers":

"In the place where the idol-makers do their work you will see tools of various kinds, made of iron and brass, such as bellows, chisels, augers, pincers, and hammers. There is a furnace made of soft clay or brick. It is about three feet high. The shape of it is square, and the walls are four or five inches thick, but the mouth of the furnace is round.

"There are many kinds of idols. Some are made of gold, some of silver, and some of brass. The small silver images are made by hammering silver until it becomes very thin. They then take a wooden model, in shape like an idol, and cover it

---

[*] Nai Chote.

carefully with the silver-leaf, and then pull out the model and pour in melted pitch instead. The second kind is made in this way: They take soft clay and sand and mix them thoroughly, and mould it in any shape as they please, and cover it again with wax about one inch thick. Then they cover it with mud and dry it in the sun. When it is dry they heat it to melt the wax out. When the wax flows out they pour in melted brass. Then, when it is cool, they knock the clay out and cover the idol with black pitch for about two days, and then plate it with gold. The third kind are those made of brick and lime. They mix the lime with molasses, and build the idol in the shape of a man. When it is finished they cover it with black pitch, and when dry they overlay it with gold. The fourth kind is made of teak-wood, by carving it with a chisel in the form of Buddha sitting or standing as the owner pleases, and sometimes they cover it with black pitch and overlay it with gold in the usual manner. Sometimes they take pieces of glass and ornament them. The fifth kind is made in this way: They make a mould of stone, and take soft clay and press it in the mould, and form a 'Pra Pim,' a printed god. They take many of these and stick them to a board about two feet long and one foot wide, and then gild them. There are other kinds of images, but they are only painted on the wall with different colors.

"When the image is not yet gilded, and when the eyes made of pearl have not yet been put in, they think that it is not a Buddha, and they do not worship it. The act of putting in the eyes is a great ceremony. After the idol is made in the form of Buddha, the owner will select a holy day to cover it with gold and put in the eyes. On the day appointed he invites priests to come and say prayers to it, and all his relatives come and cover it with gold and put in the eyes."

I have also the following account from a friend, a close observer, who went to see for himself just how the work is done:

"In making the larger idols, those varying from about one to eight feet in height, and usually in a sitting posture, they first make a model of the figure in wax. Into this model they stick small nails a few inches apart, and projecting slightly. Then the image is covered with a coating of fine sand, mixed with clay, sufficiently wet to be easily moulded. The projecting nails serve to prevent the coating from falling off before it becomes hard. After it has been dried in the sun, the idol is put into a furnace and burned, when the wax melts, and, running out, is collected for use another time. Melted brass is then poured over the image, and evenly spread, until the whole surface is covered with a thin coat of the metal. A smoothing and polishing process finishes the work, and the resplendent image is ready for the adoration of the multitude.

"The small silver idols are made in a different way. The maker has a hard-wood model called a type. He takes common coin silver, beats it out into a thin sheet, and covers the model, pressing it close in every part until it assumes the exact shape desired. It is largest at the lower end, which is left open that the model may be drawn out. Melted pitch is poured into the hollow shell of silver-leaf, and then the idol is polished, usually with fine sand. Probably there are other ways of making idols, but these two methods are all that I am familiar with, and they are the most common. But there are indications that in the not far distant future all the idols in this country will be cast—cast to the moles and the bats. May the time come quickly."

The penalties for profaning an idol are very severe. In the forty-eighth section of the Siamese Civil Code we read, that

—"if a thief steal an image of Buddha, and use various devices for getting off its ornaments, as washing or smelting, let him be put into a furnace and treated in the same way as he treated the image, and thus pay for his wickedness, and make thorough work of it.

"Section 49. If any thief strip a Buddhist image of its gold or gilding, let him be taken to a public square, and a red-hot iron rubbed over him till he is stripped of his skin as he stripped the image of its gold, and thus pay for his crime. If a thief scratch off the gold from a Buddhist image, pagoda, temple, or sacred tree, let his fingers be cut off.

"Section 52. If any malicious person dig into or undermine a Buddhist image, a pagoda, or temple, he is liable to punishment in three ways: First, to be flogged sixty lashes; second to have his fingers cut off; third, to be killed."

Buddhist images always represent a human figure, with a bland, sleepy-looking, beardless face, having all the toes and fingers of an equal length, and ears extending to the shoulders. Some deny they worship these images, saying they only serve to remind them of the great teacher, to whom they direct their thoughts. But this is only Satan's subterfuge, who is always ready with a lie when cornered.

Buddhism was introduced into China soon after the birth of our Saviour. It is a wonderful fact, that a record is made in the Chinese Mirror, or History, that in A.D. 50, the Emperor Ming saw in a dream a golden man flying about his palace, which dream was interpreted by his courtiers to mean that the "holy one" was to be found in the West. This so interested him that he sent a deputation to India, who returned with some priests and images of Buddha from Ceylon. Had the messengers gone a little further toward the west, they might have found indeed the Holy One, Christ the Son of the living God.

It is reasonable to suppose that those first images of Buddha from Ceylon became the pattern for all in China, and I have no doubt similar ones were brought to Siam with the early Buddhist missionaries from that spicy isle. In these later days other missionaries have come, telling of a purer and holier faith, and we who believe in its doctrines and predictions know that not only in China and Siam, but all over the pagan world, the image of Christ shall be reflected in countless hearts, and the people themselves will grow more and more in perfect likeness to Him. As I write this sentence there comes up to me the sound of children's voices from the mission-school chanting in concert, "Our Father, who art in heaven, hallowed be Thy Name; Thy kingdom come!" Already we hear the rustle of the banners and the tread of the Lord's hosts. Although of Siam it may be said, "Their land also is full of idols; they worship the work of their own hands, that which their own fingers have made"; yet when the power of God is manifested "He alone will be exalted in that day, and the idols He shall utterly abolish." "In that day a man shall cast his idols of silver, and his idols of gold, which they made each one for himself, to worship, to the moles and to the bats." "So shall they fear the name of the Lord from the west, and His glory from the rising of the sun."

CHAPTER XV.

MONASTERIES OR WATS.

This word "*wat*" is one that is heard all over Siam. A wat proper, includes the temple buildings, priests' houses, salas, pagodas, bell-towers, and indeed everything inside the enclosure of the temple grounds. These grounds are sometimes very extensive, covering many acres, and they hold many beautiful trees, and wide stretches of level ground, with lily-ponds, and paved paths leading from one temple to another. These wats are often surrounded by high brick walls, having ornamented gate-ways. The gates stand open day and night, for monasteries in Siam are refuges for all sorts and conditions of men. I do not hesitate to say that many of the worst characters of the land are to be found, or at least are in hiding, at these Buddhist temples. As the people are religiously careful not to take the life of any living creature, all miserable beasts, surplus pups and kittens, and old worn-out fighting-cocks, are liberated in the wat grounds, and are barely kept alive by what falls from the priests' tables. Moreover, the dying Buddhist often wills his pigs to the wat, and they are allowed to run, hunting their living where they can. As they are considered "consecrated things," no one will kill them, or buy or sell them, and they and their descendants become a public nuisance. In a remarkably short time, too, they seem to revert to their wild state. Being left to root or die, nature kindly accommodates herself to the environment: the snout lengthens and hardens, and the teeth become strong, sharp tusks capable of rending and breaking. I have seen these temple pigs come crashing through the hedges with bristles erect along the spine, and great tusk-like teeth over which it was impossible to close their lips.

Many of the wats border on the rivers and canals, and these have boats, boat-houses, and often very pretty boat-landings, with steps going down to the water. There are no inns in Siam, and nearly all travel is done by boat. You have to carry your bed and provisions along. These wats afford pleasant camping-grounds, and no one ever objected to our landing and appropriating a *sala*, or open porch, to our use. We are allowed to stroll or rest under the trees, and even sit on the temple steps. The priests usually receive us with indifference; sometimes they will answer questions, sometimes not; and if you offer them a book, or any other article, they will never receive it from a lady's hand, because they think that such an act would defile them. But you may lay it down near them, or throw it upon the ground, and they will pick it up without any compunction. I have heard of a lady whose husband indulged in costly cigars, a box of which he usually kept upon his table. Priests like them, too; and when they called, politeness demanded that they be offered. She would pass the box to each one, and then quietly place it beyond their reach with all the precious store intact.

Every wat is commenced by the erection of a temple called the Oobosot or Bote. This is to give shelter to images of Buddha. There may be many other idol-houses clustered about it, but this is to be the mother building, as it were. Every bote of a wat is publicly dedicated to the priesthood, which is a practical acknowledgment by all who have contributed to its erection, that the plot of ground defined by the eight landmarks was given by the supreme ruler of the kingdom to no one in particular, but to the priesthood in general, for the express purposes of a temple, being forever inalienable as such; and that the bote and the idol in it, and all the works in the wat, are entirely and perpetually consecrated to the priesthood. It is a remarkable fact that they have no god to whom they can consecrate them. Vast numbers of people assemble, and the dedication ceremonies sometimes last seven days, with fireworks each night. If it is a royal wat, the king himself is usually present, and when he finishes the service of dedication the representative priests respond with one voice, "Good, good; let the work go on to completion." They then join in a chant at the boundaries of the bote, which are set at each of the eight points of the compass. At these points they bury round stones overlaid with gold-leaf, and the assembled devotees cast offerings into each place—gold and silver ornaments and coins, needles and human hair—the latter with the prayer that their intellects may be as keen and sharp as needles in the next world, and their hair finer than the finest buried there. Afterward a little monument is erected over these buried treasures. On the top of each is set a stone, carved in the shape of a prickly-pear leaf. This enclosure is the most sacred place on the wat grounds. Not even an idol or a priest can be made or consecrated outside its limits. At every new and full moon the priests must assemble within the bote and listen to the reading of the two hundred and twenty-seven statutes of Buddha. The king, in his annual visitations to the royal wats, proceeds directly to the bote, and makes his offerings to the priesthood in that place. There the oath is often administered, and people go to make their vows; and as a priest must literally "owe no man anything," when he presents himself for orders he is asked if his debts are all paid. If there are any creditors who have not yet had their claims settled, they must be present to prove his indebtedness; sometimes the accusation is made before the bote, and if the claim is proven valid, proceedings stop until some one has assumed its payment, when the priest may be duly consecrated to the service of self and Buddha.

Images of the Buddha may be found by the score in every wat. They are made of brick and mortar, stone, wood, gold and silver, brass and copper, and vary in size from two or three inches to one hundred and forty feet. The larger ones of course are stationary, but others are carried about, sometimes placed in salas, and sometimes found in the little rooms of the priests. A "*sala*" is like a large ornamented room, open on all sides, where the people gather to listen to the worship, the preaching, the services for the dead and living, or to look at theatrical performances.

The priests' houses are built in rows, and what I have seen are not arranged at all like the cells of the Romish monks. Indeed, many of them are the ordinary native houses, bequeathed by their former owners to the wat, and after their death taken down and "planted" within the sacred enclosure. They are occupied by one or more priests, according to the number who have to be accommodated in the monastery. They are seldom swept or cleansed, and are infested with vermin; the cobwebs curtain the windows and hang in festoons from the inside of the roof, as there is no ceiling; and dust settles everywhere. Of what we call furniture there is none, but you may find a mat on the floor, with a stone, a block of wood, or a soiled bag of cotton for a pillow; a box, a lamp, a few old books, arrangements for betel, a spittoon, and usually a string stretched across one corner, whereon they hang their extra yellow cloths. I am now speaking of ordinary wats as found throughout the kingdom. The royal monasteries of Bangkok, I hope, are much better, but I have never visited them.

Every wat has a high-priest or abbot, and subordinate officers. Of course, the abbot's house is better than the others—more cleanly—and there are a few chairs, perhaps, a table, a chest of drawers, a clock, a brass or silver teapot with china cups, and a few metal trays for food. There may be strips of matting on the floor, and somewhere about the room his immense fan and umbrella, insignia of office, and near the door a pair of rough leathern sandals. These are made so rudely that you can count the layers of leather in the sole and every stitch with which they are held together, and they have an odd little strap near the front that comes up between the great toe and the one next to it, and with the aid of another strap across the front of the foot keeps the sandal on. Buddhism teaches that it is a sin for priests to wear shoes that cover the toes, thus proving its tropical origin and the ignorance of its Southern followers, who do not know that half the world is so cold that it would be impossible to keep such a rule and save one's toes and sole.

Many of the wats have sweet-toned bells, hanging in beautiful bell-towers. These towers are never very lofty, and are built separate from the temple. They are usually plastered brick-work, square at the base, with a rounded dome or a pagoda spire, supported by arches of masonry. They never ring these bells as we do, but climb the steps and strike them. There is one in a wat over the river from my mission-home that we often hear on Sabbath evenings. Its tones, clear and sweet, floating out on the quiet air, always remind me of home and the dear church bells ringing so far away, and in my heart is a great longing to go to the house of God and worship among my own people and kindred. We cannot help growing tired of the dusky forms and faces forever darkening the sunshine of this glorious land.

Sometimes a young man will become a Buddhist priest, and remain in the wat, often in the same one where he was consecrated, all his life—forty, fifty, and even sixty years—and these old priests are considered very holy by the people. Mothers will take their little boys, and give them to be instructed in the temple lore, as did Hannah, the Hebrew mother, her little Samuel to be with good old Eli in the tabernacle of God. The boys learn to wait upon the priests, to carry their books, betel-trays, and teapots, for in Siam it is fashionable to carry your tea with you, and take it wherever you please. These temple boys also light their cigars, and handle the money, as priests are forbidden to touch gold or silver; and to serve them while they eat, and pour water to wash their hands, as Elisha did for Elijah, and as a partial reward for these services they are graciously allowed to smoke the ends of the cigars and eat what is left. There are many rules and regulations for the wats and the priests who live there, but they are very careless of their observance. They serve more as tests of their sins than anything else, just as the ungodly in civilized lands could not know how sinful they are if it were not for the ten commandments of Jehovah, which they never pretend to keep.

Very zealous priests obey the morning bell, and rise at dawn, and dress before it is light; others get up when they please. This bell also rouses the people outside, and usually the old grandmother in every family, anxious to make merit in her old days because she knows the time is short, gets up with many a grunt and yawn, and shuffles about to have the rice cooked in time. At some wats they have worship before the priests go out for their rice. This consists of praises to Buddha, and repetitions of laws and commandments. They meet in one place and worship in concert, all speaking or chanting aloud. Then they go out to collect their food for the day, and the temple boys follow after, with a bag to hold the fruits and betel, while the priest himself carries a large iron or brass basin under his cloth in which they put the cooked rice. They go from house to house among their relatives or old neighbors, or those who live near the wat, and stand there looking and waiting. But they never ask for anything, nor do they thank the donors for gifts bestowed. Sometimes they murmur that "the food is good and clean, but when it enters the body it is defiled.".

This morning tour they call "*prote saht*," which means, "being gracious to the beasts," as they consider it very meritorious in them to condescend to go and stand where the "beasts" outside the monasteries can make merit by giving them food. The foolish donors, before and after they have made their offering, clasp their hands in holy adoration to the self-righteous, proud, yellow-robed figures before them. If they stop at the homes of any of the boys that follow, these little chaps can slip up the steps and see their friends and get a few extra things if they like. After they have gone their rounds they return to the wat and eat what they need for their morning meal. The boys scramble for their portion, and what they leave is thrown to the dogs, cats, pigs, monkeys, and chickens that wait under and about the wat houses. When breakfast is over they teach the boys to read and write; the doctors make medicine, and those who have writing to do attend to that. The sacred books are nearly all written and copied there, or by noble ladies, who present them to the wat, or to certain priests as they please. The king often orders the wats to prepare for his great occasions, and then the priests must go to work, making pictures, paper flowers, pasteboard animals and birds of impossible shapes and sizes, images and fireworks. And when they build temples or bridges, or funeral pyres for royalty, the priests even help to cut the logs in the forests, float them down, and saw them with their own sacred hands.

About eleven o'clock in the morning they strike the bell or the gong, and all assemble and eat once more. They never ask a blessing on their food, nor offer thanks for it as Christians do, but after they have eaten, they pray that the donors of the food may receive a blessing, and in doing this, they think they make merit for themselves also. From this noon-meal until the next morning they are forbidden to eat anything at all, but they may drink tea, chew betel, and smoke to their heart's content. Even medicine, if it contain aught that is used as food, cannot be taken after this meal, and they strain and boil the water they drink for fear some living creature may be swallowed. They are forbidden to eat seeds that will germinate, or eggs that have been fertilized; for this reason ducks whose eggs are intended for food are kept separate from the flock.

There are minute directions for eating, drinking, sleeping, bathing, dressing, sitting, standing, walking, talking, and indeed every action of the body, mind, and heart, but I will only enumerate a few. For priests it is a sin to meddle with royal affairs, except where religion is concerned. They should speak and do only religious things. It is a sin not to shave the head and eyebrows; to stretch out your feet when sitting, to keep the leavings of your meals, to sleep in exposed places, to climb a tree, to wash in the twilight or dark, lest some living creature be killed. It is a sin to preach in any but the sacred Pali language, or to correct the translations. It is a sin to cultivate the ground, to cover the head, to light a fire, to cook rice, to eat and talk at the same time, to let rice drop from the lips, to chew with a noise like pigs and dogs, to pick the teeth in the presence of others, and not to cleanse the teeth after meals. It is a sin to cough or sneeze to attract notice, and to ask for food or any alms. It is a sin not to love everybody alike!

The priests are at liberty through the day to go and come as they please; but all are expected to be at the wat in time for evening worship, which begins at sunset, unless they have business outside, such as preaching, prayers for the sick and dead, or attending to cremations. Then there must be two or three together, so as to watch each other.

They retire when they please, and the little boys sleep in the rooms with their relatives or friends who may be in the same wat, or at the feet of their masters like dogs.

We often hear of sacred yellow robes and priestly garments, but strictly speaking there are neither. The dress of a Buddhist priest in Siam consists of seven cloths, and they must all be yellow, for that is the sacred as well as the royal color. First, a narrow scarf next the body, called a "sweat-cloth"; then a long, wide one draped about the hips, called a "*panung*," or waist-cloth; a narrow scarf worn as a girdle; then a large cloth, three yards square, draped over the whole body from the shoulders to the ankles, and if properly arranged the folds should cover the arms to the wrists; another large cloth of the same size, folded and laid across the left shoulder, and the ends allowed to hang down a little more at the back than in front; then another girdle, two yards long and three-quarters wide, holding both these large outer cloths in place. To top all is a small piece called the "*pakrap*," or bowing-cloth, because they use it to protect their faces when they bow themselves to the earth before the idols. This cloth is sometimes ornamented with figures of pagodas or royal umbrellas, and the name of the donor, stamped in gilt, or in colors, red, brown, and black, on a yellow ground. The cloth is about a yard long, and folded lengthwise and laid carefully over the shoulder that the designs may appear to all. Besides these seven necessary cloths, they sometimes have a silk or cotton handkerchief. A pair of sandals are also considered part of a complete outfit. Priests never wear hats—their heads are considered too sacred to support them; but they carry an umbrella and a large, long-handled fan to cover their faces, and to shut out the sight of others and the wicked world generally, especially while they preach. The seven cloths are made of little pieces sewed together in imitation of the patches and rags with which the primitive Buddhists are said to have been clothed, when in their poverty and humility they were content with what they could find. Some of the cloths now worn are very costly, and are made of beautiful silk and crape; and the many seams only serve as the faintest shadows of a discarded humility. Instead of being content, too, with plain, simple food, they now expect and receive the best and daintiest the land affords.

The yellow priest-cloths are considered so sacred that no priest is allowed to die in them, and as he nears his end they are stripped from his body that they may not be defiled by the touch of death. Of course, they are never burned; when they are torn or damaged or worn out, instead of being thrown away, they are hung on the branches or wrapped about the trunks of the sacred po tree, and devout Buddhists never pass them without bowing to the yellow. If a priest leaves the monastery, to become an ordinary sinner once more, he either gives his cloths away as a work of merit to some of the inmates of the wat, or sells them. They cannot be used by other than priests.

CHAPTER XVI.

MORE ABOUT WATS.

The most beautiful places in Siam are the wats, excepting of course the palaces in the royal city. The priests select the best sites for their temple grounds, and plant trees and blossoming shrubs. They make lily-ponds for the lovely pink lotus flowers they hold so sacred; and if not bordering on a canal or river, they dig deep, wide tanks for rain-water. The temples, bell-towers, salas, and pagodas are usually built of brick, and are plastered inside and out, and ornamented with plaster figures in bas-relief. These white temples and towers, gleaming through the sacred groves, are very beautiful. They are all white, "old white, with a great deal of color in it." Originally pure white, they have been by nature tinted and brightened by warm patches of mingled sunset colors, and streaks and bars as of a shattered rainbow. There are sleepy old columns that look as though they might have stood in the sea and caught a tangle of sea-weed of the most vivid green about their feet. There are others, again, flecked with black and brown as soft and deep as velvet. Green moss and mold, ferns, air-plants, orchids, and delicate vines are everywhere. Birds sing among the trees unmolested, and bright-eyed lizards dart about in the sunshine with as indifferent an air as the "Miller of the Dee."

The temples are built in the Gothic style, and the high, steep roofs are often supported by rows of pillars. Siamese temple-roofs are peculiar. They are arranged so as to have the effect of two or three roofs overtopping each other, and the gabled ends are ornamented with gilded horns. They are covered with plain or fancy tiles, red and green and yellow, and bordered with white. The walls slope inward as they near the roof, and even the doorways and windows all have this peculiarity of narrowing toward the top. Some of the temple doors are very beautiful, inlaid with ivory and pearl, and stuccoed with curious flowers and figures, images of Buddha and his angels, and lotus lilies. This is especially true of the famous temple of the emerald idol at Wat Pra Kean, Bangkok. Often there is no floor in the temple but the earth. Sometimes they are covered with a hard cement and tiles. We have heard that there is money hidden in many of these old wats, and that in time of war the natives bury their treasures under the idols; and that the large reclining idol at *Wat Pra Non*, in Petchaburee, used to have a door in its back by which you could enter a room in its interior, where there was an altar and many precious gifts, but the door is now walled up.

Crocodiles are kept and nourished at some of the temples as a work of merit. In some corner of the wat there is always found a graveyard, where the bodies of Buddhists are usually buried with very little ceremony. Afterward, it may be weeks, months, or even years, relatives and friends assemble at an appointed time, dig up the remains, and have a merit-making and a burning. Three days after the cremation the charred bones are gathered, and if the family are wealthy they are placed in a costly urn, and taken to their home and carefully preserved. If poor, they are tied in a rag and deposited in the wat. Sometimes they are tied to the rafters, where they look not unlike bunches of seeds, or dried herbs, such as swing from garret-rafters in old farm-houses at home. I have seen them thrown under the seat in the sala where the priest sits when he preaches. Perhaps they are intended to point the moral of his discourse. These temple burial-places are to be shunned.

The graves are often so shallow that the hungry pariah dogs dig up the bodies and devour them, and the vultures hover around waiting for a feast. This is especially true of Wat Sah Kate in Bangkok, where the bodies of very devout Buddhists are cut to pieces and thrown to the dogs and birds. The bones are heaped together and burned, and the ashes scattered over the gardens. I have heard that religious fanatics were sometimes burned alive at Wat Sah Kate, but I fear that in these degenerate days there is no lazy Siamese Buddhist zealous enough to devote himself a living sacrifice. Let us rejoice that it is so, and hope that many converted ones may lay themselves upon the altar of Christian consecration and service.

At some wats they keep coffins which they rent to the poor. The body is placed in it during the religious ceremonies preceding the cremation; it is then removed to the funeral pyre, and the coffin put away to await its next occupant.

There is an order of Buddhist nuns, but very few enter it in Siam. They must be elderly women or widows. They shave the head and dress in white like mourners. They dwell in separate houses from the priests, and their services and devotions are somewhat different. They go forth at dawn to gather their food, or relatives bring it to them to the temple. They attend all the public services, they fast every holy day, and meditate, and pray too, I have no doubt—that is, the really devout ones, although they have no God to listen, and no one to grant the petitions of their longing hearts. Very few of them know how to read, and no children are committed to their care, as to the priests, to be trained for temple service. They help care for the grounds, pulling up the beautiful green grass and wild flowers, and making the yards as bare as their own desolate lives. They sweep the salas and paths, and gather up the fallen leaves of the sacred po and other trees, and pour them into the river, or burn them as a work of merit. They are forbidden to sew or do any real work, so their days must be monotonous enough.

Temple girls such as are devoted to lives of shame in India are unknown here, but I dare not say it is because the people are purer. It does not happen to be the custom, that is all.

It is distance that lends enchantment to these wats. As you draw near them, the illusion is dispelled, for there are nude figures and effigies scattered around, and on the very walls of the *bote* itself before the eyes of the blind idols are often sketched figures and scenes that should never see the light. We were present once at a cremation at one of the most frequented temples. There were scores of priests, and they had all the usual ceremonies. As we turned away we noticed a small brick enclosure, and asked what it was. They said, "A place to bathe the corpse." We looked in and saw a hideous sight, perfectly revolting. On the wall, painted as large as life, and directly opposite the door, was the nude figure of a man, to the right a similar figure of a woman, and to the left a human skeleton. If these abominations are allowed in the sacred enclosure of their holy temple grounds, what must outside heathenism be! We have heard something of the vileness of doctrine and life as preached and practiced by religious devotees in India, and hints of untellable orgies. Perhaps Siam is not quite so bad. I hope not; and yet the actual sins of the so-called holy Buddhist priests would make a black, black record. If God, to-day, visited His wrath upon existing Sodomites as He did upon the ancient city, many of the wats of Siam would be appropriate sites for Dead Seas!

There are, it is said, one hundred and eight wats in the province of Petchaburee alone. Many of them are deserted and falling into ruin now, however; but they show how costly the service of Satan is, and how it has eaten up all the wealth of this land through past centuries. While sailing along the rivers and canals I have noticed that all the best places and most beautiful buildings belonged to the Buddhist monasteries. It reminds one of the remark of a traveller in Mexico as he with others rode through some villages of earth-colored adobe huts, with its church of hewn stone overlooking them. "Poor Mexico! Many churches, no schools! All, all for the priests; for the people—nothing!" So it is in poor Siam. Only here the people are voluntary idolaters, and give these riches to the priesthood. In Mexico the natives have been taxed, and the wealth squeezed from the poor, ignorant, superstitious ones; or some proud, tyrannical Spaniard ground the faces of the poor, and then built a huge stone cathedral for the supposed benefit of his own selfish soul.

In Siam, Church and State are so closely united that I verily believe Buddhism could not exist without the fostering upholding of the king. He is crowned with religious ceremonies and priestly consecration, and he takes the oath of allegiance to the religion of Lord Buddha. He reigns and the Government is maintained for the support of Buddhism and the priesthood. These yellow-robed drones are the only ones in Siam who do not bow before the king. The king himself kneels to the high-priest. And it has been the glory of kings to pour out their treasures for the founding and repairing of temples, and the making of gold and silver idols and offerings for the priests.

What a glorious time it will be when these gorgeous temples are given up to the worship of our Lord and Saviour, the pure and holy Christ. I believe the time will come. When? That is a question we must leave with God.

CHAPTER XVII.

BUDDHIST SHRINES.

JUDGED by outward appearances, one might say that Siam is a very devout kingdom, for the land is filled from end to end with idols and priests, temples and pagodas; there are also wayside shrines, holy wells and caves, and footprints, and trees, and rocks, and shadows. Only the faithful can see the latter, and only the very ignorant believe in them all.

The most noted shrine in Siam is that of Wat Pra Kean, or the Temple of the Emerald Idol in Bangkok. It occupies a walled enclosure inside the double city walls. It is near the king's palace, and easy of access to the ladies of the royal harem; in one sense it is the king's private chapel, where he makes his daily offerings of fresh, fragrant flowers and waxen tapers, and performs his morning devotions. It is without doubt the grandest temple in Siam. It is a royal shrine, and shelters the little image which is held more precious than any other of the thousands in the kingdom. Why it is called the Emerald Idol I cannot tell, for the words "*Pra Kean*" do not translate Emerald god, but Glass or Crystal god, and in the following description of it from the pen of one who ought to have had special facilities for knowing, it will be noticed that there is no mention whatever of emerald either in its composition or adornment:

"The Emerald Idol is about twelve inches high and eight in width. Into the virgin gold of which its hair and collar are composed must have been stirred, while the metal was yet molten, crystals, topazes, sapphires, rubies, onyxes, amethysts, and diamonds—the stones crude, or rudely cut, and blended in such proportions as might enhance to the utmost imaginable limit the beauty and cost of the adored effigy. The combination is as harmonious as it is splendid. No wonder it is commonly believed that Buddha himself alighted on the spot in the form of a great emerald, and by a flash of lightning conjured the glittering edifice and altar in an instant from earth, to house and throne him there!"

No matter what is "commonly believed," no amount of faith will make that little conglomerate image an emerald. They say it has a diamond in its forehead and diamond eyes. It is said to have fallen from heaven originally, and that it was brought from Laos by Payah Lak, the first king who reigned in Bangkok, and has ever since been the pride and glory of the royal capital. Immense sums of money have been spent upon the temple, and in 1882, in honor of the Siamese Centennial, it was thoroughly repaired and rededicated with imposing Buddhist ceremonies. It is enthroned upon an altar of lofty height, reaching almost to the ceiling of the temple. The altar is pyramidal, decreasing in regular tiers from the base to the top, where there is a beautiful golden spire and a throne upon which rests the wonderful idol. Over the altar on these step-like shelves are displayed all sorts of gifts and offerings, besides innumerable gold and silver images of Buddha. There are golden umbrellas, gold and silver lamps, candlesticks and vases, trays, and incense-holders; elegant Chinese, Japanese, and other foreign vases, filled with artificial or natural flowers, and images of elephants and other beasts; also, a great variety of clocks, old and new, big and little, too fast and too slow, and some entirely run down, which seem to have entered upon that eternal rest, lifeless and timeless, of *Nipon*, the Buddhist heaven. Why do they gather all sorts of rubbish and pile it upon the altar of their gods? Who can tell?

In this temple may be seen some of those great candles made of beeswax, and as large round as the body of a man. They are gilded over the outside, and consecrated and lighted before the altar where they will burn for weeks. Here, too, is the holy fire preserved for royal and priestly cremations. Near the close of the last century the sacred fire went out, and was not relit until years after, when one of the royal buildings was struck by lightning. They took of this heavenly fire, and set it to burn once more as a perpetual offering before their god, and there it may be seen to-day. Relays of watchers are on constant guard, so that the temple is never left alone. There is too much treasure and spoil of pleasant things there to be exposed to the ruthless bands of Bangkok robbers. In a land where the ordinary people are so poor that one who has one hundred dollars is considered well-to-do, an idol worth but one-quarter of that sum is certainly a great temptation.

The walls and ceiling of Wat Pra Kean are covered with vines and flowers, pictures of gods and angels, paintings of scenes from the legend of Buddha, and strange heathen symbols. Graceful hanging lamps and chandeliers are used for illumination, while the sunlight struggles almost in vain to get in through the many small two-leaved windows and the narrow doorways. I have elsewhere spoken of these beautiful doors, inlaid with pearl and bits of colored glass, with lilies, "*tawadahs*," Buddhas, and sacred umbrellas making up their pictured surface, and all the spaces and borders covered with gilt, and yet they must be seen to be fully appreciated. Wat Pra Kean is always full of interest. Here the king in his boyhood, when his royal father, Maha Mongkut, was yet alive, was divested of his princely robes and ornaments, and clad in the plain, simple garb of a Buddhist "*Nane*." This is an order which young boys may enter when they are not yet old enough to become regular priests. After his initiation he repaired, with the officiating priests, to the royal temple at Wat Brahmanee Wade, where he spent several months in the cloisters and temples learning all the "ins and outs" of life in the monastery. "When he returned to the world and the residence assigned him," says Mrs. Leonowens, "he seemed no longer the impressible, ardent boy who was once my bright, ambitious scholar." Now as reigning king he meets the princes and highest officers of his Government, twice each year, in Wat Pra Kean. There is an elevated place just before the altar where the king kneels during his devotions, but he never sits before his god. His throne-chair is placed at one side, and his courtiers crouch on the brass-tiled floor before their king and the idol while they take the oath and drink the water of allegiance. Three times a year the king climbs up a ladder at the back of the altar, and with great ceremony changes the silken scarfs of the idol, putting on a lighter or heavier one according to the season. One of the many pagodas we visited in this temple ground is covered over with golden-hued tiles, very small, not more than one inch square, made of coarse glass and gilt. This outside layer alone is reputed to have cost $100,000. Inside is a gilt altar, with a large Buddha upon it, overlaid with gold. Another one is used as a library, and has a large, black wooden case, inlaid with silver and pearl, and holding sacred Pali books. The floor was covered with some of that wonderful silver matting, but it was so dirty you would not have known there was anything in the corners but earth. The keepers slept and cooked and ate there, and their beds and rice-pots were all huddled into the corners; and their cigars, lamps, torches, and betel-trays were laid upon the ornamented ledges of the sacred library. At the end of a rope, which opened a trap-door communicating with an upper story, they had tied some dried fish, which swung back and forth, adding not a little to the odoriferous atmosphere. Dust and cobwebs covered the walls, and the once beautiful ceiling was blackened by the smoke of their cooking.

In the king's own temple, Wat Pra Kean, the beauty of which I have been trying to describe, we found the same mixture of elegance and dirt, gold and jewels, rice-pots, dried fish, and ashes. At one side of the grand altar was a case with glass doors, filled with elegant jewels, and heavy gold chains, devoted to the temple by one of the dead princesses. But even this beautiful case was used as a screen under which to poke their old clothes and hats, for even in this, the grandest temple of the kingdom, the watchers were permitted to camp; and they had their cooking utensils, old lamps, and rubbish filling all the corners of the rear of the building, and overflowing under the altars, and on the window-sills. Surely the Buddhists have little idea of the "eternal fitness of things." The king may not sit before the blind eyes of his idol, but at its back these meanest slaves can do as they list.

Wat Chang has been mentioned in a former chapter, also Wat Sa-Kate, where so many of the dead of Bangkok are buried and burned. There is an island in the river between Bangkok and the sea, and travellers are struck with the beauty of the temple whose white wall and spires gleam out from the midst of its ever verdant foliage. The king makes an annual pilgrimage to this shrine in his elegant state barge, with thousands of boats in his train, and there are great festivities and boat races.

Wat Po is another famous resort for the worshippers of Buddha, and Wat Maha Taht, or Temple of the Holy Bones. At this latter place the Buddhists firmly believe they have enshrined some of the sacred bones of Guatama. Pagodas in Siam correspond to Dagabas in India and Ceylon, and they are always the repositories of sacred relics; so here we suppose every pile of brick and mortar with its spire pointing upward, is the monument in honor of some holy thing handed down from the far past.

There is an army of Buddhist priests in Bangkok alone; indeed we have heard so often that there are ten thousand of them, that reiteration carries with it a certain conviction of its truth. And all these yellow-robed drones are housed in monasteries, or wats, with their adherent holy places, shrines, wells, trees, stones, images, books, candles, rags, and bones.

There are no sacred monkeys, birds, reptiles, or cattle as in India. I have seen a few of those sacred Indian cattle roaming at large in Petchaburee, but their depredations are such that I can assure you they receive more curses than blessings from the enraged populace. The Chinese have tried to introduce sacred pigs, but the Siamese are too indolent to feed such hungry creatures for the doubtful merit in anticipation. At some of the wats, however, they do feed crocodiles, and a favorite pastime of the idle is to throw rice into the river and see fish come in shoals to devour it.

Last December I met one of the prince-priests, Praong Manewt, a younger brother of the present sovereign. He came to our city on a pilgrimage. He preached in the temple next door, and we went to hear him. He has been a monk five years, and refuses all offers of wealth and worldly honors from the king. He is quite small and emaciated, eats but one meal a day, and goes about without pomp or ceremony. Much of his pilgrimage is on land, where he walks with bare head and feet, from temple to shrine, from cave to sacred mountain. He prefers that mode of travel, as it is more austere and he expects to accumulate the more merit. He came to visit our schools, but would not enter the room where the girls were. They say he hates women, and will allow none to enter his wat in Bangkok. This seems strange, and if true, there must be few worshippers at that temple, for women here, as in other pagan lands, are the most constant and devout worshippers at all heathen shrines. Siamese women have their favorite resorts, especially childless wives, who go again and again to offer their petitions in vain to a god who does not and cannot hear.

At Chantaboon there is a famous pagoda which, it is declared, casts no shadow. Perhaps it is on cloudy days, or at night, or noontime when the sun is so dazzling they cannot see. You will find an account of Wat Pranon, or the Sleeping Idol of Petchaburee, elsewhere. We have here also, a Wat Maha Taht. But I have opened a mission-school at the very gateway of this Temple of the Holy Bones, where we hope to teach the children to trust in a living Christ, instead of putting confidence in the supposed merits clinging to the old bones of a dead man.

Wat Kumpang is one of the most interesting ruins in our province. It has been deserted for many years, and the crumbling walls are grass-grown and fringed with delicate ferns and orchids. Pipsissiway grows up through the earthen floor of an unfinished idol-house, and spreads its white-veined leaves before the unconscious Buddha, whose mother-of-pearl eyes were dug from their sockets long ago. This blind idol has two attendants, one on either side. The image to the right has a sacred serpent creeping up its back and spreading its seven heads above in an arched canopy. There are very few images left in the older buildings of this temple's grounds, and they breathe not a whisper of the far-away time when they were whole and new. There are several pagodas still standing, but the temple is a heap of stones. And it is these stones that make this ruin peculiar, for they are a conglomerate evidently mixed by some human process and burned. They are large and heavy, varying in size from one to three feet in length, one to two in breadth, and the same in thickness. The Siamese have lost the art of manufacturing them, if they ever knew it, and no one can now tell when or how they were made. An old legend is that Pra Rursee built Wat Kumpang, and that he found the stones in blocks as he ploughed his fields, and carried them one by one on the point of his ox-goad to their present site. As proof of the story, they show little round holes in every stone as the mark of the ox-goad. I myself have actually seen the little round holes, and yet I am so incredulous I dare not vouch for the truth of the legend. Others, when questioned, reply that they know nothing of Wat Kumpang, except that it is very old, and when the ox-goad story is mentioned they say, "Mem, don't you believe it," and so I don't. At one of the gateways is a large image of Nonsee in red sandstone, whose shoulders and breast are worn quite smooth by the natives who come to whet their knives upon its surface. Lying at its feet are the old cocoanut-shells with which they dip the needed water. I wonder if these Siamese Buddhists ever heard that it is well to "be useful as well as ornamental"? They at least apply it to this old red sandstone image with a vengeance. In one corner of the grounds is a deep, walled well, long and wide, after the fashion of these Eastern lands, which once served as a lotus-pond and bathing-place for priests. The lilies have disappeared, stray dogs lap the quiet waters, and the frogs hop in and out without fear of molestation.

There is a similar ruin at Ratburee. The temples and walls are built of the same conglomerate stone. But they are not deserted. Many priests still haunt the ancient abode. The present chief-priest, or abbot, is crazy, and pretends to be an astrologer, soothsayer, and fortune-teller. Implements of his craft, in the shape of old bottles, cracked dishes and teapots, shells, strings, sticks, banners, and charms of ancient and curious shapes, are scattered all about the grounds, and hung in the temples and pagodas. Here they have an impress of the sacred footprint at

Prabaht. It is covered with a pall, and stands in the centre of its own pagoda. If visitors ask to see it, it is uncovered with the greatest reverence. They also have an altar upon which they lay blank paper, and soon lettering appears which only the initiated can read. There are scores of large stone images in all stages of dilapidation. They are not like ordinary Buddhas, and one wonders if they are to represent Guatama at all. If so, it is not according to the Siamese conception of divine beauty. There are pictured legends upon the walls, and many ruder sketches of recent date.

Not far from Wat Kumpang in Petchaburee is another ruined shrine. On the rear gable of the idol-house is a pictured pilgrimage to Prabaht. Away up near the comb of the roof there was made in the soft plaster the impress of a giant's foot, with parallel sides and five toes all the same length, like the fabled pedal extremities of Guatama. On the wall beneath is represented a mountain, with trees and grottos, and salas in which are reclining Buddhas, with pilgrims slowly climbing up, worshipping as they go, to pay their homage to the most modern wonder of Buddhism. All this is in plastered work, which stands out from the wall, and was originally brightly colored with Chinese paint. This once popular shrine is now a refuge for stray horses. There are no doors, no priests, no worshippers. A few old women who followed us inside, clasped their hands before the dust-covered Buddhas, and then asked me why I did not restore the temple and make merit?

CHAPTER XVIII.

THE BUDDHA FOOTPRINT.

Mount Prabaht is one of the most holy places in Siam, and to it in the month of February, yearly pilgrimages are made. The pilgrims gather from all parts of the country, as a visit to Prabaht is a sure passport to Nirvana.

To reach Prabaht from Bangkok you go by boat some eighty miles up the Chow Payah River, and then inland ten or fifteen miles more. The pilgrims dress in holiday attire, and pass up the river with music and laughter, till far beyond the old capital of Ayuthia, where they go on shore, and by elephant, ox-cart, or on foot travel along a wide, pleasant road, paved with bricks, and leading into the heart of the forest. On either side of the way there are rest-houses and wells for the use of the weary pilgrims. As they near the sacred shrine they ring bells to apprise the angel of the Mount of their approach. Here they find a Buddhist monastery with triple walls. At night these walls are outlined with brilliant lamps, which look very beautiful. Inside the enclosure are the usual priest and idol houses, pagodas, salas, and rests. Scores of bells are hung round and round the temples, which the pilgrims ring for amusement.

On the western side of the mountain is the fabled footprint of Buddha. It is said to have been discovered in 1607, during the reign of Prachow Song Tam, an usurping priest-king. One writer slyly remarks that such a king had a special aptitude for such a discovery. After due examination it was pronounced a genuine impress of Buddha's holy foot. In the surrounding rocks are prints of elephants, tigers, and other wild animals, most of them, according to Mouhot, "formed by antediluvian or unknown" creatures, all of them supposed to have followed Buddha in his passage over the mountain.

The Buddha footprint is protected by a beautiful edifice covered with gilt. It is square at the base, and then dome-shaped, and is surmounted by a pyramid one hundred and twenty feet high. The walls, inside and out, are covered with curious devices, inlaid in mother-of-pearl, glass, and gilding. But, like most of their sacred buildings, it is unfinished and dilapidated. The beautiful inner walls are blackened with smoke from the incense-sticks, candles, and offerings burned before the large silver image of Buddha which reigns supreme on the jewelled throne. The floor is covered with silver matting. There are golden crowns and royal vessels; piles and piles of waist-cloths, of finest color and texture—offerings of the devout. The inner surface of the footprint is covered with innumerable layers of gold-leaf. It is estimated that $5,000 worth of this fragile but costly material is used there annually; each year, after the pilgrims leave, it is scraped off and used by the monks of the monastery for—who can tell what purpose? The temple that covers the footprint is so dark, the crowd so great, and the footprint itself is at the bottom of a hole, so that very few see the wonder, which it may have been the dream of their life to behold.

Thousands of people flock to Prabaht each year, and in such a motley crowd of heathen you may find all classes. Priests in yellow robes swarm everywhere, and receive the adoration of all. They preach to the people in the evening, and the next morning devour all the nice, dainty things the women and girls can prepare for their 11 o'clock breakfast. The day services consist of long recitations from the sacred Pali books. There are scores of beggars and gamblers, saloon-keepers and market-women, with all needed articles for sale at Prabaht prices; various troupes of theatrical performers, and the rude plays are going day and night. The ubiquitous Chinaman is there with his pigtail, and his cards, his *samsho*,* gong, and fire-crackers.

This year (1884) the king and his court and a part of his harem are among the pilgrims, and I presume the costly gifts bestowed upon the temple, the priests, and the holy footprint will be more than usually extravagant. All the royal and courtly pilgrims had to camp out, for there are neither hotels nor palaces at Mount Prabaht. Everything for their comfort and convenience had to be taken with them, and even vehicles which were to carry them from the river shore to the Mount had to be boated thither as well, for there is no good road from the capital. The king's tent was one that had taken a great prize at the Netherlands International Exhibition.

The king's company consisted of himself and harem, with all their train of personal attendants; some two thousand soldiers, royal guards, cavalry, and footmen; many of the prominent nobles, each with his slaves and followers. There were royal physicians, nurses, and cooks. The vehicles were of almost every style—fine coaches from England, with foreign horses and coachmen in livery; Japanese *jinrikishas*, drawn by men, to take the great company of ladies across the country. There were scores of sedan chairs, and some say a thousand ox and buffalo carts, to carry the food and furniture for all. The fine saddle-horses with their trappings for the king and the young nobility, so lately brought from Australia, were also out, and scores of huge elephants, with their howdahs and drivers, were there to grace the grand occasion.

Perhaps there never were so many gathered at Prabaht

---

* Chinese liquor.

at one time before. Besides pilgrims from all parts of the kingdom, the villagers and farmers from all the countryside came to see the king, and all the grand and wonderful things accompanying him. We do not know how long the king intended to remain, but the soldiers getting into trouble, one of them was shot by a comrade, and afterward six more men were beheaded at the royal mandate, and a great many pilgrims died owing to the prevalence of fever; so the king and his retinue turned back without effecting their intended trip to Patawi. We heard that a careless shot was fired in the direction of the king's tent, not with the purpose of injuring him, however, yet the excitement it occasioned must have been intense. We are glad the young king escaped both shot and pestilence, and has been permitted to return to his capital in safety.

Not far from Prabaht is Patawi, where under a shelving rock the faithful can see the shadow of Buddha. At Patawi may be seen, also, many footprints like those at Prabaht, and splendid specimens of petrified trees. The view from the summit of this rock mountain is one of the finest in the kingdom, and well repays the hardy traveller for his patience and fatigue. Hill and plain, forest and mountain form a delightful panorama to the north, while " off to the south is a vast plain, which extends from the base of Patawi to the other mountains beyond Ayuthia, whose high towers are visible in the distance, one hundred and twenty miles off. At the first glance one discovers what was once the bed of the sea, this vast plain having taken the place of an ancient gulf, proof of which is afforded by numerous marine shells, many of which have been collected in a perfect state of preservation; while the rocks, with their footprints and fossil shells, are indicative of some great change at a still earlier period."

CHAPTER XIX.

THE PEOPLE AND THEIR HOUSES.

The Siamese are undoubtedly descendants of the Laos and other northern tribes, and further back than that they claim descent from the Brahmins of India, and this latter belief accounts to my mind for the presence of Brahmins at all their great state and religious ceremonies, although the king and all his subjects are avowed Buddhists. Physically they are small and weak, with little muscle and very soft bones. The men have no beards, and all the nation, unless of mixed blood, have straight, coarse black hair, and black or brown eyes. Their features are not at all of the negro type, and some have very good looking faces, strongly reminding one of friends across the sea. The Siamese idea of beauty is to have eyes like buttonholes, with the buttons half through; black teeth, red lips, long finger-nails, straight black hair; large ears that stand out from the head at the top, and whose lobes droop toward the shoulder; small waist, and a white skin, which they mellow by rubbing it with a golden powder called "*cummin*." They usually have olive complexions, but some are very black. As a rule, they would have white, beautiful teeth, but the disgusting habit of betel-chewing disfigures the mouth wonderfully, causing the teeth to protrude and blacken, and the lips and tongue to crack. Every habitable place in Siam is defiled with the blood-red saliva they are constantly ejecting from their mouths. The cud they chew so persistently is a combination of ereca-nut, cera leaf, lime, tobacco, camphor, and tumeric. It is a very expensive luxury, but one indulged in by all classes. It is given with the sacred offerings to the priests, as well as to the meanest slaves or beggars who crouch along the streets. The natives consider it an insult if they enter another's house and are not invited to eat betel, and it is equally impolite to refuse the proffered cud. Indeed, it occupies so important a place in the economy of their social life that a wedding is called "*Kun Maak*," literally "betel-tray," because it heads the procession of gifts which are laid at the feet of the bride's parents by the bridegroom. They say "any dog can have white teeth," inferring that only those who know enough to use betel can have beautiful black ones. I have seen it in the mouths of unweaned children; and old folks no longer capable of chewing, pound it in a mortar to reduce it to the desired pulpiness, or have younger jaws and better teeth masticate it for them. It is mildly stimulating, and they can fast from food a long time if only they have plenty of betel. It costs almost as much as their food, especially among the poor. A great many young men in Bangkok are, however, giving up the filthy custom, especially those who learn to speak English, and we ardently hope the fashion will spread throughout the kingdom.

Some of the young men and women are quite handsome, and the little children beautiful in features and natural graces of form. Their eyes are specially lovely, of a rich liquid brown, and fringed with long, silky lashes. Among the nobility of Bangkok, and where the best language is used and they chat pleasantly together, their voices are low and sweet, and many of the words have a musical ring. They show a certain respect for the aged, and are very fond of little children. Motherhood is considered honorable, so infanticide is rare, and even little daughters are loved and cherished almost as tenderly as sons.

Women enjoy greater liberty than in almost any other

Oriental land. You meet them everywhere; and in the bazaars and markets nearly all the buying and selling is done by them. As servants and slaves too, they are seen performing all sorts of labor in the open streets. Still they are down-trodden, and considered infinitely inferior to men. It is a significant fact that although boys have been educated for past centuries in the Buddhist monasteries, there are not, and have never been, so far as I can learn, any native schools for girls. Quite a number, however, learn to read in their own families, but such knowledge is looked upon as a superfluous accomplishment, and they are not encouraged in it, neither is any one ashamed to acknowledge their ignorance of books.

The Siamese are a pleasant, good-natured people, but lazy and indolent to the utmost degree, and vain, shallow, and self-conceited. Their greatest vices are lying, gambling, immorality, and intemperance, although the latter is strictly forbidden by one of the commandments in their Buddhist decalogue. The vice of intemperance is fearfully prevalent. As early as 1844 the "Liquor Farmer" of Bangkok and its suburbs, paid $96,000 yearly for the privilege of making and selling it there. It is made of molasses, and costs but little, and the consumption of it is constantly on the increase. The home production is not equal to the demand, and the liquor is imported from China, Batavia, Singapore, and Europe. A certain class of foreigners have made fancy wines and liquors fashionable at court and in the higher circles of native society, and many of the young bloods are ruining both body and soul with strong drink. Native arrack and "*low*" can be purchased for sixpence a pint, and half that quantity is enough to intoxicate the ordinary tippler. So this "curse of curses" has taken possession of the land. It has been said that only "two kinds of Americans come to Siam. One class to Christianize, and the other to liquorize the natives!" In the past this was too true. Some years ago an American so dishonored our flag that now we dare not unfurl the stars and stripes above our homes, even on our national holidays, without the natives considering it the sign of a liquor establishment. It is charged that this American issued papers to venders of spirits who were thus enabled to sell imported goods, free of duty, under the protection of our dear old flag. The stars and stripes went up and down the rivers and canals on little whiskey-boats, and fluttered from doors in the principal streets of Bangkok and other cities of Siam, where the "water of sin," as my old native teacher aptly calls it, was sold.

Eating and smoking opium are also on the increase, and the law which threatens all consumers of it with confiscation of property and death, is not now enforced. There is a weed called by the natives "*Kuncha*" (which I think is Indian hemp), grown abundantly in Siam, and those who are too poor to buy opium use this instead and with similar effect. The pleasing effect of this drug lasts three or four hours, and is followed by a deep sleep. The result of its constant use is a wretched nervousness, lung complaints, dropsy, melancholy, madness, and death!

It would be hard to find a Siamese who did not use tobacco in some form. The men and boys nearly all smoke and some of the women. All chew the weed with their betel, and some use it as snuff.

Gambling is only allowed at licensed places except for a few days each year, when the king grants full liberty, and then every man, woman, and child seems determined to make the most of the chance, and everything else is neglected to indulge in the absorbing passion. This vice brings a wondrous revenue into the king's treasury, and is filling Siam with slaves.

The dress of the Siamese is very simple and comfortable, consisting of a waist-cloth, jacket, and scarf, and sometimes a hat and sandals. If all would, at all times, wear the native dress there would be no occasion for fault-finding. But as a nation they do not know what shame is, and as the climate is mild and pleasant, and the majority of the people poor and careless, their usual dress consists of a simple waist-cloth, adjusted in a very loose and slovenly manner; while many children, until they are ten or twelve years old, wear no clothing whatever. When foreigners first arrive in Siam they are shocked almost beyond endurance at the nudity of the people; and although they constantly preach a gospel of dress, their influence in this respect seems less apparent than in almost any other. Not until Siam is clothed need she expect a place among respectable civilized nations.

The old-fashioned shave, which left a patch of stiff bristles on the top of the head like a shoe-brush, is no longer the universal style. European trims are the most fashionable in the capital, and some of the young men are trying to cultivate the mustache, and the women let their hair cover the whole head, and dress it with cocoanut-oil. They shave their foreheads, rub beeswax on their lips, powder their faces, and perfume their bodies. They bend their joints back and forth to make them supple, and give the elbow a peculiarly awkward twist which they consider very graceful.

Their salutations are decidedly peculiar. The old style is to get down on all-fours, and then, resting on the knees, raise the clasped hands three times above the head, and also bow the head forward until the brow touches the floor. They kiss with their noses, by pressing them against their friends', and saying, "Very fragrant, very fragrant!" while they take long, satisfied sniffs. Many are now learning to shake hands and make graceful bows like European nations, but the imported kiss is not yet in vogue, and I do not see that it ever can be until betel is discarded, for at present the nose is a more kissable feature of the Siamese face than the mouth.

The people are exceedingly fond of jewelry, and often their gold chains and rings are the only adornment the body can boast. Many a young girl refuses to wear a jacket because it would cover up her chains, which are worn as a hunter carries his game-bag, over one shoulder and under the arm. She prefers a scarf which she can arrange and rearrange, and thus display the glitter of her golden ornaments. They wear a great many gold rings, and their earrings are often costly and beautiful. They also have gold armlets and anklets, and charms encircling neck and waist, and the higher ranks now wear gold girdles with jewelled clasps. The jewelry is of odd and unique designs,—snake-bracelets; necklaces of gold turtles, fish, and flowers, set with gems; dragon-headed rings, with diamond, emerald, or ruby eyes, and a tongue that moves. Some rings have little birds poised upon them, with outspread wings and sparkling with jewels; golden elephants, and many other rich and costly designs.

The Siamese are great bathers. Several times daily they may be seen splashing in the rivers or canals, or pouring water over themselves from jars set by the doorway. There is no privacy in Siam—eyes, eyes everywhere; and they think no more of bathing themselves and their children in the open street than of buying a bunch of lettuce from the market-woman. But it would be a mistake to suppose they are cleanly; for as they use neither soap nor towels, this drenching of the body does not cleanse it, especially when to complete the toilet they smear the body with tumeric. I am glad to say, however, that they are singularly free from vermin, owing no doubt to these frequent baths, changes of raiment, and the shaved head. Although these people are called Buddhists, they also worship devils, evil spirits, and men who are priests. Every kind of superstition is known among them—witchcraft, enchantment, sorceries, philters, conjuring of words, all the frightful secrets of the black magic, are resorted to when other means fail to arrive at their ends, which is done with the aid of demons called "*Pee.*" They are very ignorant, poor souls, and full of nameless fears—even grown men are afraid to be alone in the dark.

The nobles of Siam, under the present reign, have erected a great many handsome brick houses, which are planned by European architects, and are roomy and comfortable—that is, they are large and cool, and some of them elegantly furnished with English, French, and Chinese furniture. In these houses may be seen beautiful plate, and rich and rare old vases, vessels of gold and silver and jewel-boxes, mirrors, pictures, chandeliers, and other beautiful things in great variety, according to the rank and wealth of the owners. So little clothing is worn, and varies so seldom in style or color, that the wardrobe is usually the least part of the possessions. Some of the princes' palaces have marble and tile floors, others simple wood. Occasionally they have carpets or straw matting. All are very fond of flowers, and so these houses have beautiful gardens. Sometimes they are attached to the palaces, and sometimes they are off in another part of the city. These are filled with all the lovely trees and flowers of Siam, and many rare plants from other lands. The rich Siamese have many of the comforts and luxuries of life. They have numerous slaves and attendants. But polygamy fills the houses with immorality, bitter jealousies, and strife, and thus *there are no homes!*

The middle class dwell in houses built of wood, usually unpainted teak, and roofed with earthen tiles. They are small and illy ventilated, and here the people huddle together, from the parents to the children of the third and fourth generation. One can imagine the quarrels and fusses that arise daily where there are so many in one household. They have very little furniture, and may be said to live principally on the floor. They seem to be natural "squatters." On visiting them first you might think they had just moved in, and that the furniture would come along presently; but if you called five or ten years later you would find it had not yet arrived.

The lower class live in huts made of woven bamboo, and thatched with leaves of the mangrove tree. Nearly all dwellings are built on posts or pillars, which elevate them five or six feet from the ground, and are reached by ladders, which at night are often drawn up to prevent dogs or thieves from coming into the house. But the very poor have to content themselves with huts made of palm leaves tied to a bamboo frame, and with nothing but the bare earth for a floor.

All ordinary Siamese houses must have three rooms; indeed, so important is this number considered to the comfort of the family, that the suitor must often promise to provide three rooms ere the parents will let him claim his bride. There is the common bedroom, an outer room where they sit during the day and receive their visitors, and the kitchen. Let me begin at the latter, and try to describe the dirty, dingy place. Having no godliness, the next thing to it, cleanliness, is entirely lacking. There is a rude box, filled with earth, where they build the fire and do what they call the cooking; that is, they boil rice and make curry, and roast fish and bananas over the coals. There is no making of bread or pie, of cake or pudding; no roasts, no gravies, no soups. Even vegetables are seldom cooked at home, but are prepared by others and sold in the markets, or peddled about the streets. There they buy boiled sweet potatoes, green corn, and preserved fruits, curries, roasted fish, and ants, peanuts and bananas, sliced pine-apples and melons, and squash. Pickled onions and turnips are sold in the streets of Bangkok just as pickled beets are in Damascus. Curry is made of all sorts of things, but is usually a combination of meat or fish, and vegetables. If you want an English name for it that all can understand, you must call it a stew. The ingredients are chopped very fine, or pounded in a mortar, especially the red peppers, onions, and spices. The predominant flavor is red pepper, so hot and fiery that your mouth will smart and burn for half an hour after you have eaten it. Still, many of the curries are very good, and with steamed rice furnish a good meal. But sometimes a "broth of abominable things is in their vessels," as, for instance, when they make curry of rats or bats, or of the flesh of animals that have died of disease, and they flavor it with "*kapick*," a sort of rotten fish, of which all Siamese are inordinately fond. It is unrivalled in the strength of its fragrance and flavor. Siam is unique in that she possesses two of the most abominable things, and yet the most delicious, if we believe what we hear, and they are the durien, a large fruit found only on this peninsula, and "kapick," which I hope is not found anywhere outside of Siam.

The kitchen has no chimney, and the smoke finds its own way out, leaving black and sooty marks upon everything. There is but little furniture, except the rice-pots, kettle, and perhaps a frying-pan. There is a little stool, a foot square and four inches high, that they call a table, and on which they place the curry and fish and the sliced vegetables, while those who eat squat around it, each with a bowl of rice on the floor before them, which they replenish from a dish or basket near by, or from the rice-pot on the fire-place. The rice-pot is of coarse earthenware, round and bulging, with a small mouth and a lid. They cost but a trifle, and are easily broken, but the rice cooked in them is the most delicious I ever tasted. It is washed, then covered with cold water, and set on the fire; as soon as it comes to the boil it is skimmed and stirred. It is boiled a few moments, and then the water is drained off and the pot set near the fire for the rice to steam. In half an hour it is cooked, and when poured out is like a mountain of snow, every grain separate and whole. No wonder the natives marvel that we can live without it.

There is no regularity about their meals, and they do not wait for one another, but eat when they get hungry. In the higher families the men always eat first and by themselves, and the wives and children and dogs take what is left. The usual rule is for each one to wash his own ricebowl, and turn it upside down in a basket in a corner of the kitchen, there to drip and dry till the next time it is needed. They eat with their fingers, very few having so much even as a spoon, and they do not use the wafer-like bread so common in the Levant, which those natives double into a kind of three-cornered spoon, dip into the curds or camel stew, and eat down spoon and all.

There are no washing or ironing days. Many have no jackets, only a waist-cloth which they wear when they go to bathe. When they come up out of the water they change it for a dry one. It is then rubbed a little in the water, wrung out, and spread in the sun to dry, then they fold it up and pat it with their hands, and that is all the ironing it gets.

The kitchen floors are nearly all made of split bamboos, with great cracks between, through which they pour all the slops and push the dirt, so there is no sweeping or scrubbing to do. Near the door are several large earthen jars for water, which are filled from the river by the women or servants as often as they get empty, and here they wash their feet before they enter the house. They dip the water with a gourd or a cocoanut-shell. They also use brass basins and trays a great deal, but for lack of scouring they are discolored and green with verdigris, and I cannot help thinking the use of such vessels is one of the fruitful sources of the dreadful sores and eruptions with which the whole nation is afflicted.

The outer room is barren enough, with perhaps a mat for guests to sit upon, and a tray from which all are served with betel.

The bedroom is where things accumulate. A torn straw mat, or perhaps an ox hide or two on the floor, with brick-shaped pillows stuffed with cotton, or a block of wood itself in lieu of anything softer and you have the ordinary Siamese bed. In families of not the very poorest, you sometimes find long narrow mattresses stuffed with tree-cotton. These may be covered with an old ragged waist-cloth instead of a sheet, and over it is suspended a mosquito curtain of unbleached cotton. These things are used for years without being changed or washed. The beds and mats are filthy, and, more horrible still, are swarming with bugs. They infest the curtains, the coverings, the cracks in the floor and the wall, and the little boxes in which they store their few clothes and valuables. I have even seen them creeping over the people, and no one seems to mind them or think of being ashamed. The rooms are never cleared out or scrubbed. The cobwebs of succeeding years tangle and entangle themselves in the corners, drape the rafters and the windows, and indeed every place where the busy spinners lay their hands. There is seldom more than one window to a bedroom, and at night it is carefully closed, and if it were not for the cracks in floor and wall, the miserable inmates would surely smother. They have as great a horror of the night air as some old fogies in more civilized lands who appear to think that God only knows how to regulate the air for twelve hours out of the twenty-four. They do not bring their cattle into the house, for it is very frail and set upon posts, but they keep them under the floor, so they can hear if thieves come to steal them.

They never give any dinner or tea parties, or visit each other as we do at home. There is an occasional feast—as a wedding, a funeral, or a hair-cutting, and sometimes the neighbor girls will sit together under the same tree to sew; or by the same lamp at night to economize oil, and to chat and gossip. A great place for the latter pastime is at the temples, when they go to hear the Buddhist services, which are in Pali, usually, and not to be understood, or by the river-banks and wells when they go to fetch water. They carry water in pails, or baskets sealed with pitch, and suspended from the ends of a pole *a la Chinese*.

Thus it will be seen that house-life among the Siamese is very simple and primitive. There are no women who have worn out their lives scrubbing, or fussing over cook-stoves. They do not dread the spring house cleaning, or the fall setting up of stoves and putting down carpets. There is no canning of fruit, nor packing of butter and cheese. But alas! there is no happy home-life either, no family altar where they can worship a living God, no pleasant social board where fathers and mothers, brothers and sisters meet three times a day, and thanking God for food, eat with joy and gladness, and grow strong for His service; no sitting-room where some of the happiest years of our lives are spent, in loving companionship with those of our own household; no place for books, and no books to read, except perhaps a few vile tales, and books of superstition and witchery. God pity Siam, and plant in her kingdom many happy Christian homes. May her people be purified and cleansed and taught of Thee in all things; then will the good influence, working from the heart outward, touch, and cleanse, and beautify all their surroundings.*

---

* The reader will doubtless notice that my description of housekeeping is of Siamese life among the lower classes, not among those who have come in contact with missionaries and been improved somewhat, nor those of the higher classes in Bangkok, the princes and nobles, whose old-time home-life was neater and more orderly than that here described. These,

CHAPTER XX.

HOLIDAYS IN SIAM.

The holidays are very many. Indeed if cessation from work makes a holiday, some of the natives have a continuous one, for they never have done anything and they never expect to.

In 1884 the designated holidays, however, were "*Teep Chingcha*," or Swing Days, occurring on the 4th, 5th, and 6th of January. Swings are put up in the "swing market," and young Siamese stand in them and "work up" until they are able to take some money with their mouths from a high pole fastened in front of them. The king and others witness the feat. The awkward ones who secure nothing afford a great deal of amusement to the crowd, while the successful ones not only carry off the prize-money, but are greeted with the loudest applause. Processions of gaily-dressed natives with banners and flags parade the streets and gather to witness the fun.

Since the Chinamen have become so numerous in Siam, their New-Year marks a national holiday. It began January 27th and was celebrated for three successive days. The first day they worship idols, devils, and ancestors, and have a great racket and boom with fire-crackers. Shops are

---

through the influence of foreigners coming to Siam and visits to foreign lands, have raised themselves in the scale of living, and have foreign houses filled with foreign furniture and conveniences, order sumptuous meals from foreign bakeries, and have them placed upon their tables and served in modern style. I do not consider that true *Siamese* housekeeping.

closed and work ceases. They give themselves up to worship and fun and gambling. Their kitchen god goes to heaven for three days and then returns. They tear down the old picture of him and put up a new one, and paste red papers, with prayers and vows upon them, all over the doors and windows (ancient Hebrew custom?), begging mercy of heaven, and health and prosperity for the coming year, and promises to worship next year if the prayers are granted. All through the three days they must not quarrel nor scold in the family or in the street, and no water must be drawn or carried, and if a rice-bowl is broken during that time, it is a sign of bad luck. They also prepare food and sweetmeats, and after first offering them to the idols and their invisible ancestors, they make a feast of them for themselves and their friends, and send portions one to another. I have had more than one try of uneatable Chinese dainties presented to me at such festival times. The Chinese also burn at New-Year's, paper money, clothes, shoes, houses, horses, boats, and all sorts of things for the use of the dead.

"Prabaht," or the visiting of Buddha's supposed footprint, are the next holidays. The 11th of February the pilgrims start for the sacred shrine. To go once is a work of great merit, twice much greater, and three times will surely open the highest heaven to the weary pilgrim.

The Siamese New-Year falls on the first day of their fifth month, the 27th of March. It is called "*Krut Tai.*" The festivities, and especially the gambling, which is then free, are kept for three and sometimes five days, if the king is kind enough to grant them a few "days of grace." The first day they carry offerings to the temples and the priests, and give gifts to their friends. There are certain sweetmeats made of glutinous rice, cocoanut, sugar, and peanuts which even the poorest strive to obtain. Men, women, and children must be without restraint, and allowed to do just as they please, and go and come as they will during these three wonderful days. Even tormented souls in the Buddhist purgatory are allowed to revisit the earth and beg a share of mortal merit, and their pitiful human friends divide their small stock with them, pouring out water from brass basins upon the ground as a witness of the good deed. The people strive to visit all temples, caves, and Buddhist shrines within a reasonable distance of their homes. They bathe the idols in perfumed water, drape them in sacred yellow cloths and then bow before them in adoration, burning incense-sticks and waxen tapers. The young people play from morning till night. They gather flowers on the mountains and weave garlands, or lay them in Buddha's ever open palm. They dance and sing, they laugh and shout. All seem to be happy and in a good humor. They play tricks on each other, catching boys and girls and blacking or greasing their faces, and then pushing them into the river. I have known youngsters to stand for hours on a thoroughfare and dash water on every passer-by. They have also a pretty custom of bathing the grandmothers at these holidays. They dip water from the river and pour it over the old creatures as they sit on a board in the sunshine. No enchantments are used, but the children laugh and talk around the old ladies and sprinkle them with perfume, and powder their necks, faces, shoulders, and arms with sweet-scented powder. They are then presented with a new suit of clothes, consisting of a waist-cloth and a scarf, and money is slipped into the poor old wrinkled hands. All make merit by the operation. On the third day all Government officers drink the water of allegiance and swear loyalty to the king.

On the 11th of April another triple set of holidays began. It was the day the sun entered the sign "Aries," and was the beginning of the Siamese astronomical New-Year.

Early in May they celebrate the "*Raknah*"—beginning of seed-time. As I have spoken fully of this festival season in the chapter on Siam's Religion, I will only say here that no farmer is allowed to begin his spring ploughing and planting until after the performance of this royal ceremony and the blessing of the king's fields.

In the middle of their sixth month, which falls in May, when the moon is at its full, they celebrate a day as the anniversary of the birth, inspiration, and death of the Buddha Guatama. We will look through Mrs. Leonowens' eyes and see what she says she beheld in the city of the Nang Harm, or Royal Women, one May morning in 1864:

"I was conducted by a number of well-dressed slave-women to the residence of my pupil, the 'child wife.' Her house was a brick building, with a low wall running round it, which took in some few acres of ground, devoted to gardens and residences for her numerous slaves and attendants. I was the first, that morning, to pass between the two brick and mortar lions which guarded the entrance, and after a kindly greeting I took my place at the inner end of the hall or antechamber which gave access to the residence. The 'child wife,' a remarkably pretty little woman, dressed in pure white silk, stood in the hall beside a small marble fountain, with her two sons on either side of her. All round the fountain were huge China vases containing plants, covered with flowers, and between them were immense silver water-jars, each large enough to hold a couple of men, and each containing a huge silver ladle. Thirty or more young slave-women were engaged in filling them with cool, fresh water, drawn from a well in the garden.

"The hall was freshly furnished with striped floor-matting, and with cushioned seats for a hundred guests. In the garden, opposite the doors of the hall, was a circular thatched roof, supported on one great mast like a single-poled tent, and this was the theatre erected for the occasion. In one part was an elevated stage for the marionettes, and the whole was very prettily and gracefully ornamented, showing, as did everything around, a desire to please and to entertain. Some fifty women-porters came from an inner court, bearing on their heads massive silver dishes of sweetmeats and choice viands, and placed them along the hall; then came some maidens dressed in pure white, and arranged flowers in small gold vases beside each of the seats designed for the expected guests, and when this was done they took their places behind their mistress.

"It was early morning, just seven o'clock. But this entire women's city had been up for hours engaged in the important work of rightly celebrating the great day. The grounds around the house were all in a glow with roses, and the pure silver of the water-jars glistened resplendently in the morning sunlight. The gate was thrown wide open, and into this fairy-like scene, amid flowers and sunshine and fragrance, and the dew still trembling on the leaves, were ushered in the guests, one by one—a hundred decrepit, filthy, unsightly-looking beggar-women covered with dirt and rags and the vilest uncleanliness. And the 'child wife,' who might have numbered twenty-five summers, but who looked as if she were only sixteen, blushing with a delicacy and beauty of her own, advances and greets her strange guests with all the more respect and tenderness because of their rags and poverty, leads them gently and seats them on low stools around her sparkling fountain, removes their disgusting apparel, and proceeds with the aid of her maidens to wash them clean with fragrant soap and great draughts of cool water ladled out of the silver jars.

"What a transformation when the matted hair was washed and combed and parted and dressed with flowers, and the rags were replaced by new robes of purest white! Then she led them toward the hall, and seated them on the silk cushions beside the silver trays, and bowed on her knees before them and served to them the delicacies prepared for them, as if they each one and all deserved from her some special token of her love and veneration.

"After breakfast the music struck up and the actors and puppets appeared on the stage. The music was particularly good. The royal female bands were assembled for the occasion, and relieved each other in succession; the acting was occasionally interspersed with the plaintive notes of female voices; the priestesses of this beautiful scene, who seemed sometimes deeply moved, collected from within themselves all the charms and joys of love to pour them forth, with the inspiration of music, at the feet of their lowly listeners.

"And at length, as the curtain of the last act dropped, and the prolonged cadence of the voices and the instruments died away, a loud buzz of delight and pleasure broke from the listening crowd of old, decrepit women, who received each a sum of money from their kind hostess, and went on their lonely way rejoicing."

Wasah, a sort of Buddhist Lent, begins July 8th, and continues till October 4th. These are months of special fasting, penance, and self-mortification for the fat, lazy priests in the monasteries. There are no special rules that every one must abide by, but all are self-imposed, except that the priests must never let the dawn find them outside the temple enclosure. Some spend the night among the tombs thinking on death; others sit up all night under a tree, or in a cave, or some quiet place, denying themselves the proper attitude of repose. Others eat but once in twenty-four hours, and then only such food as is placed in their large iron bowl; outside dishes and dainties must all be avoided. But if they grow tired of these voluntary observances before the end of the three months, they can give them up whenever they choose, only they forfeit the merit they might have gained by being faithful to the end.

At the close of these holy-days the whole nation is intent on feasting them, and for every morsel of food thus prepared and given to the priests they expect to receive and enjoy an hundredfold of heavenly entertainment in the world to come, or in the "*chaatnah*," the next birth, as the Buddhists teach.

During "Wasah" all in authority or receiving Government wages must renew their oath of allegiance to the king, preceding the ceremonies attending the celebration of his birthday, September 21st. These royal natal festivities are among the grandest of the year, and include the 20th, 21st, and 22d of September. Extensive illuminations in honor of the event and fireworks are displayed every night, and day and night plays, games, and theatricals attract the throngs of idle pleasure-seekers. Birthday calls are made upon the king, and congratulatory speeches and messages are delivered by foreign ministers, consuls, and residents; gifts are presented, and a grand party given to all the *élite* of Bangkok by the Minister of Foreign Affairs at his palace, at which the king usually appears somewhere near midnight, when temperate people are so sleepy they can hardly see him, and intemperate people are so anxious to have their supper and begin drinking and dancing that they hardly care whether they see him or not. He is very gracious, and walks down the long reception hall, shaking hands and speaking kindly to this one and that.

Shortly after the royal birthday comes the first series of "*Loy Ratong.*" They are held October 3d, 4th, and 5th, and again November 1st, 2d, and 3d. The amusements of these triple holidays consist in floating fireworks and offerings to the water spirits. In Bangkok—in the vicinity of the palaces especially—night is turned into day by the multitudinous lights flashing everywhere and reflected from the water. The river seems alive with floating palaces, miniature ships, floats, and rafts, all brilliantly lighted, and riding the waves, bearing their offerings of betel and tobacco, rice, sugar, and sweetmeats to the "Great Mother of Waters" for her gracious care of them through the past year, and as a thank-offering and propitiatory sacrifice, because they have bathed in her flood, drank of her sweet waters, and rowed their boats over her bosom. There are some royal craft, resembling illuminated dragons, which are floated down the river on one side, and then slowly towed up the other. Lotus lilies, with burning tapers, are a favorite offering, or little rafts made of the pith of the plantain tree, and gaily decked with flowers, flags, and tapers. People are on the river in boats by thousands, and in all the provinces and down by the sea even the natives are setting off their fire-gifts upon the wave.

The "*Taut Katin*" holidays begin October 4th, and

last for one whole month. They are celebrated by processions on land and water. Those by water are specially magnificent. The gaily-dressed people, in beautiful boats, go on all the rivers and canals to offer their gifts at the temples, and when the religious part is finished they spend the rest of the day and night boat-racing. Even the king and his court go annually to Paknam to witness the races there. From midnight till dawn Buddhist priests are gathered at the Paknam Prachadee, reciting serious and comic chants. By daylight surging crowds in boats press up to the island to prostrate themselves before the priests and the idols, and afterward all watch the races or take part in the exhilarating exercise. The special aim of all racers seems to be to run down and upset other boats, thus throwing the gaily-dressed crews into the water, while the boats and paddles float away amid the shouts of the spectators. The Siamese are such good swimmers that seldom any one is drowned in the narrow rivers. It is interesting to read the following old account of these ancient holiday customs:

All the temples in Bangkok and its suburbs which have been made by or dedicated to the king expect a splendid visit from him annually, between the middle of the eleventh and twelfth moons. This is the season appointed by the most ancient and sacred custom for the priests to seek their apparel for the year ensuing. In conformity with this custom, the king, taking a princely offering of priests' robes with him, visits these temples.

The ceremony is called "Taut Katin," which means to lay down a pattern in order to cut patchwork by it. The pattern is the "Katin," which in ancient time the priests of Buddha used in cutting their cloth into patches, to be sewed together to make their outer and inner robes. The cloth was cut with a knife because it would be wicked to tear it. In olden time, in Buddha's day the custom was for the priests to go out themselves to seek old cast-off clothing, and the best of these they would patch together to form the seven kinds of priestly robes required. This was one conspicuous mode of self-mortification. But that mendicant custom has gradually given place to the present splendid and august one of making the patched garments from new cloth, dyed yellow; and prepared by the princely donations of thousands of the affluent and the more humble contributions of the multitudes of the poor. They begin to make preparations for this season months before the time, until in Bangkok alone there are many thousands of priests' suits in readiness by the middle of October for distribution at the temples. The cloth is dyed yellow for the purpose, as tradition says, of imitating somewhat the custom of Buddha and his early followers, who preferred a dingy yellow color for their robes for the express purpose of making themselves odious in the eyes of the world, that there might be no door of temptation left open to them to be conformed to the world. In those days it was the custom for robbers and murderers in Hindostan, where Buddhism began its course, to wear red and yellow clothing as an appropriate badge of their profession. The better classes of the world regarded them with horror, and fled from them. Now, Guatama Buddha, when a prince, had a host of ardent friends, who urged him not to abdicate his throne. But he was fully set to do it; and this was the mode he took to cut himself off from their sympathy. By assuming the robber's garb, he would rid himself of such ruinous tempters, and yet secure another class of admirers who would delight to walk with him in the road to Nipon, to which his whole heart and soul was devoted.

Although there are so many thousands of Buddhist temples in Siam, none are omitted from this annual visitation. The royal temples are visited by the first and second kings, or by some prince or nobleman of high rank who goes in the king's name. Outside the capital these royal temples are always visited by deputies of their Majesties, bearing in their arms priests' robes, and other things provided by the kings.

When either of the kings go in person, they do it with great pomp and splendor, whether by land or water. If by water they display their finest state barges. They each have ten or more of these splendid boats, with some august name attached to distinguish it from the others. These barges are called "*Rua-prateenung*," or royal throne boats. Only one appears in the royal procession at a time. They are from one hundred and fifty to one hundred and eighty feet in length, and from six to eight feet wide. They gradually become narrower fore and aft, and taper upwards. Hanging from the stem and stern are two large white tassels made of the hair of the Cashmere goat, and between them floats a golden banner. A little abaft of midships there is a splendid canopy, about twelve feet long, having the ridge curving downward at each end, and covered with cloth-of-gold, and the sides tastefully hung with curtains of the same costly material. Within is a throne, suited to this little floating palace. The bows of some of these royal throne barges are formed into heads of hideous dragons, or imaginary sea-monsters, with glaring eyes and horrid teeth and horns. The whole boat is richly carved and gilded to represent scales, often inlaid with pearl and other precious things, while the stern forms an immense tail, curving upwards to the height of twelve or fifteen feet. It is in this kind of barge that the king always rides. When he would appear in his greatest glory, he is seen seated on this his floating throne, wearing a heavy gold crown, a gold-embroidered coat, and golden shoes; and from his crown to the very soles of his sandals, he is ornamented with precious stones of various hues, and glistening with diamonds. His face appears as if a light cosmetic had been applied. So steadily does he sit, under the great weight of his glory, that he appears more like a golden idol than a living man. He has, generally, many of his little children with him when he rides in his royal barges. Sometimes the children follow him in a barge of second rank, being all beautifully attired and their faces whitened with powder. We must not forget to mention the huge jewelled fan and the many-storied royal umbrellas, white and yellow, which have their appropriate places in the dragon barge, and help to distinguish it from all others in the imposing pageant. The dragon barges are propelled by sixty or seventy paddlers, who have been trained daily for a full month for that express service. They have been taught to paddle in unison, all striking the water at the same moment, and all raising the blades of their paddles above their heads at an equal height. These royal boatmen, by their public training on the river, become a pattern for all others in the procession.

Preceding the king's personal barge there are usually from forty to sixty royal guard boats, over one hundred feet long and from five to six feet wide, going in pairs. They are modelled after the king's own boat, but smaller, and the canopy is made of whitish leaves, resembling the palm leaf, sewed together, and ornamented with crimson cloth, bordered with yellow. Under the bow and stern of these boats flaunt a pair of long gray tassels, made of the fibres of pine-apple leaves, and between each of these hangs a small golden banner. They have fifty or more paddlers, and two men in each boat beat time with a long pole decorated with white tassels, which they lift up and strike down endwise on the deck of the boat.

In the rear of the king's barge come princes, nobles, officers, and multitudes of still lower grades, who all follow the king to the temples in boats of various fashions, down to the simple one-oared skiff, with its single half-naked occupant. Each prince and nobleman sits proudly under his own canopy, attired in his best court robes, having duly arranged about him his gold or silver water-pot and teapot, and betel and cigar boxes, all of which have been given him by the king as insignia of his rank and office. And to complete the display of dignity, each one has, or rather used to have, two or more servants prostrate before him, with their heads at his feet.

The boatmen have various colored liveries. Those of the king's dragon barge and its mate usually wear red jackets and caps. On the guard-boats we see many colors; some have red jackets and leather caps of ancient style; in others the men have only short pants and a narrow fillet of palm leaf about their heads, with a point of the same on their foreheads. Brass bands follow in the procession, and companies of native performers, who furnish the music for the moving panorama.

The floating and other houses along the line of the king's advance have each prepared a little table or altar, upon which they display the choicest fruits and flowers, wax-candles, pictures, and other ornaments, as marks of respect to their sovereign. The native and foreign shipping display all their colors. The small craft on the river and canals where he is to come clear out for the time to make a wide and open passage for him. Formerly none were allowed to watch this royal procession, except from behind closed doors or windows, but now all such restrictions are withdrawn, and the people seem to enjoy the sight of the king, and take part in the general rejoicings.

The "*pa-katin,*" or priests' garments, being neatly folded and put up in bundles of a suit each, are borne with the king in the royal throne barge. When he arrives at the landing of a temple, he remains seated until several suits of the yellow robes have been carried up to the door of the idol-house, and put in care of an official, to await the approach of His Majesty, and until other officers of state and a company of infantry, together with the musicians, have had time to leave their boats and place themselves in position for receiving him. The hand-rail of the steps which the king ascends is wound with white cotton cloth, and the flagged path from the landing to the idol temple is covered with grass matting, exclusively for him to walk upon. When the king is in the act of ascending the steps of the landing, "Old Siam" blows her pipes and conch-shells, and beats her drums; the military form in double line and present arms, and the brass band plays the national anthem or some other modern air.

Having reached the door of the "*bote*," the king takes one suit of the priests' robes, and bearing them in both hands, walks in, and lays them on a table prepared for that purpose. On this table are five golden vases of flowers; five golden dishes of parched rice, tastefully arranged in the form of bouquets, five golden candlesticks with their candles, and five incense-sticks. His Majesty first lights the candles and incense-sticks. He then worships the image of Buddha, the sacred books, and the assembled priests. He next makes a request of the chief-priest to renew his covenant to observe the five rules of the Buddhist religion. These are: First, that he will not take the life of any man or other sentient creature; second, that he will not oppress any man; third, that he will not take to wife any woman belonging to another, while there is the least unwillingness on the part of the woman, or of her parents or guardians, to the transaction; fourth, that he will not lie, nor deal falsely with mankind, nor use abusive language; fifth, that he will not use intoxicating liquors as a beverage. When the king visits the temple, if it happen to be one of their four sacred days, then custom makes it necessary for him to promise to observe three other rules in addition to the above five, viz.: First, that he will not partake of any food from after midday on any sacred day until the next morning after light has appeared; second, that he will not on sacred days indulge in any theatrical or musical performances, nor in any way allow or cause his person to be perfumed; third, that he will not on such days sleep on a bed that is more than ten and a half inches high, nor use any mattress, and that he will deny himself as becometh a devout Buddhist. If the king is conscious of having transgressed any of these rules since he last renewed his obligation, he is supposed to confess his sins mentally before the idol, and to promise solemnly that he will earnestly endeavor to depart from all such sins in the future.

His Majesty having renewed his covenant obligation, then proceeds to make a formal presentation of his offering to the priests of that temple; whereupon they respond in the Pali tongue, "Satoo! satoo!" (Good! good!). The chief-priest then addresses the fraternity as follows: "This '*pa-katin*' has been given to us by His Most Illustrious Majesty the King, who being endued with exceeding great goodness and righteousness, has condescended to come hither himself, and present these garments to us, a company of Buddhist priests, without designating any particular person by whom they shall be worn." They then distribute the gifts among themselves, after which they bow down and worship the idol, reciting a few Pali sentences. This distribution of garments is not always done in the presence of the king, but sometimes after he has left the temple. The late king, Maha Mongkut, made an innovation on this old custom, by bringing with him extra suits of yellow robes, and giving them to certain priests who had distinguished themselves as Pali scholars. It is also usual to make a few other gifts to the priests of such things as they are apt to need, as bedding and table furniture; but these are not considered any part of the real "katin."

As the king is about to leave the temple, the priests pronounce a Pali blessing upon him, and he again worships the idol, the sacred books, and the priests. Then rising from his prostration, he walks out of the "bote" and descends to the royal barge, with the same ceremonies as when he ascended. He visits five or six temples in a day, and usually spends about an hour in each one. The value of each priest's suit which the king offers is supposed to be about $18.00, and so the aggregate value of the offerings he makes on these successive days is probably not less than $18,000!

And this is but one of the kings, and in but one city; while the second king follows with but little diminution of royal splendor and bounty both in his processions and offerings, and there are scores of princes and princesses, hundreds of noblemen and thousands of the people, yea, millions of them, for all who are able to do even a little join in the supposed merit-making. It is at such times that they present those immense wax candles, as large round as the body of a man, and which burn unceasingly for weeks, and the wax represents the many gifts of the very poor, some of whom cannot count on an income of four cents per day. In the land processions they often have white elephants made of wicker-work and covered with cloth or paper, upon which they pile their gifts, while the people drag his car through the streets.

With all these public holidays which receive the royal sanction we might almost call the Siamese year a circle of holidays, and when Christmas, Washington's birthday, and Fourth of July are added, besides Queen Victoria's natal day and that of all other foreign sovereigns represented by consular establishments in Siam, it will be seen that we do not live and move in a "workaday world."

CHAPTER XXI.

SIAMESE TIMES, SEASONS, AND CUSTOMS.

The Siamese have two years, civil and religious; also two cycles, one within the other, of twelve and ten years. In the first cycle, each of the twelve years bears the name of some creature. Here they are in order: First, the year of the rat; then follow, cow, tiger, rabbit, great dragon, small dragon, horse, goat, monkey, cock, dog, and hog. Those of the other cycle are simply numbered. Their sacred era is reckoned from the time it is supposed Buddha died, which was 2,427 years ago, at the full moon in May, 1884. Thus we see the Buddhist era antedates the Christian 543 years. This reckoning is never used except in their religious matters, and in counting their ages. Their civil era dates from the time Pra Ruang, one of the Siamese kings, established it, and has now reached 1245. The sacred era year begins with the new moon in December, and the civil near the full moon in April. Their years are twelve months long. Six of their months have thirty days, and six have but twenty-nine, and such a year wants eleven days to make up a full solar year. To compensate for this they have an intercalary month of thirty days once in three years. By this plan there is still a loss of about three days in nineteen years, which is supplied by adding a day to their seventh month from time to time as their Brahmin astrologers see to be necessary. Their first two months have names, and the others are simply numbered. If one is asked the time of his birth, the answer may be, "In the seventh month, year of the horse." They have the week, but no name to designate it. The first day is called Sunday, the second Moon-day; then follow Mars, Mercury, Jupiter, Venus, and Saturn, and when speaking of their weeks they say so many Sundays.

There are four watches of three hours each in the day, and the same in the night; but the constantly increasing use of watches and clocks is gradually changing their horology. Like other idolatrous nations the moon is one of their principal objects of superstition, and the first, eighth, fifteenth, and twenty-second days of the moon are holy days, and they call them days of the Lord. The Buddhist priests have their heads and eyebrows shaved the eve of the first and fifteenth of each month, and then are ready on those sacred days to preach and chant wherever invited. They are great believers in lucky and unlucky days, and astrologers are consulted concerning all things grave and foolish—as the most lucky day for a wedding, a cremation, a hair-cutting, the beginning of public works, the consecration of a temple or palace, the best day for starting on a journey, or entering a battle, or even starting to school; they say Thursday is school-day, and Sunday the most lucky day of all the week. Our mission physician would have more patients on Sunday than any other day if he would only receive them.

All festival occasions are celebrated for three days. On the first of these, at their April New-Year, they believe that the master of hell opens all the gates and lets the souls go free to feast in the bosom of their families, where they are splendidly entertained. The priests go to the palace to preach to the king, and at the close of the discourse cannons are fired to drive away the devils, and to frighten the old souls back to hell. All eternity is divided into *kops*, and a Siamese kop is measured by a stone ten miles square, and once in a hundred years an angel wipes it off with a gossamer web; and when the stone shall by these century-wipings be worn away, a *kop* will have passed. It is said that the king has a conjurer at court, who also decides the lucky and unlucky days and prophesies, but woe to him if his good predictions prove false. If evil ones fail of fulfilment, he cunningly insists that they were averted by the merit of the king and his people. When the king dies, all his subjects must put on white as mourning, and shave their heads. When a queen dies, only the women and officers of her household are required to do so.

In capital punishment the victim is usually beheaded. After taking a soothing draught, provided by merciful Buddhists who wish to make merit, his eyes are bandaged and his ears stuffed with mud, and thus he is at least partially unconscious of the stroke that destroys his life. Sometimes they are beaten and exposed through the market-places, and up and down the river, before execution. A notable instance of the latter was seen in the late Pra Pre Cha, a nobleman of high rank and a special favorite of the king, who was guilty of many crimes and misdemeanors. He received ninety lashes, was then loaded with chains, and paraded by river and road for six days, and after decapitation his head was carried on a pole. Some offenders, instead of being executed, are degraded from all titles and rank, and condemned to cut grass for elephants for life. They are branded on the forehead, and have to cut the grass themselves; no one is allowed to help them, nor can they buy it with their own money.

Agriculture in Siam is carried on in the most primitive style. The ploughs are crooked sticks, with one handle. The runner and mould-board is a natural crotch; the shorter branch is the mould-board, and the longer is left some two feet long and ten inches round, and comes to a point to receive the socket of the ploughshare, which is little larger than a man's hand, made of cast-iron in a sort of triangular' shape. It bulges out into a socket on the under side to receive the nose of the runner, and is never permanently fastened to its place, as the owner must knock it off at night and carry it home to secure it from thieves. The wood part of the plough costs about one dollar, and the iron share fifteen cents. It cuts a furrow two inches deep and five or six wide, and there is so little curve to the mould-board that it does not turn over more than half the clods broken up. The man or woman holds it by the one handle, and guides the oxen or buffalo by a rope passed through the nose. The yoke is slightly curved to fit the neck; but instead of ox-bows, such as we use, they have straight sticks run through the yoke on either side of the neck, and tied together by ropes or withes at the bottom to keep the neck in. If one animal is used, there is a short beam and a rude whiffletree with long rope traces fastened to the outside of the yoke; if two oxen or buffalo are needed, they use a longer beam and the yoke is fastened directly to it, and thus they drag the plough along. The end of the beam is often eighteen or twenty inches beyond the yoke and curves gracefully upward, and is ornamented with flowers and peacock's-feathers or red strings, and the heads of the oxen are kept up by being fastened to it by short bridles. The harrow is simply a large rake with wooden teeth, and a bamboo tongue long enough to reach to the yoke and allow the oxen to hold their heads up. It has an oval handle to aid in lifting it up to shake off the grass and stubble, and to bear down upon when the clods are hard to break.

They sprout the rice and then sew it as thick as it can grow in little patches that are easily watched and watered. When it is about a foot high it is pulled up and tied in bunches and taken to the fields that have been ploughed and harrowed and are covered with from six to eight inches of water. Then the men, women, and children turn out to *dumnah*, literally "dive into the rice-fields." They transplant the rice, thrusting the stalks with hands and feet into the soft mud beneath the water. A good diver can set out a third of an acre a day. Field hands cost from four to six dollars a month and board themselves. This planting-time may last from June to October, and then if it is a good year with proper rain and sunshine the harvest may be all gathered by Christmas. In some places it is necessary to irrigate, and the native ways are many and mostly of great antiquity. Besides ordinary ditching and flooding, "a basket holding six or eight gallons is pitched within and without to prevent its leaking, and so rigged midway between four small ropes twelve feet long, that two little girls, holding them by their ends, so swing them as to make the basket dip up several gallons of water from the canal every two seconds, and tilt it over the little dam into the rice patch. The plot near the canal being thus inundated, and protected by dikes, the surplus is distributed to more distant patches, by a large wooden scoop, so suspended that a slight movement of the hand makes it scoop up gallons of water from a little pond, and then by another jerk of the arm tilts it over the dike to the next field, and by repeating this process, in time the whole farm is properly watered. Sometimes the old-fashioned well-sweep is used and the water emptied from the buckets into an elevated trough, from which it flows to the rice-fields. Another mode consists of a series of some twenty small buckets, linked together, twelve inches apart, made to revolve on a rude wooden windlass, worked by two men holding on to a horizontal pole and treading on arms or treadles attached to the shaft around which the buckets revolve. The buckets run up in an inclined trough made to correspond quite accurately with their size, so that most of the water they dip is carried up and tilted over an embankment, when they run back again under the trough to the canal for another draught." This is "watering the land with the foot." I have never seen water-wheels in Siam, such as are so common in North Laos. If the fields are dry they reap with a sickle, and bind and stack; if the water has not yet gone down they must wade or go in boats, and cut off the heads, which resemble oats more than wheat, and gather by handfuls into baskets. Siamese rice is considered among the very best in the world, and on good ground, is very fruitful, yielding sixty and a hundred fold.

To prepare a threshing floor, the grass is taken off and the ground made smooth and level, and hardened with a coat of plaster made of cow-dung and water. A pole is planted in the centre, ornamented with a bamboo figure called *Ta Poo*, shaped like a man, and they also tie up some of the best rice-heads to the pole for the birds, and here in the moonlight nights the rice is threshed out by the treading of the cattle and buffaloes, tied side by side, the inner one fastened to a loose band around the post. A boy usually holds the tail of the outer beast with one hand, an ox-goad in the other, now twisting the tail of the poor creature, now thrusting him with the goad, and continually shouting and swearing to speed his way, that the inner one might by a slow walk keep pace with him in trotting. We have often gone to the royal threshing floor at Petchaburee. It is an exciting scene. The wild, half-naked natives shouting, and driving the cattle round and round; the nude children laughing and tumbling in the straw; the lamps swinging from the poles; the fitful bonfires; and the governor moving about in his Oriental dress and European smoking-cap.

The rice is cleaned by winnowing it in the wind, by pouring from wide, shallow baskets. It is then measured and counted as it is stored away in bins, which are built on a raised platform. These are immense bamboo hogsheads, woven in basket-work, and thickly plastered over the outside with mud. They are covered with a roof of leaves. Here the grain is kept for use or sale, and a good way to reckon a farmer's wealth is by counting his well-filled rice-bins. The rice is usually hulled by the women and slaves, who pound it in a mortar with a pestle, till the plump white grain is separated from the brown hulls. Not only the people, but their horses, cattle, dogs, chickens, birds, monkeys, everything that lives in Siam, almost, eats rice.

The farmers usually huddle together in little villages, for mutual protection and company, while their fields lie unfenced on all sides. Cattle are herded all the year round, and in spite of the utmost vigilance, they are still driven off by thieves, or trespass on the rice-fields, causing endless trouble and lawsuits.

If a Siamese wants to be regularly married, it is a source of a deal of trouble. He dare not ask for the bride himself, but must negotiate through friends in a very slow, roundabout way. When the parents' consent is given, the bride must be purchased. This price is often her redemption from the master to whom her parents have sold her, or if not a slave, the money is given to the parents, and is called *ka nom*, "the price of the mother's milk" with which the bride was nourished in infancy. Then gifts are sent to the parents and a lucky day selected for the wedding. On that day the groom goes with his friends, carrying gifts to the bride's home. These consist of trays of betel-nuts and sweetmeats. Buddhist priests are present, and they are feasted with the choicest of all the good things. Sometimes the bride and groom bow together before the priests, and are sprinkled or bathed with holy water. But this part of the ceremony is often omitted, and they are considered married as soon as the money for the bride is paid over. This money is often returned to the young mother on the birth of her first child, to aid in its maintenance. But the usual way in Siam is to fall in love with each other and run off, and then come back in three days and beg pardon, and make it up the best way they can with the outraged old folks, who ten to one did that very same way themselves when they were young.

Divorce is even easier then getting married. A man can desert his wives at will, and get others whenever he pleases; but the most genteel way to do it is to enter the priesthood at a Buddhist monastery, and be worshipped as a god for a few months, and then come forth free. There is neither law nor moral sentiment to prevent or restrain such conduct.

CHAPTER XXII.

ELEPHANTS.

Great numbers of these useful and sagacious beasts are roaming wild in the forests and jungles of Siam. A large herd belonging to the Government is pastured near Ayuthia, the old capital, and once each year the king goes up to choose from those that are decoyed or driven into the stockade such as he needs for service. They are used for travel, for beasts of burden, for timber-workers in the teak forests, and a part of the regular army is composed of elephant troops.

Siamese elephants are the usual color and size. They are from twelve to thirteen feet in height. Their ordinary pace is four or five miles an hour, and if properly fed they will travel all day and all night. They strike the ground with their trunk when weary, and make a loud sound, as a signal to the driver that they want to stop. Their trumpetings are fearful. They have only three toes on their burly feet, and, to be considered handsome, they must have black toe-nails, large, smooth tusks, and perfect tails. The drivers are called "Elephant doctors," * and usually sit perched on the animal's head. The native howdahs are made of wood, with bamboo coverings, and look not unlike a buggy-top. They are quite large; one can almost lie down in them to nap while on the creature's back. Some very beautiful and costly ones are made for the king and princes, inlaid with ivory, silver, and gold.

---

* *Mow Chang.*

Elephants are not now used in Siam as much as in Laos. There they are a daily sight in the streets of Cheung Mai. There are many more comfortable ways of travelling than on an elephant's back. The immense creature moves with a swaying, swinging motion, that to the unaccustomed very often produces sea-sickness. And yet as a means of transportation over otherwise impassable places he does very well. He is careful and sure-footed, can climb steep mountains, and when descending the opposite side will get down, and pushing, or rather supporting himself with his fore feet and letting his hind legs drag behind him, he will slowly slide down on his belly. He will swim deep rivers and make a path for himself and rider through the tangled forests, and provide his own food by gathering branches and twigs in his trunk and eating as he goes along.

Among the Laos "the thorough manner in which they go to work to break in the young elephants is remarkable. They tie the feet in pairs, and suspend the body by large ropes to a beam above, so that the feet just touch the ground, and the poor creature is unmercifully speared and pounded till he is covered with blood and wounds. He is then let down, and if not subdued, is returned to the swing and the process repeated. But when he learns his lesson well it is never forgotten, and he becomes as submissive as he is intelligent."

In the immense teak forests near Rahang, over six hundred elephants are employed in carrying wood to the river. They are valued at from two hundred and fifty to one thousand dollars each. Dr. Field, in one of his trips round the world, visited the timber-yards both at Rangoon and Maulmain, Burmah, and he says:

"I have never seen any animals showing such intelligence and trained to such docility and obedience. In the yard that we visited there were seven elephants, five of which were at that moment at work. Their wonderful strength came into play in moving huge pieces of timber. I did not measure the logs, but should think that many were at least twenty feet long and a foot square. Yet a male elephant would stoop down and run his tusks under a log, and throw his trunk over it, and walk off with it as lightly as a gentleman would balance a bamboo cane on the tip of his finger. Placing it on the pile, he would measure it with his eye, and if it projected too far at either end, would walk up to it, and with a gentle push or pull make the pile even. If a still heavier log needed to be moved on the ground to some part of the yard, the *mahout*, sitting on the elephant's head, would tell him what to do, and the great creature seemed to have a perfect understanding of the master's will. He would put out his enormous foot and push it along, or he would bend, and crouching half-way to the ground, and doubling up his trunk in front, throw his whole weight against it, and thus, like a ram, would 'butt' the log into its place; or if needed to be taken a greater distance, he would put a chain around it and drag it behind him. The female elephant especially was employed in drawing, as, having no tusks, she could not lift like her big brothers, but could only move by her power of traction and attraction. Then using her trunk as deftly as a lady would use her fingers, she would untie the knot or unhitch the chain, and return to her master, perhaps putting out her trunk to receive a banana as a reward for her good conduct. It was indeed a very pretty sight, and it gave us an entirely new idea of their value, and of the way in which they can be trained for the service of man.

"Dr. Collins, an American missionary, who made an overland trip from Bangkok to Burmah, had many opportunites for observing the nature and habits of these lordly creatures. On arriving at their resting-place for the night, it was usual to turn the elephants, partially fettered, among the bamboos, and nearly all night long they could hear the snapping of the tall reeds in order that the leaves might be stripped off for food, and they always knew where the elephants were by the tinkle of their bamboo-bells. Some of the drivers, however, were always on the watch, and some one of the elephants was sure to be a favorite.

"When they were grazing in the jungle, bright fires were kindled that blazed the long night through. The drivers on these occasions always boiled their rice in hollow green bamboo joints, and frequently the elephants would come forward for bits of rice and salt, and then retire. He was awakened one night out of a sound sleep, and looking toward the blaze, espied one of the huge brutes seated on his haunches, like an immense dog or bear, warming himself by the fire. Grave, comical, and strange the scene appeared in the solemn midnight of the tropical forest. In his journey he used fourteen different elephants, and all of them, without exception, behaved in the most gentle, intelligent, and patient manner, mutual affection seeming to subsist between master and beast. Though he would not go so far as to dignify a mere mass of matter with divine honors, as some Siamese do their so-called white elephants, yet he was fully persuaded that most of the wonderful stories told of these noble brutes are strictly true."

The elephant is reckoned by naturalists to be the slowest breeder of all known animals, and one has taken some pains to estimate its probable minimum of natural increase. As he was laboring to show how quickly the earth would be overrun with animal life if there was no corresponding destruction, he reckons a little lower than the reality. "It will be under the mark," he says, "to assume that it breeds when thirty years old, and goes on breeding till ninety years old, bringing forth three pairs of young in this interval. If this be so, at the end of the fifth century there would be alive 15,000,000 elephants, descended from the first pair."

Africa seems to be the chief source of supply for ivory. There were one hundred and twenty-nine tons offered not long since in London, and it brought £750 per ton. A large proportion of the ivory in the markets is in very small tusks, showing that many elephants are destroyed in early youth. One of the largest tusks on record is that of an African elephant, and is nine feet long, twenty-one inches in girth, and weighs one hundred and sixty pounds. I do not think elephants are ever killed in Siam for their ivory. The tusks are only gathered from those who die naturally. The killing of wild elephants is prohibited by the king, and all the ivory found belongs to him.

THE WHITE ELEPHANTS.

During a trip to Bangkok in 1876, we saw the white elephant, the lion and tiger, the large reclining idol, and the little image called the Emerald god. I should have seen all these wonderful things when I first came to Siam. They do not impress me now as they would doubtless have done then. We tried to see the Royal Museum and the King's School, but they would not admit visitors to either of them on that day. We saw enough, however, to prove there is a royal school, and we hope they will soon be multiplied all over the kingdom.

We entered the palace grounds without any trouble, the guards allowing us to pass. But when we were ready to go out an old soldier sprang up and shut the gates, saying we should not go through there. Mrs. B. argued with him a few moments, but she did not offer him a silver key, so we had to turn about and go another way. By doing so we stumbled upon the elephants. If it had not been for that crusty old soldier we would have missed our greatest sight, for we had entirely forgotten to look for them.

Before speaking of what we saw of the white elephant, let me gather a little from other writers.

"It is commonly supposed that the Buddhists of Siam regard the '*Chang Phoonk*,' or white elephant, as a deity, and worship it accordingly. This, however, is a mistaken idea. By their teachings each successive Buddha, in passing through a series of transmigrations, must necessarily have occupied in turn the form of white animals, particularly the dove, the monkey, and the elephant. Thus almost all white animals are held in reverence by the Siamese, because they believe they were once superior human beings. The white elephant especially is supposed to be animated by the spirit of some king or hero.

"From the earliest historic times the kings of Siam and Burmah have anxiously sought for the white elephant, and having had the rare fortune to procure one, have it loaded with gifts and dignities. 'King of the White Elephants' is considered one of the proudest titles of which the monarchs of these countries can boast, and was first assumed in Siam by the sixteenth king of the first dynasty, who was so meritorious as to secure seven of these noble beasts. The tenth king of the same dynasty reigned twenty-two years, but all that history records of that long period is the capture of a white female elephant in 815. King Tuang, who as early as A.D. 457 introduced the Siamese alphabet, which he handed over to a conclave of Buddhist priests, was also distinguished as the possessor of a white elephant with black tusks !—a very important fact from a Siamese point of view. The late king used to preserve the skins of the defunct creatures in alcohol.

"They are looked upon as a symbol of kingly authority and prosperity, and to be without one would be taken as an indication of the displeasure of heaven."

In the journal of an old resident in Bangkok we find the following entry:

"AUGUST 26, 1835. Bangkok is in mourning. One of the king's white elephants is dangerously ill. The king trembles on his throne. The death of such a highly revered creature seems to be regarded as ominous of the speedy death of the king himself, because, as report has it, both his father and grandfather deceased immediately after the death of a white elephant.

"The flag of Siam is a very curious one indeed, a white elephant on a red field, and very oddly it must look if ever it is necessary to hoist it upside down as a signal of distress; a signal eloquent indeed, for anything more helpless and distressing than this clumsy quadruped in that position can hardly be imagined.

"Elephants of a white color, either albinos or the result of some leprous disease—for they are not pure white, but a sort of yellowish pink—are occasionally found. Such an animal when he makes his appearance in the forest is considered sacred, and no effort is spared to capture him. When he is taken the glorious news is borne to the king. A wide path is cut through the jungles he must traverse on his way to the river, where a great floating palace of wood, ornamented by a gorgeous roof and hung with crimson curtains, awaits him. The roof is literally thatched with flowers, and the floor is covered with a gilt matting. He is surrounded by a crowd of natives, who bathe him, perfume him, fan him, feed him, and sing and play to him. His food consists of the finest herbs, the tenderest grasses, the sweetest sugar-cane, the mellowest bananas, the brownest rice-cakes, served on large trays of gold and silver, and his drink is perfumed with fragrant flowers.

"As he nears the capital the king and his court, all the chief personages of the kingdom, and a multitude of priests, both Buddhist and Brahmin, accompanied by troupes of players and musicians, come out to meet him and conduct him with all the honors to his stable palace. When he reaches the capital in a pavilion, temporary but very beautiful, he is welcomed with imposing ceremonies by the principal members of the royal household. After this, thanksgiving is offered up, and the lordly beast is knighted by pouring water on his forehead from a conch-shell. It is a sort of christening, you see; and he is also given a high-sounding name and a title. For many days he is entertained with a variety of dramatic plays. At the end of this period he is conducted with great pomp to his sumptuous quarters within the precincts of the first king's palace, where he is received by his own court of officers, attendants, and slaves, who install him in his fine lodgings, and at once proceed to robe and decorate him. First the court jeweller rings his tremendous tusks with massive gold, crowns him with a diadem of beaten gold of perfect purity, and adorns his burly neck with heavy golden chains. Next he is robed in a superb velvet cloak of purple, fringed with scarlet and gold, and then his court prostrate themselves and offer royal homage.

"When the lordly elephant would bathe, an officer of high rank shelters his noble head with a great umbrella of crimson and gold, while others wave golden fans before him. If he falls ill the king's own doctor prescribes for him, and the chief-priests pray daily for his recovery and anoint him with consecrated oil. Should he die, all Siam is bereaved. Only his brains and heart are burned. The body shrouded in fine white cloth, and laid on a bier, is floated down the river, with many mournful dirges, and thrown into the Gulf of Siam. The hairs of its tail are preserved as sacred relics. Indeed, such a hair is looked upon as one of the most precious presents by which the king can show the bestowment of his favor upon any one. They are set in handles of gold and precious stones, and one of these tufts was considered by the late king of sufficient importance to be sent to the Queen, Victoria of England."

After reading such descriptions as the foregoing, I was, dear reader, like yourself expecting to see a great deal. There were four ladies of us, and we visited four very homely animals in as many miserable old stables, where their keepers sat and smoked and gambled all day long, and—the gray-haired guide charged our company seven and a half cents. Did you ever hear of such extortion?

Evidently the elephants were not expecting company, and were in almost every state except that "royal state" in which they are always kept according to books which treat of things which are and are not in this sunny land. I do not think I ever went to see the elephants again—unless, perhaps, it was on some state occasion. I gave one of them a bunch of grass to eat; but, honestly, I did it only that I might say that I had fed them, and not from any desire to prolong their forlorn existence. They were tied with thongs to stout posts, and stood there swaying their huge bodies back and forth in the most disconsolate manner, and turning up their noses at their keepers. I did not see the least trace of scenery which adorned the walls of their "stable palaces," and was to remind them of their native jungles. But then, as I said before, they were not expecting company; and perhaps they had taken all these things down and put them away with the golden canopy, the curiously wrought mosquito-netting, and all the other elegant things, such as the "diadem of beaten gold of perfect purity," the "velvet cloak of purple, with crimson and gold fringes." Actually, I did not see a link of gold chain on any one of them, nor a ring on their long, white tusks. It was a very bad day, I think, to visit the elephants; but then I had been in Siam nearly two years, and it was my first opportunity, and I had to embrace it or come back to my home with the desire of my heart unsatisfied.

I have heard from the lordly beasts through Bangkok letters, the latest dated July 23, 1883:

"There are five white elephants now. I visited the stable of the latest arrival, and found it just the same as other stables, dingy and dirty, and the illustrious captive was confined and treated, to all appearances, in the usual way. I think it is time the popular fallacy about feeding the white elephant from gold dishes and keeping him in regal splendor was exploded. Except on state occasions it has no foundation in fact."

These "state occasions" are very few and far between. One of the oldest missionaries in Siam wrote me a few months ago that she had at last actually seen the white elephants in their trappings. They marched in procession round the king's garden during the late visit of the Prince of Wales, who was invested with the Order of the White Elephant of Siam in 1880. Edwin Arnold also received a letter from the King of Siam in acknowledgment of his praise of Buddhism, and had conferred upon him the greatest decoration, that of the Order of the White Elephant. The decoration has been proffered to several Americans holding official positions, but declined, as none of our representatives are permitted to receive titles or decorations from foreign powers.

In July, 1867, a Siamese of high rank called a famous oculist from Batavia to operate upon his eyes. He hastened to Bangkok and was successful in restoring partial sight to the left eye, and for this his grateful patient gave him ten thousand dollars. Two years later he came again to operate upon the right eye, and was the happy recipient of four thousand dollars more, and had bestowed upon him the decoration of the Order of the White Elephant, as a sign that he, also, was one whom the king delighteth to honor.

The address to the noble white elephant when first captured and introduced to all the comforts of civilized life in the capital is very high-flown and extravagant. Here is a free translation for the benefit and amusement of those unfortunate mortals who may never hear the original, and who would not understand it if they did, as they had so little merit as to be born in one of those dark *outside* lands in which the "Light of Asia" never shines:

"With holy reverence we now come to worship the angels who preside over the destiny of all elephants. Most powerful angels, we entreat you to assemble now in order that you may prevent all evil to His Majesty the King of Siam, and also to this magnificent elephant which has recently been brought. We appeal to you all, whom we now worship, and beg that you will use your power in restraining the heart of this animal from all anger and unhappiness. We also beg that you will incline this elephant to listen to the words of instruction and comfort that we now deliver.

"Most royal elephant! We beg that you will not think too much of your father and mother, your relatives and friends. We beg that you will not regret leaving your native mountains and forests, because there are evil spirits there that are very dangerous, and wild beasts are there that howl, making a fearful noise, and there too that bird '*hassadin*' which hovers round and often picks up elephants and eats them; and there are also bands of cruel hunters who kill elephants for their ivory. We trust you will not return to the forest, for you would be in constant danger. And that is not all, in the forest you have no servants, and it is very unpleasant to sleep with dust and filth adhering to your body, and where the flies and mosquitoes are very troublesome.

"Brave and noble elephant! Why should you wish to wander free? The forest is full of thorns, bushes, and marshes. Why should you wish to cross the valley and mountains? There you must drink muddy water, and there the stones will cut your feet.

"O Father Elephant! We entreat you to banish every wish to stay in the forest. Look at this delightful place, this heavenly city! It abounds in wealth and everything your eyes could wish to see or your heart desire to possess. It is of your own merit that you have come to behold this beautiful city, to enjoy its wealth and to be the favorite guest of His most exalted Majesty the King!"

CHAPTER XXIII.

THE YOUNG AND OLD FOLKS OF SIAM.

Whenever I think of the young folks who are no longer children, and have not yet reached the age of men and women, my heart is saddened. If they are girls, they will be found carrying great heavy baskets of rice or sugar from the country, or sitting in the market-stalls selling cakes, produce, and fruit. Some make cigarettes; others pound up "cummin," a yellow powder the natives use to rub on the body after the bath. A few girls make their living by sewing native jackets or Chinese trousers. If they work all day they do not average more than sixteen cents, and many do not make more than four. If they are orphans they have, no doubt, received the usual inheritance which these heathen parents leave their children, especially their daughters, and that is a load of debt. Then they have a moneyed master who requires their services as slaves, or collects an exorbitant interest on the debt. This inherited debt is a burden they accept almost hopelessly, for not more than one in a hundred ever expects to get rid of it. When the girl marries her husband must assume this debt, but her name also goes in the paper with his, and it is only a change of masters, with often a harder and much more bitter service. If the husband gets tired of his wife or quarrels with her, he deserts her, and she has to pay the debt and support the children, unless he takes them from her. Sometimes he will even charge her with the cost of the wedding, and add that to her debt. He can sell her and her children, but she can never sell him.

The young girls are very fond of jewelry, and will deny themselves needed food and clothes to buy a gold ring or a chain for their dusky bodies. They know absolutely nothing of the sweet amenities of home, and the thousand and one refining influences of Christian civilization. They never have rooms to themselves, nor the smallest space they can call their own in which to store their humble possessions. The whole family live together, and huddle into one common room. The young folks are found fault with, scolded, and even whipped in the presence of all the neighbors, and whoever happens to look or listen.

If they have any deformity, it usually furnishes them with a name, as "Blind-eye," "Crooked-elbow," "Double-toe," "Black," "Stubborn," "Hunchback." If their hair curls or waves in a way that we consider much more beautiful than the straight, wiry locks of most Siamese, they are known everywhere, and remarked in every company as "Pome Yik"—Curly-head—and there is no name that provokes them more.

They know nothing at all of the pure and pleasant social life which is the joy and blessing of young folks at home. They are never allowed to walk or ride together, or spend a quiet evening alone. They are not even allowed to talk together without being reproached, unless older persons are near enough to hear all that is said. Occasionally a pair of desperate lovers will break over these barriers and elope; sometimes they escape, but oftener they are captured and brought back to be punished. The husband's parents can beg pardon of the bride's family, and bring a peace-offering and money. If accepted, they consult together, and set the young couple up in housekeeping; if not, the husband is driven off, and the bride kept for a better market.

Although the Siamese do not kill their daughters, still the sons are a privileged class all over the kingdom. The mere fact of being a boy is a peculiar mark of merit. They are not expected to do much of anything, and they seldom disappoint the expectation. After an idle, wilful childhood, they become unmanageable, and often before they are ten years old they have been cursed and beaten and driven away from their homes, or they are placed in some monastery, with special directions that they are to be severely dealt with. Here they pretend to learn to read, but they often run off and go wandering from one temple to another, or among their relatives, learning and practicing every vice, till they are twenty-one years old. As a last hope the father and mother will receive them again, and with great ceremony have them enter the Buddhist priesthood. The young man therefore renounces his parents, his brothers and sisters, his wives if he has any, and all other relatives, his home, and his former life. He has his head shaved, is bathed with consecrated water, and clothed in yellow robes, and he vainly imagines that he has "put off the old man," and that he is now holy. Every one who sees him is expected to bow down and worship him, and he is very gracious indeed if he condescends to receive a gift from their hand. Siamese men are all called "green," unripe, until after they have donned the yellow. They remain in the monastery an indefinite length of time; then, if they come out again into the world, they soon get married, no matter how many wives they may have had before, and then they consider themselves full-fledged men, ready for anything life in Siam holds for them.

They have no ambition to excel as workmen, merchants, or scholars. There is no world of work or world of letters open to them. There is no example of good and successful men that they are urged to follow. There is no hope of advancement in the Government unless they belong to what is called the nobility. There is considerable talent displayed by some who sketch pictures on the temple walls, or for "Punch and Judy" shows. But there are no illustrated books made by the Siamese, and they know nothing of painting and drawing as an art, so there is no incentive to make themselves proficient in so elegant and pleasant a branch of the world's work.

A few writers and copyists are employed at every courtroom and at the lottery depots, but there are thousands of people who have never written or received a letter nor ever expect to. There are hardly enough workers to keep up the various trades, and so all the nicer articles of merchandise are imported from China, Japan, Europe, and America. Even the calico and muslin cloths which compose their dress are usually manufactured outside the kingdom. During a late visit to Bangkok, I saw some that had been made in Germany, perfect imitations of native designs, but of finer texture, and more beautiful in color and finish. They have no skill in making the simplest little things, such as fans, umbrellas, and shoes. They send raw material to China and buy it back again after that ingenious people have worked it up so as to derive a profit from the transaction. The natives make a few earthenware pots and jars, brittle and unglazed, but their rough blue bowls, from which the poorest of them eat their rice, and cups and plates all come from China or other lands.

If you ask a woman how she makes her living, she usually has some answer ready, for you seldom find one who has nothing to do; but if you ask a man the same question, he will often look at you in blank amazement, tell you he lives with his father, or mother, or wife, and then perhaps he will try to recall the last time he did anything, and give that as his work.

Dr. Dean tells a story of a man he hired to cut the grass in his yard. He came with an old knife, a basket, and an umbrella. After getting his umbrella advantageously planted in the hole he had dug for it, he would creep under it and whack away awhile until he reached the edges of the shade, and then with the utmost deliberation he would pull up the umbrella and proceed to replant it, when he would whack away another while, relieving the monotony by frequent smokes in its quiet shelter. If the basket ever got full and he had to go and empty it, that was quite an event in his advancement over the grass-plot. In this truly primitive fashion he managed to spend several delightful days. I think you can put the Siamese against the world for taking comfort out of their work. Who but a dweller in this lotus-land would ever think of mowing under an umbrella in the first place, and who but he could so patiently bear with his "moving tent" as it slowly crept from place to place. But then he only received thirty cents a day and had to furnish his own rice and tobacco, and when a lazy man is dependent on his own exertions for tobacco, you must not expect him to spend his strength needlessly; besides, he wanted time to enjoy his tobacco as he went along.

Many young girls are sold to managers of theatres, where they are trained to lives of folly and shame. They are taught to dance, for as a Siamese noble remarked once, "Foreigners do their own dancing, but we have a better way, we train our servants to dance for us." They also learn to bend their hands and arms, and twist their bodies about in the most approved fashion of Oriental play-houses. They learn to sing the native airs and rehearse long stories of improbable adventures of little girls who were once like themselves, and afterward became the wives of great and powerful noblemen, or even of the princes. If a prince or a noble sees a smart, pretty girl, and sends word to her friends that he wants her for his theatre, they usually have to let her go. He will make them a present, or perhaps give a small price for the child, and then she must serve him till she is grown. By that time, if he has not taken her into his harem, he may sell her to be the wife of some one else, and she will train others to play in her stead. The players are most all children or quite young folks. We try to protect those who have been in our schools from this life, but we are not able always to do so, especially if the girl herself is fascinated with the pretty dresses, the rings, the bracelets, the anklets, gold chains, crowns, and music.

Some of the actresses are children of prisoners who give their little ones to the nobles as the price of their liberty. Others have lawsuits, and, wishing to gain their point, present their children as bribes. Sometimes the parents of such children are allowed to live rent free in the market-places, or they are promoted to offices in the Government, and even given a title. We have an instance of the latter here in Petchaburee—a father who has given three of his daughters, one after the other, as they grew old enough, to the governor to be theatre-girls, and, finally, inmates of his harem. What wonder that, to a heathen mind, it seems a grand thing to so dispose of their daughters; they do not care if their hearts are broken, their lives ruined, their souls lost. Very few girls ever learn to read. The natives say, "Why should a girl learn to read, she can never make her living by it?"

The country girls have a hard life of it. If it was a civilized land I might say they work in the fields like men, but here they do a great deal more than most men; for while their brothers or husbands may be idling in the temples, or off gambling or sleeping, they are in the fields ploughing, though the water may be nearly knee-deep. Or if the ploughing is finished they are transplanting rice in the same watery fields. They crouch along with bent backs and their hands thrust into the water, placing the tender rice-stalks in the soft mud. It is very, very hard work, but transplanting rice is so much better than that which is merely sown, that they do it almost entirely in this province. The women irrigate the fields, watch the rice—for there are no farm fences—help to harvest and thresh it, and, in the country, I think it is nearly all hulled by the women. In the towns some men help, especially Chinamen; and in Bangkok and Patriew there are several steam mills which hull the rice for transportation.

In making palm sugar the men climb the trees and bring down the bamboo joints full of sweet sap to the foot of the ladder, but the women have to take it from there to the boilers and reduce it to sugar. They make it into cakes, or pour it into earthen pots, and then carry it to market and trade for what is needed.

Nearly all the country people learn to spin and weave different kinds of coarse cotton cloths, and, woman-like, the largest and handsomest ones they always give to the men, although they know the very man who receives it considers himself so much better than she, that he will hardly touch her garments even with his foot.

Notwithstanding her degradation and the scorn and reproach she has to bear, here, as everywhere, woman has a mighty influence. How true it is that "woman keeps the idol on its pedestal," and it is the mother who trains her children to idolatry. Therefore "the real conversion of one heathen woman will do more toward the advancement of Christianity than that of ten men," and yet it is more difficult to win the women to accept the truth than the men, not because they are less religious, but more so, and are more wedded to Buddhism. But let the true Gospel rays penetrate her darkened mind and heart, and to her it is joyful news indeed, that she, a woman, can go to heaven; that God thinks about her, cares for her, loves her, and will receive her into His upper kingdom with equal delight as shown to His sons!

OLD FOLKS IN SIAM.

Of course there are some like the wicked described by Asaph in the 73d psalm, "Pride compasseth them about as a chain; violence covereth them as a garment. Their eyes stand out with fatness; they have more than heart could wish. They are corrupt, and speak wickedly concerning oppression." It is not of the rich old heathen who live in palaces and whose houses are full of plenty; who seem to "have no bands in their death," and who die thinking they leave this world because they have made so much merit it is no longer a fit place to be honored by their presence, but of the masses that I now speak.

When after a life of dissipation old age comes on, and the poor man finds himself homeless, penniless, and alone, his usual resort is the Buddhist monastery. If he can find any who are willing to pay his debts, that they may have a share in his supposed merit, he enters as a priest; if not, he slips in and hangs round as a beggar or servant till death ends his earthly career. He spends most of his time in deploring his lack of merit, complaining of his diseases, troubles, and ills, and condemning everybody and everything but himself for his wretched condition. He is sure, too, that the world is growing worse, and that the people are much more wicked than in his young days. He has a great deal of good advice to give to others which he never followed himself, especially if he is a drunkard or opium-smoker. He swears fearfully, and the older he grows the more bigoted and superstitious he becomes.

You can hardly imagine a more unlovely sight than some of them present, and the old women are no better. As for both, in old age they usually shave the head quite bare, and the face, neck, and indeed the whole body is full of deep ruts and wrinkles, and often covered with blotches of white freckles, a sort of dry leprosy common to the Siamese.

Their toothless mouths are like great black holes full of red betel, and the men smoke so much tobacco that you can smell them before they come in sight. I have seen great calloused corns on their feet and ankles, and sometimes on their elbows, as large as hickory-nuts. Their hands and feet are hard and horny, and often cracked open so that they bleed, or are covered with running sores.

The old women may be widows indeed, or their husbands may have left them to enter the priesthood, or deserted them for younger wives. In either case the old mother is expected to take care of her grandchildren, and her last days are made miserable by the ingratitude of the sons and daughters she never taught to love and obey her. She tries to make merit by fasting, or by feeding priests and dogs, going to the temple services, laying her flowers and incense before the idol, and listening to long sermons, not one word of which she can understand. Her heart is all the time full of hopes and fears. She has no other expectation than that of going to hell when she dies; but still she hopes, after ages of suffering, to be permitted to be reborn as a man, and yet she is all the time afraid that she has not made merit enough for that glorious destiny.

Lest we should sometimes seem to exaggerate the difference between the condition of women in our country and that of various heathen lands, we need only quote the figures given by various heathen teachers and writers. A Chinese author, in preparing a method of keeping account of merits and demerits between the human soul and the powers above, sets down 100 demerit marks for lewd conduct in a man, and 50,000 marks for the same offence in a woman. The Buddhist teachers maintain that the sins of one woman are equal to the sins of 3,000 of the worst men that ever lived. How can we exaggerate the atrocious cruelty of such teachings? Poor, poor souls!

They are very quarrelsome, too; and they become so

angry they can no longer scold, so they just yell at each other. When things come to such a pass, the mother will often send her little children to "help grandmother swear"; and there the little black sinners stand in a row, "swearing like troopers," helping the old hags, who are so overcome with rage that all they can do is to mumble and yell, and shake their long, bony arms in impotent wrath. I never heard such commotions anywhere else as they get up sometimes in the native villages, or right in the heart of the city, for they have no shame and care not who hears their quarrel. One good thing about them is that the men usually keep quiet, and let the women scold and swear it out themselves. They seldom come to blows. But we knew a woman who became so fiery hot with anger one day that she bit a piece right out of a woman's ear, ring and all. The one who was bitten ran to the governor to complain and have the biter arrested, while the criminal dashed down to the mission compound and asked to be "baptized right away." She thought if she joined the church the officers would not arrest nor fine her. But she was not the kind of applicant for baptism missionaries are disposed to receive, and she turned away disappointed. One day in teaching the women they were asked, "Why do you quarrel so much?" One of them made this honest reply, "Before I was converted I just liked to quarrel!" I suppose that is the reason so many still keep it up.

Many old women are reduced to abject slavery, and they have to serve their masters to the utmost of their strength, by working in the fields, by grinding at the mill, or going out to beg, and to sell fruits and sweetmeats. These old slaves have no jackets, and only an old cloth about their loins, and another over their shoulders that serves to shelter their bald heads from the sun by day, or they may make a little awning of it by the sunny roadside where they sit and sell their wares. If they do not sell out, or come home with pennies lacking, they will be cursed at least if not beaten. Others die in chains, or shut up in the dungeons of Bangkok, and relatives, if they have any left, are glad to hear of their death. These old women whose religion has done nothing for their welfare in this life, and which promises absolutely nothing for them, as women, in the future, are still the most zealous adherents of Buddhism in the land. If the women of Siam would to-day cease to believe in and practice Buddhism it would soon drop from its already tottering throne, and woman could at once assume and maintain a higher and nobler position. These old folks resent our teachings because we are younger than they, and they are too old to see to read our books. Gray hairs are a crown of glory only when found in the way of righteousness. Let us pray, therefore, that the next generation may walk in the path of Life, and be crowned with the light and glory of the Gospel of Christ!

CHAPTER XXIV.

CURIOUS THINGS.

The renowned Siamese twins were the most wonderful curiosities ever found in this land. They were born at Ma Klong, a town of twelve thousand inhabitants on a river of the same name. They were early sold by their relatives, and taken to Europe and America for exhibition. In the latter country they were converted, united with the Baptist Church, and were married to two sisters. The twins died several years ago, but their families still live in the United States. By some strange freak of nature, their bodies were united by a band of flesh which reached from the right side of one to the left side of the other, and in this abnormal condition they lived their lives and died together. After the first one died, the other one's life might perhaps have been spared, but he would never consent to have his brother's body cut from his own, and so death was the inevitable consequence.

A new sensation was created some time since in London, of which I have seen the following newspaper accounts:

"THE MISSING LINK.

"There is now on exhibition at the Westminster Aquarium a hairy female child, who is introduced to the public as a talking monkey, and the nearest approach to the 'missing link' yet discovered. She is not, in the ordinary acceptation of the word, a monster, but a very bright-looking, intelligent girl of about seven years of age. She was caught, according to the account given of her by Mr. Farini, in the forest near Laos, and brought to England by Mr. Carl Bock, who, since the expedition described by him in 'The Head-Hunters of Borneo,' has been exploring Siam and the wilder states to the northeast. Hearing in various quarters of the existence of a race of hairy, tailed men, similar in appearance to a family kept at the Court of Mandalay, he offered a reward for the capture of a specimen. A man was caught, and with him the child now exhibited, and a woman of similar appearance then allowed herself to be taken. When the little one attempted to wander, the parents recalled her with a plaintive cry, 'Kra-o,' and the call has been adopted as her name.

"The father died at Laos of cholera, and the king refused to let the mother go, but Mr. Bock succeeded in getting the child to Bangkok, and obtained permission from the King of Siam to bring her to this country.

"The eyes of the child are large, dark, and lustrous; the nose flattened, the nostrils scarcely showing; the cheeks fat and pouch-like; the lower lip only rather thicker than is usual in Europeans; but the chief peculiarity apparent is the strong and abundant hair. On the head it is black, thick, and straight, and grows over the forehead down to the heavy eyebrows, and is continued in whisker-like locks down the cheeks. The rest of the face is covered with a fine, dark, downy hair, and the shoulders and arms have a covering of hair from an inch to an inch and a half long. There is, it is said, a slight lengthening of the lower vertebræ, suggestive of a caudal protuberance, and there are points in the muscular conformation and otherwise which will provoke discussion. Krao has already picked up a few words of English."

And again:

"Mr. A. H. Keane has described Krao, a seven-year-old female child, now at the London Royal Aquarium, who is sensationally claimed by her exhibitors to be the long-sought 'missing link' between man and the high apes. Krao is fairly intelligent, and her short stay among civilized people has already caused her to dislike her old savage associates. She has several physical peculiarities, the chief of which are a forehead covered with thick, black hair down to the bushy eyebrows; a growth of hair about a quarter of an inch long over her body, prehensile feet, and remarkably flexible hands. Mr. Keane finds, however, the point of chief interest to be Krao's history, which seems to indicate the existence of a hairy race of people in a part of India now chiefly occupied by almost hairless Mangoloid peoples. Krao and her parents—also hairy people—were found last year by Mr. Carl Bock, and another hairy family, which came from the same region, is said to have been known."

When I read these articles my interest was greatly excited, because I happened to know something of that little girl myself, and my knowledge was so contrary to some of the statements, that to refresh my memory I turned to my old journal, and found under date of April 16, 1881:

"The other day I saw a hairy child—a little girl about five years old. She had beautiful eyes, rather an intelligent face, could talk Siamese, and seemed like other children, except that her whole body was covered with hair as black as coal. The usual hair of the head grew clear down and met her eyebrows, which were very heavy, and then went down the sides of her face, around her ears, and under her chin. And she had short hairs all about the roots of her nose, and her body was covered with it, the heaviest, longest coat being on her shoulders, arms, and legs. I asked her: 'Whose child are you?' '*Luke cong ma*,'—'I am my mother's child,' said she.

"A Chinaman had her on exhibition, and we paid him eight cents for the sight, and gave the child a mango. She clasped her hands at once, and bowed as the Siamese all do. The school children say she belongs to the tribe of Esau, but that she does not know it, because she never heard the old Bible story. Poor little thing! she may become hideous as she grows up."

I remember well that her name was Krao, which in Siamese means hairy; and if I should happen to see the child when I go to London, I have no doubt I will recognize her. She could talk Siamese as naturally and distinctly as any of the children who crowded round to look at her. As for her "prehensile feet and remarkably flexible hands," that is characteristic of all the Siamese. From their very birth their mothers and nurses rub and bend the joints to make them supple, and the little children in the native theatres are trained to such perfection that their masters boast to one another that their troupe is the most flexible. In their pantomime and genuflexions each actress tries to outdo the others, by bending and twisting her hands, and almost unjointing her body, to gain the praise of her master and the applause of the audience. And who that has ever been in Siam can forget the awkward and unnatural projection of the elbow which all young ladies affect?

Again and again have I seen the children in the mission-schools sitting flat on the floor holding their sewing with their toes, while their little fingers were all doubled up in their strenuous effort to push the needle through the stiff cloth; and when seated on the benches, if a pencil or nut falls to the floor, they immediately pick it up with their toes. Even carpenters hold a stick with their toes while they fashion it to the desired shape with the tools in their hands. And why not? They are always barefoot, and it is very convenient sometimes when hands are full to have another available member.

As to the suggestion of a tail, by "a slight lengthening of the lower vertebræ," it is no more to be believed than the whole tale. If a reward was offered for her capture how does it happen that she was exhibited in Petchaburee months before she was taken to England? It was heads he was after in Borneo, and tails in Siam. But if he is the authority for the newspaper articles I have quoted, I fear he re-*counted* more than he found.

Here is another traveller's story:

"In Northern Siam there are curious birds, which when their nest is finished, and the eggs duly laid, it is the male bird who sets himself upon them, and the female brings mud and straw, and plasters him in. Only his head is visible, and she feeds him and hovers near to keep him company until the chirp of the little birds warns her it is time to break up the mud wall and let her lord go free."

There are little black birds with golden bills that can be taught to talk, and laugh, and sing. The love-birds are very beautiful, and sit on the same branch, nodding and winking at each other like doves.

We have some curious and interesting leaf insects and stick-bugs, that look so natural one can hardly believe they are animated until they are seen to move. The walking-fish, too, are wonderful creatures. I have seen them move over the mud-banks at a rapid rate, leaving a pretty track behind them, something like herring-bone embroidery, and I have frequently noticed little black crabs clinging to branches, six to eight feet from the ground. King-crabs are also very plentiful, that queer half-moon species, of which the male furnishes a striking example of those desperately lazy husbands who make their wives support them.

Down along the coast at Aughin and Kok Sechang, are found sea-horses, the cunning little *hippocampus*, a bony pipe-fish six or seven inches long, the head of which is very like that of a miniature horse. All honor to the brave little fellows, for unlike those miserable king-crabs, among the sea-horses the father looks after the young, as a good husband should, with real paternal solicitude. There is also the durien-fish, round as a puff-ball and covered with sharp, prickly spines.

There is in Siam a very large lizard called the *he-ah*, or *taknet*, having a split tongue. It is usually found on land, but it can live in the water, and can swim almost like a crocodile. The largest one I ever saw was some six or seven feet long, and was shot in a tree, and dragged down, when the natives at once begged for its gall to make medicine.

CHAPTER XXV.

SIAM'S CENTENNIAL EXPOSITION.

April 26, 1882, or as the Siamese count time, "sixth lunation, ninth of the waxing moon, year of the horse, fourth of the decade, fifteenth of the present reign, 1244 Siamese civil era," was the time designated for the opening of the Exposition in honor of the celebration of the one hundredth year since the establishment of the city of Bangkok as the capital of Siam. This set time was preceded by three days and four nights of Buddhist religious ceremonies and fireworks, mingled with processions and displays of royal and military power. And the king himself laid the corner-stone of the centennial memorial monument, and of the new "Palace of Justice."

The famous royal temple of the Emerald Idol, after being thoroughly repaired, was also rededicated, and the bronze statues of the four past sovereigns of the present dynasty worshipped by the king and his people. The first of these kings has left a name long to be remembered, as witness the following: "Prabaht Somdetch Boroma Rahchahteraht Ramatechaudee Praputtayautfah Chulaloke."

I went to Bangkok and visited the Exposition in May. It was certainly very good for Siam, and we hope it will lift the nation up a step or two. The missionary ladies distributed gospels and tracts, and all seemed glad to get them. I was very sorry that we had no Bible department there. One of the ladies was the very first one to go in after the doors were opened, and the king said when he heard of it, "There, the Siamese always let the foreigners get ahead of them!" He intended to secure a photograph of the first person who entered the gate, but we are sure he did not want it to be a foreigner.

The grandest display was in the queen's rooms, of royal jewels, medals, gold and silver plate, and goodly robes and garments of silk and satin and crape. But the nicest and daintiest work on nearly everything seems to have been done by Chinese rather than the natives of this kingdom. I saw in the Laos room some very curious and beautiful things which appeared to be entirely native. But Laos is an inland kingdom so far removed from outside influences that strangers have had little effect upon its manufactures.

There was a noticeable absence of thought and inventive skill in the construction of the tools and implements displayed. There was an air of rude barbarity connected with the whole which would not let you for a moment forget that you were still in Siam, and yet the Exposition is a sign of better days.

The most homelike thing I saw was a little native who was selling fans. He asked ninety cents for one; and when I showed him mine, just like it, that I only paid fifteen for, he said, "Where did you get it?" I told him, "Down the river at a floating house." "Oh!" said he; "this is in the Exposition, and it only comes once in one hundred years!"

It is worth much to have seen the royal crown-jewels, and the gems and gold and silver-plate belonging to the king and nobles, and the great cases filled with royal apparel. The queen had some very pretty things in her rooms, but I don't suppose she did much of the work herself. In one of the rooms there were curtains at the doorways, and hanging-baskets and various designs, all made of natural flowers. This room was furnished with royal chairs and sofas, gilt and covered with yellow satin. On the walls were portraits of the king, the former and the present queen, and the little heir-apparent with his black, chubby face, and his clothes a great deal too large for him. I enjoyed looking at the court dresses, embroidered in gold thread. All through the royal apartments there were effigies of pages, soldiers, courtiers, and ladies dressed in the styles of long ago—except that, almost without exception, they wore shoes and stockings, and they are a very recent addition to the Siamese costume.

The Girls' School of Bangkok had two cases in the queen's room filled with fancy-work, such as crochet, lace, mats and tidies, darnet-work and applique, zephyr afghans, rugs, and pin-cushions. I also saw the silk quilt that was presented to the king in Mrs. House's time by this school, hanging over one of the doorways among the royal possessions.

Dr. McFarland, in the interest of education and the King's School, had a room filled with all sorts of school-books, and appliances, specimens of the students' penmanship and translations, both in English and Siamese, could be seen. There were also some well-preserved specimens of native butterflies and beetles, and several beautiful mottoes and banners.

The natural products made a good display—the rices, fruits, and flowers—for Siam is wonderfully productive; but these things have never been improved by cultivation, and the vegetables especially are very small and inferior to the same kinds grown in America. Their largest onions are the size of a partridge-egg, and cabbages weighing three or four pounds to the head would be real curiosities, and their melons hardly deserve to be eaten, they are so tasteless.

The workmen's department was indifferent enough, fully proving that this nation has been standing still for centuries. Their ploughs are nothing but crooked sticks with an iron point, and knives so very blunt and rude that if I should sketch one I would have to write beneath it, "This is a knife," or you would never imagine what it was intended for.

The Siamese Exposition was remarkable for the absence of elephants. There was not one on exhibition. I cannot account for it. Perhaps the white specimens were considered too sacred for all the vulgar crowd to gaze upon, and the others are too common to show. There were tigers, bears, wildcats, foxes, mink, beavers, hedgehogs, porcupines, squirrels, rabbits, guinea-pigs, deer, and monkeys, and apes of many kinds. There was also a great variety of birds, poultry, and fishes. In the fish-room there were many beautiful and curious specimens, both living and dead; but the dead ones were preserved with carbolic oil, which made the place so offensive that visitors had to hurry through without examining anything closely. Here were several living alligators, from eighteen to twenty inches long, big-mouthed and ugly even in their infancy.

I cannot tell of all the strange and curious things, the beautiful and costly: the royal saddles and bridles, inlaid with gold and glittering with jewels; the golden throne of the old king; the old-time armor, made of bamboo and stuffed with cotton; the old flags and banners taken in almost forgotten wars; the royal bedstead; the swords and firearms; the musical instruments; the curious coins, from irregular chunks of gold and silver, brass, copper, iron, and lead, down to sea-shells (the cowries), used as money in Siam as late as 1862, and then up to the nicest and newest flat, round coins from the royal mint, stamped with the king's portrait and the centennial Siamese date 1244.

I must not forget to mention the ores and woods, the ferns and orchids; the perfumes, spices, and herbs; the elephant tusks and trappings; the fish-nets and tackle; the bamboo work; the models of houses, temples, and sacred shrines, and boats, from the little skiff, which the poorest may own, to the long, graceful boats used only by the king in his river processions; the robes and trappings for Buddhist priests, their bowls and rice-pots; and the fireworks, paper and beeswax flowers, incense-sticks and tapers for offerings and cremations.

Take it all in all, it was a wonderful thing for Siam. The king ordered the Exposition to be kept open one hundred days, and at the close the goods were returned to their owners, or sold at auction. There were entertainments every day and night, and fireworks of the most dazzling description. There were refreshment halls where one could get both foreign and native food, and there were boats and carriages and sedan chairs for the visitors. You could talk through the telephone with the old capital, Ayuthia, or send a telegram down the river to Paknam. The buildings, of course, were but temporary, made of wood and bamboo, but they were well planned, light and airy, and being painted and ornamented in the highest style of Siamese art, they presented a fine appearance.

We are glad that Siam had a Centennial Exposition, and that we were so fortunate as to see it in all its glory, and if she ever has another we hope it will be incomparable.

CHAPTER XXVI.

PETCHABUREE.

The city of Pet-cha-bu-ree is about ninety miles from Bangkok now. It used to be much farther when the only way to reach it was by crossing the Gulf of Siam, and then ascending the Petchaburee River from the sea. But now several long, straight canals have been cut, making a shorter and closer connection with the waterways of the country and rendering us independent of wind and wave.

We always travel in house-boats, which are very comfortable and make good time with four or five stout natives as rowers. Until you get fairly out of Bangkok the progress is slow, for the principal canals are often so filled with native boats coming and going that they jostle and rub and thump each other, and sometimes come to a deadlock. But as you leave the crowd and the tumult behind you the boatmen with long, steady strokes bear you quietly and swiftly along. Nearly all Siamese boatmen stand at their oars. By rowing day and night, with only short stops for rest and meals, the journey from Bangkok to Petchaburee has been accomplished in thirty-six hours, perhaps less. It is better, however, to allow yourself fully forty-eight or more, that you may have good-natured boatmen all the way, and time to enjoy the lovely scenery of this delightful land.

On our way we pass through gardens of marvellous extent, full of all tropical trees, spices, and flowers. There are great plots of ground where they cultivate the cera or betel leaves, which the natives chew with areca-nut; and fields thrown up in ridges all crowned with vegetables, and where the Chinamen with bent backs deepen the ditches, throwing the water with basket-shovels over the growing plants, or else gathering what is fit for use. We cross wide ponds full of water-lilies, gathering handfuls as we pass, and see the little boats full of the lovely lotus flowers, and their long, succulent stems all tied in bunches ready for the market, where they are eagerly purchased as a great delicacy; or piled up in tangled masses of beauty, and overflowing the boat, trail their broken stems and petals in the limpid water.

Again our way is through orchards fragrant with orange blossoms, or the mellow, luscious odor of ripening mangoes and bananas. Some of the farm-houses are built by the river's edge, and our approach is always signalled by the barking of dogs and scampering of the little ebony cupids. Sometimes we stop to buy a few pots of the delicious cocoa-nut sugar which we see them making under the trees by the bank; or to ask for eggs, ducks, and chickens, or, it may be, to teach a little, leaving books for them to read, and begging them to let us take their children to our schools. But they are afraid we will sell the children or carry them out of the kingdom, and so we have never yet succeeded in getting a single pupil in this way. I read with wonder of the mission ships going from island to island in the South Pacific and gathering boys and girls for the schools. It must be that the natives are more ready to receive the Gospel than these timid, indifferent Siamese.

As you near Petchaburee the scenery becomes more picturesque and lovely. The winding river, with its clear, sweet waters; the luxuriant foliage on either bank; the graceful bamboos swaying their plumy heads, and nodding and glancing at their own shadows in the rippling waves, and almost touching across the stream; the mangroves, with their fern-like leaves crowding into the water, and standing so close together as to be impenetrable for almost everything more delicate than the crocodile or the monkey. Whole families of the latter sometimes stand on the bank and grin at us, or smack their lips in anticipation of bananas tossed from the boat windows. They have a most comical way of quietly watching the fruit till it falls. They then run to the spot and with their long forearm fish it out of the soft mud in which it has buried itself. They often wash them and then tear off the rind and eat as daintily as you or I would do, being careful to keep all the mud from the mellow pulp.

A few native villages are found along the river, and usually a Buddhist monastery near by, a resort for most of the able-bodied men and boys of the community, who are there supported in idleness and sin. Finely cultivated rice-fields creep clear down to the river bank. The soft-eyed, fawn-colored cattle and the tame, grizzly buffalo browse quietly side by side in the meadows, while the windings of the river afford glimpses of the far-away mountains, outlined with wonderful distinctness against the summer sky. They look blue and beautiful, and you imagine quiet places of shade in their cool depths, with sweet, wild flowers under the trees, and moss covering the rocks. These you might find, but cool springs of water, and purling brooks, laughing and leaping from rock to rock, such as make the mountains of America like fairyland, I have nowhere found in Siam.

Our city was a favorite resort of the late king, Maha Mongkut, and on that account it boasts of some improvements which very few Siamese cities outside of Bangkok can show, such as the palace, temples, pagodas, and forts on *Kow Maha Sawan*, the Mountain of the Highest Heaven; the water-works, with pipes from the river to the foot of the mountain; the fine structure of solid masonry, called the Elephant Bridge, which spans the river; the two-storied brick buildings along Market Street, and the many and costly idols in the Royal Cave. The city is built on both sides of the Petchaburee River. Lying all about the city are wide-spreading plains, dotted with clusters of cocoa and sugar palms. These stately trees are so abundant that an eccentric lady once visiting us complained that she "could not look out in any direction without seeing palms." Toward the close of the rainy season the fields are clothed with verdure, and the heavy heads of rich, white rice are maturing for the harvest, which is gathered for the threshing by our Christmas time.

The sun comes up out of the sea every morning to shine on our beautiful home, and disappears at night behind the mountains in the west which stand guard between us and Burmah. There are lovely sunsets, with grand illuminations of Palace Mountain, when every roof, and spire, and pagoda is touched with fire reflected from the burnished heavens, and the palms on the plain below are bathed in the mellow glow, reminding one of pictures of the Heavenly City, with the glory shining through. Sometimes there are bands of color stretching from west to east, such as I never saw anywhere else, and the wondrous beauty of which is only eclipsed by the magnificent sunsets in Colorado, where the sun goes down in a blaze of crimson brightness, and bathes in blushes the snowy summits of the grand old Rocky Mountains.

The city has two markets, one on either side of the river, and it is along these streets that the principal business of the province is transacted. Market Street, on the east side, is lined by rows of two-storied brick buildings for nearly half a mile; but they are almost invisible as you pass along, because the merchants who live in them expose all their goods in bamboo sheds built out in front. Then the hucksters and market-women rent the space before these sheds, and sit down in the streets, in the sunshine or rain, with their trays of fish, fruit, or vegetables. The produce is nearly all brought in from the country by women, who carry it in baskets suspended from a pole across their shoulders *à la* Chinese. Of course, fish come from the sea and from up and down the river in boats. We are not far from the sea, and the boatmen or women who are bringing fresh fish blow a buffalo horn as they approach the city to let the people know of their arrival. Then women and children are seen hurrying to the boat landings, with a few pennies in their baskets, to buy the fish, which are very abundant and cheap, and there are many delicious varieties. The natives are expert in catching, in drying and salting fish, and preserving them in other ways, and great quantities are exported from Siam. There is a sort of tiny prawn gathered from the sea by the ton. They are put in tubs or large earthen vessels, salted and crushed, and allowed to stand in the sun till they are partially decayed. It is called *kapick*, and is of a purplish color, and has a dreadful odor that one can smell from one end of the market to the other. It is a favorite dish with the Siamese. No meal seems complete without it. They use it in cooking curries and in various dressings for fish, and they eat green fruits, such as tamarind pods, after first dipping them into salt and *kapick*. Once our cook told me it was "Siamese butter." They use neither milk nor butter themselves, and wonder how we can bear to use them. They hold our butter, and we their *kapick*, in mutual regard, and the sentiment is not very flattering to either of the articles in question. Just here I am reminded of a Chinese woman in Canton, who thought if she became a Christian she would have to eat foreign food, and so one day in talking to a missionary she said, pathetically, "I can love your Jesus, but I can't eat your butter!"

There are no large and handsome native stores in Siam,

but everything is mixed together, and the places where they sell their wares are just little stalls of bamboo, often not more than ten feet square. The same man or woman may have hardware and dry-goods; kerosene oil and lamps and dishes; beeswax, ropes, brass jewelry, and beads; liquor, rice, mats, rattan, fruits, betel, tobacco, priests' sandals, slate-pencils, *kapick*, Chinese fans, and umbrellas; boxes of lacquer ware, or beautiful straw-work by the Burmese and Laos; ducks' eggs, lotus-lily seeds, dried beans, split peas, indigo, sulphur, alum, camphor, spices and peppers, red, green, and dried; besides *panoongs* and *pahomes*, the two cloths which constitute the usual Siamese dress, one to drape from the waist to the knees, and the other to throw over the shoulders like a scarf. Then there are Chinese eating-stalls, where they are frying lotus stems in lard, and doughnuts in cocoa or peanut oil. They will have a pig's-head roasted and temptingly displayed, or some dried chickens hung up by the neck, and all varieties of rice-cakes and sliced and pickled onions. The Siamese make curries (a kind of highly-seasoned stew to eat with rice) of bats, rats, and frogs. They even eat white ants, which are fried crisp and sold by measure.

The afternoon is the busiest time in the Petchaburee markets, because the country people walk and carry all their loads, and they cannot get to the market in the early morning, as they do in lands where they have horses and carts and wagons, and even cars to carry produce. Here they have no such things, and I suppose the Siamese would laugh to see any one rich enough to own a wagon carrying vegetables to market in it. I never saw but one wagon in Petchaburee, and that belonged to a nobleman from Bangkok, and he rode about in it as if it was a carriage. A great many dogs go to market, for they know it is a good place to steal fish and doughnuts, so many of the women sit on the ground, and the stands are very low. It looks almost as if they set a table for the dogs, and put everything low down so the animals could reach it, and many a mouthful they snatch. The people beat them, cut them, scald them, and swear at them, but no one kills them. They think that is a terrible sin, for how can they tell but some dead friend has been reborn into the world in the form of that dog?

Some sacred cattle were given to the king when he visited Calcutta. They were sent to this province to be kept. The governor allows them to run loose and pick up their living wherever they can. They go to market regularly and lay in a supply of the nicest, freshest vegetables, the sweetest sugar-cane, and the best rice the stalls afford. The streets are so narrow, and the cattle so large and strong, they trample and push, crushing and upsetting as much more as they eat. They usually take whatever is set before them, but there is one unpleasant peculiarity about this kind of customers—they don't pay. The markets are open every day. There are no Sabbaths of rest in Siam, and the people do not observe any day of the week to keep it holy unto God. They have what they call sacred days. They go to the temples in the early morning and make offerings to the idols and the priests. Sometimes they tarry to listen to the Pali preaching service, which they cannot understand, but more frequently they go home to work, or gamble all the rest of the day.

The principal thoroughfare of Petchaburee, as of most Siamese cities, is the river. Ours is not very wide, but in the rainy season it overflows its banks, and is quite deep. Then an occasional steam-tug from Bangkok ventures upon its waters, to the wonder and admiration of all the natives, to many of whom this is the only specimen of a "fire-boat" they have ever seen. All through the day and night little native boats are going past our home.

There are no floating houses here, but quite a number of

people live in boats, especially above the Elephant Bridge. This bridge was built more than ten years ago by the Kromatah, who is now Minister of Foreign Affairs in Bangkok. He had it made strong and wide, so that elephants could cross over. It is about half a mile from the mission compound, and the last time I crossed it the old beggar-woman who so often sits there asked an alms. I suspect she is a slave and they send her out to beg, because she can get more that way than her toil would be worth, so I am opposed to giving her money. But I told her if she would sweep the bridge every Wednesday when I passed over I would give her some pennies. When I returned she had it half swept, and in the evening I sent her the pennies. Beggars here are not always poor people. It is more like a trade, and many would much rather beg than work.

Not only the city, but also this province, is called Petchaburee. It is ruled by a Governor and Lieutenant-Governor, and other nobles and officers. The two highest rulers at present are dukes, "*Phyas*," and half-brothers of the ex-regent, and they live in the best houses in the city. We cannot call them palaces, but they are built of brick, with steep tile roofs, and are surrounded by walls whose gates are shut every night. There are many houses inside these walls besides the brick ones; they are made of boards and bamboo for the servants and slaves. There are long bamboo sheds where the prisoners are confined, and still others where they keep horses and carriages and boats and goats. There are pavilions where the native players perform their dramas and dance to please their masters, as did the daughter of Herodias in the olden time. The greatest reward for fine acting in these places, is to be taken into the duke's household and assigned a place among the women of his harem. It is in these same pavilions, or *salas*, as the Siamese call them, that the judges and scribes sit when court is in session. The mode of capital punishment is beheading.

The natives themselves say, "You can even kill a man and go unpunished, that is if you have money enough to buy your head." Sometimes heads are not worth very much, and can be purchased cheaply.

The governors have a few articles of foreign furniture in their houses, such as tables, chairs, lamps, and mirrors. The latter, I can assure you, are used more than any of the others, especially the chairs. If you want to make a Siamese uncomfortable, have him sit down on a chair. Ten to one unless you watch him, he will tuck his bare black feet up on the chair too, and squat there like a mammoth frog. The women of these Petchaburee harems know nothing of true housekeeping, and everything is in a disorderly, untidy condition. The governor treats his head wife with a great deal of kindness. They are often seen out riding together in the same carriage. He sometimes goes to the country, and a few of his wives follow after, riding on horseback, with a foot on each side, like Indian squaws. He has a great many children, and seems very fond of them. Indeed, he seldom appears in public without some of his children about him. Of course these little ones are of higher rank than any others in the province, and therefore they are not permitted to attend our mission-schools, where they would have to mingle with the common people. We have visited them occasionally, and given them books, but they are very ignorant indeed of our religion, and in all the years that I have been here, they have never once been to church.

Petchaburee is said to have ten thousand inhabitants, but the houses of the city are mostly built of unpainted teak boards, or split bamboo, and covered with a curious roofing of sewed leaves, and so hidden in trees and tropical foliage that you can see but a small part of the city at a time. The streets are full of children playing, and servants and traders going about their avocations, and at all hours of the day you may meet yellow-robed Buddhist priests, or worshippers coming and going through the many beautiful temple gates. This was once a walled city, and the gates were closed and guarded every night. Traces of the old wall are still to be seen, and on Market Street, east side, the houses are designated as being below or above the city gate. I have often passed the ruins of an old fort that was built long ago as a defence against the Burmese, who frequently invaded the land. The site is now occupied by what is called the Fort temple, and the monks, with bare heads and feet, and sleepy images of the Buddha, guard its historic boundaries. This province figures in the history of Siam. A rebellion against the king was once planned here, but the leaders were captured and slain, and their followers scattered. There are records of invasions and battles, victories and defeats. This very city, where I now sit and write so quietly, has been pillaged and burned, and the inhabitants carried off as slaves. But these things all occurred before my day, and there is no sign now of these ever being repeated.

The soldiers are all drafted; such a thing as a volunteer is unheard of, and patriotism is an unknown emotion in the bosom of a Siamese. Perhaps it is because they have no graves, nor hearthstones to fight for. Their little bamboo hut, with its wretched inmates and squalid surroundings, does not inspire them with that lofty and heroic spirit which leads civilized men to die for their country.

CHAPTER XXVII.

WALKS ABOUT PETCHABUREE.

There are many interesting places about this old city; and among them one which I have often visited—"*Wat Nah Pra Taht*," or in Bangkok phraseology, "*Wat Maha Taht*,"—"The Temple of the Sacred Bones."* Buddhist priests who go to the mountains to live as hermits, dig and search in the caves and among the rocks in secluded places for little white and yellow stones which they believe are Buddha's bones. If you presume to question how they came there, they will innocently answer, "His sacred bones have power to go wherever they please." Here are the ruins of a large, unfinished pagoda, in which is deposited some of these marvellous stones. Although carried to scarcely half its intended height, it towers above everything else on the ground, and serves as a landmark for miles about the country. Great heaps of building material lie about, and the scaffolding still clings to the wall, though broken and weather-worn. The pagoda is built of bricks and has many cracks and fissures, where plants, vines, and trees even are growing in wild luxuriance. These will eventually destroy the tower as added years give them strength and weight, and the openings are widened where their roots have found lodgment. We climbed up into the pagoda and looked out from one of the windows over the city. We could see very few houses, for the trees hid them. We ascended a long flight of steps on the outside, then came to an open doorway. All beneath seems to be solid masonry. Here, however, there are two passage-ways crossing each other at right angles, cutting the pagoda into four equal parts, and at each end of these passages there is an opening. Three of them are windows, the other the door by which we entered. In this temple's grounds you can see one hundred and eighty-six large gilt idols, besides parts of a great many more that are so broken and piled together we could not count them. They are arranged mostly along the outer wall of a long, narrow building which surrounds the four sides of an open court. It was evidently built for them, as they all fit in their places. This outer wall is solid except for three or four very narrow doorways. The inner wall facing the open court is not more than a foot and a half high, with pillars at regular intervals to support the roof, which is quite heavy and covered with curious Chinese tiles. The court surrounded by these idols is about three hundred feet long and one hundred and fifty feet wide. This is only one of many buildings in the same temple grounds and perhaps cost the least money. The idols are of brick and mortar, smoothly plastered and gilded, and could not have been made for less than five thousand dollars. Tucked down by the side of one of the idols, we found a little strip of yellow cloth, and on it were written a few words in lead-pencil saying the owner wished to send it in care of Buddha to a dead woman named "*Cham.*" They have so much faith in yellow cloth that they think the merit attached to it would help redeem a soul from hell.

We saw one old temple whose great double doors were nearly covered with gold-leaf, that had been put there, a little at a time, by devout worshippers. We entered this idol-house one day and found many large and small images of Buddha arranged in tiers over the altar. The inside walls were covered with bright-colored pictures painted on the smooth plastered surface, of scenes from the stories of Buddha and the giants and angels. Another temple near by has lost its former glory and the grass and weeds grow over the door-steps once trod by myriads of feet. The room is now used as a sort of storehouse for the rubbish of the *wat*, or monastery. Here we found some strange old idols made of metal. They seemed to have been cast in moulds in pieces and then soldered together. They were standing images of the Buddha, and at one time held their proud heads ten feet high, but are now on their backs in a deserted corner. Through their broken sides we could see they were filled with a hardened clay. Hanging from the ceilings were old tattered scrolls and banners, with Chinese pictures and inscriptions, and on the altar a white-ant hill that had already buried many of the smaller idols under its dome and was slowly creeping over the open hands of the insensible Buddha.

In another temple we found priests' beds spread out before the altar. I supposed of course they were observing some special season of fasting or prayer before their gods. But that is not always the case. Sometimes they are simply watching the precious things upon the altar. On this one, besides more idols than I found time to count, were very many of the sacred storied umbrellas, an image of Buddha with the seven-headed dragon spreading itself as a shade for his sacred head, an elephant of brass offering a cup of nectar to him, and a tray with cups of tea that were refilled as often as they dried empty. The evaporation of the " cup which cheers, but not inebriates," seemed to have a very soporific effect upon the stolid images, which, since first they were placed there, have never once spoken or moved. On the outside are elaborate plaster ornaments over the windows and doors, and there are twenty-eight images of genii scattered over the roof. They look frightful enough with their drawn swords and crooked mouths, almost as dreadful as the two alligators, with wide-extended jaws and tails erect, ready to attack and swallow a blue china soup-plate that occupies the centre of a large plaster lotus-lily on the gable end of the wall.

There is a row of beautiful lotus pagodas before these temples, and each one holds in its crown some sacred relic. Temples, pagodas, sacred shrines, and po-trees are all enclosed by a high brick wall, with beautiful gateways that I have never yet seen closed, and worshippers are going in and out continually. The temple with the golden doors, of which I have already spoken, is opposite the principal gateway, and seems to be a favorite shrine for the paying of vows. Here are hundreds of theatre images stacked between the doors, brought by those who have gained their desires; and instead of the real theatre they vowed to give, they bring these miserable clay dolls and place them before the senseless idol that knows no better. There is a little altar for incense, and on it are found the two bamboo sticks they fit together with a prayer, and then toss up before the god to try their fortune.

There is no place that we visit oftener, nor enjoy more, than Palace Mountain. It is only about a mile from our home, and from the moment you leave the level, dusty plain, and pass under the shade of its trees, you seem to be in another world. The road leading up the mountain is paved with bricks, and there is a wall on either side of it to keep you from falling down the steep bank among the sharp, rough rocks. There are beautiful trees covering the mountain-side, and some of them are in bloom nearly all the year. Among the rocks are trailing vines, delicate plants, and wild flowers. There is the rustle of dry leaves under your feet, and a fragrant, woodsy smell in the air. Little birds are upon the branches, and now and then a brown bunny whisks across the path and hides under the shadow of the wall. There are pleasant resting-places built under the trees, and a new-comer might be startled at the first sight of the great white serpent that rears its scaly head among the prickly-pears at the mountain's foot, but it is just as harmless as brick and mortar in any other shape. Just in front of it is a tile-covered shed and two large wooden tanks for water, and near by are wide, pleasant seats. One of them is inlaid with marble, and is a special favorite with the natives because it is always cool. The mountain has many peaks, and each one is surmounted by some sort of a building. The most prominent are the palace, the audience-hall, the observatory, the royal pagodas, two or three small temples for idols, and the "*prasaht*," a cruciform building betokening royalty, and to be found near every palace. There are buildings for the king's retinue, rooms for the body-guard, many porches, sheds, and "*salas*." Three little forts crown as many peaks, and there are a few old rusty cannon.

There are several small caves in this mountain filled with hideous images of the dead, and of others who are torturing their own bodies, or suffering the pangs of hell. There are bland-faced Buddhas peering from every nook and corner; and in one of the caves there are plaster elephants, tigers, and crows. In another they have a model of the "sacred footprint of Buddha," the original of which they say can be seen at Mount "*Prabaht*" in this kingdom. The Siamese have a legend of Ceylon which says that fair island was formed by a clod of earth which fell from the sacred heel of Buddha as he stepped from India across the Bay of Bengal to Siam. One could almost believe the legend after seeing these giant footprints of their god!

There are two large Buddhist monasteries on this mountain. We went one morning to attend the temple service. We started before nine o'clock, but found the service had begun. All about the doorway and on the temple steps the worshippers were kneeling with clasped hands and looking toward the idols, before which five priests were offering prayers or adorations. They repeated the praises in turn, some in Pali and some in Siamese. The incense-sticks were burning, and the glare of the wax tapers tried to rival God's better sunshine, which poured in floods of glory through the open windows. After the high-priest had taken his place in the holy chair, had folded up his limbs as you always see them in images of Buddha, and placed the large feather fan before his face to shut out the distracting world, he began to repeat the liturgy, and all the people made responses. When that was finished there was a general bowing to the image, and then they waited, with hands still clasped, for the sermon. All this time we had been standing in the vestibule; now we entered, the people making way for us, and the high-priest inviting us to a place at his right hand. We seated ourselves on the floor of the temple like the rest of the audience. The subject of the sermon was Sanctification, and he said some good things—among others, that if they desired to be holy they must flee from sin. At the conclusion the people again bowed their heads and worshipped both the idols and the priests, and were then quietly dismissed. The Siamese have no singing at their religious services. The high-priest now turned in his chair and greeted us kindly. His fan had been no protection against my gaze. I hope, however, I was not a serious cause of distraction, although I was the "observed of all observers." As I could not talk to him very fluently, I left him to listen to my companion's remarks, while I wandered about the temple. In the centre of the rear sat a large gilt Buddha, with smaller idols about it, holding rods and banners, emblems of his power, I suppose. The platform on which the Buddha rested was a sort of altar, and upon it were all manner of knick-knacks and offerings. I noticed a large blue soup-tureen, filled with sand, into which they thrust the incense-sticks; glass sugar-bowls, filled with flowers, some sweet wild ones from the mountain-side, others artificial made of paper, gauze, and tinsel; wax tapers burning here and there; little betel-trays and pasteboard elephants, with bunches of flowers appearing to grow out of their backs. It seemed to be the "what-not" of the temple; and there we also saw two photographs of the present king, taken when he was in the priesthood, and clad in priestly yellow robes. On either side of the largest idol, and a little in front, stood two small tables, each containing a mirror, stands of paper flowers covered with glass globes, vases with real lotus-lilies, trays of betel, candles, paper elephants, etc. The inside walls of the temple were covered with Chinese pictures. In front and above the double doors was depicted a lofty temple, whose spire reached the clouds. All about it were pagodas, idol-houses, and salas. Crowds of people were flocking to it from all directions, some mounted upon elephants, others in two-wheeled carts drawn by oxen, while the poor trudged on foot. In the foreground was a fancy bridge crossing a river, whose waters were filled with bathers. On one of the sides of the temple was a sea view, with the blue waves rolling, and fearful-looking dragons lifting their heads and lashing their tails in the foam. There was plenty of blue and lavender sky in these pictures, and trees of the same shades, but the greenest of green for the grass underfoot. Let those who admire Chinese and Japanese paintings go into ecstasies over them if they will, but I cannot join their number. Between the doors was a small table, holding an old rundown clock; vases with paper flowers, and a few peacock's feathers; also, three images of miserable old men, who, in silent contemplation of the idol before them, or in thinking of nothing, had lost themselves all but their bones and skin. Their hair was white with age, and it was pitiful to behold the look of abject nothingness upon their faces. They were to represent Buddhist saints.

As we passed out of the temple door, after leaving some

books with the priest, and down through the paved walks of the temple grounds, we saw a part of the congregation under the trees busy eating their breakfasts, which they had carried with them that they might remain for the second service. Descending the mountain, it began to rain, and we slipped under a *sala* to wait, and we watched the crowd buying and selling bamboo sprouts. They were roasted ready to eat. There was a great deal of loud talking, and chaffering, of selling and taking back again because the money was not good or they did not give the full price, and in the midst of it all, a bull-fight over the husks that had been thrown away. It was their sacred day, too, but they have no idea of keeping it as a holy Sabbath. Being wearied with the noise and contention, we turned away and hurried home through the rain. A few hours later in the day, we met at the mission chapel for our Wednesday evening prayer-meeting. How great and yet how blessed was the contrast to the morning service!

The first little school-house I built had become too small, and I went one evening to see about having it enlarged. M. and P., two little native girls, were with me. Just as we crossed the Elephant Bridge we saw a marriage procession. There were fifteen or twenty men and boys, each with a tray of food; some of them looked very tempting, especially one filled with sugar-coated cookies. We had not gone far when we saw some donkeys quietly grazing by the roadside. We were in Temple Street, back of the governor's place, and these little creatures he had brought with him from India when he went to witness the grand display at the proclamation of Queen Victoria as Empress of India. The little natives with me had never seen a donkey before, and did not know what they were. When I told them, P. said, "Is this what Jesus rode?" "When?" said I, anxious to see what they remembered about it. "As He entered Jerusalem, and the children shouted 'Hosanna!'"

said M. "When they went to Egypt and His mother and Joseph were along. They were afraid of that king, what's his name? I forget," said P. We had no time to talk further of this, for we heard a great squealing behind us, and turning, saw two Chinamen carrying a big black pig. They had tied the poor pig's legs together, and then strung him on a bamboo pole, the ends of which rested on their shoulders, and thus they bore him squealing through the streets. Just here, too, we were passing some Chinese temples. They were ornamented in a wonderful manner with dragons, and birds, and fishes about the roof and gables, and on one side a hideous-looking head with wide-open mouth in which was thrust a sword. The children were so busy watching the pig and the temples, that they stumpped their bare toes on the bricks that stuck up in the street. Everybody we met said, "Where are you going?" They ask that instead of "How do you do?" or "Are you well?" They do not like to be asked about their health for fear the spirits will trouble them if they say they are well. If they have been sick and are getting better, they will insist they are worse.

We passed five *wats* on our way with their wide grounds and many temples, their dogs and naughty boys. There is also a monastery at either end of our walk. You can hardly go anywhere in a Siamese city without being in sight of some Buddhist temples. There are a few fig-trees on this street, but the fruit is small and inferior.

Passing through a narrow alley we came into the market which was full of all kinds of fish from the river and the sea—fresh, salt, and dry. We hurried through as fast as possible, for if fish-markets are bad at home and at Billingsgate, they are far worse in Siam, both in speech and odor.

We saw several white tents of the priests in the stubble-fields, who had come to be feasted during the Chinese holidays. They call themselves "forest priests," and they think they make a great deal of merit by leaving the temples and pretending to camp in the forests for a few days. They are careful never to do it, however, except at holiday times, when the people will nourish them with all their daintiest food. Their tents are large umbrellas with long handles which they plant in the ground, and when the umbrella is opened, they have curtains hanging from the edge down to the earth. It makes a round, cosy room with a pole in the centre.

We also saw three ox-carts all ready for a journey across the country. They are queer-looking things, with two wheels and a long, narrow bed made of sticks like the hay-racks in old-fashioned barns. These were filled with rice-straw, and in one of them I saw a fighting-cock tied by its leg. I suppose its master was the ox-driver, and he took his chicken along for company, and to gamble with by the way. On one of the racks was a covered bamboo arrangement into which the traveller was expected to crawl for the night. There he could sleep as snugly as an Indian pappoose in the wicker pocket on its mother's back. These grand preparations were all for the benefit of a young Englishman who was going off to see the hot springs about forty miles from Petchaburee. He must have a guide and servants. He must carry his food, and pots and kettles to cook it in, and dishes, and water, and indeed everything he may need.

About a month after this walk I went to see the Chinese temple we had then passed. The door was kindly opened for me by a fat, jolly-looking Chinaman, who showed me about and told me all he could in his broken Siamese. I found the inside of the temple, which looks so gay without, rough, unfinished, and dirty. On one side there was the figure of a large tigress and two cubs, made of plaster-work against the wall. Above these were little Chinese houses full of people. The porches, doors, and windows of these little houses were all bordered with buttons, and there were bright-colored trees and birds. Below the tigress was a small tank walled up, into which they throw the firecrackers when they come to worship and make merit. Crackers and other fireworks are never used by the heathen for mere play, but are a regular part of their worship, and they expect some future reward for every cracker they ever fired. I asked where their idols were, as I saw none in the temple except the tigress, and they said, "If *Mem* wants to worship we invite you into another room." My jolly Chinaman had left me to go and prepare some tea, and as there were others in the temple I found out all I desired to know. On my way to the shrine I passed the little charcoal furnace where he sat with his bellows trying his best to make the water boil. The shrine was a little place, perhaps eight feet square enclosed on three sides by curtains. Inside was an altar, upon which were placed five or six Chinese images, none of Buddha, and round about were little trays for flowers and fruit, and a candle in a candlestick. In front of the altar was a high table with a glass lantern upon it, and an oil lamp burning inside which they refill and watch with jealous care lest it go out; also a dish of sand for incense-sticks. On the altar were some Chinese books and a plate of bananas. I asked about the books, and they said the priest in his ministry read from them every night and morning before the idols. I espied a large mirror there too, but they hastened to tell me it did not belong there, but they had no other good place to put it. I asked them why they worshipped idols, and if they ever did them any good? The only reply I received was the common, thoughtless one of all Asia: "It is our custom. Our fathers and mothers did so, and we keep it up." They averred that the idols helped them, although they laughed at the idea, when I said, "Can they see, or hear, or speak, or walk?" After this tea was ready and I was invited to partake. It was served on a little table in dainty china cups. They gave me a little round stool to sit upon, and filled for me five cups of tea. There was one large cup in the centre and four little ones round it like children. I drank two cups, talking meanwhile to the people, who had gathered in to see the "foreigner," then rose to leave. My back was hardly turned when an indolent Siamese who had been lolling there got up, and said, "I'll play I'm *Mem*, and drink some tea too," and he proceeded to help himself without being invited, while the by-standers all laughed.

CHAPTER XXVIII.

THE ROYAL CAVE, PETCHABUREE.

THE morning was bright with sunshine, the air cool and refreshing. We could not have found a pleasanter day to visit the cave, which is about two miles back from the river among the mountains. We had one *jinrikisha* and two men. They were to take turns in drawing the comfortable little carriage, and as it is the only one in the city, we two ladies had to take turns in riding. We carried a lunch with us and our sketch-books, for there are many picturesque views among the hills, and even down in the cave.

We passed companies of market-women returning from the city, where they had traded their pots of palm sugar for fish, tobacco, betel leaves, matches, and empty sugar-pots. We met some of the Laos women who live in the villages beyond the mountains. They were all dressed alike with black jackets and scarfs, and blue and white striped skirts, and had their long black hair tied in a large bow-knot on the top of their heads. They carried curious pocket-shaped baskets in which were chickens, glutinous rice, or home-made cloth for the market.

The fields of rice on either side of the road were ripening for the harvest, and now and then we saw the tattered garments of the "scarecrows" fluttering in the wind. For many mornings past we had heard the natives screaming and swearing at the birds before we were ready to get up. About half-way to the cave a company of little children came running across the rice-fields, and invited us to their house to eat "Cow-mow." It is the new rice roasted and pounded, and if eaten with salt tastes very good. As they came near I noticed that four of them were pupils from our schools. We could not accept their kind invitation, but hurried on.

At the mouth of the cave we found some curious rocks, and succeeded in breaking off several good specimens. They show decided volcanic action, and appear to have been fused in a molten, bubbling state. In the cave are the greatest wonders. There are several chambers, but the first one, if you enter properly by the royal steps, is the largest, the longest, and the loftiest. It is perhaps one hundred and fifty feet long and sixty feet wide. The rocky walls arch over dome-like and solemn. At the apex there is an irregular opening through which the sun shines clear and bright, and looking up we could see the white clouds floating lazily by. Bushes and shrubs grow about the edges, vines clamber down the rough sides, and delicate mosses, ferns, and wild flowers cling to the overhanging rocks; while some great brown roots have scrambled down, down till they have reached the very foot of the cave. Pretty, bright-eyed doves have made their nests near by, and they sit pluming themselves on the ledges, and looking at us sidewise with eyes full of wonder, and then at a given signal they will all fly off together with a great whirr and rush that echoes and re-echoes through the dark, gloomy recesses.

There are many graceful stalactites depending from the vaulted roof, but the stalagmites which could climb up to meet them have all been removed, and the floor of the cave leveled and paved with large red tiles, and there is a wall of masonry with an arched doorway leading into a smaller room paved with ordinary bricks. All round about are arranged shelves and ledges that are set full of little images of Buddha, and in little niches and holes in the ceiling these vacant-looking, lifeless gods peer out at us. Not a sound is heard but the dropping of the water or the rustle of falling leaves. Now and then we hear the screeching of bats and are reminded of the old prophecy, and hope the time will soon come for its fulfilment.

There are many dark passages and winding ways leading off from these larger spaces, and the walls of the cave are full of little chambers and alcoves, and there are ledges of rock jutting out, and little pinnacles, each one crowned with an idol. The school-boys once counted one hundred and eighty-two, but I think there must be many more. One is a large reclining image having a low brick railing in front of it, and the gate-posts are ornamented with plaster lions, with their heads turned and their fierce mouths wide open. Before another large idol crouched a great gilt elephant offering to Buddha a cup of water, which it held aloft in its trunk, and a monkey also sat with its forepaws clasped in holy adoration. These figures are to perpetuate the old legend of Buddha, that when he retired to the forests as a hermit even the beasts recognized his holiness and power, and came to minister unto him. There are some Chinese inscriptions on the walls, and when some friends of ours from China were here, they translated some for us. One was, "The light of Buddha still shines"; another, "This life is regulated by a former existence, but the conditions of the next or future life depend on the preparations of the present." The latter part of this wise saying is very orthodox, and I only wish the heathen would profit by it.

There are little pocket editions of Buddha lying round loose. Nearly all the gods were undergoing repairs. They were covered with a coat of black lacquer, preparatory to being regilded. There are little tablets on many of the images, telling who made them, that the right hand may know what the left has done, and some bear inscriptions of praise to Buddha for his wisdom and merit.

In wandering about I found several hideous figures of dead bodies, and some of men, who, as hermits, have been lost in meditation until their forms are all wasted to a skeleton. Perhaps quite near by these wretched, starved hermits you will see a jolly, fat, laughing figure that looks for all the world as though it took things easy and always intended to.

Drops of clear, cool water are continually falling upon the paved floor. A circular fountain has been prepared to receive them at one place, and I have often seen it brimming full. The half of a cocoanut-shell floats on the top as a drinking-cup, and lying on the edge of the fount are some large, glossy green leaves which we brought to use instead of this too common cup.

Since we entered four other companies have come to visit the cave this morning. The first were Chinamen from Singapore, with two or three Malay servants. They were all very devout, and prostrated themselves before all the larger idols, and burned incense and a great pile of gold and silver paper money. It is thus they hope to send help to their dead friends. They then crowded about us to see what we were doing. I was sitting at the base of a pagoda which towered high above my head, and held four images of the Buddha. By my side was my sketch-book, in which I had been both writing and drawing. In my hands I had a bit of canvas work, a cluster of purple grapes with green leaves. We try at all times and places to teach this people to work, and so one of the first remarks these men made was, "They came for pleasure, yet brought their work along!" We let them look at it, and told them what it was for. And then I tried to tell them of a better God than the idols by which they had knelt. I discovered that one of them could read Siamese, and when they took their leave I asked them to stop at the *jinrikisha* outside and get a book from the servant.

After them came a band of Siamese, who wandered about in their careless, indolent fashion. They brought no offerings, and we only saw one old woman who worshipped the idols. They were more intent on looking about them, resting after their warm walk, and drinking at the fountain, than in merit-making. They were a band of travelling players who came into the city from the gardens. Not one of the women could read, and evidently foreigners are a rare sight to them, for we heard two of them discussing whether we were men or women, and finally they concluded we were men, despite our long hair, dresses, and needlework. It is a constant wonder to the natives that we are not afraid to go about alone, and that we do not have a train of servants following after to carry our things, to wait upon us, and to show what great folks we are.

The next visitors were Siamese men. One had a gun and two others carried swords. We think they had been out hunting, for there was no look of the brave soldier about them. They were full of wonderment at what they saw, but manifested no reverence. They went quickly from room to room, busy telling how things had changed since they were in the cave the last time.

We lunched in the great hall, and after our dessert of bananas and oranges, we had a drink from the fountain. We have made many visits to this Royal Cave.

CHAPTER XXIX.

DRINKING THE WATER OF ALLEGIANCE.

One year in April we went up to the "Mountain of the Highest Heaven" to see the governor and other noblemen of Petchaburee drink the water of allegiance to their king. It was a very pretty ceremony, and one that we had never seen before.

The people were gathered in the king's large audience-hall, which had been prepared for the occasion. The doors had all been thrown wide open, and as we ascended the stone steps the governor saw us and invited us to sit on his mat. It was the place of greatest honor in the hall, and there being no chairs we accepted the invitation and sat down in real Oriental fashion on a lovely Turkish mat. To our left was the governor's son, and beyond him other nobles and officers according to rank. The governor had two of his little daughters with him. They were dressed in foreign style, and one of them even had shoes and stockings on, but the elder one had bare limbs and golden anklets. He was very kind and polite to us, explaining the different parts of the ceremony and answering questions. Before him was an elegant array of costly vessels and trays, such as the king presents to those who are entitled to the honor. They are sure tokens of rank and royal favor. I think there were eleven pieces and all pure gold. There was a teapot, a water-goblet and plate, betel-trays, tobacco-boxes, and cigar-cases. All were of the most curious workmanship. The teapot was specially beautiful. It was covered with figures of Chinamen and their curious little houses and pagodas, intermingled with trees, flowers, and birds, showing plainly that if the work was not done in China, the style at least was borrowed from the Celestials. The governor's son had a set of black ware, with flowers in gold-leaf; and the *Pra Palaht*, or lieutenant-governor, next to him, but ranking higher, had a golden set that rivalled those of the governor himself. I was surprised to see that there were no gold cups for tea. The Pra Palaht had an ordinary china teacup, with a handle on one side and his monogram on the other, while the governor had a little blue china dish. They gave us tea to drink, and would willingly have supplied us with betel and cigarettes had they not known we would decline the generous offer.

The governor wore his regular court suit, consisting of a purple silk waist-cloth, a white shirt and coat, a golden girdle or belt, white stockings extending above his knees, and black shoes. It is a very simple and comfortable dress. He had the king's portrait in a golden locket tied about his neck with a pink ribbon, a gold star set with jewels on his right breast, and a silver medal on his left. The silver medal he received at Calcutta when Queen Victoria was proclaimed Empress of India. It has her likeness and new title on one side, and an Indian inscription on the other, which we could not read, and the English date "Jan. 1st, 1877." He had a white round-crowned hat, surmounted by a golden pagoda, of which he seemed specially proud, judging by the way he lifted it and tenderly turned it round and round, and finally placed it directly in front of us.

What the very beginning of the ceremony was we do not know, for we arrived too late to see. But the first thing we noticed was the feeding of priests. There were six of them in their sacred yellow robes sitting opposite us, with great trays piled with food, from which they were helping themselves, in a not very dainty way, with their fingers. And although they consider it a sin for a Buddhist priest to look at a woman, they watched us a great deal more, I think, than we did them.

The king's throne at one end of the hall was occupied by a large idol, a golden image of Buddha. Before it were arranged flowers, offerings, lighted candles, and smoking incense-sticks; while in the very front was a large brazen urn holding four or five gallons of water, and by its side a gun, a spear, and three swords. When the priests had finished their breakfast, for all this was in the early morning, a ball of unspun cotton string was attached to the idol and then carried to the priests, who, allowing the cord to pass through both their hands, sat holding it thus while they prayed at intervals. A young man stepped to the centre of the hall, and kneeling before the idol, opened one of those strange folding books and began to read the oaths of allegiance.* They were truly fearful, and I whispered to my nearest neighbor that if we believed the evil spirits, to which they appealed, had the power attributed to them, we would never dare take such an oath. After the reading of each part the priests would pray, the nobles bow their heads in assent, and with clasped hands worship the idol.

When all had taken the oath three men came forward, and as they bowed to the idol, two others who sat near an open door began to blow large conch-shells. I had not noticed these men before, and the strange, weird sound they produced with the shells startled me. They were fine-looking young men, without the least shadow of beard or mustache. They were both dressed in white robes, and had their long, heavy black hair twisted up like a woman's. One of the three men bowing to the idol belonged to the same race. They are what the Siamese call "Mons." I

---

* A translation will be found in the chapter on Siam's Religion.

have since been told that these "Mons" always take part in the religious ceremonies connected with the king, although they themselves are Brahmins. There are numerous settlements of them in Siam now, and the French Jesuits claim many of them as converts to their faith.

The three men before the idol now arose. Two of them were Siamese, and they stood one on either side of the brazen vessel filled with water. The man at the right unsheathed the swords one by one, and handed them to the "Mon," who dipped each one into the water three times, and then passed it to the Siamese on the left, who wiped the blades and put them back into their scabbards. The spear and the gun were likewise dipped into the water. This dipping of these weapons into the water has a peculiar significance. It implies that those who have taken the oath will die by these tokens of the king's power if they rebel against him. All this time the shells were sounding, the priests chanting, and the people clasping their hands to the idol. Then the "Mon" took a golden basin from the governor's mat and brought him some of the water. He also gave to the son and two or three others. Beginning with the governor, they all stood up, bowed to the idol and then to the king, in the direction of Bangkok. They drank a mouthful of the water, and with the rest they sprinkled their heads and washed their hands. After the higher nobles were served the brazen urn was carried to the rear of the hall, and the petty officers allowed to help themselves. It was amusing to see them crowd around and dip with all sorts of vessels—one with a teapot, another with a cocoanut-shell.

So they drank, and sprinkled and washed with the water of allegiance, and in great confusion the assembly broke up, and each one started for his own home, leaving everything to be gathered up by the servants. As we passed out I could not refrain from saying to the governor, "Notwithstanding all this the subjects often rebel against their king." "Yes," said he, "but they always have to submit at last." "Not according to your Siamese histories," I added, "for they tell of many a king cast down and another set up on the royal throne." At this he was silent and so was I.

CHAPTER XXX.

THE TEMPLE OF THE SLEEPING IDOL.

ON the side of Palace Mountain at Petchaburee there is an old temple, and in it lies sleeping one of the largest Buddhas in the world. The great reclining image in Bangkok measures more feet in length, but the body is not so large. The one in the capital is more costly too, the soles of the monstrous feet being inlaid with pearl and chased with gold, and traced from heel to toe with mystic circles and symbols, and the toe-nails inscribed with the supposed attributes of the man the image represents.

The one here I have seen many times. It is built of brick and mortar, then plastered smoothly, covered with lacquer, and lastly with gilt, so that it looks like a golden image. It reclines upon its right side with the feet lying one upon the other so the great toes touch. The right arm is folded under the head and is supported by several immense pillows. The left arm lies straight along the body. The ears droop to the shoulders. When the fingers and toes of a child are all the same length, and its ears come down to the shoulders, they know that another Buddha has been born into the world. But no one has ever seen such a child!

This idol's eyes are made of black lacquer and mother-of-pearl. They are only partially closed, but they have a dreamy, far-away look in them, as though forgetting the past, or trying to peer into the future. There is not a shadow of interest in the present with its living, throbbing, suffering, dying humanity. It is a fit emblem of all dead gods that gaze with stony indifference upon the woes of their worshippers. The features are regular and not unpleasant, with a hint of Ethiopia about the full lips, and the hair. The head is covered with locks of gilded hair, coiled up like little straw beehives. I found on close examination that they are made of clay and baked. They are hollow inside and are stuck on the head with plaster. There are hundreds of them on his pate, and the head is so large that it requires pillows thirty-four feet high to rest upon. By actual measurement the circumference of one of these locks of hair is seventeen inches. The soles of the feet are not gilt like the rest of the body, but red, and filled with black figures of dragons, fish, pagodas, umbrellas, lotus-lilies, Buddhas, turtles, fans, temples, and many other curious things we could not make out. In the centre of each sole is a large star.

Our old native teacher says that when the last Buddha, that is Guatama, was born, he had one hundred and eight distinct marks and figures on the soles of his feet. The feet of this idol are peculiar in several respects. The toes are all the same size in length and width, the heel round and the sides perfectly straight and parallel. The sole is flat.

The Peguins living in Siam, make yearly pilgrimages to this idol, and the women used to anoint the feet with perfume and fragrant oil, and then wipe them with their long, beautiful hair, singing and chanting meanwhile in a solemn, earnest manner. The Siamese made so much sport of them that the anointing has been abandoned. But can we not see in this traces of Mary with her alabaster box of precious ointment, very costly, and the woman that was a sinner bathing the Saviour's feet with her tears and wiping them with her hair? Verily these are of the nations who have forgotten God, because they did not want to retain Him in their knowledge, and so He has given them over to believe a lie.

We asked some priests the age of this image and what it cost. They said: "This sacred person was made long ago, and if you wish to know the cost, build one and see." They really know very little about it, and have not curiosity enough to inform themselves. I think they must have made the idol and then built the temple over it. The walls, as usual, are of brick, plastered inside and out, and when finished they were left white and clean. Now they are defaced with cartoons and rude charcoal sketches. The floor is made of cement, and must feel very cool and grateful to the hot, weary feet of the devotees as they come in from the hot sun to rest and worship. There is a row of lofty plastered pillars running down the centre to support the roof. The idol lies on one side next the wall. This leaves space before it for the pillars and the people to stand. The roof was once covered with tiles, but it is so broken now that the sky can be seen through the opening, and the hole serves as a door for the doves, which seem to have taken possession of all the rafters, which are exposed to full view.

There are three wooden doors and several windows. The idol is enveloped in cloths that have been devoted by persons wishing to make merit. I do not mean all covered, for the head and shoulders and feet stick out. These cloths do not appear ever to be removed. The new one is placed upon the old rags and tatters. The last time I was there I saw the remains of a red and yellow one showing beneath one of pure white with gilt paper flowers pasted all over it. Tradition says there used to be a door in the back of this idol, and a room inside. But I have never seen any trace of it.

When a friend from China was here, by her suggested measurement our height when standing by the feet was just equal to the width of four toes, beginning at the so-called little toe and counting up, and my upstretched arm only allowed my fingers to touch the middle of the fifth toe. But we took a tape measure one day and secured more exact figures. Here they are: Whole length of the image, 145 feet; length of ears, 14 feet 2 inches; slit for earring, 4 feet; width of ear across the top, 3 feet 6 inches; width of ear lower lobe, 2 feet; arm from shoulder to elbow, 30 feet; elbow to end of finger, 46 feet; across the neck, 18 feet; length of leg, 63 feet; length of body and head, 82 feet; length of feet, 17 feet 8 inches; length of toes, 4 feet 4 inches; length of toe-nails, 17 inches; width of foot, 7 feet 4 inches; width of toes, 1 foot 7 inches; width of toe-nails, 14 inches; height of pillows, 3¼ feet.

CHAPTER XXXI.

LOTUS-LILIES.

THE delicate fragrance of a lotus which was gathered yesterday from the lily-pond of a neighboring Buddhist monastery, fills my room as I begin to write of this peerless flower of Farther India. It bends gracefully over the rim of the glass vase holding the fountain of "heaven water" from which it draws refreshment. Its petals are rose-pink, growing brighter and redder toward the tips, where one can almost imagine the life-blood of the flower is oozing out and will soon drop upon the white mat of the table. Opening the rosy lips, the golden heart of the flower is disclosed surrounded by a silky fringe of stamens of the same bright hue, edged with pure white pollen. The leaves of the plant are dark green, almost round and lie or float upon the bosom of the lake. The stems are like long green serpents rearing their spiral forms from the black ooze beneath the water, and holding aloft their banners of green, and blossoms of beauty and fragrance.

"It is a kind of water-lily, and is considered a wonderful flower by the people of the countries in which it is found. In Egypt it was formerly sacred to the gods Osiris and Isis, and signified the creation of the world. In India the Hindoo deities of the different sects are often represented seated on a throne of this shape, or on the expanded flower. Its color in Southern India is white or red; the latter color is fabled to be derived from the blood of their god Siva when Kamadeva, or Cupid, wounded him with the love arrow." It symbolizes the world, the *meru*, or residence of the gods, and female beauty. In China and Japan the lotus seems to be specially connected with Buddha, and has a large place in the worship of that god. In the former country it also symbolizes womanly beauty, the small feet of the women being called "*kin leen*," or golden lilies. They imagine it, moreover, to have great power over the souls of the deceased. The Buddhist priests represent the dead as suffering tortures of various kinds, and ask large offerings of the surviving friends for the purpose of inducing *Kwan-yin*, the goddess of mercy, to cast the lotus upon the sufferers, and thus end their punishment. I have seen this idea illustrated in a copy of a rude drawing, taken, I think, from a temple wall. The sinner was lying on the floor of hell and the tormentor was about to crush him with a huge stamp worked by the hands and feet and resembling an instrument the Siamese use to hull rice. The victim's hands were clasped in adoration and the face turned in speechless agony toward the goddess of mercy, who occupied the upper right-hand corner of the picture. Her oblique eyes were turned down with a gentle droop, and in pity she let fall a lotus from her outstretched hand upon the sufferer.

But notwithstanding the sacredness in which the plant is held, and the fables and superstitions which are associated with it, many of the Chinese largely cultivate it. The fragrant blossoms reach a diameter of ten inches, and find a ready sale. The seeds are cooked in various ways, sometimes ground and made into cakes; they are also eaten raw; the fleshy stems supply a popular nourishing vegetable; while the fibres of the leaf-stalks serve for lamp-wicks. The ancient Egyptians also cultivated the lotus in the waters of the Nile, the beans, the stems, and even the roots being extensively used for food. The seeds were enclosed in balls of clay or mud, mixed with chopped straw, and cast into the Nile. In due season the plant appeared, followed by buds, flowers, and seeds. From this practice the inspired writer enforces the duty of self-denying zeal and faith—"Cast thy bread upon the waters, for thou shalt find it after many days."

In Siam the lotus-lilies grow in the greatest profusion, both white and pink. Indeed, on my way from Bangkok, I have sometimes sailed for miles in my boat through flooded fields covered with the lovely white lotus, which the natives were busy gathering for the markets. I could not smother a feeling of pity for the delicate beauties torn so rudely from their watery home, and thrown like any other vegetable into the bottom of the boat.

The royal lotus gardens of Bangkok are several miles from the palace of the king. There is a good carriage road leading from the city, and it is also a pleasant row by river and canal. There are beautiful temples and a palace there, which we hear is being prepared for the future home of the heir-apparent. The Duke of Mecklenburg was entertained in the lotus garden palace during his visit to the King of Siam. It is one of the most healthful and breezy sites in the city, and a favorite resort for picnics. I have enjoyed more than one pleasant party there. Dinner never tastes better than when we eat it beside the lakes where the lotus-lilies float in happy idleness. One day we found a new variety, larger than the pink ones, and pure white, with an inner row of petals crimped and fluted and tinged with delicate sea-green. The heart was golden like the others, but it had no fragrance. We gathered fresh seed-pods and ate the kernels. They are rich and sweet, with the flavor of chestnuts, but I doubt if one of us remembered Tennyson's "Lotus-eaters," although we had

—"come into a land
In which it seemed always afternoon—
A land where all things always seemed the same."

Even the idle, yellow-robed priests about the Buddhist temples on the lake shore

—"deep asleep they seemed, yet all awake,"

while their gods, the sleepy Buddhas, sit in all the temples with ever open palm, always upturned, and ready to receive, but giving nothing to the worshippers, though they fill their hands with lotus-lilies as a sure passport to Nirvana!

How many a wretched, sinful soul would buy forgetfulness if it could be purchased at such a price, and what myriads there are who never could purchase it even at so cheap a rate, for lotus-lilies do not grow all the world around, and millions live and die never having heard of the blessed flower, which, according to Buddhism, has such wonderful virtue. It is interwoven with all their religious rites and ceremonies, and there is scarcely a legend in which you cannot catch the flutter of their pink petals, or detect their delicate fragrance. It is said that "when the Buddha made his appearance in the world as a man that a halo of glory encircled him, which was visible throughout all the surrounding country, and the earth about him spontaneously produced a profusion of lotus flowers," and he is now usually represented as sitting on an open lotus-lily. It is a favorite form for pagodas, those useless piles of brick and mortar which surround every Buddhist temple. The foundation may be a round or square base, with an opened lily to support the shaft or spire, and there are sometimes several rows of petals round and round the shaft. Some beautiful specimens of this style of pagoda may be found at "Wat Na Pra Taht," or the "Temple of the Holy Bones," in Petchaburee. Lotus-lilies form the capitals of pillars for the temple porches, and indeed are so common everywhere as ornaments, that plaster flowers of almost any shape are now called by masons "*dok boo-ah*"—flower-of-lotus. They are found adorning the ceiling and doors of the wonderful temple of the Emerald Idol in Bangkok, and they are one of the thirty-two mystic signs displayed on the soles of the feet of the sleeping god. I once saw them growing in a basin at the foot of the stairway in the royal mint. Mrs. Leonowens tells us of "the lighted tapers and the vases filled with the white lotus which they set down upon the table before the gilded chairs," on the morning of her introduction to the school-room in the palace, and that the late king, Maha Mongkut, offered the white lotus and the roses to Buddha every morning in the temple erected to the memory of his mother. One of their sacred books, a legend of Buddha's life, is called "The White Lotus of the True Religion."

Last May there was discovered in Hankow, China, a secret conspiracy known as the "White Lotus." Their plan was to overthrow the present dynasty and effect a revolution in the Chinese Empire. Summary punishment was meted out to all who were caught, and no less than fifty-one heads were cut off in one week. But these Chinese secret societies are hard to overcome and almost impossible to eradicate. They may cut off the heads of the "White Lotus," but the roots are still there, and from the mire of discontent or oppression will send forth new stems and banners of defiance.

The seal of Chow Praya Praklang, one of the three noble lords who have charge of the civil government of Siam, is the figure of a lotus flower.

The faithful ones believe that the sacred bones of the Buddha often appear in the heart of the lilies placed before the priests as they sit in prayer or meditation; and I have heard that the reputed tooth of their god, held so sacred in the Temple of the Delada at Kandy, Ceylon, was found reposing in dental majesty on the heart of an opening lotus. What wonderful lilies they must have in Ceylon, and what great faith! But perhaps that monster tooth belonged to the Buddha when he was still an elephant or a mastodon. If so, the worship of that tooth as it is still carried on by elephants, seems appropriate, to say the least.

At the grand cremation of the drowned Queen of Siam, one of the companies which walked in the procession carried tridents, the triple tips of which were each crowned with the white lotus; and during the evening festivities one of the most beautiful displays was called the "lotus-lantern dance," in which the dancers held aloft the lighted lanterns, waving them to the slow rhythm of the music.

Every year thousands of real and artificial lilies are floated on the rivers and the sea as offerings to the water-spirits. They are launched at night, with their little waxen tapers bravely burning, and bearing their cargoes of sugar, sweetmeats and rice, betel, tobacco, and incense-sticks.

The Siamese use lotus-shaped cups and sprinklers for the royal bath at the hair-cutting and coronation ceremonies of the king. I have among my curiosities a beautiful lotus combination to be used as a cigar-holder. It is a piece of unique Japanese workmanship, and displays the ability of those Oriental "Yankees" to combine the useful with the ornamental. There is a coil of stem for the base, covered with a broad, green leaf, supporting the pericarp of the lily, the empty seed-cells serving to hold the cigars, while a half-opened lotus at one side may be used as an ash-cup.

I once heard a native preacher tell the people who lived near a mission chapel, but did not appreciate its privileges nor accept the blessings offered there in Christ's name, that they were like the frogs in the lily-pond—they hopped in and out of the crystal waters; they sported in the cool shade of the broad leaves; the fragrant petals dropped upon their very heads, and the rich seeds pelted them as they fell to begin a new life for themselves; yet the frogs wist not, heeded not, while the bees flew long weary miles to gather the lotus-honey and dust their tired bodies in the golden pollen. So the heathen came from the far-off country villages to sit down in the kingdom of God and enjoy the milk and honey of His abounding grace. The words were as true as the parable was beautiful.

On some of the beautiful old Japanese bells are representations of Buddha sitting in a lotus-lily while he enjoys the happy unconsciousness of Nirvana.

The King of Siam has his cigars made of the best fine-cut native tobacco, and rolled in the petals of the lotus. Chow Sye manufactures them, and furnishes not only the king, but many of the princes with the same luxurious "buree." The lilies are gathered from the royal garden, and preserved and prepared with the utmost care.

Among the Greeks the tree whose fruit gave immortality was called the lotus; and not the least beautiful among the many charming and even magnificent villas of Rome is the "Villa of Albani," built nearly a century ago by Cardinal Alessandro Albani. It is rich in works of art,—among them a bas-relief of "Antonius crowned with the lotus flower."

In Thibet the simple folk are fond of putting up what they call "Trees of the Law"—that is, lofty flagstaffs, with banners upon them emblazoned with that mystic charm of wonder-working power, the sacred words, "*Om Mani padme hum*"—"Ah, the jewel is in the lotus" (*i. e.*, "the Self-creative force is in the Kosmos"). Perhaps you are not aware that the visible world is believed by many in these Eastern lands to have sprung, or evolved itself, from the heart of a lotus. "Whenever the flags are blown open by the wind from the thrice-sacred valleys of Thibet, and 'the holy six syllables' are turned toward heaven, it counts as if a prayer were uttered; a prayer which brings down blessings not only upon the pious devotee at whose expense it was put up, but also upon the whole country-side. Everywhere in Thibet these praying flagstaffs meet the eye."

During the late prevalence of cholera in Siam, flagstaffs with little white flags displaying mysterious characters inscribed by Buddhist priests could be seen all over the kingdom. The Siamese believe cholera is the direct work of the devil and his imps, and although, when questioned, they said these flags were to show that they counted themselves in league with the spirits of the under-world and should not therefore be scourged with the dreadful plague; may there not still be some connection with the "Trees of the Law" in Thibet, and these "Spirit Flags"—"*Tong pee*"—in Siam? I am inclined to think so.

They have many beautiful fancies clustering about the lotus, and even in this warm sunny clime, they dream dreams and sing songs. Perhaps I might fill a book with them if I had time to listen to their recital, and could translate them from this Oriental tongue into smooth English strains to your ears. But we must be content with two or three. We speak of a "flowery pathway," and a "bed of roses." Hear them sing in this far-off lotus-land a song of love and beauty; the "beauty of the lilies"

> "The fragrant lilies are blooming wide,
> Trembling on the crystal tide,
> Gather, oh gather them for the bride,
> And scatter their petals on every side;
> Strew them over the nuptial bed,
> From where the feet nestle up to the head."

And here is a song to the "Lotus Nymph":

> "Oh, lovely and bright,
> Thou wast born for delight,
> In fairy bowers
> 'Midst fragrant flowers.

> "The lilies fed you
> Until you were grown,
> And then they left you
> To seek your own.

"You made your garland
    And set it afloat,
And hoped it would strand
    On your true lover's boat.

"As it passed from your sight,
    You prayed with your might,
That the brave one be stayed
    In his search for a maid.

"That the garland might cling
    To the hand of your king,
And bring him with speed
    To fill your heart's need.

"The lilies relented,
    They heard your love-prayer,
They guided your garland
    To him who should share
The life all contented
    You live with him there."

A LEGEND OF THE BUDDHA WHEN HE WAS A SPARROW.

Two happy sparrows lived in a nest, and loved and nourished their young, while the sun shone bright and warm, and the rain fell in gentle showers, and the night folded them in her quiet wings to rest. Thus in far-off India passed in sweet content the days and nights of their happy bird-life. But one day the father went in search of food. He found lotus-lilies and tried to get the seeds, but they were set fast and firm each one in its cell. As the sun grew hot the lily closed over him and he was a prisoner. The mother stayed in the nest, and a field-fire came over the plain and devoured the dry grass and delicate wild flowers. The little birdlings cried: "Father has gone to see the angels, and who will help us to escape?" The fire came nearer and nearer. The sparrow-mother beat her wings and fluttered above her nest in helpless agony, and saw her birdlings perish, and her disconsolate moans went up with the smoke to heaven, but no one answered, not the faintest rustle of an angel's wing was heard, and the hot hours passed slowly by. The day was almost gone when she broke out in bitter, indignant complainings, saying, "The fathers are of no account. They go off, forgetting their families, and flirting with other birds!" At last the long, sad day was over. The Indian sun went down in a blaze of tropical splendor. The dew fell, and the lotus unfolded its rosy petals, and the sparrow-father was free. He had been thinking of his mate and the little ones in the home-nest, and with a rich, sweet lotus seed in his bill he fairly flew to the cosy spot he had left in the morning. As he saw the blackened waste stretch before him he hastened his flight and soon alighted, with a wildly beating heart, on a burnt branch near which still fluttered his forlorn mate. In his sorrow and consternation the lotus seed dropped, and was burned in the embers which yet glowed at his feet. His angry wife flew at him and pecked him, charging him with neglect and inconstancy, and upbraiding him for the death of the nestlings. He tried in vain to defend himself, telling of the lotus-lily that enclosed him in its golden heart, and of the round, ripe seed he brought from its treasures for their evening feast, and that he was full of sorrow for the dire disaster that had befallen the birdlings he loved so well. She would not listen, but demanded, "Where is the proof of your love? Where is the lotus seed? Your words are as false as your heart, and I, if I am born again, though it be through countless generations, I will never speak to a male again!" As she ended the words of this rash vow she closed her bill with a determined snap and flew right into the fire which still burned in a neighboring copse, and perished miserably. The poor sparrow-Buddha in his despair cast one sorrowful look over his ruined and desolate home, and then followed the example of his angry spouse, and darting into the flames died with her on the same funeral pyre. But that was not the end, for the Lord and Lady Buddha were immortal, and this was but one of the fiery passages in their lives from which they came forth more and more purified, although the dross was not quite all consumed; and yet in time she did speak to him again, and learned to love him too, and the old volume of their lives was rebound.

But I cannot transcribe its pages here, for it runs through illimitable editions; and you, if you but tried to read it all would grow so sleepy you might be taken for a veritable "Lotus-eater," and there is danger you would never again be wide enough awake to finish the rest of *my* book.

CHAPTER XXXII.

CHRISTIAN MISSIONS IN SIAM.

WE cannot tell when Siam's rivers first ran to the sea, nor for how many centuries the stream of humanity, which had its rise in the North, has been flowing through the kingdom. But we do know that only a few years ago, within this present century even, was the pure Gospel introduced, and a little stream of the Gospel floods, which are yet destined to cover the whole earth, began to trickle into the hearts and lives of these poor benighted ones, bringing light, and refreshment, and glory with every drop of its life-giving waters. It was the "beginning of the Gospel of the grace of God" in this far-away heathen land, and it dates from the year 1819. There were Roman Catholics at work here long before that time. The French priests came as early as 1662, and the Portuguese had preceded them.

"At Sophaburi," says Sir John Bowring, "a city founded about A.D. 600, the ruins of the palace of Phaulcon (a Greek adventurer) still exist, and there are the remains of a Christian church founded by him, in which, some of the traditions say, he was put to death. I brought with me from Bangkok as a relic, one of the columns of the church, richly carved and gilded. The words '*Jesus Hominum Salvator*' are still inscribed over the canopy of the altar, upon which the image of Buddha now sits to be worshipped." Notwithstanding Louis XIV. sent a special embassy to the court of Siam for the express purpose of converting the king and his nobles to the Roman Catholic faith, they refused to be converted. The political designs always involved in Jesuit enterprises were also thwarted, and by a royal decree in 1780, they were banished from the kingdom.

The late Bishop Pallegoix resumed aggressive work in 1830, and the Jesuits count thousands of adherents among the Portuguese and French half-castes, the Chinese and other nationalities who desire political protection in order to evade the laws of the land, or escape punishment when they have broken them. Their converts among the Siamese are very few. They are both feared and hated by the Government, but they are gaining ground—*e. g.*: A Siamese noble lately asserted that he knew of thirty-two estates which the Jesuits had seized, and now held, through French protection, in spite of all the protestations of the native owners. The last Siam Directory gives the names of twenty foreign Jesuit missionaries, among them a vicar-apostolic and a bishop. They have a printing-press in Bangkok, five churches, and a school. They also have churches at Chantaboon, Patriew, Ayuthia, Bangplasoi, Nikhom, Prom, Sara-buree, Vat Pleng, and Kanburee. At Bann-Nok-Kwak they have both a church and a college of the Sacred Heart of Jesus.

I have read in an old book published in Bangkok in 1849, that the first effort for the conversion of the Siamese to the Christian religion was made by Mrs. Ann Hasseltine Judson, at the time of Dr. Judson's first residence in the city of Rangoon, Burmah. There were a great many Siamese there, and she, becoming interested in them, applied herself to the study of the language and then translated a tract, a catechism, and the gospel of Matthew into Siamese. The catechism was printed at the Baptist mission press in Serampore about the close of the year 1819, and was the first Christian book ever printed in Siamese. It is glorious to think that a Christian woman's heart and hand were both busy planning and working for the salvation of Siam more than sixty years ago! Ann Hasseltine is dead. They are all dead, the noble wives of that grand old missionary, Dr. Judson. "They rest from their labors, and their works do follow them"; and we of to-day yet love to do them honor. What grander work could a woman do than begin the redemption of a nation? What holier thing can we do than to strive with all our might for its completion?

Rev. W. H. Medhurst, of the London Missionary Society, was also interested in Siam about this time, not as a separate field, however, but as a portal to the Chinese Empire, and so in the same year that Mrs. Judson's Siamese productions were printed he sent Chinese tracts to Tringanu and Siam. Nearly twenty years later he sailed from Batavia for Singapore, intending to visit Siam in company with Dr. Karl Gutzlaff and the Rev. Mr. Tomlin. But he was disappointed in finding that they had sailed from Singapore just two days before his arrival. He essayed to follow them in a native prow, which was to go up the gulf as far as Singapore; but failing to get a passage from there further north, he was obliged to return. Dr. Gutzlaff and Rev. Mr. Tomlin arrived in Siam in August, 1828, and were, so far as we have been able to ascertain, the first Protestant missionaries to set foot on the soil of this kingdom. They secured permission to reside in Bangkok and labor among the Chinese, and strange to say, their best friend, and one from whom they received the greatest kindness, was a Roman Catholic, the Portuguese consul, Seignior Carlos de Silveira, who furnished them with a house on the Government property, and he even protected them when, later, the Jesuits sought their expulsion. They also found a firm friend in Mr. Robert Hunter, an English merchant, who was living, with his Portuguese wife, in Bangkok. They began at once to heal the sick, and also distributed twenty-five boxes of books in about two months.

This raised the suspicions of the natives, and they charged the missionaries with being spies, and that they intended to incite the Chinese to rebellion. The king, thinking the books were the main cause of alarm, ordered specimens to be translated, but finding nothing harmful, the missionaries were permitted to remain. They applied themselves diligently to the study of the Siamese language, and knowing that it is the "entrance of God's Word that giveth light," they attempted to translate the Scriptures, in the meantime sending appeals to the American churches, and to Dr. Judson in Burmah, for missionaries for Siam.

Mr. Tomlin was taken ill, and soon returned to his family in Singapore. Thus Dr. Gutzlaff was left alone, but he, having prepared a Siamese tract and translated one of the gospels, also went to Singapore in the latter part of 1829 to have them printed. While there he was married to Miss Maria Newell, of the London Missionary Society. She came, as a young bride, to Bangkok in February, 1830, and was the first woman to undertake personal work for Christ in Siam. She aided her husband in his unremitting toil of translating; "they hardly allowed themselves time for rest or sleep, daily employing a number of copyists." In one short year her life was ended on earth, and she and her child rest quietly in a foreign grave. Dr. Gutzlaff soon after sailed for China, where he lived to labor many years. He was but twenty-five when he reached Siam, and he entered upon the work with all the energy of his nature, and it is astonishing how much he accomplished, for during his stay of less than two years he, with Mr. Tomlin, translated the whole Bible into Siamese, a considerable portion of it into the Laosian and Cambodian languages, and prepared a dictionary and grammar of the Siamese and Cambodian.

Dr. David Abeel, who reached Bangkok in 1831—half a century ago—and just twelve days after Dr. Gutzlaff had sailed for China, was the first American missionary to Siam. His saintly life and earnest prayers seem to have left a blessing on all the lands he visited, and his name deserves a place with that of Henry Martyn. He has had a long line of successors. I will give as full a list as possible in another place. But some of them deserve special mention.

Rev. John Taylor Jones, D.D., under the care of the American Baptist Board, came over from Burmah with his family in 1833 to labor among the Siamese. He also took charge of the little flock of Chinese which Dr. Abeel had been obliged to leave. In December of that year he had the pleasure of baptizing three Chinamen. Dr. Gutzlaff had previously baptized one convert, the first-fruits of the harvest we are still reaping.

Dr. Jones labored many years in Bangkok, and we hear that he was an earnest, faithful worker, and a true Christian gentleman. He died there also, and his body rests in the Protestant cemetery.

In 1835 Dr. D. B. Bradley, of the A. B. C. F. M., reached Bangkok, by way of Maulmain and Singapore, in company with his wife, and Dr. William Dean of the American Baptist Board. They were one hundred and fifty-seven days from Boston to Maulmain. It now requires but little more than that many hours from New York to Liverpool. Dr. Bradley, being a fully trained physician, began his medical work and missionary labors immediately. He opened a dispensary, and the poor, especially the Chinese, who are more intelligent and trustful than the Siamese, flocked in crowds for healing. He also distributed books, and held a daily religious service at the dispensary. But his good works and his medical practice, which were all as free as the Gospel, soon excited the jealousy of the merit-making Buddhists. Complaints were heard that there were special days set apart by the Government and custom when all might make merit, but principally by serving Buddhist priests; while if these foreigners were allowed to show kindness to everybody every day their merit would soon outstrip that of the best men of the kingdom. About this time, too, a Captain Wellar shot two pigeons in the precincts of a Buddhist temple. This so enraged the priests, who look upon the taking of animal or insect life as one of the greatest sins, and who, moreover, had boasted that the merit of the temple grounds was so great that it was impossible to kill birds which flew there for refuge, that they attacked Captain Wellar in order to wrest the dead birds from his hand. A scuffle ensued, in which the Captain was severely wounded and his gun taken from him. Mr. Robert Hunter ran to his assistance and brought the wounded man to Dr. Bradley. He fainted several times while having his wounds dressed. The extravagant demands of Mr. Hunter in behalf of his friend, and his threats that if they were not granted he would send for foreign aid and establish British rule in Siam, produced great commotion in the Government, and so excited the people that we find the following in Dr. Bradley's journal for August 10, 1835: "It is rumored that there is a plot on foot to burn down the houses of our mission. Doubtless there are men here who would rejoice in such an event, but I do not fear that we shall at present fall into such hands. An exceedingly scurrilous and obscene placard was, a few mornings since, found on the gate of our homestead, and on it was displayed in bold relief pictures of crosses, one for each of the adult members of our mission." Before the month closed they were informed that they must leave the premises within five days. Thus the little band was scattered. One family occupied a floating house on the river, another found shelter with the kind Baptist missionaries, and Dr. Bradley moved across the river into the little Catholic village of Santa Crux, near his friend, Mr. Hunter. Those were dark days, but Christ was with them. Dr. Bradley lived to secure and occupy one of the most eligible sites in Bangkok, and there "his work as medical missionary, writer, and translator into Siamese of Christian books, printer, and preacher, continued with a zeal and hope which knew neither weariness nor discouragement until his lamented death, after thirty-eight years of toil, in June, 1873." The following words were spoken in memoriam by Dr. William Dean, who knew him intimately through all his mission life:

"The prayers of Dr. Bradley, the servant of God, are ended, but his works continue. His body sleeps, but it shall rise again. His labors are done, but his work is immortal. His labors have been long continued, faithful, and multiform.

"First, in surgery and medicine: He was the first to practice the former in Siam, and so demonstrate to the people that by the loss of a limb they might save a life. He also introduced vaccination into the country, which has saved the lives of many, and proved a rich boon to the people. His medical skill introduced him to the families of kings and nobles, and he early opened hospitals and dispensaries for the gratuitous treatment of all who came to him for healing.

"Next, his literary labors: Dr. Bradley's annual calendar has become a handbook for all classes here who use the English language. He has prepared elementary books to aid in the study of English and Siamese, and his great work, the Siamese Dictionary, which cost him years of toil, and will hand down his name to future generations. But his greatest ambition in this department was to furnish the Siamese a Christian literature. His translations of Scripture, his Bible histories, hymn-books, and tracts are known and used in Siam wherever Christ is preached. His numerous essays and publications have touched upon nearly every topic of enlightened thought and Christian science.

"Again, his evangelical labors in preaching the Gospel: In this work he has been eminently faithful, in season and out of season. Among his domestics, in the market-places, in the precincts of the palace, and wherever he met the people, he was prompt to give them the message of his Master; and you can bear me witness that he has been faithful to those who speak the English language, whether he met them in the private walks of life or the public places of prayer. He has not shunned to declare the counsel of God.

"Dr. Bradley has left a worthy Christian example and an untarnished reputation. We claim for him not infallibility nor Christian perfection, but while we may perhaps in some things have differed from him in judgment, we are all ready to yield to him integrity of purpose, and, in all the varied relations and complicated duties of life, an honest endeavor to do the right. Dr. Bradley's religion was in keeping with his natural temperament—active, ardent, untiring. His faith knew no limit within the promises of God. His foot never faltered under a divine command. His heart never feared to follow his Divine Leader. His faith amounted to an assurance, and with an unwavering expectation he looked forward to the end of his faith—the salvation of his soul. He could in all honesty say, 'I know that my Redeemer liveth.'

"As Abraham, in the dark hour when the son of promise was corded for the sacrifice and laid upon the altar, believed in God and received him in a figure as by a resurrection from the dead, so our departed brother, while looking upon the sons of promise in this land still in the darkness of death, and himself hastening to the grave, believed in God, and finished his work fully expecting that his labors would not be in vain in the Lord. A little while ago he said in our prayer-meeting, 'I expect from heaven to look down on this people, and to see them redeemed and Christianized.'

"Dr. Bradley had nearly reached the appointed limit of three-score and ten, having been born at Marcellus, New York, in 1804. Until the last month of his life he was seen walking among us, his active step, his beaming eye, and busy hands impelled with all the enthusiastic energy of youth.

"With the exception of one visit to America, and a short trip to China, his whole public life, of nearly forty years, has been one of Christian benevolence and ceaseless activity among the natives of Siam. His missionary associates have in such an example a lesson of priceless value, and his wife and children, who are also children of God, have in such a life and such a death a legacy richer than a kingdom."

His is the best known and most honored missionary

name in all Siam to this day. Wherever we go we find those who have known and loved him, have received his books, listened to his teachings, and many of them found Christ.

Dr. Wm. Dean is well known in America, China, and Siam. Not long ago he visited us at Petchaburee, and one evening gave us a sketch of his life. It was fifty years last September since he received his appointment, and it was interesting to hear him tell of the beginning of things here a half century ago, and to follow the rapidly succeeding events down to the present. He came to Siam with Dr. Bradley, but his first stay here was very short. He devoted himself entirely to the study of the Chinese language, and had the pleasure of organizing the first church of Protestant Chinese Christians that was ever gathered in the East. As soon as the ports of the Celestial Empire were opened to foreigners he hastened north. He also had the honor of organizing the first Chinese church in Hong-Kong, and baptized thirty or forty of its members, three of whom have become pastors of native churches. He spent twelve years in Hong-Kong, and later returned to Siam, and settled down to labor among the Chinese residents of this kingdom. He made his home in Bangkok, but from there went out to labor in other cities and provinces. He has baptized about five hundred disciples, seven of whom entered the ministry. When he left Boston in 1834, his friends told him he need not expect to live more than two or three years; but the members of the Missionary Society, the old Boston pastors, and nearly all his friends are dead—professors, teachers, classmates, all, all gone! while Dr. Dean has already completed threescore and fifteen years, and still lives, working and waiting for his heavenly summons to go up higher.

Drs. Mattoon and House must also be classed among the old veterans. They have both retired; not on a pension, however, unless it be paid in the gratitude of hearts which still hold them in loving remembrance. Dr. Mattoon has spent years of active service since his return to America in efforts to elevate and convert the negroes of the South, while Dr. Samuel R. House, after some thirty years in Siam, is now quietly living in his native town of Waterford, N. Y. But the agencies in Siam which these men helped to inaugurate—the church, the school, the press—still go on with ever-increasing power and blessing.

At present Dr. William Dean, and Rev. Lewis Eaton, lately arrived, are the only representatives of the American Baptist Board at work among the Chinese. They have chapels at Bangkok, Lengkiachu, Bangplasoi, Ku-Buang, Sin-Buang, and Patriew. Formerly they had quite an extensive work among the Siamese, with a full corps of missionaries, schools, printing-press, etc. But that has all been given up by the Board.

The American Board transferred its efforts to China as soon as that field was opened, and gave its work in Siam to the "American Missionary Society," by whom it was maintained a very short time, and then discontinued. Their property and printing-presses were transferred to Dr. Bradley, and are now in the hands of his widow and children. One of his sons, Rev. Cornelius Bradley, was a missionary in Bangkok for a few years, but has since gone to California, where he is now engaged in a theological seminary at Oakland. Two of Dr. Bradley's daughters have married missionaries, and, as Mrs. McGilvary and Mrs. Cheek, belong to the Laos mission. Mr. Dwight Bradley has charge of the printing-presses, and has also a lucrative position in the Foreign Minister's office, where his prompt business talents and sterling Christian manhood win for him the esteem of all. A younger brother, D. B. Bradley, is now pursuing his theological studies in the United States.

As time passed on, one agency after another left the field, until to-day the entire work of Christianizing the Siamese is left to the Board of Foreign Missions of the Presbyterian Church in the United States of America. This Board began its work by sending out Rev. W. P. Buell and wife, who arrived in 1840. They were compelled to leave the field in 1844, as Mrs. B. was stricken with paralysis, and it was not until 1847 that Rev. Mr. Mattoon and wife and Dr. House arrived to take their place. They took up the work with brave, hopeful hearts. They studied the language, and printed, and preached, and practiced medicine. The king was outwardly friendly, but became jealous of the growing influence of the missionaries and the increased "merit-making," as the Siamese called it, of the physicians. Therefore, when they desired another site for a station, they found it impossible to rent or purchase. Their native teachers were thrown into prison, the servants fled, and the people refused to sell them food. In their extremity they even cherished the painful thought of leaving the field. They looked to God for deliverance, and while waiting for a ship to carry them away, it arose from an unexpected cause. The king was attacked with an alarming disease, which soon proved fatal. The priest-king, Maha Mongkut, was then called from the seclusion of the Buddhist monastery to sit on the throne of the "Sacred Prabahts." He ascended the golden steps with a heart full of friendliness to the missionaries, to whom he owed much of his knowledge of science and languages, and from whom he imbibed the liberal policy which made his long reign a peculiarly prosperous and brilliant one. They were invited to the palace, and while enjoying the royal favor, the missionaries wrote: "The princes and nobles now courted our society; our teachers and servants returned to their places; throngs came to our houses to receive books, to talk with us respecting their contents; and we were permitted to go where we chose, and to speak in the name of Jesus with the confidence that we should not be avoided, but obtain a respectful hearing." They were soon able to secure ground and erect suitable buildings for permanent homes. In 1851 the missionary ladies were admitted to teach in the palace among the women of the royal harem. From that time to the present the missionaries have enjoyed the protection and favor of the king, and as proof of the high estimation in which they are held, we quote the following statement, prepared by the authorities, and having the sanction of the king:

"Many years ago, when there were no white men in Siam, the American missionaries came here. They came before any other Europeans, and they taught the Siamese to speak and read the English language. The American missionaries have always been just and upright men. They have never meddled in the affairs of Government, nor created any difficulty with the Siamese. They have lived with the Siamese just as if they belonged to the nation. The Government of Siam has great love and respect for them, and has no fears whatever concerning them. When there has been a difficulty of any kind the missionaries have many times rendered valuable assistance. For this reason the Siamese have loved and respected them for a long time. The Americans have also taught the Siamese many things."

"The late king always entertained the highest regard for his instructor, the Rev. J. Caswell, and besides building a tomb over his grave, presented his widow with $1,500 as a token of his esteem."

He also issued in 1870 a royal proclamation of religious liberty to the subjects of his realm, of which Dr. Bradley said when he reprinted it in the Bangkok Calendar:

"The following translation is an extract from the Royal Siamese Calendar for the current year. It is issued by authority of His Majesty the supreme king, and is to me quite interesting in many respects, but especially in the freedom it accords to all

Siamese subjects in the great concerns of their religion. Having near the close of the pamphlet given good moral lessons, the paper concludes with the following noble sentiments, and very remarkable for a heathen king to promulgate:

" 'In regard to the concern of seeking and holding a religion that shall be a refuge to yourself in this life, it is a good concern and exceedingly appropriate that you all—every individual of you—should investigate and judge for himself according to his own wisdom. And when you see any religion whatever, or any company of religionists whatever, likely to be of advantage to yourself, a refuge in accord with your own wisdom, hold to that religion with all your heart. Hold it not with a shallow mind, with mere guesswork, or because of its general popularity, or from mere traditional saying that it is the custom held from time immemorial; and do not hold a religion that you have not good evidence is true, and then frighten men's fears, and flatter their hopes by it.

" 'Do not be frightened and astonished at diverse events, fictitious wonders, and hold to and follow them. When you shall have obtained a refuge, a religious faith that is beautiful, and good, and suitable, hold to it with great joy, and follow its teachings, and it will be a cause of prosperity to each one of you.' "

The late king seemed ever ready to acknowledge the good influence of the missionaries; and to show that we make no vain boast of their power, we have only to remember that when Sir James Brooke came to Bangkok to open negotiations with the king on behalf of the British Government, he found himself treated in a manner which he considered so insulting that he indignantly took ship again with the purpose of securing assistance in the effort to open the country by main force. Before he had time to return, that old king died (1851), and when the next embassy from Great Britain reached Siam, it was to find on the throne one who could appreciate civilization, and who claimed to be himself quite a scholar even by European standards. Maha Mongkut knew how to treat them, and to treat with them, in an intelligent and regal manner. Years after, the late ex-regent remarked to Mr. Seward, United States Consul-General to Shanghai, that "Siam had not been disciplined by English and French guns as China, but the country had been opened by missionaries." And God is using them still to help lead this old-new nation, which is waking up from its sleep of centuries, into the only way of truth and righteousness.

CHAPTER XXXIII.

THE CHURCH IN SIAM.

"Let us surround the wicked with truth and light, and God will come down from above and capture them." As I have already spoken of other churches, in this chapter I will confine myself entirely to those of our own Board.

Bangkok was the first station occupied by the Presbyterian Board, and although Mr. Buell arrived in 1840, and a church was organized in 1849 that the missionaries themselves might have a place of their own in which to celebrate the Lord's Supper, and one Chinaman was received on certificate as a member of the church, it was not till after twelve years of weary waiting that the first Siamese convert openly abandoned the religion of his fathers and made a public profession of his faith in Christ. Two more were received in 1861; and several years later the first Siamese woman ventured to join the church. Since then the church has gone on increasing year by year. This first church now numbers 53 communicants, 22 of whom are women, and 25 baptized members who are still little children. I am sorry I am not able to give the full number admitted since its organization; of course it is much greater than that now represented. Many have died, and others have fallen away, either gone back to Buddhism, or sinned so as to be cut off from the communion. They are quite liberal, and with their contributions help to support a native preacher in Ayuthia, the old capital of the kingdom. Several of their members have become ministers, and are still preaching the Gospel,—two of them at Ayuthia, and one at the Second church, Bangkok.

An interesting incident is handed down of how the foreigners of Bangkok took great pride in raising money for an organ for the mission. A man who was not a Christian started out with the subscription paper. He would not let the missionaries subscribe, and meeting a Christian captain at the hotel who wished to give something, he would not receive it, saying, "None but sinners are to have anything to do with this business." They raised the money and sent to Singapore and bought the organ, and it served to lead the service of song for years.

A second church was organized in Bangkok in 1878, and has had about 45 members, 22 of whom are girls from the Boarding-school.

In 1872 a station was begun at Ayuthia. Rev. Messrs. Carrington and Arthur, with their families, lived there a short time. Six confessed conversion and received baptism, but no church has been organized. There were several more natives baptized at a later date. The work is now left to the care of two native helpers, but it is very discouraging, and should be either abandoned or reinforced. The Siamese are not yet ready for aggressive work alone. They need foreign leaders.

Petchaburee "was first visited by Rev. Mr. Buell in 1843, when the governor treated him and his companion with indignity. The books and tracts they distributed were either returned by the people, or were seized and destroyed; and several who received them were arrested and would have been whipped by the governor of the province had not a Buddhist high-priest (the prince who was afterward king) been present at the time and interceded for their release." But better times were coming, and in 1861, just eighteen years after Mr. Buell's efforts for the good of the people were rejected, at the urgent request of the new acting governor, Petchaburee was selected as a station, and his friendly aid rendered then and afterward did much to make the missionaries comfortable. Drs. McFarland and McGilvary came, with a knowledge of the language, from Bangkok in June, and began at once to preach and teach. In 1863 a church was organized and three converts received. Since then the work has gone on, not without vicissitudes and discouragements, it is true, and yet to-day the Petchaburee church is the largest one in the kingdom. When I came in 1874 it numbered less than 20 communicants; now there are nearly 200 and over 50 baptized children, and the whole number of members since the beginning is 319. A colony left the parent church several years ago and were organized at Bangkaboon in 1878; and since then another colony has begun a new, separate life as a church at Paktalay, and still others at Baulam and Ta Rua. The training of native ministers began at this station; six have been educated for that work, and three more are now under instruction. Where there are no colleges and no theological seminaries, such work demands a great deal of care and labor from the one or two missionaries at the station, who have everything else to attend to as well.

The province of Petchaburee presents a wide and inviting field. Besides the city proper, said to contain about twenty thousand people, there are many outlying villages among the farms and along the sea-coast. From thirteen of these villages no less than 30 converts were baptized in 1883, and the whole number added to the church during the year was 69. A new chapel has been finished at Paktalay, a fishing village on the coast, and besides 20 converts almost the whole village have pronounced in favor of Christianity.

At Bangchan there are quite a number of members, and a new chapel has been built, and our people are giving money now to help the Christians at Ta Rua to secure a chapel. Collections are taken up at all these out-stations whenever services are held, and our pastor, Mr. Dunlap, is trying to teach all to abound in the grace of giving; these converts already give more in proportion than church members at home.

Two important factors of the work in Petchaburee are the numerous schools and the hospital, but of both of these I will speak in subsequent chapters. The following is as complete a list as I have been able to make of all the Protestant missionaries who have ever labored in Siam to date, 1885.

LIST OF PROTESTANT MISSIONARIES TO DATE.

PRESBYTERIAN MISSIONARIES, SIAM.	CAME.	LEFT.
Anderson, Miss Arabella..	1872	1876
Arthur, Rev. R.	1871	1873
Arthur, Mrs. R.	1871	1873
Buell, Rev. Wm. P.	1840	1844
Buell, Mrs. Wm. P.	1840	1844
Bush, Rev. Stephen	1849	1853
Bush, Mrs. Stephen	1849	1851
Carden, Rev. Patrick L.	1866	1868
Carden, Mrs. Patrick L.	1866	1868
Carrington, Rev. John.	1869	1875
Carrington, Mrs. John.	1869	1875
Coffman, Miss S. M	1874	1882
Cort, Miss M. L.	1874	
Culbertson, Rev. J. N.	1871	1881
Culbertson, Mrs. J. N. (Miss B. Caldwell)	1878	1881
Cross, Mr. S. (Layman)	1883	1884
Cross, Mrs. S. (Miss L. Linnelle)	1882	1884
Dickey, Miss E. S.	1871	1873
Dunlap, Rev. Eugene P.	1875	
Dunlap, Mrs. Eugene P.	1875	
George, Rev. S. C.	1862	1873
George, Mrs. S. C.	1862	1873
Grimstead, Miss Susie D.	1874	1877
House, Rev. S. R., M.D.	1847	1876
House, Mrs. S. R.	1856	1876
Hartwell, Miss Mary E.	1879	1884
McCauley, Rev. J. M.	1878	1880
McCauley, Mrs. J. M. (Miss Jennie Kerser)	1878	1880
McClelland, Rev. C. S.	1880	1882
McClelland, Mrs. C. S.	1880	1882

	Came.	Left.
McFarland, Rev. S. G., D.D.	1860	1878
McFarland, Mrs. S. G.	1860	1878
McDonald, Rev. Noah A., D.D.	1860	
McDonald, Mrs. Noah A.	1860	
McDonald, Miss H. H.	1879	1882
McDonald, Miss M. H.	1879	
MacLaren, Rev. C. David*	1882	1883
MacLaren, Mrs. C. David.	1882	
Mattoon, Rev. S.	1847	1866
Mattoon, Mrs. S.*	1847	1866
Morse, Rev. Andrew B.	1856	1858
Morse, Mrs. Andrew B.	1856	1858
Neilson, Miss Jennie	1884	
Odell, Mrs. J. F.*	1863	1864
Olmstead, Miss Laura A.	1880	
Sturge, Ernest A., M.D.	1880	1885
Sturge, Mrs. Ernest A. (Mrs. Turner)	1881	1885
Vandyke, Rev. J. W.	1869	
Vandyke, Mrs. J. W.	1869	1880
Wachter, Rev.	1884	
PRESBYTERIAN LAOS MISSION.		
Cheek, Marion A., M.D.	1875	
Cheek, Mrs. Marion A. (Miss S. B. Bradley)	1875	
Campbell, Miss M. M.*	1879	1881
Cole, Miss Edna S.	1879	
Griffin, Miss Isabella	1882	
Hearst, Rev. John P.	1882	1883
Hearst, Mrs. John P.	1882	1883
McGilvary, Rev. Daniel, D.D.	1858	
McGilvary, Mrs. Daniel	1860	
Martin, Rev. Chalmers.	1883	
Martin, Mrs. Chalmers.	1883	
Peoples, Rev. Samuel, M.D.	1882	
Peoples, Mrs. Samuel (Miss Sadie Wirt)	1882	
Vrooman, C. W., M.D.*	1871	1873
Wilson, Rev. Jonathan	1858	
Wilson, Mrs. Maria*	1858	1860
Wilson, Mrs. Kate*	1866	1875
Warner, Miss Antoinette	1882	
Wishard, Miss Florence	1882	1883
Westervelt, Miss Lizzie	1884	
BAPTIST MISSIONARIES, SIAM.		
Ashmore, Rev. Wm., D.D.	1857	
Ashmore, Mrs. Martha*	1857	
Chandler, Mr. J. H. (lay missionary)	1843	1871
Chandler, Mrs. J. H.	1843	1871

	CAME.	LEFT.
Chilcot, Rev. Cyrus A.*	1865	1867
Dean, Rev. Wm., D.D.	1835	1884
Dean, Mrs. Wm. (Mrs. Slafter)*	1839	1881
Dean, Miss Fannie	1864	
Davenport, Rev. Robert	1836	1845
Davenport, Mrs. Robert	1836	1845
Eaton, Rev. L. A.	1882	
Fielde, Miss Adele M.	1866	1871
Goddard, Rev. Josiah.	1840	1848
Goddard, Mrs. Eliza Abbott	1840	1848
Jones, Rev. John Taylor, D.D.*	1833	1851
Jones, Mrs. Eliza Green*	1833	1838
Jones, Mrs. Judith Leavitt*	1841	
Jones, Mrs. Sarah Sleeper	1847	
Jenks, Rev. Erastus N.	1846	1848
Jenks, Mrs. Erastus N.	1846	1848
Lion, Rev. Wm.	1867	
Lion, Mrs. Wm.	1867	
Morse, Miss Harriet.	1848	
Partridge, Rev. S. B.	1869	
Partridge, Mrs. S. B.	1869	
Reid, Rev. Alanson*	1835	1837
Reid, Mrs. Alanson.	1835	
Slafter, Rev. Cowdon*	1839	1841
Slafter, Mrs. Cowdon* (afterward Mrs. Dean)	1839	1882
Smith, Rev. S. J.	1849	
Telford, Rev. Robert	1854	1863
Telford, Mrs. Robert	1854	1863
MISSIONARIES OF OTHER BOARDS AND SOCIETIES.		
Abeel, Rev. David, M.D.	1831	1832
Bradley, Rev. D. B., M.D.*	1835	1873
Bradley, Mrs. E. B.*	1835	1845
Bradley, Mrs. S. B.	1850	
Bradley, Rev. Cornelius.	1871	1874
Bradley, Mrs. Cornelius.	1871	1874
Benham, Rev. N. S.*	1840	1840
Benham, Mrs. N. S.	1840	1840
Caswell, Rev. Jesse.	1840	1848
Caswell, Mrs. Jesse.	1840	1849
French, Rev.*	1840	1842
French, Mrs.	1840	1843
Gutzlaff, Rev. Karl, M.D.	1828	1831
Gutzlaff, Mrs. Karl (Miss Newell)*	1830	1831
Hemmenway, Rev. Asa.	1840	1849
Hemmenway, Mrs. Asa.	1840	1849
Johnson, Rev. Stephen.	1834	1846
Johnson, Mrs. Stephen.	1834	1846

	Came.	Left.
Lane, Rev. L. B., M.D.	1850	1855
Lane, Mrs. L. B.	1850	1855
Lisle, Rev. Wm.*		1839
Lisle, Mrs. Wm.		
Peet, Rev. L. B.	1840	1846
Peet, Mrs. L. B.	1840	1846
Pierce, Miss M. E.*	1840	1844
Robinson, Rev. Charles.	1834	1845
Robinson, Mrs. Charles.	1834	1845
Robins, Rev. Mr.	1838	1839
Robins, Mrs.	1838	1839
Silsby, Prof. J.	1850	1854
Silsby, Mrs. J.	1850	1854
Tomlin, Rev. Jacob.	1828	1831
Tracy, Rev. Stephen, M.D.	1838	1839
Tracy, Mrs. Stephen	1838	1839

CHAPTER XXXIV.

OUR SCHOOLS IN SIAM.

ALTHOUGH some may teach that "ignorance is the mother of devotion," it is not the mother of Christianity, nor of any religion that will save the soul. Education has always been a pet scheme of the Presbyterian Church, and wherever you find such an organization, you will find that schools are planted and fostered, and the wiser her people become the better Christians they are.

The missionaries had only been in Bangkok a few years when they tried to gather children into a school. Their first efforts resulted in securing six little boys and girls who were willing to be taught. In 1852 the present Boys' School was opened at Sumray, as the lower compound at Bangkok is called. They receive both boarding and day pupils, and afford them the advantages of a common school education. English is a prominent feature, and is the inducement which secures most of the pupils. They desire to gain sufficient knowledge of that language to enable them to secure positions as clerks or servants among the foreigners of the capital. They try to learn English, but nothing else, unless compelled. Some 300 boys have been taught in this school during the thirty years of its existence. Let us hope that all have had their faith in Buddhism shaken. Some have been converted, and have since occupied positions of trust and usefulness. Two are now in the ministry, and one is a teacher in the school. He has lately translated "Peep of Day" into Siamese, and he did it very well, too. A former pupil and teacher translated

"Pilgrim's Progress" years ago, and a new illustrated edition will soon appear fresh from the press.

In the *Foreign Missionary* for May, 1883, is an engraving, and an interesting account of a former pupil of this Boys' School, now an attaché of the Siamese Embassy which we hope will visit America. He sent his photograph recently from London to Dr. S. R. House, with a letter in which he says:

> "I suppose Dr. House will be much surprised at receiving this from one of his old pupils, who has long been under his tuition and care in Siam through his benevolence. I promise myself much pleasure at meeting my old teacher. May our Lord spare us that we may see each other again in this world. God giveth and taketh away everything. The position I am holding is His gift; I am quite firm and confident in Him. I cannot inform you now of the certain time of our arrival in America. No doubt we shall all be pleased, and enjoy very much in coming to the beautiful country that we have never seen before."

He then speaks of the great changes and improvements going on in Siam; names two of his old fellow-pupils in the mission-school who are now employés in the telegraph department of the Government, and another who is the surgeon of the same regiment in which he is captain. The writer of this letter was placed by his father, a native goldsmith of Bangkok, in the Boys' Boarding-School of that city, in the year 1865, when a lad of thirteen. Of amiable disposition, good mind, and pleasing manners, he always had the love of his teachers. In his sixteenth year he became convinced of his duty to acknowledge the Saviour he had learned to love and trust, and with a young schoolmate, now an elder in the First Church at Bangkok, he was baptized by Dr. House, November, 1867. After being connected with the school four or five years, he left it, and was variously employed. While a clerk in the Government custom-house he married a native Christian girl. He has, of late, been an officer in the Siamese regular army, and was appointed attaché to the Siamese Embassy commissioned by His Majesty to visit the various courts and capitals of Europe and America.

The school was never more prosperous than when under the care of Rev. J. M. McCauley and wife, now of Tokio, Japan. They were both earnest, experienced teachers, and loved their work, and they were anxious to increase the attendance and elevate the standard of education. Mr. McCauley's continued ill-health compelled him to leave Siam, but he has found unwonted strength and a wide field of usefulness in the Tokio Union College.

The Bangkok school has suffered many vicissitudes and a constant change of teachers. We hope the time will come when this school shall have developed into a college, with a faculty of experienced teachers, who will have time to devote to its best interests.

The Girls' Boarding-School of Bangkok was opened in 1873 by Mrs. Dr. House and Miss Anderson. They hoped to secure the attendance of daughters from the families of princes and nobles; but although a few of this class came in the earlier years of the school, of late no children of rank have been enrolled. When we think of the indifference of the Siamese to the education of girls, we rejoice over the success of this school. During the eleven years of its existence seventy-two pupils have been admitted. Of this number perhaps twenty-five have remained three years, and ten four years. Only five have been entered for five years, and two for a longer period, neither of which, however, remained over five years. Very few leave before their term of contract expires, but the majority of them only engage to stay three years. Of the seventy-two enrolled, eighteen were day pupils. Of the whole number, fifteen have been converted, ten have already married, and three have gone to live with foreigners.

It is a wonderful advantage to secure pupils for a term of years, and have them under your constant and direct influence. No attempt is made at a thorough education, as many of these girls do not even know the alphabet when admitted, and three or even five years is far too short a time in which to produce a finished scholar. They are taught to read and write their own language, and English if desired, and the simpler branches of a common education. They spend an hour and a half each day in sewing and fancy-work. They learn to make their own clothes, to wash and iron, and to cook native food. They are taught quiet, womanly habits, and to keep their apartments neat and clean. Siamese girls reach maturity, and are usually married so young, that at present there is but one student in this school over fifteen years of age. A few of the pupils pay their board at $1.80 per month, and there is a small income from the sale of fancy articles. In 1882, during the Bangkok Centennial Exposition, the teachers and pupils of this school were permitted to place their goods on exhibition in one of the queen's apartments in the grand hall. They attracted the attention of the king, who purchased the whole display, and afterward presented the school a silver medal. During the same exhibition I saw in one of the king's rooms a beautiful silk quilt, which the school, while still under the superintendence of Mrs. Dr. House, presented to His Majesty on one of the royal birthdays.

Special provision is made for the education of destitute orphans, but children who have parents living are expected to be clothed by them, and to have at least a part of their expenses defrayed. But this is done very grudgingly by the natives. They love to think that their "merit" secures them every advantage. This poor school has in the last ten years been in charge of no less than eight different American teachers, all, except three, coming to it with new ideas and plans of work, and utter ignorance of the Siamese language. They have had the advantage, however, of the faithful and constant services of "Ma Tuan," who is an exceptional Siamese woman, and was educated and trained for her position by Mrs. House, and she has also gained something from each of that lady's successors. She has been chief teacher and matron for the school ever since it began, and interpreter between the new missionaries and the old pupils, as she understands English very well. It is through her influence that many of the pupils have been secured and retained. She is dignified and kind, and each year should add to her wisdom and usefulness. The future of this school is brighter and broader than the past. Miss Olmstead, one of the teachers, has opened two branch schools for day pupils right out among the people, to allay prejudice and finally gather the girls into the boarding department. There is no good reason why, in a city like Bangkok, the capital of this kingdom, so anxious for progress and civilization, this Girls' School should not number hundreds of pupils and scores of graduates, and as time passes parents will learn to appreciate an education enough to be willing to pay for it, thus diminishing the number of assisted pupils and bringing the school nearer self-support. At present it is sustained by contributions from American churches, which support scholarships at $30 per annum. There are thousands of girls in Bangkok, and this is the only school for them in all that idolatrous city; and when we know that women are always more conservative than men, and that old, false religions depend on them for support and propagation, we should redouble our efforts and prayers for their release from the thraldom of Buddhism.

Years ago the missionary ladies had access as teachers to the royal palaces. Maha Mongkut himself invited them to visit the women of his harem. These visits began in 1851, and it was "the first zenana teaching ever attempted in the East." A somewhat similar work was started in Hindostan six or seven years later; but during the present reign I have heard of no such visits. A few English ladies have access there, and teach their language and fancy-work. The queen takes English lessons, and annoys her teacher not a little by her determination to learn the whole of that redundant language from a translated copy of "Æsop's Fables." But we can learn of no effort being made to impart a knowledge of Christianity, the only religion which recognizes the rights and blessings of womanhood.

PETCHABUREE SCHOOLS.

Mrs. Dr. McFarland had the distinguished honor of opening the first school for girls in Siam. It was begun at Petchaburee in 1865, just eight years before the one in Bangkok. She did not despise the day of small things, for she commenced with but one pupil, a half-grown girl she had induced, by the promise of a slight reward, to leave her idle companions and try to learn to read and sew. Others watched the result, and seeing nothing serious happen to the first brave soul who ventured to take a step from ignorance toward knowledge, they followed too. They had no school-books, but were taught to read from charts prepared by the missionary's Siamese teacher, and the tracts and gospels printed for distribution. Oral instruction was given in the rudiments of arithmetic, astronomy, and geography. We still use a small outline map of Siam which Mrs. McFarland drew and colored with her own hand. That first school has continued to grow and increase. Scores have been taught to read and to sew. Nine other schools have been opened and hundreds of pupils enrolled. Nearly forty women and quite a number of boys have entered the church through the school-room door. Many of the pupils remained for several years, and scores of others a shorter time. But may not all have learned enough of Jesus to save them if they but believe in and love Him? We may meet many in heaven whom we never recognized here as God's children.

In 1878 there were already six schools and 240 pupils. That was by far the most prosperous year of the school work. The "Howard Industrial" numbered seventy-seven, and there were no less than forty-three enrolled among the Laos. But there were then three strong, well women to oversee and teach these 240. The very next year Mrs. Dr. McFarland went with her husband to open the King's School at Bangkok. Soon clouds began to gather here. They grew thicker and darker until, bursting upon our station, we and our work were deluged in storms of trial and tribulation. In the seventeenth annual report (1882) no name appeared but mine, as the schools were then left entirely to my care and teaching. Our city and province had been scourged with cholera for more than a year. Many of the old pupils fell victims, and others feared to go to the schools lest they be carried home dead, so sudden and irresistible was the power of the mighty plague. Yet we kept up five schools and a boarding department, and there were 108 pupils in all, women and children, with ages ranging from six to thirty-five years. The next year we opened two more new schools, and the others were also kept up. They were taught by seven native teachers, all of them trained in the Howard School, and these teachers, I am glad to say, are learning to be more and more efficient, patient, and persevering. There were 167 pupils, but only four of them boarders. Dr. Sturge took charge of boys who had been under our care and reported forty-seven at the end of the year. The attendance was very irregular, and until parents are more interested in the education of their children, we see no remedy for it. Those who are constant make commendable progress. The industrial class for 1883 numbered fifty-four; of these, twenty-seven received wages for their work, the highest eight cents per day, and the lowest two cents. The other twenty-seven worked for the school. There were 894 garments made and twenty patchwork quilts. The income from sales was $237. The profit was very small indeed; the idea not being to make money, but to furnish employment. The workers are neither neat nor tidy, and persist in chewing betel, and if but one drop of their blood-red saliva falls on a white garment, it can hardly be sold at all. Many garments, of course, had to be given away to the pupils who came unclothed to school. The children in the outside or district schools, also learned to sew, and made most of their own clothes, and seventeen quilts, which when finished were given as rewards to the little workers. It is a comical sight to see them on cool mornings going about the city wrapped in their patchwork quilts, like an Indian in his blanket. The native teacher in the industrial department is held responsible for all work; instructs the others in sewing; cuts and prepares the work; runs the sewing-machine; attends to a part of the buying and selling; and is paid twenty-four cents per day, but works all the time, while the others are required to spend half the day with books. Those women who have lately been employed as successful teachers in the district schools have learned all they know by this half-day method.

It is thought by some that in such a school there is danger lest the natives should think they are paid for learning to read. May not the same objection be made to free boarding-schools? In one sense ours might be called a boarding-school, but the pupils are expected and required to do some sewing for the pennies they receive for food, and then they are allowed to buy and eat what and where they please, instead of having all their food purchased and prepared for them and then invited to sit down and eat it together. While this industrial school is not all that mission workers would like, still, under existing circumstances, where all women and girls are expected to earn their own living, and we cannot induce them to enter the boarding-school, although both tuition and board are offered free, it presents the only available means we know by which their attendance upon our instructions can be secured.

It is a well-known fact that when ladies began zenana work in India, they gave their time; they gave every book needed; they gave materials for needle-work, and what was completed belonged to the worker; their attendance was even then considered a favor. But now what do we see there? India has 26,000 schools, over 80 colleges, and nearly 3,000,000 pupils. She will soon be the most enlightened of all the Eastern nations, and one gratifying feature of her education is that the women of the land are found by thousands in schools opened expressly for their benefit by the Government, and by native princes and noblemen. By their diligence and talent they are proving themselves worthy of their advantages, and in the competitive examinations, open to all who have pursued a certain course of study, both young men and women, some of the latter have taken prizes of the first rank. When the women of a country are elevated to walk side by side with their husbands and brothers in paths of usefulness and learning, then, and not till then, will the nation be truly civilized. When God so blesses the women and girls of Siam that they will be willing to go to school and study because they desire to learn; and further, when they will be ready to pay for the privilege of doing so, none will rejoice over it more than those who have always been ready and anxious to do much for hundreds more who still stand aloof from our schools in spite of every effort and inducement to have them enter. There is very little encouragement by the

Government for female education, and provincial cities cannot well go ahead of the capital, and yet the king made a generous donation toward the Girls' School Building in Petchaburee. We very much wish they would establish a Government school for girls in Bangkok, as they already have several schools for boys. Many hoped that the Memorial Building to the late queen would be devoted to the education of the young women of Siam, but as it nears completion other purposes are manifest. If through the king's sorrow and pain, and the death of the bright young queen, other women could have had the door opened before them into light and knowledge, that dark calamity would indeed have proved a "blessing in disguise."

But to return to our local work. In 1883 three pupils were graduated from one of the schools, and put in training for teachers. Several attempts have been made at teaching English, but there is no demand for it here, and the pupils take no interest in the study; but they never tire of the Bible, and their Scripture lessons are taught to them as the most important of their studies, and not merely slipped in among the rest. The pupils attend church and Sabbath-school, and lately nine of them have been baptized. Wednesday services are held at the district school-houses. Many gospels and tracts are there disposed of, and the good seed of the Word scattered far and wide. For the sake of hundreds of interested friends who have followed our work in Petchaburee for the past decade, I will here insert the names of our schools, with the number of pupils, according to the latest report: Howard Industrial, 54—the pupils were gathered from several of the other schools; Glendale, 72; Bethany, 19; Colorado, 15; Market Street, 25; Graham, 20; Hunter, 16; Dr. Sturge's Boys' Schools, 47; and since then the Hardin School has been opened with 19 pupils.

In this year of 1885 the work still goes on, ever widening

and deepening. Wherever a chapel is built in the village there is a call for a new school, and we cannot furnish teachers enough to supply the demand, but we try to be patient and look forth with hope and courage.

In 1877 a new building was erected in Petchaburee for a boarding-school and orphanage, and a refuge for homeless women and girls. As I have already said, the king gave $1,000, and some of his noblemen contributed $1,200. The structure cost about $4,500, and is large enough to furnish a home for the missionary teachers; wide, pleasant dormitories for fifty or sixty pupils; two school-rooms, and a chapel for morning and home services. As the highest number never exceeded twenty, it has not yet proved a success as a boarding-school. We can hardly persuade the natives to live in the house with us, and to sleep up-stairs. They are afraid of the night, and of evil spirits which they believe float round in the upper air, and, according to native custom, masters and teachers should always occupy the upper rooms of a house (that nothing inferior may be above their heads), while pupils and servants are kept below, and our attempts to make Western ideas prevail have not been a success. They like their own native bamboo huts best. Besides, we have never been able to find a matron like Ma Tuan of Bangkok, nor parents willing to consign their children to us for a term of years as they do there. But we can wait and hope for better days.

My faith is strong enough to see in the future a large and flourishing Girls' Boarding-School in Petchaburee. We must have it, not only for girls, but one for boys also. There is no other way to reach the children of our church members scattered abroad on farms and in fishing villages. If neglected the boys will drift into the Buddhist temple schools, and the girls grow up in ignorance.

An interesting work has sprung up among the Laos of the province. Mrs. Dr. McFarland inaugurated it. Schools have been opened and carried on with fluctuating success At present we have a few Laos girls and quite a number of boys in the boarding departments. The future will reveal better and more earnest work among this peculiarly attractive people.

Years hence new missionaries may find much to criticise in the work and methods of their predecessors; but they should not forget that laying foundations is hard work, and that until a nation is prepared for radical changes, it is much easier to criticise than to correct or improve the attempts made by those who did, not what they would, but what they could. "The life-work of a missionary at longest is so soon over; at the moment often when one seems fully trained and skillful, he is set aside and another less skillful takes up the work. Or, however serviceable the work has seemed, yet the growth of wisdom puts it all to shame, so that one is tempted to regard it as utterly useless. Improved methods of work, new ardor in the workers, and grand new successes cast a suspicion of failure on all that has preceded them. Yet the poorer work of the pioneers may have been the sufficient scaffolding, and in ways we know not of, our failures are worked into the texture of the eternal plans, which cannot fail and never falter."

I am glad to know there are many who not only have faith in mission work, but also patience to wait for its outcome. How foolish to expect every pupil in these schools of heathen to turn out well. How many of those in the schools of Christian America become what they ought to be, considering the time, toil, and money expended on them? The good seed often lies dormant in the heart for years, but it does not die. "God's word shall not return unto Him void." Hundreds have drifted through our mission-schools, of whom we now have no trace whatever—we have even forgotten their names and faces; yet we believe that each one of them had tasted of "morsels of bread which the Master had blessed and broken," and that they carried in their hearts, out into the heathen world, some germ which, if they are God's elect, He will yet quicken to His honor and glory. The missionaries believe there are thousands of secret disciples in India; there may be hundreds in Siam.

> " Where we but see the darkness of the mine,
>   God sees the diamond shine;
>   Where we can only clustering leaves behold,
>   He sees the bud they fold.
>   We only see the rude and outer strife:
>   God knows the inner life;
>   And those from whom, like Pharisees, we shrink,
>   With Christ may eat and drink."

14

CHAPTER XXXV.

MEDICAL MISSIONS.

In the third annual report of Dr. Ernest A. Sturge, of Petchaburee, he says:

"Medical mission work is as old as the Gospel dispensation. Our Saviour Himself was the first medical missionary, and the early disciples followed closely in His footsteps, holding in their divinely-joined relationship preaching and healing. Statistics prove that where these two agencies are properly combined the work is most successful."

I notice in connection with the work in South China,

—"every attempt to get hold of a new city failed until our medical missionaries first won the confidence of the people by healing, or at least relieving, cases where the skill of the native physicians would not avail." "Even while the heathen through prejudice stand aloof from the preacher, they will seek the physician more and more after he has performed some of those cures which to them seem almost supernatural."

The very earliest missionaries to Siam were also doctors of medicine, and while preaching Christ for the salvation of the soul, they practiced medicine for the healing of the body. The natives to this day call all missionaries "*Mow*," the Siamese word for doctor, and they expect to get medicines whenever they come and ask for them. Indeed, the missionaries are expected to cure, prevent, or produce all manner of impossible things. As early as 1828 Dr. Karl Gutzlaff reached Bangkok, and began to dispense medicines and to care for the sick and suffering. He was followed by Dr. David Abeel, and later by Dr. D. B. Bradley, who a few days after his arrival was taken to call upon a Siamese nobleman, who began to question him at once as to his purpose in coming to Bangkok. He also asked Dr. B. if he had any vaccine virus, and if he could cure small-pox and cholera, and amputate tumors, legs, and arms? He also expressed his sorrow that the doctor had not come a little sooner that he might have saved the life of the second king, who had recently died of cholera. About a week later he was requested in the name of the king to go immediately and try his skill on a company of slaves and captives who were sick of small-pox and cholera. On the way he was told that the king did not care much for these people, and therefore he was willing to let him experiment on them first, and if he proved skillful the great men would employ him. Dr. B. found them thickly huddled together on the damp ground under boat-sheds. They seemed quite destitute of food, and had neither nurse nor friend to care for them. Many were in the last stages of spasmodic cholera, others very low with small-pox, and some deplorably wretched with other diseases. Although the prospect was so discouraging, he ventured to prescribe for some of them. All were exceedingly anxious to obtain medicine, thinking it had power almost to restore life to the dead. The doctor returned home, thinking the king would not be likely to prize his humble talents as a physician since he stood so powerless among those dying slaves. But on the 5th of August, 1835, he opened a dispensary, and on the 22d he wrote: "The sick crowd upon me, our compound being literally filled from sunrise to sunset with wretchedly diseased bodies and priceless souls, who are as sheep without a shepherd." His work and his fame increased till he soon had from ninety to one hundred patients daily. His first surgical operation was for the removal of an ulcerated tumor, which completely covered the left eye of the patient. He felt not a little nervous about it, lest the astonished multitude who witnessed the operation should publish evil reports. It was, however, quite successful. There was a great desire among all who could read to get books; some even feigned sickness and took loathsome medicines that they might be entitled to a tract. He was one day called upon to prescribe for a Chow Phayah, a man high in authority. He had a disease in his legs of twenty years' standing. But he would only consent to have one leg treated. He said he would wait and see what the foreign doctor would do with that first. He experienced so much relief at once that the next day he gave him charge of both. In three days the patient presented the doctor with delicious fruits in token of thankfulness, and in eight days sent him word that he was well, with many thanks and a request that the doctor should attend him in future if he had need.

Dr. Bradley had the honor of introducing vaccination. It was first successful in 1840, and since then has increased in favor more and more. The people have no superstitious fear of it here as they have in India, where they say "one of their gods, Krishnu, is to become incarnate, and will have milk in his veins instead of blood, and the English, knowing this, have adopted vaccination as a mode of finding Krishnu, and when they find him will kill him."

Dr. House came to Siam in 1847 and found plenty of work, for during the first eighteen months he treated 3,117 patients; but after a few years he gave up his medical practice entirely, much to the regret of all. He, however, spent a long life, some thirty years, laboring for the spiritual welfare of the natives, and still lives to pray for their salvation.

The next physician who labored any length of time was Dr. M. A. Cheek, who from 1874 to 1883 helped battle with disease and superstition among the Laos, a people tributary to Siam. He labored under many disadvantages, having at first no hospital, assistants, or nurses. He came equipped with neither medical nor surgical outfit. He studied the language, and threw himself into the work, adapting himself as much as possible to the circumstances. Patients were treated and served on his veranda, his wife helping to distribute medicines and food, and often acting as interpreter; being a daughter of Dr. Bradley, she knew the Siamese language perfectly, and could easily adapt herself to the somewhat similar tones and expressions of the Laos. In time a bamboo hospital was put up, and the work increased year by year. He taught the natives to help him, and in 1882 he wrote:

"The last year has been one of almost ceaseless toil. The number who have received medicines directly or indirectly, is about 13,000, and applicants for medicines and advice have, in many cases, come from districts from which we had not previously had patients. Many of the princes, and others, from the city and in our immediate neighborhood, who had kept aloof from any contamination with the hated foreigner, have been compelled to seek, for themselves or their slaves, the remedy which had proved to be life-saving to so many others. Hence the foreign medicines have been more generally and more thoroughly tested than ever before, and their effects, contrasted with the native methods of combating disease—incantations, spirit worship, sacred water, with or without some rude empiricism with native herbs, the bones, teeth, and gall of various reptiles and mammals—have given them a wide recommendation.

"The Laos believe all disorders of the human body to be due directly to the influence of offended spirits; the theory is comprehensive and the method of treatment logical. Strange to say, the results are not always satisfactory. With a fidelity to their theory 'worthy of a better cause,' they attribute any want of success to some neglect in the ceremonies observed—there was not enough of them—rather than to anything defective in the system. But notwithstanding the capacity of the average Laosian for general credulity and his special readiness to accept whatever absurdity he believes to be supernatural, spirit worship in the treatment of diseases has lost some of its sanctity, and many, even of the heathen, have entirely renounced it. By breaking down these superstitions, our medical system removes a chief obstacle to Christianity.

"One singular superstition of the Laos is their belief in witchcraft. This is one of the greatest social evils, and involves more serious injury than all other beliefs and practices combined. It is a greater evil even than the vicious misrule of ignorant Laos princes. The people believe that the spirit of one person may enter another and inflict serious injuries, and even destroy life. Anything like hysteria is considered a sure indication that the patient is 'possessed.' The exorcism involves a practice full of savage cruelty to the patient, and barbarous injustice to the unfortunate neighbor who is accused of bewitching him.

"There are some discouragements connected with the medical work. First, too small a proportion of those receiving medicines really come within our reach. Friends of the sick come and describe the symptoms, and from the information obtainable in this exceedingly unsatisfactory way, a conclusion must be arrived at and a prescription made. The results of such treatment could not be very highly satisfactory, even with intelligent nursing and faithful observance of directions. The nursing of the sick among the Laos is of a kind to insure the recovery of none but the strongest. To any one acquainted with the careful and skillful nursing of a well-conducted American hospital, or the kind and loving attentions of the sick-chamber in our homes, it would seem almost impossible that any one should recover under the rough treatment practiced here. In very many cases my directions are followed with a degree of freedom which is often amusing. Besides consulting the inclinations of the patient, and the advice of neighbors and friends, and then making some kind of a compromise between these and my instructions, spirit worship is also considered an essential part of the treatment. It is almost impossible to prevent this sorcery in cases to which I attend personally in the houses of the sick, and it is highly improbable that one in a hundred neglects some spirit-offerings during illness, or 'a bribe to the spirits,' to use a literal translation of the Laos. In all these cases, of course, recovery is attributed partially to the spirits, and the results are equally unfortunate from a professional and missionary point of view.

"During last year I was requested to attend a princess, the wife of the chief, in a prolonged and dangerous illness. She recovered, and after her restoration half a month was consumed in making preparations for a thank-offering; many presents were distributed among the priests, and readings from the Buddha scriptures were attended by the princess and all her relatives for two days. Not one word of thanks was considered due to the foreign doctor. The utter absence of gratitude in the Laos heart is, I believe, conceded by all to be one of their most characteristic features.

"Notwithstanding all the discouraging aspects of the work here, and all the inconveniences of living in so isolated a place, and the inconsiderable success of the medical work, still there is much to encourage us as we look back over the history of the past year; through all these months of toil and ill-health we have been strengthened and cheered by the many promises of Him whose command is, 'Go ye into all the world and preach the Gospel to every creature.'"

At present there is no medical missionary in Bangkok. There are several foreign physicians, however, who practice for their own private interests, and one native, Dr. Tein Hee, who received his medical training in America. He acquired his earlier education at the missionary boarding-school in Bangkok, and was afterward graduated, through the kind aid of a Christian gentleman, from the medical school of the University of the City of New York. He is now in the employ of the king, and has charge of a hospital for sixty patients that was erected and given for the use of the public by a native nobleman. During the late prevalence of cholera dispensaries were opened, by order of the king, in different parts of the capital, where the sick could obtain medicines free, and I have no doubt many lives were saved. The medical work appeals strongly to the interest and sympathy of the natives, and I do not hesitate to say that a hospital in Bangkok could be supported by the contributions of the benevolent, just as the same work is maintained in Canton, China, and has been for years. Although

Bangkok is one of the healthiest of Oriental cities, a hospital is greatly needed. Indeed the city should have several of them, and there should be asylums for all classes of wretched humanity, and especially for the insane, who are now allowed to wander about as they please, or are kept in confinement at temples or private dwellings, and no attempts are ever made to cure them.

Dr. Ernest A. Sturge came to Siam in 1880, and has occupied the Petchaburee station ever since. The first year he had no hospital, and the cholera raged for months. The sick and dying were all about us, on our veranda and in our very rooms. We received them until our hands were more than full, but the terror-stricken natives were helpless and useless before the terrible scourge. We were imprudent, I acknowledge, doctor and all, and we would advise no one else to follow our example. But God kept us in safety, and verified the rich promise of deliverance "from the noisome pestilence," and we were not afraid " for the terror by night " " nor for the destruction that wasteth at noonday." Scores and hundreds all about us died, but not one of those whom we received into our house; and the majority of all who were willing to accept, and who followed Dr. Sturge's directions, recovered.

Home physicians do not sufficiently appreciate the intelligence of the sick, and their friends and nurses who do as they are told, and thus help in the restoration of every patient. All this is wanting in heathen lands, and cases are not unknown where the medicine has been rubbed on the outside and the mustard plaster eaten, or the quinine divided and half taken before the ague chill and half after.

When Dr. S. began his work the natives were afraid, and yet the first year he had over 1,300 patients. Fearing they would consider him mercenary if he charged for drugs, according to the custom already established at the station, he gave away all his medicines and had no fees; but he found that the voluntary gifts of the natives amounted to less than three dollars for the year, so willing were they to reap the benefit of their supposed merit. But now better counsels prevail, and he is even more willing to receive than they are to give. Missionaries always find in dealing with any people, that they appreciate and prize most that which costs them something. The next year he built a hospital, having received a donation for it from a relative in England. During the twelvemonth he treated 4,552 patients, and the work is constantly increasing, and the spiritual results are becoming manifest. His fame has spread abroad. Thousands of natives have been helped or cured through his care and medicines. The influence of his work has been to disarm opposition to missionary labor, and to gather many about us as friends who, but for him, might never have come near our compound.* But I will quote again from his report, as he gives a better record of his own work than I could write :

"In establishing a hospital in Petchaburee our object was not only to give bodily healing to the people, but also to bring the life-giving Gospel to many who would not otherwise be reached; to break down any opposition which might exist, and raise the company of missionaries in the estimation of the natives, who appreciate the services of a physician more than the preaching of the Gospel. Every morning, except Sabbath, directly after chapel service, the dispensary is open to all afflicted ones from eight o'clock until noon. The number who have received benefit the past year is as follows: At the dispensary—Siamese men 1,637, Siamese women 1,431; Chinese, 685; Laos, 306; Buddhist priests, 209; Hindoos, 12; Burmese, 60; surgical operations, 140; vaccinations, 78; professional visits to homes, 814; total, 5,372. Among the patients were twelve Chinamen treated for the opium habit. Of these, three have returned saying they have entirely left off the use of the deadly drug. The result of the other cases is unknown. The principal diseases were what one

---

* Texts of Scripture are printed on the prescription papers.

would expect to find in a moist, tropical climate, among a poor people, namely: malaria in its various forms, dysentery, rheumatism, and skin diseases. The surgical operations were small, and worthy of little notice. The total expense of the hospital for 1883 was 834 ticals and two salungs, equal to $500.70; sale of medicines, 130 ticals, or $78. There were thirty in-patients, of whom five confessed conversion. One of them wishes to study for the ministry. He has already been the means of bringing several of his relatives to the Saviour. Of the out-patients, two received baptism in their homes, being too ill to come to the chapel. One of these died shortly after being baptized, firmly trusting in Jesus. The other one is now much improved in health, though still unable to walk. He is doing much good in his village, Paktalay, telling others of his new-found joy. At our last communion two others received baptism who were first brought to a knowledge of the truth through benefits received at the dispensary. Tracts were given to many, and much good may have been done through their teachings."

Medical missions present a wide and inviting field to the young doctors graduating from the home schools. There is neither crowding nor lack of patients, and every man who devotes his life to such a work is sure to become famous. Who does not covet the golden opportunities well improved of such men as Dr. David Livingstone; Dr. Hepburn, of Japan; Dr. Kerr, of Canton; Dr. Van Dycke, of Beyrout; and the late Drs. Southon and Calhoun, and a host of others, noble men, whose records are in heaven and on earth!

CHAPTER XXXVI.

LIFE ON THE COMPOUND.

A "MISSION COMPOUND" includes all inside of the enclosure of the mission premises. Ours at Petchaburee covers several acres, and is very pleasantly situated on the bank of the river, and a little below the city. There are three good dwelling-houses for missionaries, large, cool, and comfortable; two of them are built of brick and have tile roofs; the other is wood, thatched with *attap*-palm leaves.

The "Petchaburee Home" is quite large, with rooms for boarding pupils and teachers, and a chapel that fronts the river, where we meet every day for morning prayers. Besides these there is the new brick hospital, a room for the industrial school, and in the back-yard there is a cluster of native houses, occupied by the families of native preachers, teachers, servants, etc. As they are directly under our care, we hope better things of them than of those who live outside. Many of them own the houses in which they live; others occupy huts belonging to us. Of course these people are not all Christians, but they are expected to abide by the rules of the compound, which are these: All must attend religious services, observe the Sabbath, be careful not to quarrel or swear, be in by nine o'clock at night, not steal from each other or from us. All who cannot read are expected to come to school until they learn. They must receive and lodge no strangers without permission, and they must not gather the fruit or flowers in our gardens, or hang about our kitchens, or borrow utensils from the cook. They must not worship idols, nor engage in their heathenish rites in the compound, and all must wear clothes. This last is, I believe, the very hardest to make them do. Of all the missionaries who have ever lived here, no one has ever yet succeeded in making them obey this rule. Parents and servants are talked to, and children are switched, and yet almost every day some ebony cupid has to be sent home to be dressed. We have a watchman who is expected to patrol the premises all night and see that there are no thefts or fires. He locks all the gates at dusk except one, and that is closed at half-past nine, and should not be opened again till the next morning. There are no foreigners in the city to visit us, and the natives should have no business in or out after that time, unless they are sick and come to see the doctor. There is almost always some one sick in the compound. We try to teach them to eat regularly three times a day, but they do not try to control their appetites, and eat at all hours, and all sorts of trash, sweet and sour, ripe and unripe fruits. They usually boil rice once a day, in the morning, and then eat what is left cold. Sometimes it is not cooked enough, and it swells in the stomach, causing great distress. Then they send in great haste for the doctor, or to beg some medicine. They are just like a lot of overgrown children, and a great deal harder to manage because they think they are "big folks." Some imagine they can do as they please, so long as the missionaries do not know of it; and they become so angry at any one who tells of their misdemeanors, that many of the best cannot be induced to tell what they know even when cited as witnesses.

In some of the houses you will find an old heathen grandmother, who thinks she has a right to control everything. These poor old creatures interfere a great deal with the progress of Christianity. Their children may be converts and desire to bring up their little ones in the fear of the Lord, but the grandmother, or "*Yi*," as they call her, has the care of the children while the parents are at work, and teaches them all sorts of superstitions, and takes them with her to the heathen temple. She makes them afraid of evil spirits and fills their young minds with frightful tales. If they are sick she wants to change their names, although they have already been baptized. She ties charm-strings about them, and puts iron rings on their ankles, and ties the heads of field-beetles about their wrists. They shave the head, and leave little tufts of hair here and there as charms against the evil one. After seeing Siamese youngsters with little tufts scattered promiscuously over their heads, one can have a clearer understanding of Samson's "seven locks." These old grandmothers cling with the utmost persistency to old customs, and when we try to tell them they are hurtful, they say, "My mother raised me that way, and I have lived to be old as you see." They never mention all the brothers, and sisters, and neighbors' children who have died under the treatment, but because they did not die themselves, they contend that the old ways are best. They, too, are the most persistent advocates of "*cummin*" versus clothes. In their day babies were all besmirched with yellow powder, and this, with their gold and silver ornaments and charm-strings, was considered enough. Now, that all must wear clothes too, is in their eyes a most needless superfluity. They contend that the cummin makes the body sweet and keeps off the mosquitoes, and the idea of dress for modesty's sake is entirely beyond their comprehension. They also teach the youngsters that there is no beauty without black teeth and mouths full of betel. But nevertheless we take courage by the contrast between the parents and the grandparents, and hope the next generation will be many grades higher still. It will be impossible for the children in our mission-schools to become old folks like that class who are now fast dying out. As a rule old folks will not listen to our teachings. They say, "We are too old to change; please let us be; we cannot understand the new way of salvation, and we dare not throw away the merit we have made in all the past." For this reason there is only here and there a gray head in all the congregations.

I thank God day after day that I was not born a Siamese, and yet the Lord has thoughts of mercy and love toward them, and it is being manifested in these latter times. One wild olive-branch after another is being grafted in, and the wound in the Saviour's side is wide enough to receive them all, these heathen nations, naughty branches which ran wild in ages past. God has sent us here to gather them up, and to bring them in. The hope of Siam is its children, dear little black-eyed creatures, ready to learn in Christ's or Satan's school.

Siam is a pleasant mission field, healthful, hopeful, and perhaps as home-like as any other in the world, for no heathen land can be like America till after it is converted. Life in a heathen land is very different from what many imagine. There are, no doubt, personal suffering, privation, and exposure in some countries, but I have never seen them here. We have good houses, with wide, cool verandas. They are two stories high, and the basements are used for store-rooms, school-rooms, printing-office, and book depository, while we all live up-stairs. This is the coolest and most healthful plan. The windows are all doors, and have no glass, but shutters instead, that can be opened or closed to admit air and keep out the rain. There is no bell or knocker, for the doors stand open all day long, and the Siamese usually cough as they approach, and we expect no other visitors. We have no chimneys, for we need no fires. Our floors are covered with Chinese matting, and we have home and home-made furniture; some pictures on the walls, and portraits of the far-away father and mother and other dear ones. The kitchens are sometimes built of bamboo and set back a little from the house. We have cook-stoves from home and ordinary utensils. We do not find it incompatible with God's service to supply ourselves with some conveniences, even though we, like you, might "get along" without them. We have good food, plenty of it, and cheap, too; and clothing can be either purchased here, and made up by yourself or native tailors, or sent from home, having been prepared by the hands of loving friends. Servants are plenty and cheap—only five or six dollars a month—and they are just as good as you train them to be. Many of them are patient, faithful, and trustworthy; and if they have been with you for several years, they learn to regard your goods as theirs, and are very careful of them. Indeed, they are more careful of some things than we would be, and they can do much better marketing and buying native supplies than we can. Chickens are the cheapest meat we can eat. We often get them for six and eight cents apiece; so please do not blame missionaries for eating *chicken* salads, stews, and curries, *because they cannot afford anything else!* I must not forget to speak of the delicious rain-water we have to drink. It is caught in the rainy season and filtered into large porous jars. These jars are so large a man could actually hide in them, as in the famous story of the "Forty Thieves." Although porous, they do not seem to leak, and water stored in them keeps cool and sweet the whole year round. Filtering through sand and charcoal takes all the rain-taste away. Thus you see we have the purest, best water in the world, for it comes right down from heaven, and is more wholesome than ice-water. There are no springs, and well-water is not good.

We are so shut up among the heathen here that we must make our own little social world, so national holidays, Christmas, New-Year, birthdays, and anniversaries are not allowed to pass unnoticed. We see each other every day, and we try not to forget or leave off the old home manners and customs. We talk English for our own benefit, and to help the little children, if there are any, to learn their mother tongue. We must strive against the native influence, and do all we can to lift the people up to the Gospel standard. Now and then we take a holiday, and go up the river or to the mountains for a picnic, and once in the past ten years I have gone to the seashore and spent a fortnight at Anghin.

We have a semi-monthly mail bringing letters, magazines, and papers, and an occasional "box," as a proof that, though far away, we are not forgotten in the old home circle. We rise early and breakfast, then the morning bell rings for prayers at half-past seven. At eight work begins. Mr. Dunlap is off teaching or preaching, or has his class of theological students at his study. Dr. Sturge goes to his hospital and receives patients, dispensing medicines, kind words, and good books. The ladies take charge of the schools. Some are on the compound, and others in the city must be visited.

It is a glorious thing, this freedom which lets us do all the good we can, and in so many places. Single ladies are a great wonder to their heathen sisters, and they are often asked, "Is it true that you have no master, and that you can go and come and do as you please?" They are bought and sold and held in cruel bondage, and the way the loving husband exacts obedience from his wives is by threatening to sell them. It is the old, old story, of man oppressing woman, that has been enacted in every land under the sun, and would still be the same for us had not Christ the Saviour of women appeared with His blessed Bible and the golden rule. We never can pay that lowly Nazarene the debt we owe.

The work of mission ladies is varied, and consists in teaching schools, conducting Bible and prayer meetings, visiting from house to house, translating and distributing books, teaching the Christian women how to take care of themselves, their families, and homes; caring for the sick, the dying, and the dead; comforting the sorrowing and cherishing little orphans; settling quarrels; teaching the people to work and sew, and to make and wear clothes—this last one of the most difficult branches we ever attempted; touring among distant villages, and going from house to house begging for pupils, and explaining our work and good intentions. Last, but by no means least, "keeping up an interest" in home societies and bands by writing innumerable letters, and collecting and sending curiosities. It is a blessed work, and we enjoy it all as done for Christ.

The natives often ask permission to have their weddings in our houses. Then they bring in fresh flowers and green branches, and make everything bright and beautiful. Even wedding presents are not wanting, for their friends "help them," as they call it, by bringing useful things with which to set up housekeeping. They furnish their own refreshments, and pass the tea and cakes with evident enjoyment. Of course the ceremony is performed by the pastor, who sometimes adds a little lecture on the duties of married life to these ignorant ones who know so little of what is right and proper. Sometimes there are funerals, and we must always take charge of them. The converts cannot bury with Buddhist customs, and they know no others. We have a little chapel and a quiet churchyard about half a mile from the compound, and there all our dead are buried. Although this station has been occupied for nearly a quarter of a century, there are no foreign graves among them.

We travel mostly by boat, but the "house boats" are very comfortable. Overland journeys are performed on elephants, or, if not too long, with horses or ox-carts. At this station we never use elephants, but have boats, horses, wagons, and jinrikishas, and hire ox-carts when needed.

We have also a good cloth tent as a very comfortable part of our camping outfit. With these we often go to the surrounding villages, and visit and teach the country people. Quite a number of them, however, come to church here, walking from two to ten miles and back again the same day. When we celebrate the Lord's Supper they call it the "Great Sabbath," and all try to be present. Extra chairs and benches are carried into the chapel, and every place is filled. These are always glad and happy days to the missionary when he sees the "work of the Lord prospering in his hands." When things go smoothly, and all labor together for the glory of God, it is a pleasure to be with them, and we feel that a blessing follows us day by day. But when there are murmurings and divisions—when those who should be an example of good bring reproach upon the name of Christ—the clouds darken and the burden grows almost too heavy to be borne. But somehow grace and strength have always been sufficient, and hope and courage never fail. Among our saddest days are those when loved workers leave us in search of lost health, and the brightest are when we welcome new helpers to our little band.

A mission compound soon becomes a resort for all in sorrow or distress. They want refuge and a helper. They offer themselves and their families and a life-long service, if we will *only pay their debts and release them from their masters and the payment of the Government taxes!* They see us living here without earning any money in their way of working, and so they imagine we have an inexhaustible treasury somewhere, and that we should draw from it for every one's needs. During the day, when the gates are open, peddlers of all kinds drift in, and beggars singing their songs and rattling bones and cymbals as an accompaniment; the sick and wounded, widows and orphans, and visitors from the lowliest to the loftiest. Some are earnest inquirers after truth, others but idle curiosity-seekers who wish to see for themselves who and what the "farangs" (foreigners) are, and what they have in their houses. Others will come to purchase clothing that has been made by the pupils in the industrial school, and we have seen many a one pass out with a new coat having a copy of the Gospel in its pocket.

Several times have the people of the province thrown written papers full of complaints into our yard, begging that we take their part against the cruel oppression of Government officers. The governor and lieutenant-governor often come followed by trains of servants. When the king came to Petchaburee on a visit, his princes and nobles filled our yard and houses day after day. I suppose that nearly every one came to our compound then except the king himself. The "mission compound" is truly a centre of attraction in all this region, and that man or woman who has never been here or does not know some of the missionaries, is looked upon as very ignorant by his fellow-natives.

We are isolated and alone, nearly one hundred miles from Bangkok, and we seldom see a white face that does not belong to our own number, yet we live in a little world of our own, and the light we have kindled shines farther and wider each year, and round about us circle influences that will reach to eternity!

CHAPTER XXXVII.

THE PRESS.

The preparation of a Christian literature in a language all the people can understand, is one of the most practical ways of attacking a heathen nation. Although quite a cargo of such ammunition entered Siam with the first missionaries, the books were nearly all Chinese. They were scattered broadcast, however, and were the first seed-sowing, and a foretaste of what was to follow. The Press, when properly used, is a great power for good, and the presses of Bangkok, until of late years, have issued little but what was for the uplifting of the Siamese.

Nearly all the men and boys of Siam can read, and a few of the women, and by means of books knowledge may be scattered over the kingdom which could not possibly be disseminated in any other way. These good books are splendid preachers, and natives are constantly coming for baptism who trace their interest to the reading of this or that book.

Those earnest and patient harbingers of civilization, the Protestant missionaries, first introduced the printing-press into Siam. It was established in Bangkok in 1836. Previous to that time some 20,000 volumes of Chinese books had been distributed. In Siamese much less had been done, because tracts could not be obtained and the Bible was not yet translated. Before Dr. Bradley's arrival only one small tract and the first four or five chapters of St. John's gospel had been printed and circulated in Siamese. How strange to learn of sending out a few leaves of the Bible at a time.

While Dr. B. was in Singapore on his way to this land, 700 copies of St. Luke, translated by Dr. Gutzlaff, were printed there, and Dr. Bradley brought them with him to Bangkok. Soon after, Dr. Jones had his translation of St. Matthew, and some 2,000 copies of a small tract, printed in Singapore also. Dr. Bradley had the honor of printing, with the assistance of Mr. Davenport, the first tract in Siam. He soon had three others ready, but no printer. Workmen were soon found, however, for by 1844 we read of an English newspaper in Bangkok, and that the "Life of Christ," translated by Dr. Bradley, had already reached its third edition, and that the whole number of copies, 6,000, were given away to Siamese readers. Portions of the Bible, as soon as translated, were published and bound up in separate volumes, and so distributed. The whole Bible is now finished, and they have even attempted a sort of revision of the New Testament. The new Bible is being bound in three volumes—the Old Testament in two, and the New in one; for even with the smaller type now in use one complete volume would be much too large for convenient handling, almost as large as a Webster's Unabridged Dictionary.

The expense of the publication of the Scriptures in Siamese is borne by the American Bible Society. The cost is one cent for every ten pages printed, and Dr. McDonald says the whole Bible, if properly bound, could not be sold under $3 per copy and cover the cost. No earnest attempt has ever yet been made to sell the Scriptures in Siam. The people are willing to accept it for nothing, but very few will buy it. I think I have only sold one Gospel, a copy of St. Matthew, for fifteen cents, in all the ten years of my sojourn. The Petchaburee church lately purchased eighty copies of the New Testament to distribute to her converts after their baptism.

There are at present three large printing establishments

in Bangkok, notably that of Mr. D. B. Bradley, a worthy successor to his honored father, who might well be called the Father of the Press in Siam: not because he began the work, exactly, but because he continued steadfastly for thirty-eight years, and did more than any other one man in translating, writing, printing, and distributing good books. His industry and perseverance seemed boundless, and only ended with his life. But the work he did lives after him in many valuable books and tracts yet destined to bless future Siamese generations. Quite a number of presses are employed in the Bradley office, and all seem busy. Job work is done neatly and with dispatch. There is a translating department and also a type foundry in connection with this office.

The Presbyterian Mission Press was established in 1861. It is under the care of Dr. McDonald. He has long had control of it, and has translated and revised quite a number of books. Five native printers are employed, and the annual expense of the office is about $1,000. They do not seek for work, but do a few odd jobs that may be brought to them, provided they are unobjectionable matter. This is the main depot for missionary literature. Here a new edition of the Bible has just been completed, and they are now issuing an illustrated "Pilgrim's Progress." How that sturdy old "Pilgrim" has marched through the past, and with unflagging footsteps presses into the future. I wish you could all see a Chinese copy, with Celestial illustrations! "Stories of Jesus," by M. L. Cort, is among the latest Siamese books; a "History of the United States," by Mrs. Dr. McFarland, is now in press; a Theology, by Dr. McFarland, and a Physiology, by Dr. Sturge, are in process of preparation. The earlier missionaries have nearly all helped at the translation of the Bible.

The following is a partial list of books written, translated, and published in Siam: "Hints to the Wise,"

"Golden Balance," and others, by Dr. Jones. "Life of Christ," "Old Testament History," and many others, by Dr. Bradley. Vocabulary of Siamese and English, "Church History," "Confession of Faith," "Shorter Catechism," "Evidences of Christianity," "Siamese Hymnal," and four Sermons, by Dr. McFarland. Bible Lessons, Second Reader, and U. S. History, by Mrs. Dr. McFarland. "Stand by the Truth," "Questions on New Testament History," and "Child's Catechism," by Dr. and Mrs. House. Astronomy, Philosophy, Quantitative Analysis, Photography, and Medicine, by Dr. McDonald. Arithmetic, 2 vols.; Geography with maps, Philosophy, First Reader, The Atmosphere, and two Sermons, by Rev. J. W. Vandyke. "Bible Blessings," by Miss Anderson; "Way to Heaven," a tract, by Miss S. M. Coffman; "Soul's Cry, and God's Answer," a tract, translated by M. L. Cort; also, "Stories of Jesus," by the same. Of the following I do not know the authors' names, but they were all prepared by the earlier missionaries: "Killing Animals," "Counterfeit Money," "Catechism on Prayer," "Patty Parsons," "Ride on the Calf," "Faith and Practice," "Creator and Saviour," "Child's Book of the Soul," "Truth Made Simple," etc. Kru Noa, a native teacher of Bangkok, translated "Pilgrim's Progress"; Kru Poom, the "Peep of Day"; Mr. Mah, a native Christian, wrote "The Light of Europe" a poem, and "Contrasted Religions"; Kru Yuan, the native preacher at Ayuthia, wrote "The Gospel Gate," and "Proofs of Christianity"; and Kru Phoon, of Petchaburee, is writing the Life of Christ in blank verse. Of the foregoing list, the Geography, Arithmetic (part first), Bible Lessons, First Reader, and Hymnal were all printed at Petchaburee on a private press, besides various tracts.

The Roman Catholic Bishop Pallegoix had a splendid Siamese Dictionary published in Paris years ago, and that Church has prepared some books, both in the Romanized and genuine Siamese text, which they print on their press in Bangkok; also books for their various schools.

The present king has a Royal Press, and there are several others among the Siamese, but they are very quiet, and we see and hear little of their productions beyond a few school books and Buddhist volumes for the priests. The Siamese are not a literary people, and until they invent a new system of writing, which is now as slow as making English printed letters by hand, they cannot expect to produce daily enough copy to make even one good-sized newspaper. The monks in the monasteries have unlimited leisure, but they are also afflicted with unlimited indolence, and they even allow poor, persevering women to make merit by writing their sacred books for them. The late king, Maha Mongkut, while a priest, had a printing-press at his temple, and he knew how to use it too. We hear nothing of the present ruler's literary attainments, and whether he writes at all or not I cannot tell. His public addresses and state speeches read very well.

CHAPTER XXXVIII.

LAOS, THE NORTH-LAND.

The Siamese call the Laos provinces "Muang Lao," or "Muang Nuah," the latter appellation meaning the "North-Land." The extent of territory covered by the Laos provinces is supposed to be one-half as great as Siam, and the population as dense. If so, we find a country almost as large as Italy, and containing from four to five millions of people. It is an inland country, and only reached from the south by small boats or elephants. The territory is divided into states, which a long time ago were independent kingdoms, each one having its own chief or king. Their very independence proved their weakness. If they had been united their combined resistance might have repulsed the frequent invasions of Siam, Burmah, and Pegu, to which kingdoms the Laos states became, time and again, wholly or in part a prey. This state of affairs continued until the beginning of the present Siamese dynasty, something over a century ago, when five of the states lying north of Siam became tributary to this kingdom. According to Dr. Cheek, these five states measure 220 miles north and south and some 420 east and west, and sustain a population of 2,000,000. Although bound in a common interest to Siam, they have a certain independence of each other even yet; but their kings must now come to Bangkok to be invested with regal titles and to receive their kingdom.

Many of the Laosians speak the Siamese language, and nearly all the princes and nobles can read it. Even a Laosian princess, Ooboonla Wannah, is a subscriber for one of the Bangkok papers. They have a written language of their own, and some books, original and translated. The first Laos tracts were distributed in 1861. They must have been written, as I have never yet heard of any printing having been done in that language. It is true the missionaries there have a press and a good font of type brought from the United States, but the force has been so small that no one could be spared from the regular ministering to the religious needs of the people to attend to printing. A portion of the Bible has been translated, and we hope it will soon be completed and given to the natives. At present there is an earnest desire on the part of the Siamese rulers to have their language prevail among the Laos, and the latter are eager also to learn it. Thus the Scriptures in Siamese can be used to good effect; yet the vast majority of the people will not get the Siamese soon enough nor well enough to depend on this Bible for their enlightenment. They should by all means have one of their own, as the best way to reach the heart of any nation is through their mother tongue.

At the Centennial in 1882 I had the pleasure of meeting the king of the Laos and his courtiers, who had come to honor the king and to place their contributions among the many strange and wonderful things in the Exposition building. The Laos department made no mean display. In the Royal Museum at Bangkok I have also seen a beautiful ivory "howdah," or elephant saddle, richly carved and inlaid, which was presented by one of the kings of Laos to the ruler of Siam. When the king came from the "North-Land" he had a fleet of forty boats, and they anchored under the shadow of Wat Chang. These Laos boats are very pretty as well as curious. Some were painted in blue and gold, and others were decorated with white elephants, but all had the stern finished like a fish-tail reared high in air.

Quite a number of the Laos states belong to Burmah, and it is said there are no less than thirty-seven Shan, or Laos princes, under the jurisdiction of King Thebaw.

Of those states tributary to Siam, that of Cheung Mai seems to be the most important, and its king, residing in his capital of the same name, makes a triennial visit to the King of Siam as his Suzerain, bringing with him the usual tribute of a gold tree, a silver tree, a gold chain, and finger-rings richly set with gems. I have seen several of these trees. They are quite beautiful, and if they were solid gold and silver, and the jewels all true gems, they would be quite valuable. The trees are seven or eight feet high. The trunk is a tin cylinder heavily plated, and the branches are made of copper wire also covered with the precious metals. The leaves and petals of the flowers are pure gold and silver, very beautiful, and so delicately wrought as to show the ribs and veins as in the natural plant. They are miniature and graceful imitations of the clove-tree found in great abundance in Laos.

Very few Europeans have ever penetrated this North-Land, and for what information we have been able to gather, we are indebted to the hasty notes or observations of stray travellers, and the journals and letters of missionaries who have occupied Cheung Mai as a station since 1867. At that time the missionaries were eighty-nine days accomplishing the journey from Bangkok by boat. The time may be shortened by taking elephants from Rahang to Cheung Mai. But if there was a railway direct from Bangkok, by making twenty miles an hour, in twenty-four hours after bidding Bangkok friends "good-bye," one could be shaking hands with, and receiving a cordial welcome from, others in the Laos capital. None would rejoice more over this apparent annihilation of space than those isolated workers who are now laboring for Christ in the very "ends of the earth."

All who have seen this beautiful land are enthusiastic in their descriptions of its natural scenery; its elevated plains, palm-dotted and covered with rice-fields, and widening off into jungles of bamboo and valuable teak forests; its mountains, rivers, streams, and cascades; its caves and rapids. No less than thirty-five of the latter have to be crossed in the ascent of the river between Rahang and Cheung Mai. Often the boats have to be emptied of their cargo and hauled over these rapids by ropes, and in descending they must also be let down gently by ropes to prevent their being broken on the rocks or swamped in the waves. The river is very winding and in places deep and rapid, and has an ever-changing channel, caused by the rapid current and constant destruction and formation of sand-bars. The pleasantest season and the best time to make the up-river journey is during the winter months. There is no danger of being frozen in, for one voyager records that in February the thermometer was as low as 48° Fahrenheit! If one has a good Laos boat, large and comfortable, an abundant and varied supply of food, pleasant company, some books, and plenty of time, the trip is really enjoyable. If the gentlemen of the party are hunters, they can keep the table supplied with game, such as venison, mountain goat, and wild boar. There are also wild ducks and turkeys, and other birds less rare and delicate. A tiger or two may also be shot at, at least, if not taken; but if the latter, there is great satisfaction in having killed so ferocious a beast and being able to trample his skin under your feet, where as a beautiful rug it will serve you for years. On the way you pass many villages, and a few cities of more or less importance. "Kumpang Pet," or Diamond Wall, is an old decayed city, and the inhabitants, like most of the Siamese further south, are not very enterprising. The large teak forests are worked principally by Burmans of Rangoon or Maulmain.

Not many hours from Kumpang Pet are the ruins of a large Buddhist temple, said by the natives to have been built about four centuries ago, when the city was the capital of an independent kingdom. A traveller who visited the site says: "The space occupied by the ruins of this temple prove the great dimensions of the ancient monument; whilst its construction of enormous blocks of dark red sandstone testifies to its antiquity." Further up the river is Rahang, the most important city of Northern Siam. Here the river is some four hundred feet wide, and divided into many channels made by little islands which are no doubt overflowed at high water.

Carl Bock, a Danish traveller, strongly advocates a railway between Bangkok and Rahang. The distance between the two points would be only fifteen hours, while by boat even the most energetic foreigners require twelve days for the three hundred miles. Rahang is the seat of considerable trade. Here also the teak forests are actively worked by British Burmans. This appears to be the most profitable business. Over six hundred elephants, valued at from $225 to $900 each, are employed in carrying wood to the river. The district also exports a great quantity of sapan-wood, cut into small blocks, and has an active trade in gum, hides, rice, and wax. In the markets or bazaars may be found cloth of English and German manufacture, colored pictures, iron and earthen ware, and other imported articles. A few miles north of here the lordly Chow Payah, or Manam, as the river at Bangkok is usually called, changes its name and becomes the Maping. Rahang is a flourishing town of some ten or fifteen thousand inhabitants. Its forests of precious woods are a great source of wealth, and the soil of the surrounding country is extremely fertile, but as yet vast tracts are left uncultivated. Wayfarers bound for the north, who are in haste to reach their destination, here leave their boats and baggage to go by river, while they take elephants and guides, and strike out through the jungles and forests. The jungle grass is often ten or fifteen feet high, so that the traveller perched in his howdah on the elephant's back can just look out over its waving masses. In some places the elephant trail from Rahang is strewn with enormous blocks of granite, of which valuable stone I do not hear that the natives make any use. The cultivated lands produce great quantities of rice and tobacco. Between the plains the country is rough and hilly.

"At last we arrived," says C. B., "on an immense plateau containing many villages, the inhabitants of which are chiefly engaged in rearing cattle. Everywhere large farms were to be seen with thousands of cattle and buffalo. They are employed as beasts of burden by those who cannot afford elephants. They are also exported in large droves to British Burmah. I met one dealer conducting a herd of over one hundred buffalo for sale to Maulmain.

"This district produces large quantities of excellent cotton, which is sold principally to merchants of Yunnan. Sticlac and gum (dammar) are found in the neighboring woods, and also exported. Two days later I arrived at Lakon, a Laos town of nearly fifteen thousand inhabitants, surrounded by the usual wall, some six feet thick, built of small bricks."*

A former traveller says:

"It is a fine country for some distance before reaching the city. The houses are comparatively neat and comfortable. We noticed here, for the first time, a curious custom of stacking the rice in the forks of the trees until ready to be threshed. Here also we first met several long droves of oxen in single file, their burdens being carried in double baskets placed like a pair of saddle-bags across their backs. The leader, or foremost ox, always has a mask fancifully made of shells to cover the whole face, and a large peacock's tail extending up from it between the horns, and waving rather comically and gracefully over the

---

* Dr. and Mrs. Peoples have gone this year (1885) to occupy Lakon as a mission station.

back. Everything that is not carried on elephants is borne by oxen, in these baskets, all over the Laos country. Thousands of them are to be seen daily in Cheung Mai. Often most of the drove have little bells, similar to sleigh-bells, fastened all over them, which jingle merrily and add not a little to the life of the place."

Lakon is noted as a great market for elephants; the natives say there are over a thousand in the place, most of them having been caught by the Karens in the mountains. These same mountains have rich mines of iron, lead, and copper ore.

The last city before reaching Cheung Mai is Lampoon. It is not on the river, but several hours' walk inland. There is, however, a large creek by which boats can reach it at high water. There is nothing peculiar about the city, except that its wall is circular instead of the usual square. It has a fine market, and a royal temple, with a tall, glittering spire. The people are all Buddhists and devil-worshippers. Rice-fields are on every side, extending in some places as far as the eye can see, and they succeed each other until you reach the very gates of the royal city of Cheung Mai. It is interesting to translate some of these foreign names—Cheung Mai, for instance: *Cheung*, town, burg, or ville; *Mai*, new. Thus Cheung Mai is only Newtown or Newville, as commonplace a name as one could find anywhere in America. *Cheung Rai*, Fieldburg; *Cheung Toong*, Meadowville, etc.

If one goes by boat from Rahang the journey is much longer, but the tedium of the "time-devouring river" is relieved by the grand and romantic scenery, especially among the rapids, which are nearly forty in number, and begin where the mountains come down to the river on either side. In places they form an almost perpendicular bank of solid stone, first on one side, then on the other. The beautifully veined strata are plainly visible, and laughing waterfalls, and leaping cascades, and pendant stalactites, moss-covered or fringed with ferns and vines, enhance the loveliness of the wild and enchanting scene, while the more gently sloping ascents are covered with rich foliage and graceful bamboo. Again the river rushes through a narrow rocky gorge not more than thirty or forty feet wide, but whose upright walls extend skyward at least six hundred feet, and a cascade dashing from an overhanging cliff falls on the other side of the boat. "One has an indescribable feeling of awe as he passes through that deep chasm, as if in some deserted street of an old city built by giants of a former age, but of which no trace remains." There the sun only smiles upon the waters a short time at noon, and through the other hours of daylight there is a sense of dawn or twilight hanging over the passage. The place is called "*Peen-fa*," which means vaulting the sky. The longest rapids are nearly a mile in length. Over some of them the traveller is compelled to prepare a channel for his boat by gathering out the stones, and building a dam back of the boat, and then dragging the boat till the water is so shallow that another dam is necessary, and so little by little they overcome every obstacle, and at last find smoother sailing. Good ropes and a pulley, and some long, strong bamboo poles, with iron hooks to them, are almost indispensable. The long native boats, called "*Rua-Chalas*," are better than any other kind for this river, except in point of comfort, and then the wider Laos boats, with cabin accommodations, are a great improvement. The rua-chalas take but three oarsmen, and make the trip in half the time that the large Laos boats do, consequently at half the expense.

As you approach Cheung Mai you are reminded of the scenery of Petchaburee, with its river, its plains, and mountains, only the Laos mountains are more lofty and beautiful. The country is elevated and usually healthy, with a comfortable climate, and all the tropical fruits and flowers. There are iron, lead, and copper mines in her mountains, and even gold is found in her river beds, and to the north of Cheung Mai there are petroleum wells. There are numerous caves in the mountains which the natives have turned into Buddhist temples, and filled with their idols and idolatrous rubbish. A late traveller speaks of visiting *Muang Fang*, a place only resettled a twelvemonth, and the men and women were yet busy cutting down the jungle and clearing the ground where there was formerly a great city, at one time even the capital of Western Laos. All that remains of its ancient glory are the city walls, pierced and broken; a few ruins of temples, pagodas or prachadees, and thousands of bronze idols. Near Muang Fang is the famous cave "Tum Taptan." The entrance is seventy or eighty feet above the plain, while the height of the limestone mountain is perhaps three hundred feet. At the mouth of the cave bricks and plaster had been shaped to form a doorway. Above the portal are some carved figures in sandstone of "*hoalaman*," and more especially of a bird, representing a peacock, an evident sign that it had formerly belonged to the Ngious or Burmese. To the left of the door is a narrow niche, holding a broken figure of a Buddha, said to be a doctor, at whose feet the pious pilgrims laid a number of decanters, pots, and jars made of clay in the Ngiou country. The cavern itself is high and lofty, and in the middle, on an elevated platform, lay a gigantic Buddha, surrounded by smaller images, sitting and praying with uplifted hands. They were covered with yellow rags, and had caps on their heads which the priests had left in token of devotion. To the right was an altar, on which was an immense collection of idols of bronze, wood, and stone, together with a curious assortment of priests'-cloths, water-jars, rice-trays, spittoons, streamers, and tufts of hair. The travellers' servants

15*

bowed in adoration, and made offerings of wax-tapers, parched rice, and flowers; besides, a couple of gorgeously colored photographs of a Chinese man and woman brought from Bangkok. At the back of the cave, some thirty feet aloft, was an erect figure of Buddha in the act of giving blessing. Before the altar was a miscellaneous assortment of old mattresses, pillows, and mats, swarming with roaches, lizards, and other disgusting vermin. The natives say that at its source the head-waters of the lordly Chow Payah come gushing from the mouth of a cave in the Laos mountains.

There is a large pagoda in the river near Cheung Mai, and the river itself is full of life, with boats coming and going, fishers at work, etc., walking about, busy night and day with prod and basket and seine. The Laos women, too, wade through the shallow water to cultivate their little gardens upon the exposed sand-bars. They raise patches of sweet potatoes, cucumbers, and beans. They are all planted and harvested while the river is low. When the rains descend again their gardens are overflowed, and entirely disappear under torrents of rushing water; and the great water-wheels, twenty feet in diameter, turning ceaselessly and bringing the water up to the houses and fields. The natives depend on the yearly overflow of the river and on irrigation for their fields and gardens, which are very productive. The missionaries can raise nice home vegetables in the greatest abundance, and one of their dwellings has a grape-vine climbing to the roof.

Cheung Mai is a city variously estimated to contain from twenty to thirty thousand souls. A great deal depends on the number you count outside the city wall, for like most Laos cities the royal and business part of the town is surrounded by a brick wall. The streets are wide and pleasant, having double rows of trees, and streams of running water brought by an aqueduct from a mountain two or three miles distant. The houses are uniform in style and built of teak-wood and bamboo; the former are covered with burnt tiles and the latter thatched with long grass, or chaak, made from the leaves of the mangrove. They are elevated on posts several feet from the ground like Siamese dwellings, and have verandas and open courts, and usually ground room enough for a garden. Bricks are used for Buddhist temples and shrines, and are therefore held too sacred for human habitations.

For an Oriental city the walled portion of Cheung Mai is kept very neat and clean. The markets are held within the gates in the early morning, and for only a few hours at a time. Everything is carried in by women in baskets, and arranged in the most orderly manner. There are pork and chickens for sale, and fruits, vegetables, and flowers. While not trading the market-women work away on their embroidery, which is used for their clothing, pillows, and mattresses.

Occasionally one sees a few "*nantok*," the old silver coinage of the Laos, worth six rupees each; but the present medium of exchange are the bright silver rupees bearing Queen Victoria's stamp as Empress of India, together with salt! When the latter is used the article sold is usually worth its weight in salt. This commodity is so precious because the Laos are entirely shut off from the sea, and, having no salt mines, are dependent on boats, elephants, and cattle to bring the useful article to their inland markets.

A Government agent has lately been appointed to look after British interests in Cheung Mai, as the city occupies a favorable position between British Burmah and Siam, and may sometime become a point of commercial and political importance, especially if the projected railway between Maulmain and the Laos capital should be built.

The merchants of Yunnan come south to Cheung Mai with caravans of horses and mules and return laden with cotton. The Laos also export lacquer, betel-nut, wax, gum, tobacco, silk, and rice. The women spin and weave nearly all the cotton cloth used for garments. They have no sheep, and know nothing of the use of wool. The silkworms flourish and provide them with plenty of the raw silk, but the mulberry-trees which nourish them never bear fruit.

The men dress very much like the Siamese, and wear the same tuft of hair on the top of the head. The women have long, shining black hair, combed straight back and looped into a beautiful knot, which needs no pin to secure it. If they are unmarried they wear a flower in the hair, and the asking for this flower by a young man is equivalent to offering his heart and hand. The dress of the Laosian women is very unlike that of the Siamese; it is more complete and modest. It consists of a skirt made of varying widths sewed together so that the seams pass round the body. The upper strip is white, the next red, the next woven of white and black stripes and shaded with motley colors. This is the widest piece and goes about the knees. The bottom strip is red and about fourteen inches wide. The skirt is long, reaching to the ankles, and "is kept in place by using the upper white strip for a belt as a band of a sheaf of wheat is twisted and tucked in under itself." Rich and poor all dress alike, except that the higher classes vary the universal style a little by inserting a very showy strip of wrought silk into the skirt near the bottom. Some are beginning to wear jackets or waists, but the usual style is for the women to have a brightly-colored cotton or silk scarf tied around their chests just under the arms.

The Laosians are a finer, hardier-looking race than the average Siamese. They are taller and better formed. In some of the tribes the common men disfigure their bodies by tattooing from the waist down to below the knees. An old writer says:

"One of the princes told me that persons of his class seldom follow this singular custom, as they do not reckon themselves among those born to take the rough-and-tumble of life, and very rarely become soldiers. Those who are tattooed do it because they glory in being men, and not women—men who can fight like the devils pictured on their thighs, and run like deer when occasion calls, through jungles and swamps, with but little to cover their tattooed nudity. There is no religious element connected with the custom. It is a painful operation and some die in consequence. The coloring matter deposited under the cuticle is chiefly soot and hog's lard, or cocoanut oil. The usual fee for a single person is $1.20, but when figures are required demanding more of the time and skill of the operator the fee is greater. It requires many *lyings* and much patient endurance to complete the work on one man."

The Laos burn their dead, and the following account of a funeral fête in Cheung Mai is from the graphic pen of Rev. J. Wilson, who for nearly a score of years has been laboring for the spiritual welfare of the Laosians:

"The cremation of the late second king took place this afternoon. Several thousands of people were present, among them the chiefs and their suites from several of the other provinces. There had been great preparations, and there was a good deal of display. The funeral-car was large and bore the expressive token of a huge dragon with an elephant's head and trunk. Upon the back of this dragon rested the pagoda-shaped pyre, gaudy, like the dragon, with gilt and silver tinsel. The spire of the pagoda reached some forty feet from the ground. This funeral-car was dragged by ropes, at which more than a thousand persons assisted in pulling. The first king and higher princes led the van of the procession. In the foremost part of it was the king's elephant, decked with gold trappings. In the funeral procession came also the favorite horse of the late second king, richly caparisoned in silver ornaments, and saddle covered with silver-cloth. Just after the horse came the second king's elephant wearing silver trappings worth hundreds of rupees, as the gold trappings already mentioned are worth thousands. They are both of heavy beaten work, highly polished, and of a quaint pattern. To see the huge animals move slowly along, these polished pieces of silver and gold flashing in the sunlight, reminds one that he is in the East. There is nothing just like it in the Western world. These gold and silver trappings were the only costly articles in the parade. The pagoda pyre, as it moved slowly along, had a graceful look, a costly glitter, but all this came from pretty tinsel worth but little. Some of the princes wore diamond rings and costly garments; a few of the princesses wore diamonds also in their ears and on their fingers. Many of the people were dressed in gaudy colors.

"The vast assemblage had the appearance of some holiday gathering. The constant hum of voices, rising to merry laughter, dispelled the idea that the people were come to render their last homage of respect to their dead chief. But so it is in regions where only the 'Light of Asia' has shone. Fear and dread of death in its approaches, wailing over the corpse, and then loud and merry festivity, and oftentimes the most arrant buffoonery when it is prepared for and borne to the funeral pyre. Even then the bodies of the great cannot rest in the flames in quiet, but rockets must haunt the pyre, bearing to the flaming pile caricature shapes of men and beasts, birds and reptiles. We Westerners even cannot resist the ludicrous effect of such figures scudding along the ground, and in many cases dashing right into the flames. It is only when it is all over that the thought, 'Death has been here and borne a great man from the people,' resumes its place. It would be impossible to give the full details of the ceremony, nor could one understand it from even the fullest description. Eyesight alone can comprehend it."

The Laosians are civil and respectful. Theft is a capital crime, and there is more morality among them than most Eastern nations can boast. They are Buddhists and devil-worshippers, evince great veneration for the spirits of their ancestors, and are full of superstitious fears. They believe that nearly all illness is produced by witchery, and whoever is accused of being the witch, or "*Pee-ka,*" is banished, with his family, from the city or town where he lives, his property confiscated forever, his houses burned down, and trees destroyed. Hundreds of poor unfortunates are yearly driven from their homes on account of this terrible superstition. The missionaries of Cheung Mai have sheltered a great many by allowing them a refuge in the mission compound. To this the outside natives offer no objections—imagining, perhaps, that the evil spirit "Pee-ka" loses all power in the presence of the wonderful foreigners from the outside world. An effort has been made in the United States to raise money for the purchase of refuge farms for these poor persecuted people.

"I had repeatedly," says Dr. Cheek, a medical missionary to the Laos, "requested permission to witness an investigation of a case of witchcraft, and I was at last granted an opportunity. I found upon inquiry that the patient, a girl of about sixteen, had some months previously suffered from a protracted fever, probably typhoid, and that upon recovery had lost the power of speech, though in other respects she seemed quite well.

"One day she went with a party of children to a temple, and while there she spoke a few words more or less distinctly. Immediately the children became alarmed and ran home. Supposing the case to be one of witchcraft the owner (for the patient was a slave) sent for the spirit-doctors. Three of these professionals were present when I reached the place, and one of them, who seemed to be considered more eminent than his fellows, assumed the *rôle* of chief inquisitor. After becoming thoroughly infused with the inspiration of a rather large bowl of *arrack*, this eminent doctor began muttering some gibberish, and, taking up a tiger's tooth, he drew it along the side and back of the patient, leaving deep scratches, while the patient of course writhed and struggled. At length a rather deeper and more skillful incision, which drew the blood, elicited a cry of pain, and this cry was interpreted by the ferocious, drunken spirit-doctor as indicating the seat of the spirit. Then, with a vigorous thrust between the ribs, while his assistant pressed a bluntly-pointed piece of wood against the unhappy patient, he, with foul and abusive language, ordered the spirit to leave. The exorcism was a failure, and the patient refused to speak, although pressingly flattered to do so by the combined efforts of these two drunken savages. The patient is in such cases, for the time, supposed to be the not altogether 'unconscious envelope' of the infesting spirit; and any injury inflicted by the spirit-doctor is directed against the spirit, and any answer given to the questions put by the spirit-doctor, or the friends of the patient, are from the spirit. So the witch-doctor asks its name and abode, and the names of relatives, and sundry questions concerning domestic relations, supposed to be known only to members of the family. If to all these questions the desired answers are given, the person whose spirit it is, is accused of witchcraft, and, together with all the members of the family, he must leave the neighborhood; nor can they settle anywhere in the vicinity of their home again. Everything belonging to them, except such articles as can be easily removed, is committed to the flames. They cannot sell their rice-fields, gardens, houses, or any other possession, since no one will risk the supposed contamination. Hundreds of families become outcasts yearly. We have attempted to aid individual victims by making our premises places of refuge, and enabling those who had been driven from home to find work and protection; but we are helpless before this wide-spread and degrading prostitution of the human intellect."

Leprosy is also quite common among the Laosians, and whenever the disease manifests itself, the poor victim is banished to the leper villages, and must spend the remainder of his wretched life in company with others as hopeless as himself. How like the day of doom the morning of their banishment must dawn upon the lepers when they go forth from all they have known and loved. Over the entrance to these leper villages might well be written the old inscription, "Who enters here must leave all hope behind." There is no more going to the market with flowers in her hair, chatting with friends and neighbors in the pleasant streets. They cannot go to see the prince, nor follow the grand procession on holidays, nor mingle with the worshippers in the beautiful temples when they lay their offerings of incense and fragrant flowers before the gilded images of Buddha. Not so much to be deprived of, according to our way of thinking, but it is all that constitutes the life of a heathen, and when shut out from it all, life seems dark indeed.

Missionaries are in Cheung Mai now, and have been for nearly twenty years, and God is blessing their work. They have churches, a school, and hospital. For particulars concerning the latter work I refer you to my chapter on "Medical Missions." The Rev. Messrs. McGilvary and Wilson are the pioneers who began the work, and the veterans who are still carrying it on. They have been cheered by the arrival of new helpers, and saddened by their speedy departure; and it was this mission that was called to mourn the loss of Miss Mary Campbell, whose bright young life was quenched in the waters of the Chow Payah. Since then her companion, Miss Cole, has returned to America for rest and a change. At present the missionaries are Dr. and Mrs. McGilvary, Rev. Mr. Wilson, Dr. and Mrs. Peoples, Rev. Mr. and Mrs. Martin, and Misses Griffin, Warner, and Westervelt.

The Laos Church has had its vicissitudes, its times of persecution and martyrdom. Two of the converts suffered death for Christ's sake. Nan Inta, their first convert, was one of the bright and shining lights that the Spirit of God is kindling for Himself in heathen lands. Twice has the Laos Church been relieved by the sudden death of a fierce persecutor, who was taken away while his hand was uplifted to destroy. In 1869 the old king died soon after the murder of the martyrs, just as the missionaries were preparing to flee for their lives, and in 1882 Chow Hawma, the second king, died. It was his funeral fête of which I have spoken in this chapter. One of the missionaries writing of him says:

"He has always been our bitter enemy. After the first king went to Bangkok he had letters sent throughout the country forbidding the people to come to us for any purpose whatsoever, and that if any more joined the church they would be severely punished. The governors were told to require the converts to obey all the laws of the land. This we felt was only opening the doors for all kinds of oppression. Just a few days before his death another and stronger letter was sent to all the villages, but we were unable to learn its contents, or get a copy of it, as we did of the first. Now, however, we have nothing to fear, for no one in the country has the power to follow his commands, and we will doubtless be left alone to do our work until the return of the king and princes from Bangkok, and whether we are again troubled will depend much on who is made second king. But we can trust and not be afraid, for our Father is the first and only King of this land that is to be given to Jesus for His possession. Our work is just as interesting as it has ever been, and these letters have kept none away from us, and we know they will not."

All seems to be peaceful and happy now (1885), and last September, when the birthday of the King of Siam was celebrated at Cheung Mai, a dinner was given, to which the great officials and the missionaries were invited. The king of Cheung Mai sat at the head of the table, and Dr. McGilvary was placed opposite, and both were called on for a toast and speech suitable to the occasion, and both responded. A rich volume might be written concerning this North-Land and its people, and the Gospel work among them.

CHAPTER XXXIX.

THE CAPTIVE LAOS IN SIAM.

EVER since the conquest of several of the Laos states by Siam at the beginning of the present dynasty, large numbers of the Laosian captives, and refugee adherents of an unsuccessful prince, who had fled to Siam, have been detained as hostages and slaves. At present their descendants number some twenty or thirty thousand and are scattered through the various provinces, especially those lying near the capital, that they may be easily drafted for soldiers, or other Government service whenever needed. They have that inherited dread of the sea common to all inland tribes and therefore make poor sailors. But being strong and robust they are better-looking soldiers than the ordinary Siamese. I will not venture to say much as to their fighting capacity, for having a natural love of life, and an equally natural lack of patriotic regard for the land of their captivity, we should not expect much from these drafted bondmen. They are a down-trodden and oppressed people. Able-bodied men are required to serve the Government, at their own charges, three months out of the year, and as much more as the petty Siamese officers can exact in the various districts where they are settled. They must plant and reap the king's rice-fields; go into the fever-haunted forests and cut timbers for the royal cremation buildings; make and repair roads and bridges; build temporary shelters of bamboo and palm-leaves for parties of royal travellers, and attend them in their journeys. They are literal "hewers of wood and drawers of water," bearers of burdens, watchmen, boatmen, and so on to the bitter end of the servile catalogue. And yet with all this unrequited labor, they are so industrious and frugal that if you go into their homes there will be found a greater appearance of thrift than in the ordinary houses of the Siamese.

The Laos captives are of various tribes and languages, and a difference in dress will be noticed. There seems to be no chief over the whole tribe, but each village has its "headman." The people are usually divided into three classes: woodmen, stock-raisers, and farmers. The latter live in the villages and cultivate the outlying fields, going and returning daily, except in harvest-time, when they are compelled to camp in the fields to watch their rice until it is cut and gathered.

The Laos villages near Petchaburee look, at a distance, like a cluster of weather-beaten haystacks, and the wonder is where the people live, for they are seen along the roadway, or in the fields with their herds of oxen and buffalo. As you draw nearer you discern that these haystacks are hollow, and elevated a few feet from the ground. By climbing a bamboo ladder you enter dark, smoky apartments, seldom more than three in number, which look to our unaccustomed eyes very little like a home. They are dark and uninviting, for the surrounding roof comes down so low as to shut out not only the rain, but most of the sunlight and air. As you look up, this roof appears like a great umbrella with bamboo poles for ribs, and instead of oaken rafters, or beams of polished wood, these ribs of bamboo are kept in place by twisted ropes of rattan, to which is fastened by withes the long, coarse swamp grass used for thatch. An old tradition says that at first the men did not know how to thatch roofs, for they began at the top and tied down. But the old widows, who had to do the work themselves, taught them a better way by starting at the edge and working up. Thus the overlapping grasses were not disturbed or broken. There are no doors, properly speaking, nor windows, nor chimney. The fire-place is a box filled with earth, having a few bricks or stones set up, on which to place the cooking utensils. The smoke finds its own way out as best it can. I used to have serious objections to this wholesale smoking of everything in the native huts, the people themselves not excepted, but I have come to look upon it with greater favor, and even consider it a blessing to human beings living in this rude way; for smoke, as is well known, is one of the best disinfectants in the world; it drives off the mosquitoes and ants; it helps to preserve the dried fish, beef, buffalo meat, peppers, and other food in the hut. The very materials of which the hut is made, and the ox-hides upon which the people sit and sleep, are made more durable by the daily clouds of incense from the kitchen altar. Their baskets, and other useful articles made of rattan and split bamboo, would need constant renewing were it not for the good smoking they receive, for there is an ingenious little borer who soon makes havoc of the nicest and best wicker-work if left to revel undisturbed among its pith and fibre.

The floors of these huts are made of split bamboo, with great cracks between them, so they never need sweeping. Delicate lace curtains the color of "London smoke" depend from the roof, and are daily renewed or repaired by the same cunning little weavers we find in "kings' palaces." A few rattan-stools and three-cornered pillows lying upon the floor, baskets, rice-trays, bowls and plates, cocoanut dippers, betel-trays, and spittoons complete the list of furniture; save that in some corner you may find the men's fishing-tackle, also hatching-baskets full of silk-worms, a cotton separator, reels, and spinning-wheels, just such as you find in China, Siberia, and Brazil. That is the women's special domain, and their busy fingers are seldom idle. The manufacture of cloth for all domestic purposes is left entirely to her. She can gather the cotton under the burning sun, trudge weary miles with her baby tied on her back to the city to buy pails of dyestuff from the Chinese dyers, or to gather mulberry leaves wherever she can find them for her silk-worms. They boil the cocoons to loosen the silk, and when they have wound off all the thread they eat the worms. These are regarded as quite a delicacy. I had a dish presented to me once, but I could not bear to taste them even; and yet why should they not be food as well as oysters or snails, birds'-nests or horse-flesh? The woman can card and spin and weave, dye and embroider, until back and eyes are completely tired out. She can embroider scarfs, pillows, and shrouds. I have never seen embroidered skirts among these Laos, but they weave bright silken threads among the blue and white cotton, and make very pretty stripes.

The cotton separator reminds one of a patent clothes-wringer, except that the rollers are not rubber and do not turn on cog-wheels, but on themselves, being made of hard wood, and having the outer ends finished like screws, with the threads running in opposite directions. Their looms are very simple and primitive, and they weave nothing but the coarsest cloth. The loom is usually set up under the house on the "ground floor," and near by swings the hammock in which baby sleeps while mother weaves. Gathered about, so as to be under shelter, are the dye-pots and the large mortar where the daily rice is hulled, also the pens for cattle, buffalo, pigs, and chickens. No wonder they need a smudge, and enjoy the smell of smoke. Then, too, these evening fires are pleasant places around which the young girls sit and spin and embroider, or play games when the young men come to visit them. Their simple, unromantic ways remind one of old Bible times, and they even have a custom of serving for a wife, as Jacob did for his beloved Rachel. They are very fond of music, and love to sing and dance. Many of the young men have curious reed organs upon which they play skillfully. They are light and sweet-toned, and are very well adapted to their wild and weird melodies. You can hear them answering each other through the night as they come from far away to visit the pretty, black-eyed girls in the distant villages, and you can imagine those same girls listening intently for the familiar notes they love best in all the band. Then they will adjust their silver bracelets, recount their rings, and give their black scarf, embroidered with bright silks, a graceful toss over their shoulder, and prepare to look as careless and unconcerned as shy maidens do in every other land. They all expect to marry, and therefore begin to prepare their wedding outfit ere they enter their teens. They spin and weave diligently, and care not how much they are teased because their hands are stained with dye, and on their wedding-day they are very proud of the baskets of cloth and garments carried in the bridal procession. Their dress is a black jacket with silver buttons, a scarf, and a blue and white striped skirt. The stripes in the skirt run up and down, instead of round the body, as those of the North Laosians do. The skirt is of three pieces, and is kept in place by drawing it tightly round the body, giving it a twist, then a nip and a tuck. The entire absence of strings, pins, hooks, and eyes seems very strange. Their scarf is sometimes worn as a headdress, and they tie little packages in one end of it, or money in the corners. They have a set of pockets, something like an old-fashioned housewife, that they can roll up, in which they carry tobacco, betel, and ceri-leaf, that they may refill their mouths whenever they dispose of a useless quid; for, like the Siamese, all are addicted to the filthy habit of betel-chewing.

Their jewelry is all silver. They have great holes in the lobe of the ear, in which they wear silver ornaments like cuff-buttons. They have silver hoops for necklaces, and bands and coils for anklets, bracelets, and rings. Some of the latter are very curious. I purchased several made of coils of silver wire that had sixteen spirals in each. The women have long black hair, and when young care for it, combing it nicely and looping it into a large glossy bow-knot like a butterfly perched on the top of their heads; and they also put flowers under its wings after the fashion of their great-great-grandmothers in that far-away North-Land before their captivity. The men wear respectable suits—pantaloons and coat of plain black cotton, the latter fastened with silver buttons. They also have silver rings on their fingers. They have a sort of overcoat they wear on special occasions. It is long and wide and embroidered with silk, and ornamented with strips of colored cloth, both silk and cotton. The women often come to us to beg scraps of bright cloth for this purpose. They also have a robe of similar design, though modified in shape. These garments are usually kept for gala-days, weddings, and funerals, and finally become the wearer's shroud when he lies in state to be wailed over, feasted, and worshipped before he is cremated.

The Laos have clear, olive complexions, bright eyes, and beautiful teeth, and their features are decidedly European. Full negro lips are rarely seen, and I have never met a curly head. The men have no beards. Some of the children are quite beautiful; but when they grow old and weather-beaten, tanned by exposure to wind and sun, they become swarthy, and remind me of the Ute Indians in the Rocky Mountains. And yet we find some venerable-looking old men and gray-haired women for whom we fain would wish a better fate than the life and death of a heathen. Their language is rough and guttural, and usually spoken in a loud tone. In the villages we hear nothing but Laos, yet all learn the Siamese as they grow older and begin to trade in the market towns. Their food is very plain and coarse. They literally eat "locusts and wild honey." They often bring the honey in the comb, and still clinging to its bamboo branch, to sell to us. I do not know how they catch the locusts, but they roast them, and think them very rich and good. They also eat the bee-bread and the half-formed bees, frogs, snails, certain kinds of snakes and lizards, turtles, bats, and the roots, bark, twigs, and leaves of trees. They gather wild vines and herbs from the mountain-side, and wild fruits from the forest, mushrooms from the bogs, and food from every available place; they even eat the flesh of beasts that die, and say it is purified by the fire that cooks it, and the Siamese do the same.

They are kind-hearted and very fond of children. Drunkenness is their chief vice. They sit around a pot of home-brewed rice-beer, and suck it through slender pipes till they are "too full for utterance." They compel one another to drink, and one might often find a whole village, even the women, the boys, and the girls, so tipsy they could hardly find the way to their own huts. Drinking is a daily sin. As the women grow older they seem to give it up and go to making merit, but the old men do nothing but drink and carouse. They seldom fight hard enough to kill.

The religion of these Laos is a strange jumble. They believe, first and best of all, in a Great Spirit who dwells in the sky. But they add to this lesser spirits of earth, air, and water, a god of the hills, like Pan of old, and a god of the valleys. They believe in demons, devils, and the ghosts of their ancestors; and all these are their enemies, and must be appeased by worship, gifts, and feasting. They are not usually idolaters, and in many of their villages have neither temple nor holy place.

A few of their young men are beginning to enter the Buddhist monasteries as priests, but it is contrary to their ancient customs. Of course their relatives must feed them and worship them as other Buddhists do, but as yet it is no throwing away of the old devil-worship, but only the addition of the more prominent Buddhist customs to their own old rites and ceremonies. They have no sacred day corresponding to our Sabbath or the Buddhist's seventh day, but every twelfth day is sacred to these Laos; and having no calendars, that they may not lose their count, they have twelve shells in a little box with two compartments, and each day they remove one shell from one side to the other, until all are gone, when that is a sacred day, and the same process is repeated throughout the year. Each of these twelve days has a name—as the day of the turtle, the lizard, and so forth.

Spirit altars are in every house, upon which they place offerings for their ancestors every twelfth day. The time for offerings is counted from the death-day of the father of the family; so there is no uniformity in their sacred days, and no special concert of worship. They place food, such as the old man loved to eat, and betel and tobacco upon the altar. It is left there as long as it takes an ordinary person to consume that amount, when it is carefully removed and eaten by the members of the household. An incredulous observer once asked an old woman how the spirits partook of the food, as there always seemed to be as much left as had been placed on the altar. "Ugh," she grunted, "grasshoppers take it to them."

The number twelve is of great significance and enters into their old legends and tales; for instance, they tell that in the beginning of the world there were twelve couples, the parents of twelve tribes and languages. Once every year they build an altar to the Sky Spirit, or "*Pee Fa*," having twelve steps or tiers, and on them are placed twelve trays of meat curry, prepared from the flesh of buffalo. They take two of these animals, a white one and a black one, and offer them in sacrifice, in the vain hope that they will thereby be protected from plague and death. They pour out the blood like the old Israelites, but sometimes a thrifty fisherman saves it to dye his fish-nets, and make them tough and strong. In times of cholera or any other prevalent disease they erect an altar to this "Pee Fa," and repeat the sacrifices already mentioned. A few years ago when the cholera raged so fatally some of the lesser Laos villages were entirely deserted, and whole families died out. In their desperation they slew their cattle in sacrifice and left the bodies to decompose around their dwellings, which but added to the virulence of the plague. They know nothing of prayer as we understand it, for instead of asking the higher powers to come near and help and bless them, they entreat them to keep far away from their dwellings and not to harm them. They beg the ghosts of their ancestors not to trouble them, nor take any off by death to the world of spirits.

They do not believe in witchcraft as the North Laos do, yet they do hold to spirit-possession, and they pretend to drive out the evil one by exorcism. Placing food at the head of the ladder leading into their huts they invite the evil spirit, after it has gone out of the person, to eat its fill and begone. But instead of waiting for it to go peaceably the spirit-doctor goes to the spot, and wildly slashing the air with knives and other weapons pretends to cut it to pieces. For the ordinary patient they make offerings to the spirits without trying to drive them out, believing that some diseases are the effect of outside influences. They kill an ox every four or five days, if the man is wealthy, and make a feast for the entire village; if poor, they content themselves with pigs and chickens; of course these savory curries are accompanied by great baskets of steamed, glutinous rice, vegetables, and fruit, with a generous dessert of rice-wine, betel, and tobacco. But if, after all, the patient dies, both he and his impoverished friends are consoled by the thought that he will reap the benefit of all these foolish feasts in the world to come. Their ideas of the future life are vague, but all believe in immortality and think that in heaven all will be masters and can eat and drink their fill without having to work for it.

They have many strange legends and spirit stories, "old wives' fables." They tell of the flood during which it rained seven days and seven nights, and all the birds were set free instead of only the raven and dove of Noah, and all the people perished. "*Pratan*" then sent down a couple of persons from heaven to repeople the earth. In time they became great and had many languages.

They say that long ago the rice grew in very large grains. But a poor man died before the rice harvest, and his widow had to gather in the grain alone. The rice grains were so large and heavy she could not lift them, therefore she took a knife and cut them into small bits, and ever since the rice has grown in small grains. Perhaps that is the reason why nearly all these chivalrous Orientals still leave the rice harvest to the women. The grains are now too small for the men to stoop for.

Another strange set of stories are, that the sky used to be so close down to the earth that when the people hulled their rice in the mortar the pestle struck the vault overhead and caused it to thunder all through heaven; and that there was a tall tree, called the "Sky Opener," up which good people climbed into heaven. One can but wonder if those discontented and desperate mortals in other parts of the earth who threaten to "leave this world and climb a tree," ever heard this old Laos myth, and had a vague longing to follow them to the abodes of bliss. But these captive Laos are learning better, truer things than this. There is a tree that opens heaven, a wondrous, bitter tree, and Christ who hung upon it said, "I, if I be lifted up will draw all men unto me," and already more than one of these poor heathen has been made willing to go by way of the cross.

A Laos widow, who lived with us for several years, told me of some of their customs. They burn the dead, like the Siamese, with protracted ceremonies and funeral feasts. For a rich man an ox is slain each day and prepared for the guests. The body is laid in state and the table set before him; there all assemble, and after the spirit-doctor has finished his incantations (they have no priests), and invited not only the dead man to partake, but all his ancestors, they wait a reasonable time for the spirit-feast, and then the living friends devour the food. If they cannot afford oxen, they substitute pigs and chickens, and all who help furnish food for these funeral feasts hope thereby to escape the molestations of the ghost. Sometimes, as in the cholera season, the body is buried without being burned. But the usual custom is to bury only the charred bones. Over the grave they erect a small bamboo house, and in it lay gifts for the dead. If a man, costly silk cloths, and from ten to fifty pieces of native cotton cloth; for a woman, from five to twenty pieces of cloth, also garments such as the Laos wear, and a rice-pot containing various articles of food, betel, and tobacco. They vie with each other in the costliness of the funeral feasts and the quality and quantity of goods left to rot upon the grave. The Laos are buried in the long black robes already described as gala dresses. In the neck-band a piece of silver money is fastened for the use of the spirit in its journey—to pay the ferryman over the river Styx, perhaps. They do not put this money in the mouth like the Siamese, because it might be dropped in crossing the dark river to the other world, and the departed could not talk to those he met if he had money in his mouth.

There is a peculiar kind of withe they use in tying on the thatch of their huts. They roll this up into balls, and throwing it into the grave-house, say: "Take this; it will become silver in the other world; use it for your needs."

Ma Ting had a little son named "You," whom we all loved. He was in the mission-school for several years, and learned that best of all knowledge, to love Christ. He fell sick, and as we had no physician here, his mother took him to her native village. But he would not permit the Laos doctors to perform their heathen ceremonies or spirit-incantations over him. He stoutly maintained that "he belonged to God," and that "he believed in his grandfather's way," who is a Christian. He was sick a long time, and at last died, trusting in Jesus. He left word that they should bury him with his Bible in his hands. His mother's last question was, "How are you now?" "My heart is well," said he, and died. Since then the widow also has died, and a little brother, and we trust all are safe. The dear old grandfather still lives, earnest and steadfast in the faith. His conversion was truly wonderful. He was first awakened by reading one of Dr. Bradley's old calendars that somehow fell into his hands. He was struck with the tables telling of the sun and moon, and he concluded that if the foreigners knew so much more of the sun and moon than the Laos, they must also know more of heaven and how to get there. He procured portions of the Scriptures and read them diligently, and was converted before he ever heard a sermon. Here is another picture, of Nan Inta, the first-fruits of the Gospel among the Northern Laos, and as we contemplate the two, we may get a new realization of how wonderfully "the heavens declare the glory of God," and that "His ways are past finding out":

"Nan Inta," says Rev. Dr. McFarland, "being of an inquiring mind and unsatisfied with Buddhism, which he had thoroughly studied, he, from curiosity, visited the missionaries on their arrival, and was pleased with the story of the Gospel, and particularly with the plan of salvation therein revealed, if true. But how shall he know that it is true?

"One week before the great solar eclipse which occurred on the 18th of August, 1868—one of the most remarkable that has ever been witnessed—he visited the missionary, and was told that on a certain day there would be an eclipse of the sun. Their religious belief concerning an eclipse is, that it is caused by a huge monster in the air trying to swallow the sun and the moon, and the idea that any one could foretell such an occurrence seemed wonderful. How anxiously did he wait to see the result!

"The very day and hour predicted the phenomenon occurred. Nan Inta seemed to be bewildered. The foundation of his trust in Buddhism was shaken. It had deceived him in things relating to this world, and could he trust it for the future? This was doubtful. But could he trust in the Christian's Saviour? He was so aroused to thought and impressed with the ability of those who believe in the Christian religion, that he began the study of the Gospel with eagerness, and was soon baptized.

"The eclipse referred to was witnessed by the late King of Siam, his courtiers, and many of the European residents in the country, at a temporary observatory erected in a dense jungle at 'Hua Wean'—'Whale's Head'—on the western shore of the Gulf. It was while visiting this place to witness the eclipse that the king contracted the fever which ended his earthly life. This eclipse was referred to in January of 1869 by Prof. Proctor, in a lecture in Association Hall, New York, as having settled the interesting fact of those solar prominences which before that were supposed by astronomers to belong to the atmosphere of the moon. By this eclipse they were proved to be on the sun.

"How interesting a fact, that while scientists were gazing upon this phenomenon and settling great facts in astronomy, God was making use of it to bring a dark-minded heathen into the glorious light of the Gospel!"

But let us now return to *Pa Ang*, our captive Laos. For a score of years he was the only convert in the Laos village. Although a bamboo chapel had been built and frequent services held, the villagers met together in council and deliberately said, "We will not give up our old beliefs and accept Christ." The former missionaries, Mr. McGilvary and Mr. Wilson, who had been deeply interested in them, removed to Cheung Mai to labor more directly among the Laos in their native land. The little chapel went to ruin, but old Pa Ang, ever faithful, trudged to church at Petchaburee Sabbath after Sabbath. At last a nephew professed Christ, and the old man's heart was filled with joy, and he delighted in his little grandson, and rejoiced over his happy death with chastened gladness. Then his daughter came seeking salvation, and a granddaughter united with the church, and two other members of his family. And since I began to write this chapter, *La*, a little granddaughter, came to tell me she wished to be baptized. "Why do you wish to join the church?" said I. "Because Jesus loved us so that He came down from heaven and died upon the cross." "Do you love Him?" "Yes, I love Him." "And do you think you can serve Him?" "If God does not help me I cannot, but if He helps I can." And God will help not only La, but all others in the tribe whom He has chosen for His own. La has been in one of my schools for several years. She is fitted for a teacher, but is not yet old enough to have charge of a school, as she is not quite twelve, but we use her as an assistant.

A school has been opened among the people, and we have had perhaps a hundred pupils from the different villages, but the boys come very irregularly, and the girls begrudge the time taken from the preparation of their wedding outfits to learn to read. Last month a party of us went in the wagon to one of their villages to give a magic-lantern entertainment. Some four hundred gathered to look and listen as the scenes from Christ's wonderful life were thrown, one at a time, upon the canvas and explained by Mr. Dunlap. We greatly enjoyed the outdoor meeting—the pleasant evening air, the darkness, the upturned faces, the glowing pictures full of life and light and salvation, if they will but believe in Him who was there portrayed. They were delighted, and wanted the canvas to glow all night, and then invited us to come again and again.

What an interesting people they are! We are hopeful, too, for their future, and believe that a brighter, better day will dawn for these captive Laos.

16*

CHAPTER XL.

SEETONE AND HIS ANGEL-BRIDE, MONORA—A LAOS LEGEND.

In the far-away land of Chumpah lived Seetone, renowned for his bravery and beauty. One day, as he was wandering through the forests, he came upon a pool of clear, cool water, fringed about with ferns and wild-wood flowers. A few stray sunbeams that glinted through the overhanging branches danced upon its rippling surface; the birds dropped down to bathe, and the deer came to the brink to allay their thirst.

As he stood gazing upon the lovely scene he was startled by the rustle of wings and peals of silvery laughter. He retreated into the shadow, and looking up saw with amazement a band of angels flying from heaven. They laved their beautiful forms in the cool waters of the lake, and swam and played and splashed about in perfect abandonment of delight. As he caught glimpses of their faces one by one, each seemed more beautiful than her companion.

Attracted by some flowers on the brink, one of the angels, named Monora, or Luklatan, swam near his covert; and when, at the impulse of his love, he caught her fluttering wings, the others flew with a startled cry to their native heaven. Very gently he wooed her to his home; and when he had gained her love and confidence, he removed her wings, and consigned them to his mother for safe keeping.

The days and months flew quickly by, and Seetone was perfectly happy with his angel-bride. But a brave prince from a neighboring realm, hearing of her wondrous beauty, came with an army to secure her for his own. Seetone went out to battle, having a garland of fragrant flowers about his neck which Monora had woven and placed there, saying, "Take these, my true love, and as long as they are fresh and fragrant, be assured of my welfare and safety." During the long, weary march, and in many a pitched battle, the garland retained its freshness and beauty. But one day near the close of a desperate battle, when Seetone had almost gained the victory, the garland suddenly withered and dropped dry and scentless at his feet. With one great heart-throb of agony he fainted away. Immediately he was at his home, when his mother told him that, hearing no tidings from the battle-field, and fearing for the safety of his angel-bride, she had restored the hidden wings, when Monora at once soared sunward and was lost to sight.

Seetone, taking a ring which she had given him, and bidding farewell to his mother and to earth, by the exercise of his inherent power mounted up, and riding upon the clouds soon came to the river which flows between earth and heaven. He could not cross, for the waves devoured every one who attempted the passage. So he changed himself into a mosquito, and clinging to the tail of a crow was borne safely to the other side. He resumed his natural form, and sat down to rest in a *sala* by a river of clear, sweet water. Soon a maiden came tripping down the path, with her buckets swinging lightly over her shoulder to dip water for her mistress' bath. He craved a drink, which she kindly granted. While quaffing the sweet water, he quietly slipped Monora's ring into the vessel, and the maiden bore it with her into the heavenly palace. As her waiting mistress threw up her hands to receive the grateful shower which she poured upon her lovely form, the ring fell with the sparkling drops and encircled her finger. That instant she felt a thrill of the old love which once animated her being; and seeing the ring, her own ring which she had once given to Seetone, she inquired if the maid had seen any one by the river bank. When told of the noble stranger to whom she had given drink, the mistress' heart trembled with delight, and hastily summoning Seetone, they renewed their vows of love and devotion. Monora gave Seetone wings, mightier and stronger than her own, and endowed him with immortality and—there my Laos friend stopped, saying: "There is more of the story, but I have forgotten it." "Never mind," said I; "that is a good place to leave them: happy in heaven."

CHAPTER XLI.

BUDDHA'S CRYSTAL TOOTH.

HERE is the Siamese version of the story of Buddha's tooth: When the great teacher died his disciples burned his body, and then the bones were heaped together as sacred relics. Kings and princes from all lands where his teachings were believed came to secure a share of them. Each was anxious to get the largest and best. But a Brahmin high-priest, taking up a golden basin, said he would divide the precious store, giving to all the same measure. To this they agreed.

As he filled and refilled the basin he discovered one of the large eye-teeth. Thinking it the most precious relic of all because it grew in the mouth of him who spake such wonderful words, he slyly hid it in his long hair, which was knotted at the back of his head. Then he gave away all the bones to the kings and princes, who, seeing he reserved nothing for himself, remonstrated; but he said he needed none. They returned to their kingdoms with gladness and great joy, to build dagabas, pagodas, prachadees, wats, and shrines for the holy bones.

Pra In, the god who sees and knows everything, saw the tooth in the Brahmin's hair, and concluding that such a deceiver ought not to have that most precious of all the holy relics of Buddha, he caught it away from the wicked man. When the Brahmin put his hand up to make sure the priceless treasure was safe, he discovered to his great grief that the tooth was gone, and of all his grand opportunities nothing remained in his hand but the empty golden basin. He thought of the many times he had filled it and given the holy contents to those far-away kings and princes. And now he would have given his life almost for one little bone. But the way was long and weary, and besides, as he was ashamed to go and beg for what he had once refused, he was left in despair. Finally he set up the golden basin, and it has been worshipped ever since.

Here the legend ended, and when I asked the woman who told me, "What became of Buddha's tooth?" she said, "*Mi saap*"—"I do not know." I suggested the legend I had heard of its being found in the heart of a lotus, and now enshrined in a curious old temple in Ceylon. "Oh!" said she, "I suppose Pra In put it there to be found by whoever had merit enough to see the sacred crystal." *

The sequel to the story was told me later by one who said Pra In carried the tooth to the second heaven, called "Dawahdhung," and put it in an emerald pagoda, and that many devout Buddhists place flowers and tapers in the hands of the dead to offer at this emerald shrine in heaven. He also said that four teeth of the holy Buddha have been preserved—the right upper eye-tooth in heaven, the left upper in Ceylon, the lower right in India, and the lower left is with the god of dragons and serpents in the underworld.

The stories of Buddha's tooth and its adventures are truly wonderful. I will quote two more. The first is found in "Indian Pictures":

"From the fourteenth century downwards Kandy, the ancient capital of the Highland Singalese, has been distinguished as the

---

* Siamese call many sacred things "crystals," no matter what the material.

headquarters of Buddhism, finding its centre in the temple of the Dalada, the shrine of Buddha's tooth, round which the Buddhist hierarchy gather. This, with the adjoining palace, is the most interesting building in Ceylon. There is an octagonal stone edifice of two stories, in the upper part of which is an Oriental library, containing several valuable Pali manuscripts, and the Buddhist scriptures written on wood and sumptuously bound. A balcony runs outside on which the kings of Kandy were wont in former times to appear before the people and to witness performances on the green below. The relic of the left eye-tooth of Guatama Buddha, here said to be enshrined, has a curious history. Rescued from his funeral pile B.C. 543, it was preserved for eight centuries at Dantapura, in South India, and brought to Ceylon A.D. 310. The Malabars afterward captured it and took it back to India, but the great Prakrama recovered it. The Portuguese missionaries got possession of it in the sixteenth century, carried it away to Goa, and after refusing a large ransom offered for it by the Singalese, reduced it to powder and destroyed it at Goa in the presence of witnesses. The account of this destruction of the tooth is most circumstantial in the Portuguese records. Nevertheless the Buddhist priests at Kandy produced another tooth, which they affirmed to be the real relic, that taken by the Portuguese being counterfeit; and they conducted this to the shrine with great pomp and ceremony. This is the relic now treasured with such care and reverence. It is probably not a human tooth at all, being, as those who have seen it affirm, much too large ever to have belonged to man." [I would suggest that it may still be a Buddha tooth, preserved from a remote time, when that changeable god was still passing through some of his beastly transmigrations.]

"When the British got possession of it in 1815 there was great excitement, the relic being regarded as a sort of national palladium. They allowed it, however, to be restored to its shrine amid great festivities. The sanctuary in which it reposes is a small chamber without a ray of light, in which the air is stifling hot, and heavy with the perfume of flowers, situated in the inmost recesses of the temple. The frames of the doors of this chamber are inlaid with carved ivory, and on a massive silver altar stands the golden shrine, jewelled and hung round with chains. In front of the altar is a table upon which worshippers deposit their gifts."

The second account is quite similar, and is given in connection with the visit of the Prince of Wales to India:

"At Kandy the prince was vouchsafed a sight of the 'Dalada,' or sacred tooth of the Guatama Buddha. He died, it is said, some twenty-five hundred years ago, and the sacred incisor was preserved in the capital of Kalinga, where it remained five hundred years, when it was taken to Ceylon, where it reposed for more than fifteen hundred years, when a prince from the mainland came to the island and captured the venerated relic. The king of Kandy recaptured it, and for some troubled centuries after it had a varied fortune, being borne from one hiding-place to another.

"At last, in 1560, the Portuguese Dom Constantine of Braganza got it, as he supposed, at the capture of Jaffna, and carried it to Goa. The king of Pegu offered four hundred thousand cruzadoes for its ransom, but the pious Archbishop of Goa was resolved upon the destruction of the idolatrous relic. However, the Portuguese chronicler says he placed poor Buddha's tooth 'in a mortar, and with his own hand reducing it to powder before them all, cast the pieces into a brazier which stood ready for the purpose, after which the ashes and the charcoal together were cast into the river in the sight of all those crowding to the verandas and windows which looked upon the water.' But, if the Singalese are to be believed, the archbishop had better have taken the money; for it was not the genuine tooth after all, but a sham one made for the occasion; while the genuine, original one was spirited away from the captured city, and found its way to Kandy.

"The 'Dalada' is deposited in a bell-shaped, golden casket, glittering with diamonds, emeralds, and pearls. When the prince and some of his suite were gathered in the chamber, a priest brought the key of the casket from a secret receptacle. The outer casket being opened, inside of it was seen a second, then a third, fourth, and fifth, all of gold. Within the last, lying upon a golden lotus-leaf, was the sacred tooth which no mortal hand may touch. The eldest priest, quivering with unfeigned emotion, covered his hand with a piece of silk, and, taking up the golden leaf, held up the sacred relic for the prince's gaze. There was not much to see, and without faith nothing to admire. The 'Dalada' is a piece of bone, or, as some say, of ivory, with a suture up the side. It is nearly two inches long and one inch round, tapering toward the end, which is rounded. If the article ever was in Buddha's mouth, and if he had a complete set to match, he must have possessed a wonderful jaw and a remarkable stomach; for it is easy to see that the tooth is not a human molar or incisor. It has been suggested that it was modelled after the canine teeth which are seen in some images of Vishnu and Kali; but it by no means resembles a true canine."

CHAPTER XLII.

NEW SIAM.

There have as yet been no such marvellous revolutions in Siam, affecting the whole kingdom in its private, public, and political life and interests, as have astonished and electrified the world in the history of the Japan of to-day. But the Siam of 1885 is very different from the Siam of even fifty years ago. Then a selfish and jealous policy controlled the first and second kings, and was upheld by the sanction and advice of the nobles. It was in those old days that Chinese junks were sunk at the mouth of the river, and chains stretched from shore to shore to prevent the foreign ships from steaming up to Bangkok. The Siamese were content with their condition, and wished no outside element to be introduced that would surely disturb the Buddhist Nirvana-like lethargy that had lulled them in its senseless intoxication for centuries.

Protestant missionaries had but just found their way to these shores, and were busy learning the language and preparing books for the people. They were casting up a highway for the fulfilment of God's eternal purposes. After these pioneers of civilization, came the American and English ambassadors to make treaties with Siam. Since then many changes have taken place, and many improvements adopted, until now the traveller visiting Bangkok is surprised at the various outward tokens of Western civilization. Now upon the bank of the river may be seen the custom-house, where dues are collected from all the foreign shipping in port, and the flags of almost every land are floating from the mastheads; there, too, is the royal mint where all the money of the realm is coined; the museum where are gathered many rare and curious things from their own and other countries; the telegraph and telephone offices; the barracks full of soldiers in uniform; the king's pleasure yacht, built in England and elegantly furnished; the post-office with its letter-boxes in all parts of the city; and over the triple walls of the palace grounds may be seen, glittering in the sunshine, the triple towers of the king's new palace, designed and executed by foreign architects and filled with beautiful things from London and Paris, and illuminated with electric lights.

A few months before I left Siam one of our native assistants was sent down the coast to purchase a sea boat. He was providentially detained, but at every province and island where the boat stopped in which he had taken passage, he told the people of Christ; and his words had such effect that when he returned, having made his purchase, there came with him a fleet of boats, carrying nearly three hundred men and women, many of them inquirers. And so they voyaged up the coast, day after day and week after week, seeking the one missionary who could tell them more perfectly of the way of life. They anchored in the bay, and a messenger was sent for Mr. Dunlap, who hastened down the river on his glad errand.

Our chapels in Petchaburee are growing too small, and there are additions to the churches at every communion. They are increasing their contributions regularly. It was proposed to build a new chapel at one of the stations, and nearly half the required sum was given the first day funds were asked for. At Bangkaboon they are enlarging the chapel, and the people nobly say, "We will defray the expense as a gift to the Master." Mr. Dunlap writes: "Please do not ask for money to build chapels for this station; better let the native Christians do it themselves." It will be their home mission work and church extension.

The very latest news is that Mr. D. has just returned from an extended tour of three hundred miles down the west coast from Petchaburee. He travelled in a native boat, and visited six provinces. He reached all the governors and officers, and was kindly received everywhere. He carried with him a letter from the Prime Minister of Siam, commanding his subordinates to aid the travellers in procuring food and suitable lodgings, and forbidding them to place any obstacle in their way. Surely such aid from high officials, and so great liberty, is wonderful when we recall former days of opposition and hindrance. They were specially well treated in the Cheya province, which has a population of over 47,000, and a governor who is an enterprising man, and earnest as to the welfare of his people. Mr. Dunlap says:

"He received us kindly, placed a well-furnished house at our disposal, visited us frequently, and urged us to come and settle in his province—offering, as an inducement, lumber and lot for a house. I told him that I had Bible pictures to show, by means of a sciopticon. He at once offered me a place in his park, and sent his men out to announce it in the surrounding villages. That night we had about a thousand people, to whom I preached the Gospel for more than an hour. The governor and his family being present, the people were orderly and listened attentively.

"The next day I noticed a court in session at the governor's palace, and asked his permission to preach in the court-house, which was granted. The court adjourned to hear the sermon; and when I left, the judges and scribes were reading the Gospels aloud to the crowd assembled. We also preached in several villages, and, at the governor's request, to the prisoners. Is not this a wide-open door?

"Our next stop was in the Langsooen province, the population of which is 20,000. This is the Florida of Siam as far as fruits are concerned. It also produces large quantities of tin. We preached for two days in the capital and ten days in the villages. Several expressed deep interest, and some requested baptism, among them two Government officials. One man, who had previously received instruction, we found teaching others in this province; and, through his influence, four wish to adopt our religion.

"We aimed to reach the Lakon province with its 230,000, as yet unvisited by the missionary, but unfavorable winds and high sea prevented. We left our native assistant here, in his own province, to teach the people, and then set sail for home. We were forty-two days making the three hundred miles.

"Now is the time to make consecrated effort for the Master in this land. There is not an obstacle in the way. In fact, we believe the way is providentially open to us, and that we should go forward."

No mission-field stands in greater need of workers than Siam. Oh, that I could persuade scores to enlist in this holy crusade! Life in that land is not an exile, nor a dreary, lonely burying of one's self away from the rest of the world. We have daily telegrams published in an English paper at the capital, and regular fortnightly mails. The sturdy pioneer workers of fifty years ago have prepared the way for us, so that now we find pleasant homes and kind friends awaiting us, and a people whom God is making ready for His salvation. Although "length of days" is not usually expected in foreign lands, yet even that may be vouchsafed us. But we must not count our lives dear unto ourselves. "Duties are ours; events are God's." When England would send forth her troops to India or Egypt, the best, the bravest of her sons are given up, and thousands go voluntarily to be shot or butchered the moment they come in conflict with Arab rifle or scimetar. They fall by hundreds, and their bodies fill the shallow trenches hastily scooped in the desert sands. When I passed through Egypt on my way home, I saw the graves of many a brave Highlander; and who can tell how many more of Britain's blue-eyed sons have gone to certain death in the dark Soudan? But how many missionary graves are there in Egypt? I verily believe you could count them on your ten fingers. Yet what if there were scores? Shall the armies of the

Queen of England excel the soldiers of God in their conquest of the world? Shall they be more brave and willing and valiant than we, when God is also our King and our Father, and these perishing ones are our brothers and sisters?

In all this wide kingdom of Siam, with her open ports, her doors ajar, inviting missionary effort from all Christian lands, and her ten millions of Buddhist heathen, there are but a handful of American workers, including but three ordained ministers who can teach and preach in the native tongue. Think of it! Three men for ten millions—more than three millions for each! And America is full of Christian men and women who profess to have given themselves to the Lord, and to have consecrated all they have to His service.

Already the day is breaking in this dark land, morning dawns, and it is the entrance of God's Word that giveth the light. The tree of knowledge has also taken root, and her branches will extend yet farther and wider, hung with rich and tempting fruits for all who will but pluck and eat. There is an earnest desire on the part of Young Siam to learn English, and in the city of Bangkok may be found quite a number of Government schools established by the king or his princes, and supported from the royal treasury.* Although particular care is taken not to have religion taught, it is impossible to separate Christianity from the English language, and the very school-books furnished by the king are full of its sublime teachings.

A short time ago a foreigner went to visit the royal schools near the palace, where some of the highest princes

---

* The Queen has also opened two schools. One of them is industrial, and the pupils are taught to make supplies of clothing for the soldiers in the royal army, thus economizing what was formerly paid to English clothiers.

and nobles are learning English, and as he crossed the threshold of the school-room door he heard the boys reading of "the Good Shepherd who careth for the sheep." I have heard that the old king, Maha Mongkut, told Mrs. Leonowens, when he employed her as governess for the royal children, that she was not to teach religion; and then, in keeping with his erratic, contradictory nature, he ordered that as a first lesson in English she teach them to sing "God save the King!"

The mother of one of the highest nobles in the kingdom came to Petchaburee on a visit, and she invited us to assemble our schools and let them sing before her. They were very kindly received. Some of the children repeated the Lord's Prayer, at the request of a Buddhist priest, who sat near by and saw and heard all that was going on. The noble lady said to us during the call, and in the presence of all her people: "Your religion is sure to prevail in Siam." And there comes to us the good news that one of the most intelligent of the Laos princes has made the same acknowledgment concerning his own country.

To those of us who believe, how comforting are these verifications of God's grand old promises: "The knowledge of the Lord shall cover the earth as the waters cover the sea." "All the ends of the earth shall see the salvation of our God. To Him every knee shall bow, every tongue confess." It is true there are only about eight millions of Siamese, and, compared with some other nations, that is a very small number; but eight million saved souls would make a glorious setting for one of Christ's many crowns. If any one should ask, "What are your hopes for the salvation of Siam?" I would reply with Dr. Judson, of Burmah, "They are bright as the promises of God." "To-day stands on the shoulders of yesterday. It sees farther and wider." We will take the wheel, the old symbol of Buddhism, for our symbol to denote the progress that is rolling over Asia in this nineteenth century. See how it moves forward. It never can turn back! Confucius, Mahomet, Buddha, all the founders of the most widespread religions in the world to-day, were sons of Asia; and now before all these hoary systems stands the great Asiatic Christ; from everlasting to everlasting He is God, the Alpha and the Omega of the eternal past, the eternal future; and all in heaven and earth and hell will one day bow before Him, and with reverence and awe acknowledge His supremacy and almighty power.

THE END.

APPENDIX.

I.

SIAMESE FACTS AND FANCIES.

I.

In the Buddhist millennium in Siam the water will flow up the river on one side and down on the other, so these poor indolent creatures will never have to row against the current, but by crossing from side to side can float idly to their destination, however remote. They will have to do no work either, but will live happy and content, as the birds do.

II.

Thunder—"crying of the sky"—is caused by a horrible giant who lives in the air; when he growls at his wife he causes the earth to tremble; but not always content with grumbling, he sometimes follows her, hatchet in hand, and, if in the paroxysm of his fury he throws the hatchet, it produces a thunderbolt.

III.

The World. The earth is flat, and it takes two hundred years to sail round it, at the rate of two hundred miles a day. Mt. Mah Mene, or Mt. Meru, is 840,000 miles high, and heaven is at the top. It takes a soul seven days to ascend to heaven, being led along the way by Arahang, the god-like guide; and for this belief they cry his name into the ears of the dying till they are deaf to all earthly sounds. In the midst of heaven is a great basin, where the angels bathe. When there are too many bathing at once, they splash the water over and cause rain. Another theory is, that a great fish one thousand miles long shakes its tail in the sea.

IV.

Lightning. A woman shakes a mirror in the air in mockery, or the angels strike fire with bricks. They believe in mermaids and water-sprites, and fairies, genii, and spirits of earth and air. When the wind sighs or rustles through the tree-tops, the mothers say they hear the voices of their dead babies crying in their hammocks. And falling stars are the spirits pitching torches.

Rainbow. Glory drinking water.

V.

Tides. A monster crab going in and coming out of his hole causes the waters to rise and fall.

The words crocodile and tiger are never spoken by the natives when near their haunts. They fear they will hear.

VI.

Cats. Many curious and beautiful specimens of this animal exist in Siam. Among the most curious are the tailless cats with blue eyes.

VII.

Pottery. I have never seen nor heard of a beautiful piece of Siamese manufacture. They seem utterly devoid of taste and skill such as characterize their northern neighbors in China, Japan, and Corea. The native workmen confine themselves to the manufacture of the rudest and simplest articles—water-jars and bottles, rice and curry-pots, fire-places, and basins and griddles for cooking fish, rough, unshapely, and unglazed; tiles for ordinary dwellings—the handsome green and golden tiles for temple and palace roofs are all Chinese. A few little cups with lids, for temple offerings, for pomades and salves, are made in Bangkok. They are rudely painted, and glazed on the outside only, and are sold for one or two cents apiece.

VIII.

Macaroni and Vermicelli. These articles of diet are manufactured in Chinese style all over the kingdom. They are made of rice flour, the lump of dough being squeezed, or, rather, pressed through a colander into a kettle of boiling water. When properly set and cooked, they are dipped out with baskets and spread on huge bamboo trays to dry in the sun. They are not hollow like the Italian macaroni, neither are they so palatable to the Western appetite. This rice vermicelli, however, is very delicate, and makes a fine addition to the soup. They are tied in bunches and stacked up in the native boats or shops like bundles of straw or dried herbs.

IX.

Chantaboon (nutmeg country) is a stronghold of the French Jesuits, who have for decades been laboring among the Chinese who have settled in large numbers in that part of Siam. They have established churches, courts, and prisons, and would like to govern the province in the interests of Catholicism and French Asia, and doubtless receive much sympathy, and, perhaps, help, from the Government representatives at Saigon and other French ports of Cochin China. Chantaboon borders on Cochin China, and is very fertile and populous, and furnishes lumber, tin, coal, iron, gold, and precious jewels, and being regarded as an important outpost of the kingdom, the Siamese have built costly and extensive fortifications there. It has an excellent harbor noted for its fine scenery, especially the prominent " Lion Rock," which is seen from the deck of every ship which enters the wide and beautiful river. The extensive teak forests covering the neighboring mountains, furnish timber for ships that are here built after European models in the Government shipyards.

X.

Native Doctors. There is a college of native physicians in Bangkok who are trained for service in the royal palaces, but their practice is far from praiseworthy, and is full of ignorance and superstition. Many of the Buddhist priests are also physicians. The people like to have it so, believing their merit will help cure the sick. We often find recipes for medicines posted up in the public rest-houses. The drug-stores in the native bazaars present a fine array of dried roots and leaves, besides shells and buffalo horns, old bones, tiger teeth and eyes, lizard and alligator gall, and many other pretended medicines as useless and even more disgusting. The blind and ignorant heathen doctor, conscious of a higher power which controls disease and the issues of life and death, places his medicine in the hand of his god and hopes that the merits of the merciful Buddha will impart efficacy to the drug or lotion. The sick like to boast of the quantities of medicine they have taken, and it is not uncommon for them to swallow several gallons during an illness—mostly weak teas and solutions. They anoint with holy oil, and sprinkle with consecrated water, spurting it from the mouth in a fine spray over the patient, as a Chinese laundryman sprinkles clothes; and they knead the body when the joints are stiff and sore.

A medical missionary once called on a patient; he was an old convert, and near his end. He told Dr. S. he had great faith in his prayers, but he would not take his medicine. When the doctor left, the old man's sons were searching all through the town for buffalo bones, and even summoned a native doctor from the city, who, with owl-eyed wisdom, pronounced the case a violent attack of colic.

Women care for each other in times of need, and some have gained quite a reputation in attending at the birth of children, but some of their customs are almost too horrible to relate on this page, and it is a great wonder that mothers and their little ones survive the treatment. The child is not permitted to have its natural nourishment, but is stuffed with rice and bananas, and nursed by the other mothers of the village. Thousands of these little creatures die on the eighth day after birth of lockjaw, and hundreds of delicate mothers cannot endure the fiery ordeal of the peculiar treatment, and so perish also. Many who thus die are denied the right of cremation, as being considered unworthy the sacred privilege. As yet no ladies have ever been sent to Siam as medical missionaries, but here is a wide field for the exercise of their skill, tact, and patience.

II.

A WONDERFUL MONUMENT OF THE PAST—PRA PRATOM CHEDEE.*

THE history of the Pra Pratom Chedee is involved in much darkness. It is reported that a finger-ring had been found in digging there, which bears indubitable marks of having been made more than eight hundred years ago. There appears to be no written document extant which throws any light on the questions when and why that pagoda was built. But there are various traditions. One of the most interesting is that it was once the seat of a rajah's rule called Payah Pan; that all the plains of Siam were then divided among petty chiefs who were frequently at war with one another; that on a certain occasion a collision took place between Payah Pan and his son Payah Kong, when, being seated on elephants, they fought with each other, and that the son by one stroke of his lance severed the head of his father from his body, and hence won the day. But he, not long afterward, became greatly distressed at the thought that he had killed his father. Having suffered a long time the bitterest remorse, a Buddhist oracle at length extended to him the comforting thought that he might do much to atone for his sin of patricide, by erecting on the spot where his father fell,

---

* For the contents of this chapter I am indebted to Dr. Bradley's "Bangkok Calendar" of 1871.

and where Buddha once slept, a pagoda reaching above the highest flight of doves, and enshrining in it a bit of the most sacred relics of Buddha. With this Payah Kong was delighted, and in obedience to the oracle began to build the pagoda, and gave to it all his great wealth and after-life.

About 1829, when the late Supreme King was chief priest at Temple Saman-rie in Bangkok, he caused an image of Buddha to be cast for his own personal benefit, and about the same time caused a small portable pagoda to be removed from the old city, and had a new layer of silver cast about it. The next dry season he, with a great company of minor priests, made a pilgrimage to the ancient pagoda of Pra Pratom. One evening he went up to the sacred pile and worshipped in the holy place, when he is said to have offered the following prayer in the Pali language:

"I have great reverence for this pagoda, and consider it to be the most ancient monument of Buddha in all Siam, which is proven to be a fact from the form and style of it, there being none like it in modern times, so that the present generation of men hardly recognize it to be a pagoda. And it would appear that the founder of it did indeed enshrine in it that which makes it worthy of being a place to be held in the highest reverence, and that hence he expended upon it a large amount of property, making it so large and firm that it has successfully resisted the wear and tear of many ages. And now, if there be in truth any sacred relics of Buddha anywhere in this world, I think there must be portions of them enshrined somewhere within this sacred structure; and if it be so, I beg that the angel in charge will be pleased to divide unto me about two pieces of the same, as I desire to enshrine one of them in the idol and the other in the pagoda which I have made, that I may have them near me in the great city to worship, and before which to present continual offerings, as would be most worthy. And this I desire because this Pra Pratom Chedee is now far off in the wilderness, and not in a suitable place for the people generally to resort to worship. Hence, I beg that the guardian angel will be pleased to distribute unto me of the sacred relics about two pieces."

Having offered this prayer, he then sent one of his personal attendants to take a precious calipot, borne on a salver, and place it in a niche of the pagoda on the east side. In the afternoon of that day, as the Chief Priest was about to descend from the place of worship, he sent a servant to invite the calipot to return, and behold there had been nothing deposited in it by the angel. A month or more after this, the Chief Priest having returned to his temple in Bangkok, the following event is said to have transpired at Temple Maha-Taht (Temple of the Holy Bones), where the king graduated in his youth. There was a very precious image of Buddha in the temple, one of great antiquity. On a certain night about eleven o'clock a company of priests went in and worshipped in the holy place. When they were about half through their devotions, they beheld something like smoke of a reddish color ascending from the idol, and which had a pleasant fragrance like burning incense. The smoke increased until the idol seemed to be of a red complexion like betel. The priests were all quite startled at the sight, and rose up to examine the phenomenon, thinking that it might be a fire which had caught there. But they saw nothing except the reddish smoke, and returning to their devotions, finished their rehearsals. They then proceeded to examine more narrowly into the cause of the smoke, expecting to find that it had arisen from some fire without the temple. But they found nothing to solve the mystery. Early next morning they reported this phenomenon to the Chief Priest at Wat Saman-rie. He arose and went at once to Temple Maha-Taht to examine into the wonder. In pursuing his investigations he found in the urn employed for the purpose of preserving the sacred relics two more pieces than there had been before. When he asked the priests of the temple if they had ever before noticed them, their reply was that they had not. He then inquired of the keeper of the doors if he knew of any one placing them there. His reply was that he did not. He then summoned a meeting of many persons to witness the two sacred relics. They were all unanimous in the opinion that they could not have been put there by human hands, and that they must have come there themselves.

The two new relics were different from any that are seen in modern times, being each about the size of a mustard-seed, of a whitish color, like the flowers of the *peekoon*. They had each two or three white dots in a straight line. Prince Sopon was the first to discover this peculiarity. These two relics are now enshrined in a pagoda of precious stone, within the *Praratana Sotsa-daram*.

The foregoing account of the wonderful relics is a translation from the Siamese. A legitimate inference to the priest and to all his councillors was that the two relics having been sought for at Pra Pratom and expected from thence, were by superhuman power brought to Temple Maha-Taht and given as described. Hence the great respect now paid to that pagoda.

Dr. Bradley visited Pra Pratom twice—once in 1865, and again five years later. It is about sixty miles from Bangkok, near *Nakon-Chisee*, a small village on the Tacheen River, but the seat of government for one of the most important provinces of Siam. The wonderful shrine is some seven and a half miles nearly due west from this village. It is reached by a straight canal through a level prairie, with but here and there a small forest tree. The late king had this canal excavated, doubtless for the primary object of making a convenient way of access to a place which is destined to become a very popular shrine for the worship of Buddha, and to transmit the name of Maha Mongkut to future generations as a sovereign of great wealth, and of sincere devotion to Buddhism, such as he taught when a priest at the head of a reformed Buddhist school, and such as he upheld with the right hand of his kingly power, in faithfulness to the oath he took when he ascended the throne.

The original name of the pagoda was Pra Pratom Chedee, literally *a pagoda of a god that slept*. But for reasons best known to such as have authority to change names, a slight alteration has been made in the writing of that original name, so that it can now be literally rendered, *a pagoda of the god of the beginning*, or *the most ancient pagoda*. The change is only in the letter *o* in the word Pratom, which formerly had no rising inflection, but now has, and when Romanized is written Prât'óm.

According to the original name it is commonly understood that Guatama, or the Buddha, when journeying in Siam, "on a certain time," slept at that place, which idea harmonizes well with other traditions concerning him; as, for example, that he found shelter at one time under a great shelving rock, some fifteen miles east of Prabaht, during a tremendous storm, and that consequently from that time to this the ceiling and siding made by the rock becomes brilliant to the view of every devoted follower of Buddha when looking at it, and is therefore called *Prá-Chi;* that he put one of his feet in a small mount at *Prabaht*, and left his footprint in a rock, and hence the name; and that he reclined on a rock at the top of a small mount twenty or thirty miles from Pratom, and therefore that place is called *Pra-taan—the lounge of a god*.

In 1865 Pra Pratom Chedee stood in the midst of a vast wilderness of jungle grass, bushes, and scraggy bamboos, with scarcely a hill in all the field of vision, or a large tree, and nothing to bound the outlook but the horizon. The upper half of it had not then been enclosed by the new brick work, and was much like the tops of some of the Bangkok pagodas. It would appear that the original size of its base was not a quarter what it is now. The artificial mount on which it stands is a regular circle, not far from 4,000 feet in circumference, and about 15 feet high. The new work had been carried up 200 feet, and at that height was over 300 feet in circumference. Radiating from the old spire were heavy four-inch planks laid flatwise, upon which the work was to be built up. Several such strata had already been placed in the pile below to prevent the masonry from splitting. Such an accident had occurred four or five years previous, while many men were at work on the top; the mass of brick and mortar suddenly parted from the old spire on all sides, and came down with a great crash, and—marvellous to relate—so great was the merit of working upon it, that, report says, only one of the men was killed by the accident. The confused pile made by this avalanche was at length levelled, and now forms the mound already spoken of.

Ascending to where the workmen were busy with trowel and mortar, a widely extended view could be obtained, revealing a vast plain covered with the usual jungle productions of Siam. Here and there could be seen small plats of cultivated land, and round about them a few grass-thatched huts indicating poverty.

At the immediate base of the pagoda were being erected a circle of extensive buildings with splendid porches, guarded by huge figures of Nak, a kind of demigod. At the northern entrance was a small artificial mountain, with a great variety of caverns and subterranean recesses. On the exterior of the mount were sundry pools of water, little pagodas, and miniature temples. On the west side was a reclining god, fifty feet in length, in process of formation, under the plastic hands of two Chinese masons. Near by were fifteen or twenty small brick houses, all after the same model, designed for the accommodation of Buddhist priests; and on either side of the canal which terminates near the pagoda are numerous substantial brick salas, or pavilions, some fifty rods apart, built for the shelter of pilgrims coming to worship Buddha.

The king was also having a palace erected on the east side for his own convenience and pleasure when he would come to consecrate all those new works to the Buddhist religion, and to lead the devotions of his great family at that rising shrine. Among other buildings of the palace was the usual accompaniment everywhere seen at the royal residences in city or country—a large, open hall for theatrical performances; for such plays are quite in harmony with the modern worship of Buddha. An almost incalculable amount of treasure had been already expended, and many hundreds of thousands of dollars would be required to complete the plans laid out.

After viewing all this waste nearly twenty years ago, that good and wise old man, Dr. Bradley, wrote: "Would that the king could see how much better it would be for his name and his people, if he would employ his great wealth for the complete exploration and survey of all his dominions, that their vast hidden treasures might be brought to light, their rivers accurately mapped, their towns, cities, and provinces all clearly bounded, with railways and telegraphs bringing them into close proximity to the great metropolis, and the whole into lightning communication with all the western kingdoms and nations."

In 1870 he again visited Wat Pra Pratom, and had a view of "that most magnificent monument of Buddhism which Siam contains." He says: "We had not seen it since 1865, when the work of restoring the old pagoda, which had stood there for not far from one thousand years, had been going on for ten years or more. When you get out of your boat and ascend the steps nearest the pagoda, then—and not till then—will you be struck with wonder at the vast amount of work and treasure expended, for you had until then seen only its dome and its spire. Your sight will be fixed at first on the unique building in front of the shrine, which is about 750 feet in length, 15 feet wide, and 30 feet high to the ridge of the roof; and this you are told forms one of four sides of a perfect square, with the same style of buildings on the other three sides. You will be singularly impressed with the deep red color of the earthen tiles that cover the roof, and the yellowish red of all the brick stuccoed walls. At each corner is a more lofty structure of fine proportions, giving grandeur and symmetry to the whole as being the external boundaries of the monument. And there are, besides these, elevated structures over as many gates into the enclosure on each side, giving variety and magnificence to the whole view. One of these beautiful gateways I noticed was especially designed for the king, at times when there are theatrical plays on the wide lawn in front. These long buildings, forming the four sides of the sacred enclosure, are divided lengthwise into a narrow hall, with verandas on each side extending their entire length, broken only by the doors. On entering one of these doors you ascend three or four feet, and passing through you find yourself on a neatly paved plateau, twenty feet or more in width, extending all round the pagoda. This is bounded internally by a brick stuccoed wall, much more diversified in structure than mere walls usually are. You next ascend a flight of marble steps, and passing through a tasteful porch, stand in the second plateau, still better paved and more richly furnished with curiosities of Buddhistic reminiscences, artificial rocks, mountains, caves, miniature pagodas, and temples. This space is bounded by an unbroken circle of buildings. The width of the plateau is about twenty feet, excepting at places opposite the four corners of the outer wall, where it is a good deal wider. From this you go up six or eight feet by stone steps to the third story. Here, if we remember rightly, you will stand on a marble floor, beautifully shaded by trees and shrubs of many varieties, and richly furnished with granite circular tables and benches, flower-pots, and marble couches. From a measurement we made by pacing the entire circuit of this floor, we think it not less than 2,000 feet by 30 feet in width. The fourth story is reached by another set of steps, only three or four feet high, into another circle of buildings, with a narrow hall. This hall is sun-lighted externally by scores of oval windows, and internally by arched avenues of white mason-work. The floor is of artificial marble, and extremely well done. From its ceiling throughout the entire circuit are suspended, about ten feet apart, chandeliers of Siamese manufacture. Each one is intended to hold several tumblers of cocoa or peanut oil, and on special religious occasions to be all lighted up.

"This circular hall is divided into four equal parts by idol sanctuaries or temples, which are quite large and commanding, having the same graduated roofs as are in vogue in Bangkok. You will find enshrined in each several gilded images of Buddha from the size of a man to an enormous giant. On the wall, between the oval windows, are moral lessons, written in the ancient Siamese character, occupying each a space four feet square. The letters are made with a kind of putty, and stand embossed on the wall hard as stone. We paced this hall, and found it to be about 1,030 feet circuit. On the same level with the hall there is an open space fifteen feet wide all round the pagoda, and this is bounded internally by another circular structure, having somewhat the appearance of Siamese city walls, with its closely studded embrasures. But each of these is so constructed as to form a little house for a lamp, which is shielded from the wind by a large pane of colored glass in its arched front, and at the back is a small opening in which the lamp is put. There are two hundred and thirty of these miniature lighthouses, and they stand some three feet apart, and when lighted must make a fine display.

"In the rear of these is another open space, which may be called the fifth story of the monument. It is about ten feet above the one next below. By pacing we judged it to be 900 feet in circuit. Hence, the pagoda at this elevation, if our measurement approximates to truth, is about 300 feet in diameter, its height 30 feet from the ground, and the distance from this to the pinnacle some 384 feet. There seems to be no reason to doubt that the whole central structure below and above this, from bottom to top, is of solid mason-work—that is, without any cavities. What a huge pile of brick and mortar!

"Above this fifth story there are no more places left for promenading, and from this point the pagoda takes the usual form of the largest dagabas in the city of Bangkok. It is belted with seven rounded zones, in regular, ascending gradations, until the upper and smaller one is some sixty feet from the fifth story. Then begins the even face of the pagoda, extending upward from the seventh zone, it may be, 100 feet. Here the pagoda again changes form, very much resembling the upper part of the royal pramanes or cremation buildings, and is crowned with a metallic framework, having many arms, and a lance-shaped spire. On its arms are suspended little bells which are rung by the breezes of heaven, and which, the people say, are of the most precious gold, but hung too far heavenward ever to tempt the cupidity of mortals.

"All the upper parts down to the top of the dome, or smooth, even surface, are finished, and it was the last work His Grace the late President of the Foreign Department had accomplished under his direction. The dome is still unfinished, and, with its scaffolding and the zigzag footpath going up to its top, has an unsightly appearance.

"Standing on the scaffolding near the top of the dome we saw men at work finishing from above downward, and then removing the scaffolding as they descend, thus cutting off all possibility of unlawful access to the gold at the pinnacle. The workmen were so high up as to look like little children. We walked up the footpath until our head began to swim and we dared venture no further. But from that point of observation we had a grand view of a vast extent of level country, without the least highland, except in the direction of Petchaburee, whose mountains appeared like small black clouds on the horizon.

The number of brick and bamboo houses clustering about its base now appeared like quite a little city.

"The monument fronts to the east, and the palace for the king stands forty or fifty rods opposite its front. The houses for the settled priests, forty or fifty in number, and for many of their order who come on pilgrimages, are on the west side.

"Much time and money are still required to finish all these works as their chief patrons, the King and the Foreign Minister, had contemplated, and now since they have been summoned into the spirit world to render to their Maker an account of all their doings here on earth, it may be many years before the whole is finished. Let us fervently hope that all spirit and heart for such useless and wicked expenditure will have died away ere its possible completion, and that it will therefore be abandoned to the speedier ruin."

www.ingramcontent.com/pod-product-compliance
Lightning Source LLC
Chambersburg PA
CBHW050849300426
44111CB00010B/1185